Artificial Neural Systems Handbook

Volume I

Artificial Neural Systems Handbook
Volume I

Edited by **Sophia Nelson**

CLANRYE INTERNATIONAL

New Jersey

Published by Clanrye International,
55 Van Reypen Street,
Jersey City, NJ 07306, USA
www.clanryeinternational.com

Artificial Neural Systems Handbook: Volume I
Edited by Sophia Nelson

International Standard Book Number: 978-1-63240-070-3 (Hardback)

Printed in the United States of America.

Contents

Preface

The easiest way to define a neural network would be the following- It is a computing system or network which consists of simple and highly interconnected processing elements. These processing elements process information and data through their dynamic state response to external inputs and stimuli. In computer science and in fields related to it, artificial neural systems or networks usually refer to models that are inspired by a living organism's central nervous system, focussing on the brain. It is a system that is capable of pattern recognition as well as machine learning. This field does not use traditional programming. Instead it involves the creation of huge parallel networks and the training and programming of those networks towards solving specific problems. There are other machine learning systems as well and like those systems neural networks are often used to solve a huge variety of tasks which are difficult to solve using common and ordinary rule based programming, including processes like speech recognition and computer vision. These are biologically inspired methods of computing and are often believed to be the next major advancement in the computing industry. These have major ramifications in our daily lives and thus skilled technicians and researchers are of course required.

This book is an attempt to compile and collate all available research on artificial neural systems under one aegis. I am grateful to those who put their hard work, effort and expertise into these research projects as well as those who were supportive in this endeavour.

Editor

Sleep Stage Classification Using Unsupervised Feature Learning

Martin Längkvist, Lars Karlsson, and Amy Loutfi

Center for Applied Autonomous Sensor Systems, Örebro University, 701 82 Örebro, Sweden

Correspondence should be addressed to Amy Loutfi, amy.loutfi@oru.se

Academic Editor: Juan Manuel Gorriz Saez

Most attempts at training computers for the difficult and time-consuming task of sleep stage classification involve a feature extraction step. Due to the complexity of multimodal sleep data, the size of the feature space can grow to the extent that it is also necessary to include a feature selection step. In this paper, we propose the use of an unsupervised feature learning architecture called *deep belief nets* (DBNs) and show how to apply it to sleep data in order to eliminate the use of handmade features. Using a postprocessing step of hidden Markov model (HMM) to accurately capture sleep stage switching, we compare our results to a feature-based approach. A study of anomaly detection with the application to home environment data collection is also presented. The results using raw data with a deep architecture, such as the DBN, were comparable to a feature-based approach when validated on clinical datasets.

1. Introduction

One of the main challenges in sleep stage classification is to isolate features in multivariate time-series data which can be used to correctly identify and thereby automate the annotation process to generate sleep hypnograms. In the current absence of a set of universally applicable features, typically a two-stage process is required before training a sleep stage algorithm, namely, feature extraction and feature selection [1–9]. In other domains which share similar challenges, an alternative to using hand-tailored feature representations derived from expert knowledge is to apply unsupervised feature learning techniques, where the feature representations are learned from unlabeled data. This not only enables the discovery of new useful feature representations that a human expert might not be aware of, which in turn could lead to a better understanding of the sleep process and present a way of exploiting massive amounts of unlabeled data.

Unsupervised feature learning and in particular deep learning [10–15] propose ways for training the weight matrices in each layer in an unsupervised fashion as a preprocessing step before training the whole network. This has proven to give good results in other areas such as vision tasks [10], object recognition [16], motion capture data [17], speech recognition [18], and bacteria identification [19].

This work presents a new approach to the automatic sleep staging problem. The main focus is to learn meaningful feature representations from unlabeled sleep data. A dataset of 25 subjects consisting of electroencephalography (EEG) of brain activity, electrooculography (EOG) of eye movements, and electromyography (EMG) of skeletal muscle activity is segmented and used to train a deep belief network (DBN), using no prior knowledge. Validation of the learned representations is done by integrating a hidden Markov model (HMM) and compare classification accuracy with a feature-based approach that uses prior knowledge. The inclusion of an HMM serves the purpose of improving upon capturing a more realistic sleep stage switching, for example, hinders excessive or unlikely sleep stage transitions. It is in this manner that the knowledge from the human experts is infused into the system. Even though the classifier is trained using labeled data, the feature representations are learned from unlabeled data. The architecture of the DBN follows previous work with unsupervised feature learning for electroencephalography (EEG) event detection [20].

A secondary contribution of the proposed method leverages the information from the DBN in order to perform anomaly detection. Particularly, in light of an increasing trend to streamline sleep diagnosis and reduce the burden on health care centers by using at home sleep monitoring technologies, anomaly detection is important in order to rapidly assess the quality of the polysomnograph data and determine if the patient requires another additional night's collection at home. In this paper, we illustrate how the DBN once trained on datasets for sleep stage classification in the lab can still be applied to data which has been collected at home to find particular anomalies such as a loose electrode.

Finally, inconsistencies between sleep labs (equipment, electrode placement), experimental setups (number of signals and categories, subject variations), and interscorer variability (80% conformance for healthy patients and even less for patients with sleep disorder [9]) make it challenging to compare sleep stage classification accuracy to previous works. Results in [2] report a best result accuracy of around 61% for classification of 5 stages from a single EEG channel using GOHMM and AR coefficients as features. Works by [8] achieved 83.7% accuracy using conditional random fields with six power spectra density features for one EEG signal on four human subjects during a 24-hour recording session and considering six stages. Works by [7] achieved 85.6% accuracy on artifact-free, two expert agreement sleep data from 47 mostly healthy subjects using 33 features with SFS feature selection and four separately trained neural networks as classifiers.

The goal of this work is not to replicate the R&K system or improve current state-of-the-art sleep stage classification but rather to explore the advantages of deep learning and the feasibility of using unsupervised feature learning applied to sleep data. Therefore, the main method of evaluation is a comparison with a feature-based shallow model. Matlab code used in this paper is available at http://aass.oru.se/~mlt.

2. Deep Belief Networks

DBN is a probabilistic generative model with deep architecture that searches the parameter space by unsupervised greedy layerwise training. Each layer consists of a restricted Boltzmann machine (RBM) with visible units, $\mathbf{v}$, and hidden units, $\mathbf{h}$. There are no visible-visible connections and no hidden-hidden connections. The visible and hidden units have a bias vector, $\mathbf{c}$ and $\mathbf{b}$, respectively. The visible and hidden units are connected by a weight matrix, $\mathbf{W}$, see Figure 1(a). A DBN is formed by stacking a user-defined number of RBMs on top of each other where the output from a lower-level RBM is the input to a higher-level RBM, see Figure 1(b). The main difference between a DBN and a multilayer perceptron is the inclusion of a bias vector for the visible units, which is used to reconstruct the input signal, which plays an important role in the way DBNs are trained.

A reconstruction of the input can be obtained from the unsupervised pretrained DBN by encoding the input to the top RBM and then decoding the state of the top RBM back to the lowest level. For a Bernoulli (visible)-Bernoulli (hidden) RBM, the probability that hidden unit h_j is activated given

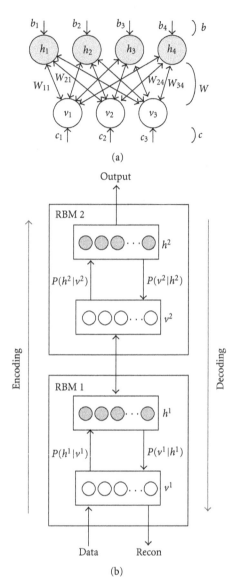

FIGURE 1: Graphical depiction of (a) RBM and (b) DBN.

visible vector, $\mathbf{v}$, and the probability that visible unit v_i is activated given hidden vector, $\mathbf{h}$, are given by

$$P\left(h_j \mid \mathbf{v}\right) = \frac{1}{1 + \exp^{b_j + \sum_i W_{ij} v_i}}$$

$$P(v_i \mid \mathbf{h}) = \frac{1}{1 + \exp^{c_i + \sum_j W_{ij} h_j}}. \tag{1}$$

The energy function and the joint distribution for a given visible and hidden vector are

$$E(\mathbf{v}, \mathbf{h}) = \mathbf{h}^T \mathbf{W} \mathbf{v} + \mathbf{b}^T \mathbf{h} + \mathbf{c}^T \mathbf{v}$$

$$P(\mathbf{v}, \mathbf{h}) = \frac{1}{z} \exp^{E(\mathbf{v}, \mathbf{h})}. \tag{2}$$

The parameters $\mathbf{W}$, $\mathbf{b}$, and $\mathbf{v}$ are trained to minimize the reconstruction error. An approximation of the gradient of the log likelihood of **v** using contrastive divergence [21] gives the learning rule for RBM:

$$\frac{\partial \log P(\mathbf{v})}{\partial W_{ij}} \approx \left\langle v_i h_j \right\rangle_{\text{data}} - \left\langle v_i h_j \right\rangle_{\text{recon}}, \qquad (3)$$

where $\langle \cdot \rangle$ is the average value over all training samples. In this work, training is performed in three steps: (1) unsupervised pretraining of each layer, (2) unsupervised fine-tuning of all layers with backpropagation, and (3) supervised fine-tuning of all layers with backpropagation.

3. Experimental Setup

3.1. Automatic Sleep Stager. The five sleep stages that are at focus are awake, stage 1 (S1), stage 2 (S2), slow wave sleep (SWS), and rapid eye-movement sleep (REM). These stages come from a unified method for classifying an 8 h sleep recording introduced by Rechtschaffen and Kales (R&K) [22]. A graph that shows these five stages over an entire night is called a hypnogram, and each epoch according to the R&K system is either 20 s or 30 s. While the R&K system brings consensus on terminology, among other advantages [23], it has been criticized for a number of issues [24]. Even though the goal in this work is not to replicate the R&K system, its terminology will be used for evaluation of our architecture. Each channel of the data is divided into segments of 1 second with zero overlap, which is a much higher temporal resolution than the one practiced by the R&K system.

We compare the performance of three experimental setups as shown in Figure 2.

3.1.1. Feat-GOHMM. A Gaussian observation hidden Markov model (GOHMM) is used on 28 handmade features; see the appendix for a description of the features used. Feature selection is done by sequential backward selection (SBS), which starts with the full set of features and greedily removes a feature after each iteration step. A principal component analysis (PCA) with five principal components is used after feature selection, followed by a Gaussian mixture model (GMM) with five components. The purpose of the PCA is to reduce dimensionality, and the choice of five components was made since it captured most of the variance in the data, while still being tractable for the GMM step. Initial mean and covariance values for each GMM component are set to the mean and covariance of annotated data for each sleep stage. Finally, the output from the GMM is used as input to a hidden Markov model (HMM) [25].

3.1.2. Feat-DBN. A 2-layer DBN with 200 hidden units in both layers and a softmax classifier attached on top is used on 28 handmade features. Both layers are pretrained for 300 epochs, and the top layer is fine-tuned for 50 epochs. Initial biases of hidden units are set empirically to −4 to encouraged sparsity [26], which prevents learning trivial or uninteresting feature representations. Scaling to values between 0 and 1 is done by subtracting the mean, divided by the standard deviation, and finally adding 0.5.

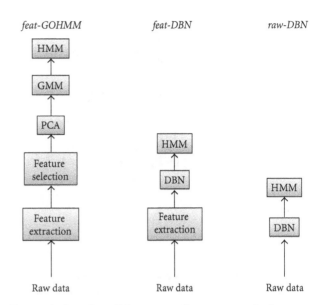

FIGURE 2: Overview of three setups for an automatic sleep stager used in this work. The first method, *feat-GOHMM*, is a shallow method that uses prior knowledge. The second method, *feat-DBN*, is a deep architecture that also uses prior knowledge. And, lastly, the third method, *raw-DBN*, is a deep architecture that does not use any prior knowledge. See text for more details.

3.1.3. Raw-DBN. A DBN with the same parameters as *feat-DBN* is used on preprocessed raw data. Scaling is done by saturating the signal at a saturation constant, $\text{sat}_{\text{channel}}$, then divide by $2 * \text{sat}_{\text{channel}}$, and finally adding 0.5. The saturation constant was set to $\text{sat}_{\text{EEG}} = \text{sat}_{\text{EOG}} = \pm 60\,\mu\text{V}$ and $\text{sat}_{\text{EMG}} = \pm 40\,\mu\text{V}$. Input consisted of the concatenation of EEG, EOG1, EOG2, and EMG. With window width, w, the visible layer becomes

$$v = \begin{bmatrix} \text{EEG}_1^{64} & \text{EOG1}_1^{64} & \text{EOG2}_1^{64} & \text{EMG}_1^{64} \\ \text{EEG}_{1+w}^{64+w} & \text{EOG1}_{1+w}^{64+w} & \text{EOG2}_{1+w}^{64+w} & \text{EMG}_{1+w}^{64+w} \\ \vdots & \vdots & \vdots & \vdots \end{bmatrix}. \qquad (4)$$

With four signals, 1 second window, and 64 samples per second, the input dimension is 256.

3.2. Anomaly Detection for Home Sleep Data. In this work, anomaly detection is evaluated by training a DBN and calculating the root mean square error (RMSE) from the reconstructed signal from the DBN and the original signal. A faulty signal in one channel often affects other channels for sleep data, such as movement artifacts, blink artifacts, and loose reference or ground electrode. Therefore, a detected fault in one channel should label all channels at that time as faulty.

Figure 3 shows data that has been collected at a healthy patient's home during sleep. All signals, except EEG2, are nonfaulty prior to a movement artifact at $t = 7$ s. This movement affected the reference electrode or the ground electrode, resulting in disturbances in all signals for the rest of the night, thereby rendering the signals unusable by a clinician. A poorly attached electrode was the cause for

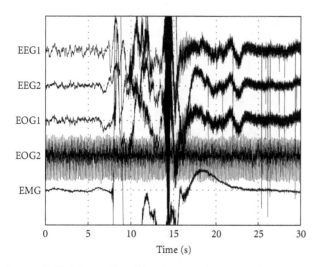

FIGURE 3: PSG data collected in a home environment. A movement occurs at $t = 7$ s resulting in one of the electrodes to be misplaced affecting EOG1 and both EEG channels. EOG2 is not properly attached resulting in a faulty signal for the entire night.

the noise in signal EEG2. Previous approaches to artifact rejection in EEG analysis range from simple thresholding on abnormal amplitude and/or frequency to more complex strategies in order to detect individual artefacts [27, 28].

4. Experimental Datasets

Two datasets are used in this work. The first consists of 25 acquisitions and is used to train and test the automatic sleep stager. The second consists of 5 acquisitions and is used to validate anomaly detection on sleep data collected at home.

4.1. Benchmark Dataset. This dataset has kindly been provided by St. Vincent's University Hospital and University College Dublin, which can be downloaded from PhysioNet [29]. The dataset consists of 25 acquisitions (21 males 4 females with average age 50, average weight 95 kg, and average height 173 cm) from subjects with suspected sleep-disordered breathing. Each acquisition consists of 2 EEG channels (C3-A2 and C4-A1), 2 EOG channels, and 1 EMG channel using 10–20 electrode placements system. Only one of the EEG channel (C3-A2) is used in this work. Sample rate is 128 Hz for EEG and 64 Hz for EOG and EMG. Average recording time is 6.9 hours. Sleep stages are divided into S1: 16.7%, S2: 33.3%, SWS: 12.7%, REM: 14.5%, awake: 22.7%, and indeterminate: 0.1%. Scoring was performed by one sleep expert.

All signals are preprocessed by notch filtering at 50 Hz in order to cancel out power line disturbances and downsampled to 64 Hz after being prefiltered with a band-pass filter of 0.3 to 32 Hz for EEG and EOG, and 10 to 32 Hz for EMG. Each epoch before and after a sleep stage switch is removed from the training set to avoid possible subsections of mislabeled data within one epoch. This resulted in 20.7% of total training samples to be removed.

A 25 leave-one-out cross-validation is performed. Training samples are randomly picked from 24 acquisitions in order to compensate for any class imbalance. A total of approximately 250000 training samples and 50000 training validation samples are used for each validation.

4.2. Home Sleep Dataset. PSG data of approximately 60 hours (5 nights) was collected at a healthy patient's home using a Embla Titanium PSG. A total of 8 electrodes were used: EEG C3, EEG C4, EOG left, EOG right, 2 electrodes for the EMG channel, reference electrode, and ground electrode. Data was collected with a sampling rate of 256 Hz, which was downsampled to match the sampling rate of the training data. The signals are preprocessed using the same method as the benchmark dataset.

5. Results

5.1. Automatic Sleep Stager. A full leave-one-out cross-validation of the 25 acquisitions is performed for the three experimental setups. The classification accuracy and confusion matrices for each setup and sleep stage are presented in Tables 1, 2, 3, and 4. Here, the performance of using a DBN based approach, either with features or using the raw data, is comparable to the *feat-GOHMM*. While the best accuracy was achieved with *feat-DBN*, followed by *raw-DBN* and lastly, *feat-GOHMM*, it is important to examine the performances individually. Figure 4 shows classification accuracy for each subject. The *raw-DBN* setup gives best, or second best, performance in the majority of the sets, with the exception of subjects 9 and 22. An examination of the performance when comparing the F_1-score for individual sleep stages indicates that S1 is the most difficult stage to classify and awake and slow wave sleep is the easiest.

For the *raw-DBN*, it is also possible to analyze the learned features. In Figure 6, the learned features for the first layer are given. Here, it can clearly be seen that both low and high frequency features for the EEG and high and low amplitude features for the EMG are included, which to some degree correspond to the features which are typically selected in handmade feature selection methods.

Some conclusions from analyzing the selected features from the SBS algorithm used in *feat-GOHMM* can be made. Fractal exponent for EEG and entropy for EOG were selected for all 25 subjects and thus proven to be valuable features. Correlation between both EOG signals was also among the top selected features, as well as delta, theta, and alpha frequencies for EEG. Frequency features for EOG and EMG were excluded early, which is in accordance to the fact that these signals do not exhibit valuable information in the frequency domain [30]. The kurtosis feature was selected more frequently when it was applied to EMG and less frequently when it was applied to EEG or EOG. Features of spectral mean for all signals, median for EMG, and standard deviation for EOG were not frequently selected. See Figure 5 for errors bars for each feature at each sleep stage.

It is worth noting that variations in the number of layers and hidden units were attempted, and it was found

TABLE 1: Classification accuracy and F_1-score for the three experimental setups.

	Accuracy (mean ± std)	F_1-score				
		Awake	S1	S2	SWS	REM
feat-GOHMM	63.9 ± 10.8	0.71	0.31	0.72	0.82	0.47
feat-DBN	72.2 ± 9.7	0.78	0.37	0.76	0.84	0.78
raw-DBN	67.4 ± 12.9	0.69	0.36	0.78	0.83	0.58

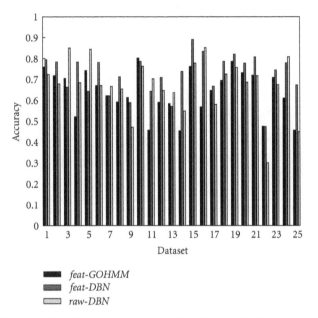

FIGURE 4: Classification accuracy for 25 testing sets for three setups.

TABLE 2: Confusion matrix for *feat-GOHMM*.

%	Classified				
	Awake	S1	S2	SWS	REM
Awake	72.5	16.8	3.0	2.5	5.2
S1	29.4	31.1	25.6	1.5	12.4
S2	2.0	8.4	71.9	7.1	10.6
SWS	1.1	1.3	9.6	87.8	0.2
REM	11.7	13.3	29.4	2.7	42.9

TABLE 3: Confusion matrix for *feat-DBN*.

%	Classified				
	Awake	S1	S2	SWS	REM
Awake	75.8	18.2	1.8	0.2	4.1
S1	26.0	37.6	25.1	0.7	10.6
S2	1.0	9.8	73.1	7.2	9.0
SWS	0.4	0.1	13.9	85.5	0.1
REM	1.9	4.0	10.3	0.1	83.7

TABLE 4: Confusion matrix for *raw-DBN*.

%	Classified				
	Awake	S1	S2	SWS	REM
Awake	68.4	13.4	2.5	0.7	15.1
S1	20.3	33.1	24.8	1.6	20.2
S2	1.0	6.3	76.5	9.1	7.1
SWS	0.1	0.0	11.1	88.8	0.0
REM	21.1	6.9	11.1	0.8	60.1

that an increase did not significantly improve classification accuracy. Rather, an increase in either the number of layers or hidden units often resulted in a significant increase in simulation time, and therefore to maintain a reasonable training time, the layers and hidden units were kept to a minimum. With the configuration of the three experimental setups described above and simulations performed on a Windows 7, 64-bit machine with quad-core Intel i5 3.1 GHz CPU with use of a nVIDIA GeForce GTX 470 GPU using GPUmat, simulation time for *feat-GOHMM*, *feat-DBN*, and *raw-DBN* were approximately 10 minutes, 1 hour, and 3 hours per dataset, respectively.

5.2. Anomaly Detection on Home Sleep Data. A total of five acquisitions were recorded at a patient's home during sleep and manually labeled into faulty or nonfaulty signals. A DBN with the *raw-DBN* setup was trained using the benchmark dataset. The root mean square error (RMSE) between the home sleep data and the reconstructed signal from the trained DBN for the five night runs and a close-up for night

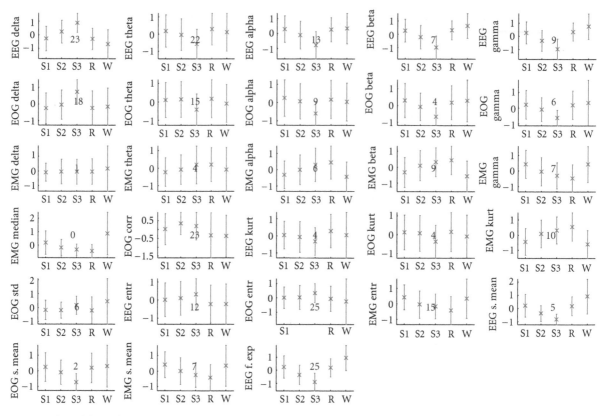

Figure 5: Error bar of the 28 features. Gray number in background represents how many times that feature was part of best subset from SBS algorithm (maximum is 25).

2 where an electrode falls off after around 380 minutes can be seen in Figure 7.

Interestingly, attempts on using the *feat-GOHMM* for sleep stage classification on the home sleep dataset resulted in faulty data to be misclassified as awake. This could be explained by the fact that faulty data mostly resembles signals in awake state.

6. Discussion

In this work, we have shown that an automatic sleep stager can be applied to multimodal sleep data without using any handmade features. We also compared the reconstructed signal from a trained DBN on data collected in a home environment and saw that the RMSE was large where an obvious error had occurred.

Regarding the DBN parameter selection, it was noticed that setting initial biases for the hidden units to −4 was an important parameter for achieving good accuracy. A better way of encourage sparsity is to include a sparsity penalty term in the cost objective function [31] instead of making a crude estimation of initial biases for the hidden units. For the *raw-DBN* setup, it was also crucial to train each layer with a large number of epochs and in particular the fine tuning step.

We also noticed a lower performance if sleep stages were not set to equal sizes in the training set. There was also a high variation in the accuracy between patients, even if they came from the same dataset. Since the DBN will find a generalization that best fits all training examples, a testing set that deviates from the average training set might give poor results. Since data might differs greatly between patients, a single DBN trained on general sleep data is not specialized enough. The need for a more dynamic system, especially one including the transition and emission matrices for the HMM, is made clear when comparing the hypnograms of a healthy patient and a patient with sleep disordered breathing. Further, although the HMM provides a simple solution that captures temporal properties of sleep data, it makes two critical assumptions [13]. The first one is that the next hidden state can be approximated by a state depending only on the previous state, and the second one is that observations at different time steps are conditionally independent given a state sequence. Replacing HMM with conditional random fields (CRFs) could improve accuracy but is still a simplistic temporal model that does not exploit the power of DBNs [32].

While a clear advantage of using DBN is the natural way in which it deals with anomalous data, there are some limitations to the DBN. One limitation is that correlations between signals in the input data are not well captured. This gives a feature-based approach an advantage where, for example, the correlation between both EOG channels can easily be represented with a feature. This could be solved by either representing the correlation in the input or extending the DBN to handle such correlations, such as a cRBM [33].

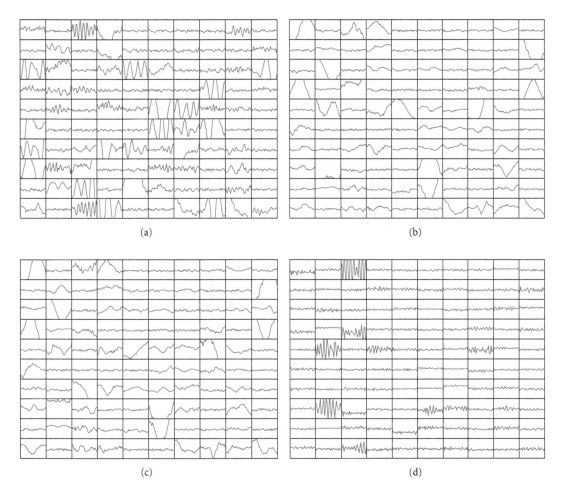

(a)

(b)

(c)

(d)

FIGURE 6: Learned features of layer 1 for (a) EEG, (b) EOG1, (c) EOG2, and (d) EMG. It can be observed that the learned features are of various amplitudes and frequencies and some resemble known sleep events such as a K-complex or blink artifacts. Only the first 100 of the 200 features are shown here.

Regarding the implemented *feat-GOHMM*, we have tried our best to get as high accuracy with the setup as possible. It is almost certain that another set of features, different feature selection algorithm, and/or another classifier could outperform our *feat-GOHMM*. However, we hope that this work illustrates the advantages of unsupervised feature learning, which not only removes the need for domain specific expert knowledge, but inherently provides tools for anomaly detection and noise redundancy.

It has been suggested for multimodal signals to train a separate DBN for each signal first and then train a top DBN with concatenated data [34]. This not only could improve classification accuracy, but also provide the ability to single out which signal contains the anomalous signal. Further, this work has explored clinical data sets in close cooperation with physicians, and future work will concentrate on the application for at home monitoring as sleep data is an area where unsupervised feature learning is a highly promising method for sleep stage classification as data is abundant and labels are costly to obtain.

Appendix

A. Features

A total of 28 features are used in this work.

Relative power for signal y in frequency band f is calculated as

$$y_{P_{\text{rel}}}(f) = \frac{y_P(f)}{\sum_{f=f_1}^{f_5} y_P(f)}, \quad (A.1)$$

where $y(f)_P$ is the sum of the absolute power in frequency band f for signal y. The five frequency bands used are delta (0.5–4 Hz), theta (4–8 Hz), alpha (8–13 Hz), beta (13–20 Hz), and gamma (20–64 Hz).

The median of the absolute value for EMG is calculated as

$$\text{EMG}_{\text{median}} = \text{median}\left(\sum_{k=1}^{N} |\text{EMG}(k)|\right). \quad (A.2)$$

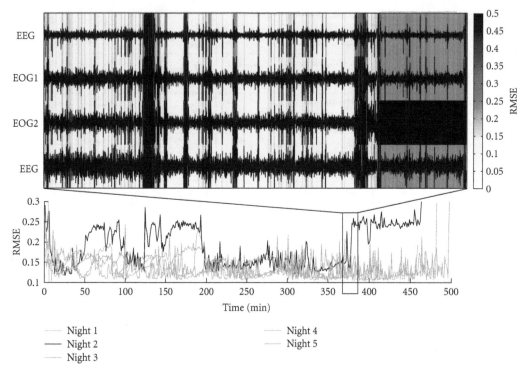

FIGURE 7: RMSE for five night runs recorded at home (bottom). Color-code of RMSE for night run 2 where the redder areas more anomalous areas of the signal. EOG2 falls off at around 380 minutes (top).

The eye correlation coefficient for the EOG is calculated as

$$\mathrm{EOG_{corr}} = \frac{E\left[\left(y_1 - \mu_{y_1}\right)\left(y_2 - \mu_{y_2}\right)\right]}{\sigma_{y_1}\sigma_{y_2}}, \qquad \text{(A.3)}$$

where $y_1 = \mathrm{EOG_{left}}$ and $y_2 = \mathrm{EOG_{right}}$.

The entropy for a signal y is calculated as

$$y_{\mathrm{entropy}} = -\sum_{k=1}^{8} \frac{n_k}{N} \ln \frac{n_k}{N}, \qquad \text{(A.4)}$$

where N is the number of samples in signal y, and n_k is the number of samples from y that belongs to the kth bin from a histogram of y.

The kurtosis for a signal y is calculated as

$$y_{\mathrm{kurtosis}} = \frac{E[y - \mu]^4}{\sigma^4}, \qquad \text{(A.5)}$$

where μ and σ are the mean and standard deviation, respectively, for signal y.

The spectral mean for signal y is calculated as

$$y_{\mathrm{spectralmean}} = \frac{1}{F} \sum_{f=f_1}^{f_5} y(f)_{P_{\mathrm{rel}}} \cdot f, \qquad \text{(A.6)}$$

where F is the sum of the lengths of the 5 frequency bands.

Fractal exponent [35, 36] for the EEG is calculated as the negative slope of the linear fit of spectral density in the double logarithmic graph.

Normalization is performed for some features according to [37] and [30]. The absolute median for EMG is normalized by dividing with the absolute median for the whole EMG signal.

Acknowledgments

The authors are grateful to Professor Walter T. McNicholas of St. Vincents University Hospital, Ireland, and Professor Conor Heneghan of University College Dublin, Ireland, for providing the sleep training data for this study. They would also like to thank senior physician Lena Leissner and sleep technician Meeri Sandelin at the sleep unit of the neuroclinic at Örebro University Hospital for their continuous support and expertise. Finally, special thanks to D F Wulsin for writing and sharing the open-source implementation of DBN for Matlab that was used in this work [20]. This work was funded by NovaMedTech.

References

[1] K. Šušmákováemail and A. Krakovská, "Discrimination ability of individual measures used in sleep stages classification," *Artificial Intelligence in Medicine*, vol. 44, no. 3, pp. 261–277, 2008.

[2] A. Flexer, G. Gruber, and G. Dorffner, "A reliable probabilistic sleep stager based on a single EEG signal," *Artificial Intelligence in Medicine*, vol. 33, no. 3, pp. 199–207, 2005.

[3] L. Johnson, A. Lubin, P. Naitoh, C. Nute, and M. Austin, "Spectral analysis of the EEG of dominant and non-dominant

alpha subjects during waking and sleeping," *Electroencephalography and Clinical Neurophysiology*, vol. 26, no. 4, pp. 361–370, 1969.

[4] J. Pardey, S. Roberts, L. Tarassenko, and J. Stradling, "A new approach to the analysis of the human sleep/wakefulness continuum," *Journal of Sleep Research*, vol. 5, no. 4, pp. 201–210, 1996.

[5] N. Schaltenbrand, R. Lengelle, M. Toussaint et al., "Sleep stage scoring using the neural network model: comparison between visual and automatic analysis in normal subjects and patients," *Sleep*, vol. 19, no. 1, pp. 26–35, 1996.

[6] H. G. Jo, J. Y. Park, C. K. Lee, S. K. An, and S. K. Yoo, "Genetic fuzzy classifier for sleep stage identification," *Computers in Biology and Medicine*, vol. 40, no. 7, pp. 629–634, 2010.

[7] L. Zoubek, S. Charbonnier, S. Lesecq, A. Buguet, and F. Chapotot, "A two-steps sleep/wake stages classifier taking into account artefacts in the polysomnographic signa," in *Proceedings of the 17th World Congress, International Federation of Automatic Control (IFAC '08)*, July 2008.

[8] G. Luo and W. Min, "Subject-adaptive real-time sleep stage classification based on conditional random field," in *Proceedings of the American Medical Informatics Association Annual Symposium (AMIA '07)*, pp. 488–492, 2007.

[9] T. Penzel, K. Kesper, V. Gross, H. F. Becker, and C. Vogelmeier, "Problems in automatic sleep scoring applied to sleep apnea," in *Proceedings of the 25th Annual International Conference of the IEEE Engineering in Medicine and Biology Society (IEEE EMBS '03)*, pp. 358–361, September 2003.

[10] G. E. Hinton, S. Osindero, and Y. W. Teh, "A fast learning algorithm for deep belief nets," *Neural Computation*, vol. 18, no. 7, pp. 1527–1554, 2006.

[11] Y. Bengio, P. Lamblin, D. Popovici, and H. Larochelle, "Greedy layer-wise training of deep networks," in *Advances in Neural Information Processing Systems (NIPS '06)*, vol. 19, pp. 153–160, 2006.

[12] M. Ranzato, C. Poultney, S. Chopra, and Y. LeCun, "Efficient learning of sparse representations with an energy-based model," in *Proceedings of the Advances in Neural Information Processing Systems (NIPS '06)*, J. Platt, T. Hoffman, and B. Schölkopf, Eds., MIT Press, 2006.

[13] Y. Bengio and Y. LeCun, "Scaling learning algorithms towards AI," in *Large-Scale Kernel Machines*, L. Bottou, O. Chapelle, D. DeCoste, and J. Weston, Eds., MIT Press, 2007.

[14] Y. Bengio, "Learning deep architectures for AI," Tech. Rep. 1312, Department of IRO, Universite de Montreal, 2007.

[15] I. Arel, D. Rose, and T. Karnowski, "Deep machine learning—a new frontier in artificial intelligence research," *IEEE Computational Intelligence Magazine*, vol. 14, pp. 12–18, 2010.

[16] V. Nair and G. E. Hinton, "3-d object recognition with deep belief nets," in *Proceedings of the Advances in Neural Information Processing Systems (NIPS '06)*, 2006.

[17] G. Taylor, G. E. Hinton, and S. Roweis, "Modeling human motion using binary latent variables," in *Proceedings of the Advances in Neural Information Processing Systems*, 2007.

[18] N. Jaitly and G. E. Hinton, "Learning a better representation of speech sound waves using restricted boltzmann machines," in *Proceedings of the IEEE International Conference on Acoustics, Speech, and Signal Processing (ICASSP '11)*, 2011.

[19] M. Längkvist and A. Loutfi, "Unsupervised feature learning for electronic nose data applied to bacteria identification in blood," in *NIPS Workshop on Deep Learning and Unsupervised Feature Learning*, 2011.

[20] D. F. Wulsin, J. R. Gupta, R. Mani, J. A. Blanco, and B. Litt, "Modeling electroencephalography waveforms with semi-supervised deep belief nets: fast classification and anomaly measurement," *Journal of Neural Engineering*, vol. 8, no. 3, Article ID 036015, 2011.

[21] G. E. Hinton, "Training products of experts by minimizing contrastive divergence," *Neural Computation*, vol. 14, no. 8, pp. 1771–1800, 2002.

[22] A. Rechtschaffen and A. Kales, *A Manual of Standardized Terminology, Techniques and Scoring System for Sleep Stages of Human Subjects*, U.S. Government Printing Office, Washington DC, USA, 1968.

[23] M. Hirshkowitz, "Standing on the shoulders of giants: the Standardized Sleep Manual after 30 years," *Sleep Medicine Reviews*, vol. 4, no. 2, pp. 169–179, 2000.

[24] S. L. Himanen and J. Hasan, "Limitations of Rechtschaffen and Kales," *Sleep Medicine Reviews*, vol. 4, no. 2, pp. 149–167, 2000.

[25] L. R. Rabiner and B. H. Juang, "An introduction to hidden markov models," *IEEE ASSP Magazine*, vol. 3, no. 1, pp. 4–16, 1986.

[26] G. E. Hinton, *A Practical Guide to Training Restricted Boltzmann Machines*, 2010.

[27] S. Charbonnier, L. Zoubek, S. Lesecq, and F. Chapotot, "Self-evaluated automatic classifier as a decision-support tool for sleep/wake staging," *Computers in Biology and Medicine*, vol. 41, no. 6, pp. 380–389, 2011.

[28] A. Schlögl, C. Keinrath, D. Zimmermann, R. Scherer, R. Leeb, and G. Pfurtscheller, "A fully automated correction method of EOG artifacts in EEG recordings," *Clinical Neurophysiology*, vol. 118, no. 1, pp. 98–104, 2007.

[29] A. L. Goldberger, L. A. Amaral, L. Glass et al., "PhysioBank, PhysioToolkit, and PhysioNet: components of a new research resource for complex physiologic signals," *Circulation*, vol. 101, no. 23, pp. E215–220, 2000.

[30] L. Zoubek, S. Charbonnier, S. Lesecq, A. Buguet, and F. Chapotot, "Feature selection for sleep/wake stages classification using data driven methods," *Biomedical Signal Processing and Control*, vol. 2, no. 3, pp. 171–179, 2007.

[31] G. Huang, H. Lee, and E. Learned-Miller, "Learning hierarchical representations for face verification with convolutional deep belief networks," in *Proceedings of the IEEE Conference on Computer Vision and Pattern Recognition (CVPR '12)*, 2012.

[32] D. Yu, L. Deng, I. Jang, P. Kudumakis, M. Sandler, and K. Kang, "Deep learning and its applications to signal and information processing," *IEEE Signal Processing Magazine*, vol. 28, no. 1, pp. 145–154, 2011.

[33] M. Ranzato, A. Krizhevsky, and G. E. Hinton, "Factored 3-way restricted boltzmann machines for modeling natural images," in *Proceedings of the 30th International Conference on Artificial Intelligence and Statistics*, 2010.

[34] J. Ngiam, A. Khosla, M. Kim, H. Lee, and A. Y. Ng, "Multimodal deep learning," in *Proceedings of the 28th International Conference on Machine Learning*, 2011.

[35] A. R. Osborne and A. Provenzale, "Finite correlation dimension for stochastic systems with power-law spectra," *Physica D*, vol. 35, no. 3, pp. 357–381, 1989.

[36] E. Pereda, A. Gamundi, R. Rial, and J. González, "Non-linear behaviour of human EEG: fractal exponent versus correlation dimension in awake and sleep stages," *Neuroscience Letters*, vol. 250, no. 2, pp. 91–94, 1998.

[37] T. Gasser, P. Baecher, and J. Moecks, "Transformations towards the normal distribution of broad band spectral parameters of the EEG," *Electroencephalography and Clinical Neurophysiology*, vol. 53, no. 1, pp. 119–124, 1982.

Activation Detection on fMRI Time Series Using Hidden Markov Model

Rong Duan[1] and Hong Man[2]

[1] *AT&T Labs, Florham Park, NJ 07932, USA*
[2] *Department of Electrical and Computer Engineering, Stevens Institute of Technology, Hoboken, NJ 07030, USA*

Correspondence should be addressed to Rong Duan, rongduan@research.att.com

Academic Editor: Anke Meyer-Baese

This paper introduces two unsupervised learning methods for analyzing functional magnetic resonance imaging (fMRI) data based on hidden Markov model (HMM). HMM approach is focused on capturing the first-order statistical evolution among the samples of a voxel time series, and it can provide a complimentary perspective of the BOLD signals. Two-state HMM is created for each voxel, and the model parameters are estimated from the voxel time series and the stimulus paradigm. Two different activation detection methods are presented in this paper. The first method is based on the likelihood and likelihood-ratio test, in which an additional Gaussian model is used to enhance the contrast of the HMM likelihood map. The second method is based on certain distance measures between the two state distributions, in which the most likely HMM state sequence is estimated through the Viterbi algorithm. The distance between the on-state and off-state distributions is measured either through a t-test, or using the Kullback-Leibler distance (KLD). Experimental results on both normal subject and brain tumor subject are presented. HMM approach appears to be more robust in detecting the supplemental active voxels comparing with SPM, especially for brain tumor subject.

1. Introduction

Functional magnetic resonance imaging (fMRI) is a well-established technique to monitor brain activities in the field of cognitive neuroscience. The temporal behavior of each fMRI voxel reflects the variations in the concentration of oxyhemoglobin and deoxyhemoglobin, measured through blood oxygen level-dependent (BOLD) contrast. BOLD signal is generally considered as an indirect indicator for brain activities, because neural activations may increase blood flow in certain regions of the brain.

1.1. Characteristics of fMRI Data. fMRI data are collected as a time series of 3D images. Each point in the 3D image volume is called a voxel. fMRI data have four important characteristics: (1) large data volume; (2) relatively low SNR; (3) hemodynamic delay and dispersion; (4) fractal properties. Typically, one fMRI data set includes over 100-K voxels from a whole brain scan and therefore has 100-K time series. The observed time sequences are combinations of different types of signals, such as task-related, function-related, and transiently task-related (different kinds of transiently task-related signals coming from different regions of brain). These are the signals that convey brain activation information. There are also many types of noises, which can be physiology-related, motion-related, and scanning-related. The signal to noise ratio (SNR) in typical fMRI time series can be quite low, for example, around 0.2 to 0.5. For different regions and different trails, the SNR level also varies significantly. Such noise nature causes major difficulty in signal analysis. Hemodynamic delay and dispersion further increase the complexity of fMRI signal structure. Special efforts have been made to construct flexible hemodynamic response function (HRF) which can model the hemodynamic delay and dispersion through various regions and different subjects [1, 2]. fMRI data also have fractal properties, which means that a class of objects may have certain interesting properties in common. In other words, fMRI data are approximately scale invariant or scale free.

1.2. Methodology of Analyzing fMRI Data. Two areas of fMRI-based neural systems study have attracted lots of attention over the past two decades: functional activity detection and functional connectivity detection. Functional activity detection aims to locate the spatial areas that are associated with certain psychological tasks, commonly specified by a predefined paradigm. Functional connectivity detection focuses on finding spatially separated areas that have high temporal correlations [3]. Generally, functional connectivity detection is conducted under the resting-state condition. The differences in biophysical motivations and experiment designs of these two studies are reflected in their methodologies. Functional activity detection compares the temporal series of each voxel with the excitation paradigm and functional connectivity detection compares the voxel timeseries with other series in a predefined spatial region, that is, Region of Interesting (ROI), or "seed" region. Functional activity detection is more on the temporal correlation and functional connectivity detection is more on spatial correlation. Even though the two areas have some differences, they share many common statistical modelling strategies. Both of them attempt to build models to abstract the spatial and temporal relations from the observed fMRI data. To choose a model that can capture the properties of the time series accurately and efficiently is essential in both study areas.

A large number of methods have been proposed to analyze fMRI data. Most of them can be characterized into one of these two categories: modelling based approach and data driven approach. Reference [4] provided a detailed review. Even though the authors claimed the methodologies as functional connectivity detection, certain amount of the reviewed methods were commonly used in functional activity detection study too. This paper focuses on constructing a model to extract voxel temporal characteristics and test the voxel activities using functional activity detection as example. All the models referred following are for this task if no further clarification.

An established software called statistical parametric map (SPM) is a typical functional activity detection modelling package based on general linear model (GLM) [5], general linear model transforms a voxel time series into a space spanned by a set of basis vectors defined in the design matrix. These basis vectors include a set of paradigm waveforms convolved with hemodynamic response function (HRF), as well as several low-frequency DCT bases. The residual errors of this linear transform is modelled as Gaussian pdf. The key component of this method is how to constitute the design-matrix which can accurately model the brain activation effects and separate noises. Using GLM to analyze fMRI data has following intrinsic assumptions:

(i) the activation patterns are spatially distributed in the same way for all subjects,

(ii) the response between input stimulation and brain response is linear,

(iii) the HRF function is the same for every voxel,

(iv) the time series observation has a known Gaussian distribution,

(v) the variance and covariance between repeated measurements are invariant,

(vi) the time courses of different factors affecting the variance of fMRI signals can be reliably estimated in advance,

(vii) the signals at different voxels are independent, and

(viii) the intensity distribution of background (nonactive areas) is known whereas the distribution of active areas is not known.

Reference [6] substituted paradigm with the average temporal series of ROI as seed and applied SPM on functional connectivity detection. And the most recent release of SPM incorporates dynamic causal modelling to infer the interregional coupling, but it is designed more on EEG and MEG data [7].

There are some other methods which can be considered as special cases of GLM. For example, direct subtraction method subtracts the average of "off" period from the average of "on" period. Voxels with significant difference will then be identified as active. Students' t-test can be used to measure the difference in the means by the standard deviations in "off" and "on" periods. The larger the t-value is, the larger the "on-off" difference is, and the more active the voxel is. Correlation coefficient is another special case of GLM. It measures the correlation coefficient between a reference function waveform and each voxel temporal signal waveform. Voxels with large correlation coefficient are considered to be connected. If the reference function waveform is defined by paradigm [8], it is functional activity detection, and if the reference function waveform is defined by some seed time course, it is functional connectivity detection [9].

There exist some problems in GLM-based methods. For example, GLM assumes one HRF function for all voxels. The BOLD signal is only an indirect indicator of neural activity, and many nonneural changes in the body could also influence the BOLD signal. Different brain areas may have different hemodynamic responses, which would not be accurately reflected by the general linear model. Also, GLM method typically requires grouping or averaging data over several task/control blocks, which reduces sensitivity for detecting transient task-related changes, and make it insensitive to significant changes not consistently time-synched to the task block design. Low SNR makes it possible for nontask-relevant components overshadow task-relevant components and further reduces the sensitivity and specificity. GLM only considers the time series and ignores relationships between voxels, hindering the detection of brain regions acting as functional units during the experiment. Another problem is that the GLM method does not extract the intrinsic structure of the data, which may significantly weaken its effectiveness when the a priori of fMRI signal in response to the experimental events is not known or may not be constant across all voxels.

Besides GLM-based methods, a few methods have been proposed to improve the accuracy of modelling fMRI temporal signals. Reference [10] introduced a Bayesian modelling method which used a two-state HMM to infer an optimal state sequence through Markov Chain Monte Carlo sampling. The method assumed the observation is a linear combination of a two-state HMM, which infer hidden psychological states, plus constant and trend. The model is designed as the combination of offset, linear trend and a set of two-state HMMs state sequences start at different time points. MCMC is used to estimate the optimal state sequence for each voxel. This method is good in interpreting the dynamics in each voxel, but the computing complexity is big concern as mentioned by the authors, and also the totally paradigm-free approach might introduce noise that irrelevant with the experiment design. Reference [11] applied state-space model and Kalman filter to model the baseline and stimulus effect without any parametric constrain. Reference [12] employed multiple reference functions with 100 ms shift to find the highest correlation coefficient reference function for specific voxels, which avoids the common practice of using a single-reference function for all voxels. Reference [13] proposed Gaussian mixture models to describe the mutually exclusive fMRI time sequence. Reference [14] introduced an unsupervised learning method based on hidden semi-Markov event sequence models (HSMESMs) method which had the advantage of explicitly modelling the state occupancy duration. The method decomposed an observation into true positive events, false positive events, and missing observations. The "off-on" paradigm transitions were modelled as left to right HMM true positive states, and the other periods were considered as semi-Markov false positive states. The likelihood of HSMESM was calculated iteratively to detect activity base on predefined threshold. Reference [15] used first-order Markov chain to estimate the time series, t-test, and mutual information to detect the actions. All these methods are essentially two-stage approach. The temporal property is modelled at each voxel independently and then spatial modelling is performed based on the summarized statistics from temporal analysis. Fully Bayesian spatiotemporal modelling [16] considered spatial and temporal information together. This method decomposed the observation data into spatiotemporal signal and noise, and space-time simultaneously specified autoregressive model (STSAR) was employed to construct noise model. Half-cosine HRF model and activation height model were used to construct fMRI signal models.

Granger causality analysis [17] and dynamic causal modelling [18] are two popular methods in functional connectivity detection in recent years. A series comments and controversies [19–22] have been dedicated to comparing these two methods on model selection, causality, and deconvolution from biophysiological view. Reference [23] criticized dynamic causal modelling from computation complexity and model validation from mathematical perspective. The advantage of these two methods are that they consider the spatial and temporal information at the same time, but the disadvantage is the model complexity.

All the modelling-based approaches mentioned above are either too simple to capture the temporal or spatial dynamics for different voxels and subjects, or too complicated to estimate parameters accurately and inference easily.

In addition to these modelling-based methods, there are also data driven methods in analyzing fMRI data. One popular example of this approach is independent component analysis (ICA). ICA decomposes a 4D fMRI data volume (3D spatial and 1D temporal) into a set of maximum temporal or spatial independent components by minimizing the mutual information between these components. ICA does not require the knowledge of stimulus or paradigm in data decomposition, and similar voxel activation patterns will usually appear in the same component. ICA is also called blind source separation, because it does not need prior knowledge, and it is able to identify "transient task related" components that could not be easily identified by the paradigm. The first application of ICA in fMRI data was the spatial ICA (sICA) [24]. Temporal ICA (tICA) was introduced later by [25]. Reference [26] compared the sICA with tICA and reported that the beneficial of each method depends on the independence of the underlying spatial or temporal signal. sICA maximizes independence spatially and the corresponding temporal information might be highly correlated, and vice versa for tICA. To consider the mutual independence between space and time simultaneously, [27] proposed a spatiotemporal independent component analysis (stICA). Extended from entropy-based one-dimension ICA decomposition introduced in [28], the authors embedded the spatial and temporal components at the same time and also incorporated the spatial skewed probability density function to replace the kurtosis and symmetric probability density function in decomposing the independent signals. As pointed out in [29], the disadvantages of the Infomax and entropy-based stICA algorithms used in [27] are that the number of parameters needed to be estimated is large, the local minima and sensitive to noise characteristics of the gradient descent optimization methods. To improve the stability, robustness, and simplify the computing complexity, [29] adopted the generalized eigenvalue decomposition and joint diagonalization on both spatial and temporal autocorrelation to achieve spatial and temporal independent signals simultaneously. ICA methods have showed promising results in fMRI analysis, but similar as all other data-driven methods, it is hard to interpret the output and it usually requires special knowledge and human intervention. Also, ICA does not specify which component, among many output components, is the activation component, and there is no statistical confidence level of each components extracted.

Clustering is another well-developed data driven approach in brain activity and connectivity detection. It has been used to identify regions with similar patterns of activations. Common clustering algorithms include hierarchical clustering, crisp clustering, K-means, self-organizing maps (SOM), and fussy clustering. The major drawback of most clustering methods is that they make assumptions about cluster shapes and sizes, which may deviate in observed data structures. The optimization techniques used in clustering may also result in local maxima and instable results. In addition, the number of clusters is frequently determined heuristically and randomly initialized, which makes the output inconsistent with each trial.

In this paper, we propose a simple dynamic state space model, which attempts to model the voxel time series as a random process driven by the experimental paradigm or some ROI area seed series. For a given voxel, its behavior is described by a two-state hidden Markov model with certain state distributions and state transitions. The HMM parameters are estimated from the prior statistics of the paradigm as well as from the testing time series. Two methods are introduced to detect the voxel activation based on the estimated HMM. The first method calculates the likelihood of each time series, given its HMM, and forms a likelihood map for all the voxels reside in a fMRI slice. A simple Gaussian model is also used to improve the contrast of this likelihood map. The second method uses the t-test or the Kullback-Leibler distance (KLD) to measure the distance between the on-state distribution and the off-state distribution. These distributions are estimated based on the most likely HMM state sequence, which is calculated through a Viterbi algorithm. The contribution of the method is that it unifies the robustness, stability, and reliability under the same framework in estimating paradigm driven fMRI study. First, it incorporates the dynamic characteristics of fMRI time series by adapting 2-state HMM model, which is robust in detecting active voxels with different delay and dispersion behaviors. Second, the proposed method utilizes paradigm prior knowledge in parameter estimation, which is not only to simplify the computing compared with the approach in [10], but also to improve the stability and reliability of the output due to the stability of paradigm.

The rest of this paper is organized as follows. In Section 2, we introduce the two-state hidden Markov model approach for fMRI data. In Section 3, we discuss activation detection methods base on the estimated HMM. In Section 4, we present the experimental results on two sets of fMRI data, one is normal subject and the other is brain tumor subject, and compare the results with GLM-based statistical parametric mapping package (SPM) [5].

2. Hidden Markov Model for fMRI Time Series

2.1. Hidden Markov Model. HMM is a very efficient stochastic method in modelling sequential data of which the distribution patterns tend to cluster and alternate among different clusters [30]. A hidden Markov model consists of a finite set of states. In a traditional Markov chain, the state is directly visible to the observer, and the state transition probabilities are the only parameters. In an HMM, only the observations influenced by the state are visible. Each of the hidden state is associated with a probability distribution. Transitions among the states are measured by transition probabilities. The most common first-order HMM implies that the state at any given time depends only on the state at the previous time step.

HMM is well developed in temporal pattern recognition applications. It was first applied to speech recognition [31].

Now it is widely used in multimedia [32], bioinformatics [33, 34], informational retrieval [35], and so forth.

An HMM can be described by the following elements [31]: (1) a set of observations $O\{T\}$, where T is the number of time samples; (2) a set of states $Q\{N\}$, where N is the number of states; (3) a state-transition probability distribution $A = \{a_{ij}\}$, where $a_{ij} = P[q_{t+1} = S_j \mid q_t = S_i]$, $1 \le i, j \le N$; (4) observation probability distribution for each state $B = \{b_j(x)\}$, where $b_j(x) = P[o_t = x \mid q_t = S_j]$, $1 \le j \le N$, $x \in \mathfrak{R}$ is a possible observation value; (5) an initial state distribution $\pi = \{\pi_j\}$, where $\pi_j = P[q_1 = S_j]$, $1 \le j \le N$.

An HMM is therefore denoted by $\lambda = \{A, B, \pi\}$. We further model each state distribution as a Gaussian pdf:

$$P\big[O_t = x \mid q_t = S_j\big] = \frac{1}{\sigma_j\sqrt{2\pi}}e^{-(x-\mu_j)^2/(2\sigma_j^2)}, \quad j \in \{0, 1\}. \tag{1}$$

Let $Q = q_1, q_2, \ldots, q_T$ be a possible state sequence and assume that the observation samples are independent, the likelihood of an observed sequence given this HMM can be calculated as:

$$\begin{aligned} P(O \mid \lambda) &= \sum_Q P(O \mid Q, \lambda)P(Q \mid \lambda) \\ &= \sum_Q \pi_{q_1}b_{q_1}(o_1)a_{q_1q_2}b_{q_2}(o_2)\cdots a_{q_{T-1}q_T}b_{q_T}(o_T). \end{aligned} \tag{2}$$

Given the observation O and the HMM, the most likely state sequence $Q = \{q_1, q_2, \ldots, q_T\}$, which maximizes the likelihood $P(Q \mid O, \lambda)$, can be calculated through the Viterbi algorithm [36]. The Viterbi path score function is defined as:

$$\delta_t(i) = \max_{q_1, q_2, \ldots, q_{t-1}} P[q_1q_2\cdots q_t = i, o_1o_2\cdots o_t \mid \lambda], \tag{3}$$

where $\delta_t(i)$ is the highest probable path ending in state i at time t. The induction can be expressed as:

$$\delta_{t+1}(j) = \max_{1 \le i \le N}\big[\delta_t(i)a_{ij}\big]b_j(o_{t+1}). \tag{4}$$

In an application of HMM, multiple HMMs are trained by different groups of labeled data. The HMM parameters are estimated based on these training data. The test data will be assigned to the one which has the maximum likelihood.

2.2. Brain Activation Detection

2.2.1. HMM Likelihood Methods. In our unsupervised learning methods, HMM parameters are estimated directly from the experimental paradigm or the voxel time series under examination. This is different from conventional HMM applications where HMM parameters are usually estimated from some training data. The attempt of avoiding training process is motivated by the fact that the true activation behavior varies from voxel to voxel and from patient to patient. Therefore, it is not advisable to use the parameters from certain set of voxels to characterize other voxels.

Since the simple block paradigm has only two levels, "on, off," in this work we let the number of state $N = 2$, that is, on-state S_1 and off-state S_0.

Because of the first-order Markov assumption, that is, $P(q_t = j \mid q_{t-1} = i, q_{t-2} = k, \ldots) = P(q_t = j \mid q_{t-1} = i)$, the distribution of a state duration is exponential, and the expected value of a state duration can be expressed as:

$$\bar{d}_i = \frac{1}{1 - a_{ii}}. \tag{5}$$

Given an experimental paradigm, let the length (i.e., time samples) of the ON period be L_{on}, and the length of off period be L_{off}, the transition matrix A can be estimated as $a_{00} = 1/(1 - L_{\text{off}})$, $a_{01} = 1 - a_{00}$, $a_{11} = 1/(1 - L_{\text{on}})$, $a_{10} = 1 - a_{11}$.

The parameters in B can be estimated from the voxel time series O. Assuming that the time samples are normalized, let p_{on} denote the paradigm ON periods, and p_{off} denote the paradigm off periods, the off-state S_0 Gaussian parameters are

$$\mu_0 = \frac{1}{|p_{\text{off}}|} \sum_{t \in p_{\text{off}}} o_t, \qquad \sigma_0 = \sqrt{\frac{1}{|p_{\text{off}}|} \sum_{t \in p_{\text{off}}} (o_t - \mu_0)^2}, \tag{6}$$

and the on-state S_1 Gaussian parameters are

$$\mu_1 = \frac{1}{|p_{\text{on}}|} \sum_{t \in p_{\text{on}}} o_t, \qquad \sigma_1 = \sqrt{\frac{1}{|p_{\text{on}}|} \sum_{t \in p_{\text{on}}} (o_t - \mu_1)^2}, \tag{7}$$

where $|p_{\text{off}}|$ is the total number of time samples in the off periods, and $|p_{\text{on}}|$ is the total number of time samples in the ON periods.

Because the paradigm always starts at the off state, the parameters in π are set as $\pi_0 = 1$ and $\pi_1 = 0$.

Given a 2-state HMM as specified, if an observation sequence does have two distinguishable states in consistence with the paradigm states, the resulting $\{\mu_0, \sigma_0\}$ will be clearly different from $\{\mu_1, \sigma_1\}$, and the likelihood of such sequence given this model will be relatively high. If an observation sequence does not have such clear 2-state characteristic, the corresponding state transition will be somehow random and will not fit well with the specified A matrix. In such situation, the likelihood of this sequence will be relatively low. Therefore, the value of voxel sequence likelihood can provide an indication about the activation of this voxel. A likelihood test on an fMRI slice will be able to produce a likelihood map with each point representing the likelihood of a voxel on this slice.

To enhance the contrast of this likelihood map, we introduce a simple Gaussian model for the p_{off} samples. This model is consistent with the S_0 state distribution in the 2-state HMM. The likelihood of the entire sequence is calculated based on this model. The expectation is that if a voxel is non-active, its distribution in p_{off} periods and p_{on} periods should be similar, and therefore the likelihood to this model should be relatively high; on the other hand, if the voxel is active, its distribution in p_{on} periods will be quite

different from the distribution in p_{off} periods, and therefore the likelihood of the whole sequence on this model will be relatively low. The substraction of the HMM log likelihood map and the Gaussian log likelihood map is equivalent to a general likelihood ratio test, and it provides an activation map with enhanced contrast.

2.2.2. State Distribution Distance Methods. If a voxel is active, its fMRI time series can be partitioned into segments associated with two states, and each state can be described by a distribution. The assumption is that if the on-state distribution is significantly different from the off-state distribution, we have high confidence to declare a voxel as active, and vice versa. Therefore, the second method we are investigating attempts to measure the distance between the presumed on-state and off-state distributions.

There are many techniques available for measuring the distance of two distributions. We study two of such measures in this work, one is the t-test, and the other is the Kullback-Leibler divergence. Both on-state and off-state distributions are models as simple Gaussian pdfs.

Given the Gaussian parameters, $\{\mu_0, \sigma_0\}$ and $\{\mu_1, \sigma_1\}$, the t-test calculates the difference of two mean values corrected by their variance values

$$t = \frac{\mu_1 - \mu_0}{\sqrt{(\sigma_{\text{on}}^2/|p_{\text{on}}|) + (\sigma_{\text{off}}^2/|p_{\text{off}}|)}}. \tag{8}$$

A t-map is produced after the t-test is applied to all the voxels on an fMRI slice. High t values in the map usually indicate active voxels.

The Kullback-Leibler divergence [37] is frequently used as a distance measure for two probability densities, although in theory it is not a true distance measure because it is not symmetric. In general it is defined in the form of "relative entropy,"

$$D\big(p_i(x) \| p_j(x)\big) = -\int p_i(x) \log \frac{p_j(x)}{p_i(x)} dx. \tag{9}$$

For two Gaussian pdfs, a close form expression for KLD is available:

$$D\big(p_i(\cdot; \mu_i, \sigma_i) \| p_j(\cdot; \mu_j, \sigma_j)\big)$$
$$= \frac{1}{2}\left[\log\left(\frac{\sigma_j^2}{\sigma_i^2}\right) - 1 + \frac{\sigma_i^2}{\sigma_j^2} + \frac{(\mu_i - \mu_j)^2}{\sigma_j^2} \right]. \tag{10}$$

These are well-established methods. However a critical issue in fMRI analysis is how to estimate the correct on-state and off-state distributions. A simple assumption is to let all time samples in the paradigm ON periods be the on-state samples and let all samples in the paradigm off periods be the off-state samples. We refer to this approach as the "paradigm state" approach. The SPM takes a similar approach, except that the block paradigm is convolved with an HRF, which is normally a low-pass filter characterizing

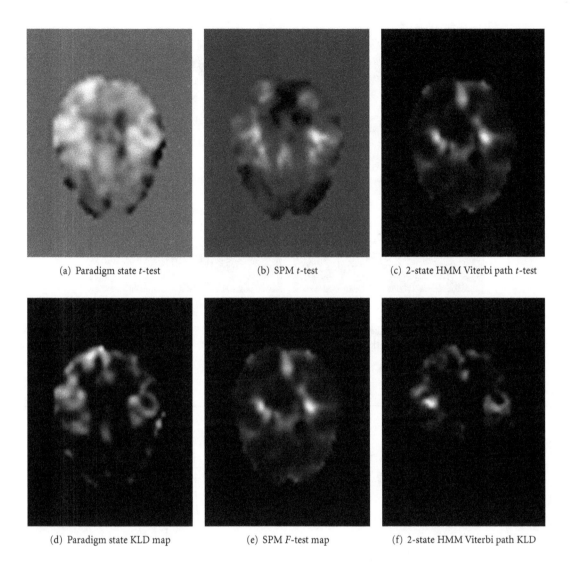

(a) Paradigm state *t*-test (b) SPM *t*-test (c) 2-state HMM Viterbi path *t*-test

(d) Paradigm state KLD map (e) SPM *F*-test map (f) 2-state HMM Viterbi path KLD

FIGURE 1: (a), (b), and (c) are *t*-test map for paradigm-defined state, SPM method, and 2-state HMM Viterbi path map respectively; (d), (e), and (f) are KLD map for paradigm defined state, SPM *F*-test, and 2-state HMM Viterbi path KLD map, respectively. The HMM Viterbi path methods (c) and (f) produce more compact and clearly highlighted regions than paradigm state estimation (a) and (d); HMM Viterbi path methods perform similarly to SPM with some minor differences.

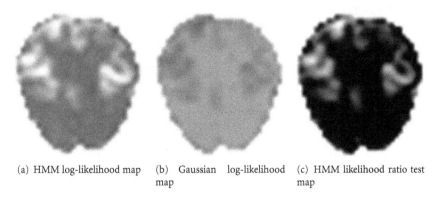

(a) HMM log-likelihood map (b) Gaussian log-likelihood map (c) HMM likelihood ratio test map

FIGURE 2: (a) HMM log-likelihood map—2-state HMM model is applied to all voxels. The active voxels with obvious 2-state on/off patterns will have relative high likelihood given this model; (b) Gaussian log-likelihood map—"off"-state Gaussian model is applied to all voxels. The nonactive voxels with obvious 2-state on/off patterns will have relative high likelihood given this model; (c) HMM likelihood ratio test map—subtraction of HMM log-likelihood map and Gaussian log-likelihood map equivalent to general likelihood ration test, and it enhances the contrast for activation map.

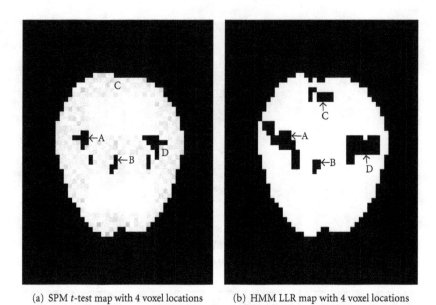

(a) SPM *t*-test map with 4 voxel locations   (b) HMM LLR map with 4 voxel locations

FIGURE 3: Glass map for SPM *t*-test and HMM likelihood ratio and 4 voxel time series. "A" and "B" are detected by both SPM and HMM methods, while "C" and "D" are only detected by the HMM log-likelihood ratio method.

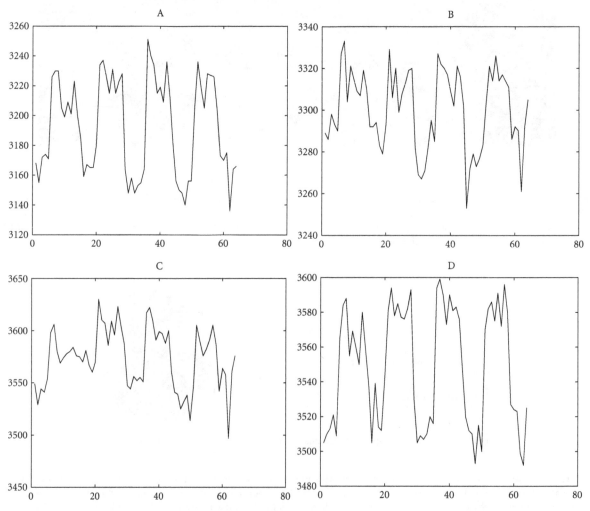

FIGURE 4: The time series of four active voxels. "A" and "B" are detected by both SPM and HMM methods, while "C" and "D" are only detected by the HMM log-likelihood ratio method.

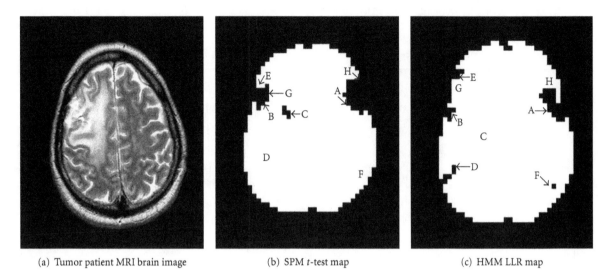

(a) Tumor patient MRI brain image   (b) SPM *t*-test map   (c) HMM LLR map

FIGURE 5: Tumor patient high-resolution image and glass maps for SPM test and 2-state HMM likelihood ratio test. The patient has a tumor on his left frontal lobe from (a). No supplemental voxels from SPM *t*-test (b). "D" and "F" are supplemental voxels detected from HMM LLR map in (c).

the nature voxel response to a stimulus. The μ_0 and μ_1 are obtained by projecting the time series to the HRF convolved paradigm waveform, and the σ_0 and σ_1 are set to be the same to model the residual error between the voxel time series and the weighted paradigm waveform.

We take a different approach by applying the 2-state HMM on each voxel series and calculate the most likely state sequence using the Viterbi algorithm. We refer to this approach as the "Viterbi path" approach. Then the on-state and off-state statistics are calculated according to the optimal state assignment for each time sample. The $\{\mu_0, \sigma_0\}$ are obtained from all samples belonging to the off-state, and $\{\mu_1, \sigma_1\}$ are obtained from all samples belonging to the on-state.

3. Experimental Results

3.1. Normal Subject. The data set is collected from a test with self-paced bilateral sequential thumb-to-digits opposition task. The task paradigm consists of a 32 sec baseline followed by 4 cycles of 30 sec ON and 30 sec OFF. The time series is sampled at 0.25 Hz, which produces 68 time samples for each voxel. The first four samples are ignored during analysis because of initial unstable measurement. The BOLD image is acquired in a 1.5 T GE echo speed horizon scanner with the following parameters: TR/TE = 4000/60, FOV = 24 cm, 64 × 64 matrix, slice thickness 5 mm without gap, and 28 slices to cover the entire brain. Following acquisition of the functional data (with a resolution of 3.75 × 3.75 × 5 mm³), a set of 3 mm slice thickness, high resolution (256 × 256 matrix size), gadolinium-enhanced images are also obtained according to clinical imaging protocol. The data is aligned to remove the limited motion between data sets then smoothed with a Gaussian kernel before further processing [5]. We further normalize each time series with the mean and variance of its paradigm off period. In order to compensate DC drifting in

many voxels, each time series is partitioned into four equal-length segments, and normalization is performed separately on each of these segments. In the reported results, only one fMRI transverse slice is shown.

We first compare three methods based on two different distribution distance measures. These include the SPM with a *t*-test or an *f*-test, and our HMM Viterbi path method with a *t*-test or a KLD measure. The results are shown in Figure 1. From these results we can see that the primary motor and secondary motor areas are effectively highlighted by all these methods. We also have the following observations: (1) the HMM Viterbi path methods produce more compact and clearly highlighted regions, which indicates that Viterbi path estimation is more accurate than paradigm state estimation; (2) the HMM Viterbi path *t*-test method performs similarly to SPM *t*-test with some minor differences, mostly along the outer frontal regions; (3) the KLD methods have resemblance to SPM *F*-test in the sense that their results are pure positive, while *t*-test results are signed.

To test the effectiveness of our HMM likelihood ratio method, we compare its result with an SPM *t*-test result. In Figure 2, (a) shows the two-state HMM log-likelihood map; (b) shows the Gaussian log-likelihood map of the same slice; (c) shows the log-likelihood ratio test map. It can be seen that HMM log-likelihood map is almost the reverse of Gaussian log-likelihood map, which validates our expectation in Section 2.2.1. (c) is similar to (a), yet with enhanced contrast. This result resembles the SPM *t*-test result, although their magnitude scales are quite different.

We examine several active voxels detected by SPM and by HMM likelihood ratio test. In Figure 3, the SPM t-map and the HMM log likelihood ratio map are thresholded at certain level to yield similar number of active voxels. The corresponding voxel time series marked with "A," "B," "C," and "D" are shown in Figure 4. The voxels "A" and "B" can be detected by both SPM and HMM likelihood ratio test.

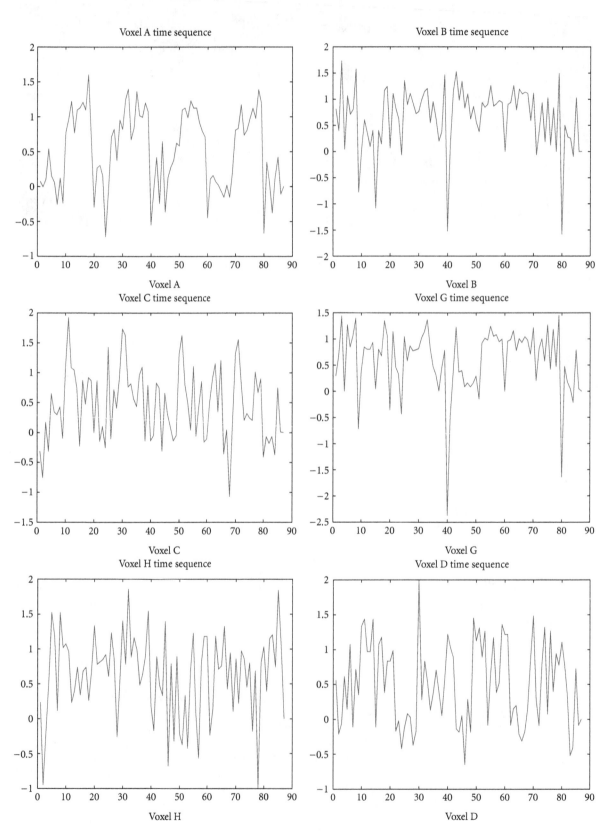

FIGURE 6: Continued.

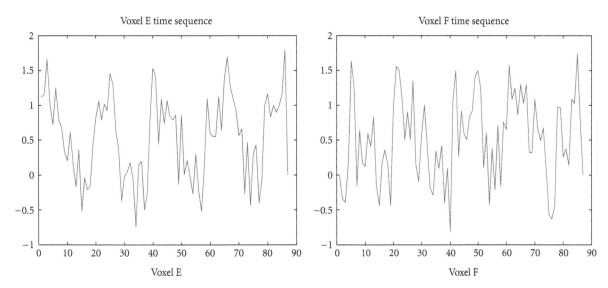

FIGURE 6: Voxel time series, voxels "A" and "B" are detected by both SPM t-test and 2-state HMM likelihood ratio test; voxels "C," "G," and "H" are detected by SPM t-test only. "D," "E," and "F" are detected by 2-state HMM likelihood ratio test only.

The voxels "C" and "D" are only highlighted by the HMM likelihood ratio test.

3.2. Brain Tumor Subject. Functional MRI is not only used for normal brain function mapping, it is also widely used for neurosurgical planning and neurologic risk assessment in the treatment of brain tumors. The growth of a tumor can cause functional areas to shift from their original locations. Large tumors can cause these critical regions to shift dramatically. Localizing the motor strip and coregistering the results to a surgical scan prior to a neurosurgical intervention can help guide the direct cortical stimulation during an awake craniotomy and possibly shorten operation time. In some cases, using fMRI to confirm the expected location of the motor strip may avoid awake neurosurgery altogether.

The HRF for brain tumor patient is more complicated than that for normal healthy subjects. We compare our unsupervised 2-state HMM model with GLM-based SPM on brain tumor patient and found 2-state HMM model is more robust to HRF and it is more sensitive in detecting supplemental motor activation.

The machine specification and the functional data acquisition for a tumor patient is the same as for the normal subject described above. The experiment design is different. The test is self-paced bilateral sequential thumb-to-digits opposition task. The task paradigm consists of a 20 sec baseline followed by 4 cycles of 20 sec ON and 20 sec off. Each point is 2 sec for a total of 3 min. The time series is totally 90 time samples for each voxel. The first 3 samples are ignored during analysis because of initial unstable measurement. The patient has a tumor on his left frontal lobe. As seen in the high resolution fMRI image in Figure 5(a).

Figure 5(b) is a thresholded SPM t-test map, both left and right motor areas are detected by SPM and there is no supplemental voxels. SPM t-test shows that the tumor does not impact the patient's motor area. Thresholded HMM

likelihood ratio test result shown in Figure 5(c) indicates some weak motor activation in the left side motor area. In addition, there are some supplemental motor activation detected on surrounding areas. We further study several active voxels from Figures 5(b) and 5(c). The locations of selected active voxels are marked as "A," "B," "C," "D," "E." "F," "G," and "H" in each figures, respectively. The corresponding voxel time series are shown from Figure 6. From these results, we can see that there are three types of voxels. The voxels "A" and "B" are detected by both SPM and HMM likelihood ratio test, which exhibit strong activation patterns. Voxels "C", "G," and "H" are detected only by SPM, and in fact they are either very weak activations or false positives. Voxels "D," "E," and "F" are detected only in HMM likelihood ratio test and their time series have strong activation patterns related to the paradigm but with different delay and dispersion. These results reaffirmed our understanding that SPM has difficulty in locating active voxels with unexpected delay and dispersion behaviors.

4. Conclusion Remarks and Future Works

In this paper we have presented HMM-based method to detect active voxels in fMRI data. A 2-state HMM model is built based on paradigm on/off periods, and a 1-state HMM model is built based on paradigm off period. A log-likelihood ratio map is generated using the two log-likelihoods. Viterbi path is obtained for the 2-state HMM model. According to the Viterbi path, t-test map and KLD map are generated. From experiments we see that HMM methods are as effective as SPM method, and sometime HMM methods can detect supplemental active voxels that SPM may miss, especially in complicated cases with such as tumor patients. Overall we consider that the HMM methods are complementary to the SPM method, because SPM focuses on capturing fMRI signal waveform characteristics while HMM method attempts to describe fMRI signal stochastic behaviors. In other words, the HMM methods can provide a second opinion to the SPM test results, which can be very helpful in practical situations.

References

[1] M. W. Woolrich, T. E. J. Behrens, and S. M. Smith, "Constrained linear basis sets for HRF modelling using Variational Bayes," *NeuroImage*, vol. 21, no. 4, pp. 1748–1761, 2004.

[2] P. Ciuciu, J. B. Poline, G. Marrelec, J. Idier, C. Pallier, and H. Benali, "Unsupervised robust nonparametric estimation of the hemodynamic response function for any fMRI experiment," *IEEE Transactions on Medical Imaging*, vol. 22, no. 10, pp. 1235–1251, 2003.

[3] L. Lee, L. M. Harrison, and A. Mechelli, "A report of the functional connectivity workshop, Dusseldorf 2002," *NeuroImage*, vol. 19, no. 2, pp. 457–465, 2003.

[4] K. Li, L. Guo, J. Nie, G. Li, and T. Liu, "Review of methods for functional brain connectivity detection using fMRI," *Computerized Medical Imaging and Graphics*, vol. 33, no. 2, pp. 131–139, 2009.

[5] K. J. Friston, A. P. Holmes, K. J. Worsley, J. P. Poline, C. D. Frith, and R. S. J. Frackowiak, "Statistical parametric maps in functional imaging: a general linear approach," *Human Brain Mapping*, vol. 2, no. 4, pp. 189–210, 1994.

[6] M. D. Greicius, B. Krasnow, A. L. Reiss, and V. Menon, "Functional connectivity in the resting brain: a network analysis of the default mode hypothesis," *Proceedings of the National Academy of Sciences of the United States of America*, vol. 100, no. 1, pp. 253–258, 2003.

[7] J. Ashburner, "Spm:a history," *NeuroImage*, vol. 62, no. 2, pp. 791–800, 2012.

[8] G. K. Wood, "Visualization of subtle contrast-related intensity changes using temporal correlation," *Magnetic Resonance Imaging*, vol. 12, no. 7, pp. 1013–1020, 1994.

[9] J. Cao and K. Worsley, "The geometry of correlation fields with an application to functional connectivity of the brain," *Annals of Applied Probability*, vol. 9, no. 4, pp. 1021–1057, 1999.

[10] P. Hojen-Sorensen, L. Hansen, and C. Rasmussen, "Baysian modelling of fmri time series," in *Proceedings of the 13th Annual Conference on Advances in Neural Information Processing Systems (NIPS '99)*, pp. 754–760, 2000.

[11] C. Gossl, D. Auer, and L. Fahtmeir, "Dynamic models in fmri," *Magnetic Resonance in Medicine*, vol. 43, no. 1, pp. 72–81, 2000.

[12] M. Singh, W. Sungkarat, J. W. Jeong, and Y. Zhou, "Extraction of temporal information in functional MRI," *IEEE Transactions on Nuclear Science*, vol. 49, no. 5, pp. 2284–2290, 2002.

[13] V. Sanguineti, C. Parodi, S. Perissinotto et al., "Analysis of fMRI time series with mixtures of Gaussians," in *Proceedings of the International Joint Conference on Neural Networks (IJCNN '2000)*, vol. 1, pp. 331–335, July 2000.

[14] S. Faisan, L. Thoraval, J. P. Armspach, and F. Heitz, "Unsupervised learning and mapping of brain fMRI signals based on hidden semi-Markov event sequence models," in *Proceedings of the 6th International Conference on Medical Image Computing and Computer-Assisted Intervention (MICCAI '03)*, pp. 75–82, November 2003.

[15] B. Thirion and O. Faugeras, "Revisiting non-parametric activation detection on fMRI time series," in *Proceedings of the IEEE Workshop on Mathematical Methods in Biomedical Image Analysis*, vol. 1, pp. 121–128, December 2001.

[16] M. W. Woolrich, M. Jenkinson, J. M. Brady, and S. M. Smith, "Fully bayesian spatio-temporal modeling of FMRI data," *IEEE Transactions on Medical Imaging*, vol. 23, no. 2, pp. 213–231, 2004.

[17] A. Roebroeck, E. Formisano, and R. Goebel, "Mapping directed influence over the brain using Granger causality and fMRI," *NeuroImage*, vol. 25, no. 1, pp. 230–242, 2005.

[18] K. J. Friston, L. Harrison, and W. Penny, "Dynamic causal modelling," *NeuroImage*, vol. 19, no. 4, pp. 1273–1302, 2003.

[19] K. Friston, "Dynamic causal modeling and Granger causality comments on: the identification of interacting networks in the brain using fMRI: model selection, causality and deconvolution," *NeuroImage*, vol. 58, pp. 303–305, 2011.

[20] O. David, "fMRI connectivity, meaning and empiricism. Comments on: Roebroeck et al. The identification of interacting networks in the brain using fMRI: model selection, causality and deconvolution," *NeuroImage*, vol. 58, pp. 306–309, 2011.

[21] A. Roebroeck, E. Formisano, and R. Goebel, "Reply to Friston and David. After comments on: the identification of interacting networks in the brain using fMRI: model selection, causality and deconvolution," *NeuroImage*, vol. 58, pp. 296–302, 2011.

[22] A. Roebroeck, E. Formisano, and R. Goebel, "Reply to Friston and David. After comments on: the identification of interacting networks in the brain using fMRI: model selection, causality and deconvolution," *NeuroImage*, vol. 58, pp. 310–311, 2011.

[23] G. Lohmann, K. Erfurth, K. Mller, and R. Turner, "Critical comments on dynamic causal modelling," *NeuroImage*, vol. 59, pp. 2322–2329, 2012.

[24] M. Mckeown, S. Makeig, G. Brown et al., "Analysis of fmri data by blind seperation into independent spatial components," *Human Brain Mapping*, vol. 6, pp. 160–188, 1998.

[25] B. B. Biswal and J. L. Ulmer, "Blind source separation of multiple signal sources of fMRI data sets using independent component analysis," *Journal of Computer Assisted Tomography*, vol. 23, no. 2, pp. 265–271, 1999.

[26] V. D. Calhoun, T. Adali, G. D. Pearlson, and J. J. Pekar, "Spatial and temporal independent component analysis of functional MRI data containing a pair of task-related waveforms," *Human Brain Mapping*, vol. 13, no. 1, pp. 43–53, 2001.

[27] J. V. Stone, J. Porrill, N. R. Porter, and I. D. Wilkinson, "Spatiotemporal independent component analysis of event-related fMRI data using skewed probability density functions," *NeuroImage*, vol. 15, no. 2, pp. 407–421, 2002.

[28] A. J. Bell and T. J. Sejnowski, "An information-maximization approach to blind separation and blind deconvolution," *Neural Computation*, vol. 7, no. 6, pp. 1129–1159, 1995.

[29] F. J. Theis, P. Gruber, I. R. Keck, and E. W. Lang, "A robust model for spatiotemporal dependencies," *Neurocomputing*, vol. 71, no. 10–12, pp. 2209–2216, 2008.

[30] G. McLachlan and D. Peel, *Finite Mixture Models*, John Wiley & Sons, New York, NY, USA, 2000.

[31] L. R. Rabiner, "Tutorial on hidden Markov models and selected applications in speech recognition," *Proceedings of the IEEE*, vol. 77, no. 2, pp. 257–286, 1989.

[32] G. Xu, Y. F. Ma, H. J. Zhang, and S. Q. Yang, "An HMM-based framework for video semantic analysis," *IEEE Transactions on Circuits and Systems for Video Technology*, vol. 15, no. 11, pp. 1422–1433, 2005.

[33] A. Krogh, M. Brown, I. S. Mian, K. Sjolander, and D. Haussler, "Hidden Markov Models in computational biology applications to protein modeling," *Journal of Molecular Biology*, vol. 235, no. 5, pp. 1501–1531, 1994.

[34] R. Durbin, S. Eddy, A. Krogh, and G. Mitchison, *Biological Sequence Analysis: Probabilistic Models of Proteins and Nucleic Acids*, Cambridge University Press, 1999.

[35] D. Miller, T. Leek, and R. Schwartz, "A hidden markov model information retrieval system," in *Proceedings of the 22nd Annual International ACM SIGIR Conference on Research and Development in Information Retrieval*, pp. 214–221, ACM, 1999.

[36] G. D. Forney, "The viterbi algorithm," *Proceedings of the IEEE*, vol. 61, no. 3, pp. 268–278, 1973.

[37] S. Kullback and R. Leibler, "On information and sufficiency," *Annals of Mathematical Statistics*, vol. 22, no. 1, pp. 79–86, 1951.

3

An Efficient Constrained Learning Algorithm for Stable 2D IIR Filter Factorization

Nicholas Ampazis[1] and Stavros J. Perantonis[2]

[1] *Department of Financial and Management Engineering, University of the Aegean, 82100 Chios, Greece*
[2] *Institute of Informatics and Telecommunications, NCSR "Demokritos", 15310 Athens, Greece*

Correspondence should be addressed to Nicholas Ampazis; n.ampazis@fme.aegean.gr

Academic Editor: Tingwen Huang

A constrained neural network optimization algorithm is presented for factorizing simultaneously the numerator and denominator polynomials of the transfer functions of 2-D IIR filters. The method minimizes a cost function based on the frequency response of the filters, along with simultaneous satisfaction of appropriate constraints, so that factorization is facilitated and the stability of the resulting filter is respected.

1. Introduction

Factorization of 2D polynomials is an important problem in the design of IIR filters in two-dimensional signal processing because a factorized filter transfer function can be efficiently implemented in cascade form. However, the fundamental theorem of Algebra, concerning polynomial factorization, cannot be extended to the two-dimensional case; that is, a bivariate polynomial $F(z_1, z_2)$ cannot, in general, be factored as a product of lower-order polynomials. The 2D IIR cascade structure may be considered as an attractive circuit design alternative, because of its relative insensitivity to coefficient quantization, the requirement of smaller number of arithmetic operations for a given filter size, and finally, because issues related to the stability of the filters are easier to deal with for filters with a smaller number of denominator coefficients [1]. Hence, an efficient method for the factorization of 2D IIR filters would be most beneficial.

Many methods have been proposed for dealing with the two-dimensional polynomial factorization problem [2–6]. Most of those methods, however, adopt a conventional numerical method of roots finding (e.g., Laguerre's, Newton-Raphson's, Jenkins-Traub's methods, etc.), in which successive approximations to the roots are obtained. In addition, almost all numerical methods can only find the roots one by one, that is, by deflation method, where the next root is obtained by the deflated polynomial after the former root is found. This means that numerical root-finding methods are inherently sequential.

In an earlier work we have proposed a neural network-based Constrained Learning Algorithm (CLA) for factorizing 2D polynomials using constrained optimization techniques [7]. Using that approach we were able to obtain exact solutions for factorable polynomials and excellent approximate solutions for nonfactorable polynomials. The technique offers the advantage of incorporating a priori information about the relations between the coefficients of the original polynomial and the coefficients of the desired factor polynomials. By incorporating additional stability constraints into the formalism, the stability (in the sense of Huang [8]) of a transfer function with the resulting factorized polynomial in the denominator (of up to second order) is also made possible. Our CLA method has been explored further in [9] by utilizing root moments, in [10] with an adaptive neural network architecture, and in [11] for handling complex root cases.

Despite its success in 2D polynomial factorization, CLA suffers from disadvantages which can limit its effectiveness for its application to IIR filter factorization. CLA's cost function is not directly related to a proximity measure between the frequency response characteristics of the filters, but is based on the Mean Square Error (MSE) criterion between the output of the original polynomial and the output of the resulting factorable polynomial for various real values of $|z_1| < 1$ and $|z_2| < 1$. Thus, CLA requires separate factorizations for the numerator and denominator polynomials of the IIR filter, while better solutions, in terms of the proximity of filter characteristics, could be achieved by simultaneous variation of all available parameters (numerator and denominator coefficients). In this paper we apply constrained optimization techniques to the more general problem of implementing a stable cascade IIR filter, given the specifications of an original 2D filter. This is achieved by suitably modifying our previous formalism as it is explained in the following section.

2. Derivation of the Algorithm

Consider the polynomial

$$f(z_1, z_2) = \sum_{i=0}^{N_A} \sum_{j=0}^{N_A} a_{ij} z_1^i z_2^j \qquad (1)$$

with N_A even and $a_{00} = 1$. For the above polynomial, we seek to achieve an exact or approximate factorization of the form

$$f(z_1, z_2) \approx \prod_{i=1,2} f^{(i)}(z_1, z_2), \qquad (2)$$

where

$$f^{(i)}(z_1, z_2) = \sum_{j=0}^{M_A} \sum_{k=0}^{M_A} w_{jk}^{(i)} z_1^j z_2^k \qquad (3)$$

with $M_A = N_A/2$.

To this end, we can utilize a feedforward neural network architecture in order to learn the appropriate weights $w_{jk}^{(i)}$ as we proposed in [7]. For example, Figure 1 shows the architecture of such a network for the case where $N_A = 2$. The units in the hidden layer have a logarithmic activation function ln, and the output unit is linear. This architecture has been preferred to the $\sum$-$\prod$ architecture employed in [12], because it produces smoother cost function landscapes avoiding deep valleys and thus facilitates learning. As we showed in [7], this neural network can be trained using a Constrained Learning Algorithm (CLA) that achieves minimization of the MSE criterion along with simultaneous satisfaction of multiple equality and inequality constraints between the polynomial coefficients. Using that method, we are able to obtain very good approximate solutions for nonfactorable polynomials.

Now consider the 2D IIR filter transfer function

$$H(z_1, z_2) = \frac{B(z_1, z_2)}{A(z_1, z_2)}, \qquad (4)$$

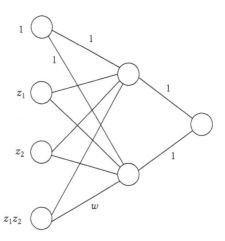

FIGURE 1: Neural network architecture used to solve the factorization problem.

where

$$B(z_1, z_2) = \sum_{i=0}^{N_B} \sum_{j=0}^{N_B} b_{ij} z_1^i z_2^j,$$

$$A(z_1, z_2) = \sum_{i=0}^{N_A} \sum_{j=0}^{N_A} a_{ij} z_1^i z_2^j \qquad (5)$$

with N_A, N_B even and $b_{00} = a_{00} = 1$.

For the above polynomials, we seek to achieve an exact or approximate factorization of the form

$$B(z_1, z_2) \approx \prod_{i=1,2} B^{(i)}(z_1, z_2), \qquad (6)$$

where

$$B^{(i)}(z_1, z_2) = \sum_{j=0}^{M_B} \sum_{k=0}^{M_B} u_{jk}^{(i)} z_1^j z_2^k, \qquad (7)$$

$$A(z_1, z_2) \approx \prod_{i=1,2} A^{(i)}(z_1, z_2), \qquad (8)$$

where

$$A^{(i)}(z_1, z_2) = \sum_{j=0}^{M_A} \sum_{k=0}^{M_A} v_{jk}^{(i)} z_1^j z_2^k \qquad (9)$$

with $M_A = N_A/2$, and $M_B = N_B/2$ so that the transfer function of (4) can be approximated by

$$\widehat{H}(z_1, z_2) = \frac{\prod_{i=1,2} B^{(i)}(z_1, z_2)}{\prod_{i=1,2} A^{(i)}(z_1, z_2)}. \qquad (10)$$

Unfortunately, if it were to apply CLA in this problem we would have to derive two separate factorizations for the numerator and denominator polynomials. Such an optimization scheme, however, is not directly related to a proximity measure between the original and the factorized filter frequency response characteristics. In terms of the proximity of filter characteristics, obviously a better approximation can be achieved by a simultaneous variation of both the numerator and denominator coefficients.

In this case, we should ask: in what sense are $H(z_1, z_2)$ and $\widehat{H}(z_1, z_2)$ similar? The answer to this question is that we would at least expect the amplitude spectra of $H(z_1, z_2)$ and $\widehat{H}(z_1, z_2)$ to be roughly equal so that the specifications of the original and of the factorized filter match as close as possible. Hence, the main purpose of the factorization algorithm is to minimize an MSE cost function based on the magnitude of the frequency responses of the original and the resulting filter:

$$
E = \frac{1}{2} \sum_{\theta_1=-\pi}^{\pi} \sum_{\theta_2=-\pi}^{\pi} (T - O)^2,
$$

$$
T = \ln\left(\left|H\left(e^{j\theta_1}, e^{j\theta_2}\right)\right|\right), \tag{11}
$$

$$
O = \ln\left(\left|\widehat{H}\left(e^{j\theta_1}, e^{j\theta_2}\right)\right|\right).
$$

The double summation is carried over a regular grid of points. Logarithmic functions are used also in this case in order to suppress deep valleys and thus facilitate convergence. However, E is still a highly nonlinear function of the polynomial coefficients, and therefore gradient-based techniques can run into problems in the presence of valleys or ridges in the cost function landscape. For such cases it has proved beneficial to incorporate into the adaptation rule additional a priori problem-specific information. This often facilitates the convergence of the algorithm and leads to better solutions.

For the problem at hand, additional information is available in the form of constraints between the coefficients of the given numerator and denominator polynomials and the coefficients of the corresponding desired factor polynomials. More explicitly, if we assume that $B(z_1, z_2)$ and $A(z_1, z_2)$ are factorable, then these constraints can be expressed as follows:

$$
\Phi^u_{j+(N_B+1)i}
$$

$$
= b_{ij} - \sum_{l=1}^{i} \sum_{m=1}^{j} u^{(1)}_{lm} u^{(2)}_{i-l,j-m} = 0, \quad 0 \le i \le N_B, \ 0 \le j \le N_B,
$$

$$
\Phi^v_{j+(N_A+1)i}
$$

$$
= a_{ij} - \sum_{l=1}^{i} \sum_{m=1}^{j} v^{(1)}_{lm} v^{(2)}_{i-l,j-m} = 0, \quad 0 \le i \le N_A, \ 0 \le j \le N_A. \tag{12}
$$

Thus, for the general case in which $B(z_1, z_2)$ and $A(z_1, z_2)$ are nonfactorable, the objective of the adaptation process is to reach a minimum of the cost function of (11) with respect

to the variables $u^{(i)}_{jk}$ and $v^{(i)}_{jk}$, which satisfies as best as possible the constraint $\Phi = 0$, where $\Phi^T = (\Phi^u, \Phi^v)$ with

$$
\Phi^u = \left(\Phi^u_{j+(N_B+1)i}, 0 \le i \le N_B, \ 0 \le j \le N_B\right),
$$

$$
\Phi^v = \left(\Phi^v_{j+(N_A+1)i}, 0 \le i \le N_A, \ 0 \le j \le N_A\right). \tag{13}
$$

The strategy which will be followed in order to solve this problem is similar to the method we proposed in [7], but with appropriate modifications in order to take care of the above constraints, as well as the new cost function that we introduced in (11).

At each iteration of our algorithm, the vector of unknown coefficients $\mathbf{w} = (\mathbf{u}, \mathbf{v})^T$ is changed by $d\mathbf{w}$, so that

$$
d\mathbf{w}^T d\mathbf{w} = (\delta P)^2, \tag{14}
$$

where δP is a small constant. Thus, at each iteration, the search for an optimum new point in the $\mathbf{w}$ space is restricted to a small hypersphere centered at the point defined by the current vector $\mathbf{w}$. If δP is small enough, the changes to E and to Φ induced by changes in the coefficients can be approximated by the first differentials dE and $d\Phi$. Also, at each iteration, we seek to achieve the maximum possible change in $|dE|$, so that (14) is respected and the change $d\Phi$ in Φ is equal to a predetermined vector quantity $\delta \mathbf{Q}$, designed to bring Φ closer to its target (zero).

Maximization of dE can be carried out analytically by introducing suitable Lagrange multipliers. Thus, a vector $\mathbf{v}$ of Lagrange multipliers is introduced for the constraints in (12) and a multiplier μ is introduced for (14).

Consider a function ε, whose differential is defined as follows:

$$
d\varepsilon = dE + \left(\delta \mathbf{Q}^T - d\Phi^T\right) \mathbf{v} + \mu \left[(\delta P)^2 - d\mathbf{w}^T d\mathbf{w}\right]. \tag{15}
$$

On evaluating the differentials involved in the right-hand side, we readily obtain

$$
d\varepsilon = d\mathbf{w}^T \mathbf{J} + \left(\delta \mathbf{Q}^T - d\mathbf{w}^T \mathbf{F}^T\right) \mathbf{v} + \mu \left[(\delta P)^2 - d\mathbf{w}^T d\mathbf{w}\right], \tag{16}
$$

where

(i) $\mathbf{J}$ is a vector with elements $J_i = \partial E / \partial w_i$;

(ii) $\mathbf{F}$ is a matrix given by $F = \begin{bmatrix} \mathbf{F}^u & 0 \\ 0 & \mathbf{F}^v \end{bmatrix}$;

(iii) $\mathbf{F}^u$ and $\mathbf{F}^v$ are matrices with elements $F^u_{mi} = \partial \Phi^u_m / \partial u_i$ and $F^v_{mi} = \partial \Phi^v_m / \partial v_i$, respectively.

To minimize $d\varepsilon$ (maximize its magnitude) at each iteration, we demand that

$$
d^2\varepsilon = \mathbf{J} - \mathbf{F}^T \mathbf{v} - 2\mu d\mathbf{w} = 0, \qquad d^3\varepsilon = -2\mu > 0. \tag{17}
$$

From (17) it immediately follows that

$$
d\mathbf{w} = \frac{\mathbf{J}}{2\mu} - \frac{\mathbf{F}^T \mathbf{v}}{2\mu}. \tag{18}
$$

Equation (18) is the update rule for the coefficients of the factor polynomials, but μ and $\mathbf{v}$ must still be evaluated in terms of known quantities.

Noting that $d\mathbf{\Phi} = \delta\mathbf{Q} = \mathbf{F}d\mathbf{w}$, we can multiply both sides of (18) by $\mathbf{F}$ and solve for $\mathbf{v}$ to obtain

$$\mathbf{v} = -2\mu\mathbf{I}_{FF}^{-1}\delta\mathbf{Q} + \mathbf{I}_{FF}^{-1}\mathbf{I}_{JF}, \quad \text{where } \mathbf{I}_{FF} = \mathbf{FF}^{T}, \mathbf{I}_{JF} = \mathbf{FJ}. \tag{19}$$

To evaluate μ, we substitute (18) and (19) into (14) and obtain

$$\mu = -\frac{1}{2}\left[\frac{I_{JJ} - \mathbf{I}_{JF}^{T}\mathbf{I}_{FF}^{-1}\mathbf{I}_{JF}}{(\delta P)^2 - \delta\mathbf{Q}^{T}\mathbf{I}_{FF}^{-1}\delta\mathbf{Q}}\right]^{1/2}, \quad \text{where } I_{JJ} = \mathbf{J}^{T}\mathbf{J}. \tag{20}$$

Note that due to the block-diagonal form of matrix $\mathbf{F}$, it is possible to avoid the tedious evaluation of $\mathbf{I}_{FF}^{-1}$ by rewriting the quantities I_{JJ}, $\mathbf{I}_{FF}$, and $\mathbf{I}_{JF}$ as follows:

(i) $I_{JJ} = (\mathbf{J}^u)^T\mathbf{J}^u + (\mathbf{J}^v)^T\mathbf{J}^v$, where $J_i^u = \partial E/\partial u_i$ and $J_i^v = \partial E/\partial v_i$,

(ii) $\mathbf{I}_{FF} = \mathbf{I}_{FF}^u + \mathbf{I}_{FF}^v = \mathbf{F}^u(\mathbf{F}^u)^T + \mathbf{F}^v(\mathbf{F}^v)^T$,

(iii) $\mathbf{I}_{JF} = \mathbf{I}_{JF}^u + \mathbf{I}_{JF}^v = \mathbf{F}^u\mathbf{J}^u + \mathbf{F}^v\mathbf{J}^v$.

Hence, (19) and (20) can be rewritten as

$$\mathbf{v} = -2\mu(\mathbf{I}_{FF}^u)^{-1}\delta\mathbf{Q}^u - 2\mu(\mathbf{I}_{FF}^v)^{-1}\delta\mathbf{Q}^v$$
$$+ (\mathbf{I}_{FF}^u)^{-1}\mathbf{I}_{JF}^u + (\mathbf{I}_{FF}^v)^{-1}\mathbf{I}_{JF}^v,$$

$$\mu = -\frac{1}{2}\left[\frac{I_{JJ} - (\mathbf{I}_{JF}^u)^T(\mathbf{I}_{FF}^u)^{-1}\mathbf{I}_{JF}^u - (\mathbf{I}_{JF}^v)^T(\mathbf{I}_{FF}^v)^{-1}\mathbf{I}_{JF}^v}{(\delta P)^2 - (\delta\mathbf{Q}^u)^T(\mathbf{I}_{FF}^u)^{-1}\delta\mathbf{Q}^u - (\delta\mathbf{Q}^v)^T(\mathbf{I}_{FF}^v)^{-1}\delta\mathbf{Q}^v}\right]^{1/2}, \tag{21}$$

since the matrices $(\mathbf{I}_{FF}^u)^{-1}$ and $(\mathbf{I}_{FF}^v)^{-1}$ can be computed more easily than the composite matrix $\mathbf{I}_{FF}^{-1}$.

We next discuss the choice of $\delta\mathbf{Q}$. It is natural to choose the elements δQ_m of $\delta\mathbf{Q}$ proportional to Φ_m with a negative constant of proportionality $-k$, $k > 0$, so that the constraints move towards zero at an exponential rate. Then, the bound $k \leq \delta P(\mathbf{\Phi}^T\mathbf{I}_{FF}^{-1}\mathbf{\Phi})^{-1/2}$ set on the value of k by (20) forces us to choose k adaptively. The simplest choice for k will be used; namely, $k = [\xi(\delta P)^2/((\mathbf{\Phi}^u)^T(\mathbf{I}_{FF}^u)^{-1}\mathbf{\Phi}^u + (\mathbf{\Phi}^v)^T(\mathbf{I}_{FF}^v)^{-1}\mathbf{\Phi}^v)]^{1/2}$, where $0 < \xi < 1$. Thus, the final update rule has only two free parameters, namely, δP and ξ.

3. Stability Constraints

For the filter $H(z_1, z_2)$ defined in (4), it is reasonable to assume that for most practical purposes the numerator polynomial $B(z_1, z_2)$ does not affect the system stability [1]. In the important special case of a second-order denominator polynomial $A(z_1, z_2)(N_B = 2)$, the stability conditions according to Huang [8] for the factor polynomials can be written as $X_k < 1$, $k = 1, \ldots, 6$, as shown in Table 1. These conditions can be incorporated in the formalism as follows:

TABLE 1: Stability constraints for the denominator polynomial.

$X_1 = (v_{10}^{(1)})^2$

$X_2 = (v_{10}^{(2)})^2$

$X_3 = (v_{01}^{(1)})^2 + (v_{11}^{(1)})^2 + 2v_{01}^{(1)}v_{11}^{(1)} - (v_{10}^{(1)})^2 - 2v_{10}^{(1)}$

$X_4 = (v_{01}^{(1)})^2 + (v_{11}^{(1)})^2 - 2v_{01}^{(1)}v_{11}^{(1)} - (v_{10}^{(1)})^2 + 2v_{10}^{(1)}$

$X_5 = (v_{01}^{(2)})^2 + (v_{11}^{(2)})^2 + 2v_{01}^{(2)}v_{11}^{(2)} - (v_{10}^{(2)})^2 - 2v_{10}^{(2)}$

$X_6 = (v_{01}^{(2)})^2 + (v_{11}^{(2)})^2 - 2v_{01}^{(2)}v_{11}^{(2)} - (v_{10}^{(2)})^2 + 2v_{10}^{(2)}$

at a certain iteration of the algorithm, let a number M of the stability constraints be violated, so that $X_{k_r} \geq 1$, $r = 1, \ldots, M$. We can augment the vector $\mathbf{\Phi}^v$ of the previous section by adding extra components $\Phi_{[j+(N_A+1)i]+r}^v = X_{k_r}$, $r = 1, \ldots, M$. By following the formalism of Section 2 using the augmented vector $\mathbf{\Phi}^v$, the quantities X_{k_r} are driven towards the stability region. Note that the dimensionality of the vector $\mathbf{\Phi}^v$ is adaptive, as only the violated constraints are included in each iteration. Iterative application of this scheme can lead to a final stable solution.

4. Experimental Results

We seek an approximate factorization of the second-order 2D IIR filter whose numerator and denominator polynomial coefficients are shown in Tables 2 and 3, respectively. Note that both polynomials are nonfactorable.

Figure 2(a) shows the amplitude spectrum of the original low-pass IIR filter, and Figure 3 shows the error curve of the *unconstrained* gradient descent method applied to (11) using a regular grid of 32^2 points with an adaptation gain of 10^{-6}. From the latest figure we can see that after an initial error reduction, an undesirable flat minimum is reached followed by unbounded oscillations caused by a transition into a region of the parameter space in which the denominator polynomial is unstable. The amplitude spectrum of the filter corresponding to the factorization result achieved at the flat minimum is shown in Figure 2(b) and is clearly unacceptable.

Using the constraints Φ_1^u, Φ_3^u, Φ_4^u, Φ_1^v, Φ_3^v, and Φ_4^v and all stability constraints of Section 3, we have applied both CLA, as described in [7], and the method proposed in the present paper using a regular grid of 32^2 training points. Figure 2(c) shows the amplitude spectrum of the filter obtained from the original CLA approach (with $\delta P = 0.01$ and $\xi = 0.99$) applied sequentially to the numerator and denominator polynomials. Obviously CLA outperforms gradient descent in all aspects. However, there are still small (but not negligible) differences between the amplitude spectra shown in Figures 2(a) and 2(c).

Figure 2(d) shows the amplitude spectrum of the filter obtained by the proposed method, with $\delta P = 0.07$ and $\xi = 0.99$. Clearly, there is very good agreement between the amplitude spectra of Figures 2(a) and 2(d). In order to visualize this better, in Figure 4, we present the differences in the amplitude spectra between the original filter and each of the filters obtained by gradient descent (Figure 4(a)), CLA (Figure 4(b)), and the proposed method

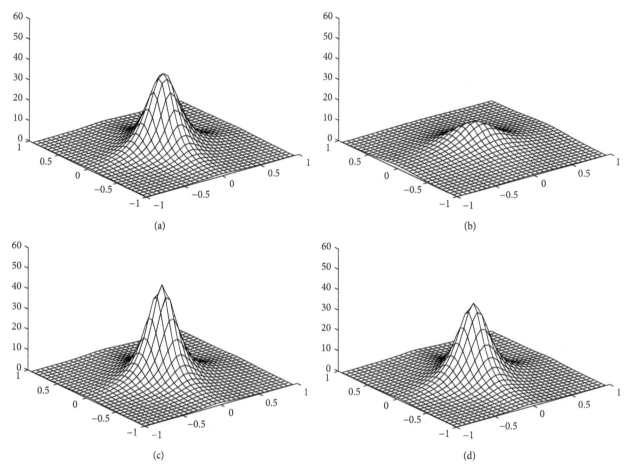

FIGURE 2: Amplitude spectrum of (a) original filter. (b) Filter obtained with gradient descent. (c) Filter obtained with CLA. (d) Filter obtained with the proposed method.

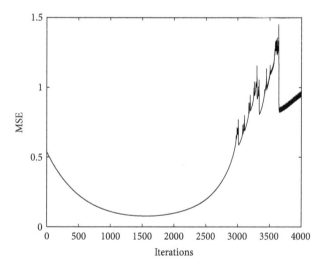

FIGURE 3: Error plot of gradient descent method.

(Figure 4(c)). From this figure it is clear that, of all the methods, the one proposed in the present paper achieves the maximum proximity to the original amplitude spectrum, leading to the design of a cascade filter that meets as closely as possible the specifications of the original nonfactorable filter.

The factorization results are summarized in Tables 2 and 3. Note that the separate factorization of the CLA approach produces coefficients that are closer to those of both the numerator and denominator polynomials of the original filter, while the proposed method achieves maximum similarity between the frequency responses in expense of a smaller coefficient similarity, distributed along both the numerator and denominator coefficients.

5. Conclusions

In this paper, an efficient algorithm was proposed for factorizing simultaneously the numerator and denominator polynomials of the transfer functions of 2D IIR filters. The method is useful for designing IIR filters in cascade form for more efficient hardware implementation. By introducing a cost function based on the difference of frequency responses

TABLE 2: Factorization results for the numerator polynomial.

	Original non-factorable	Proposed method	CLA
Numerator polynomial coefficient matrix **B**	$\begin{bmatrix} 1 & 0.4000 & 0.0300 \\ 0.2500 & 0.4500 & 0.0700 \\ 0.0125 & 0.0350 & 0.0100 \end{bmatrix}$	$\begin{bmatrix} 1 & 0.4001 & 0.0384 \\ 0.2501 & 0.4649 & 0.0809 \\ 0.0078 & 0.0451 & 0.0427 \end{bmatrix}$	$\begin{bmatrix} 1 & 0.4000 & 0.0276 \\ 0.2500 & 0.4418 & 0.0602 \\ 0.0156 & 0.0484 & 0.0318 \end{bmatrix}$
1st factor polynomial coefficient matrix	—	$\begin{bmatrix} 1 & 0.1598 \\ 0.0368 & 0.1678 \end{bmatrix}$	$\begin{bmatrix} 1 & 0.0888 \\ 0.1212 & 0.1141 \end{bmatrix}$
2nd factor polynomial coefficient matrix	—	$\begin{bmatrix} 1 & 0.2403 \\ 0.2133 & 0.2542 \end{bmatrix}$	$\begin{bmatrix} 1 & 0.3111 \\ 0.1287 & 0.2785 \end{bmatrix}$

TABLE 3: Factorization results for the denominator polynomial.

	Original non-factorable	Proposed method	CLA
Denominator polynomial coefficient matrix **A**	$\begin{bmatrix} 1 & -0.9636 & 0.2321 \\ -0.9636 & 0.8360 & -0.1791 \\ 0.2321 & -0.1791 & 0.0445 \end{bmatrix}$	$\begin{bmatrix} 1 & -0.9638 & 0.2315 \\ -0.9638 & 0.8910 & -0.2030 \\ 0.2320 & -0.2065 & 0.0438 \end{bmatrix}$	$\begin{bmatrix} 1 & -0.9635 & 0.2320 \\ -0.9635 & 0.8332 & -0.1778 \\ 0.2317 & -0.1767 & 0.0335 \end{bmatrix}$
1st factor polynomial coefficient matrix	—	$\begin{bmatrix} 1 & -0.5087 \\ -0.4649 & 0.2518 \end{bmatrix}$	$\begin{bmatrix} 1 & -0.4902 \\ -0.4616 & 0.1625 \end{bmatrix}$
2nd factor polynomial coefficient matrix	—	$\begin{bmatrix} 1 & -0.4551 \\ -0.4989 & 0.1739 \end{bmatrix}$	$\begin{bmatrix} 1 & -0.4733 \\ -0.5019 & 0.2062 \end{bmatrix}$

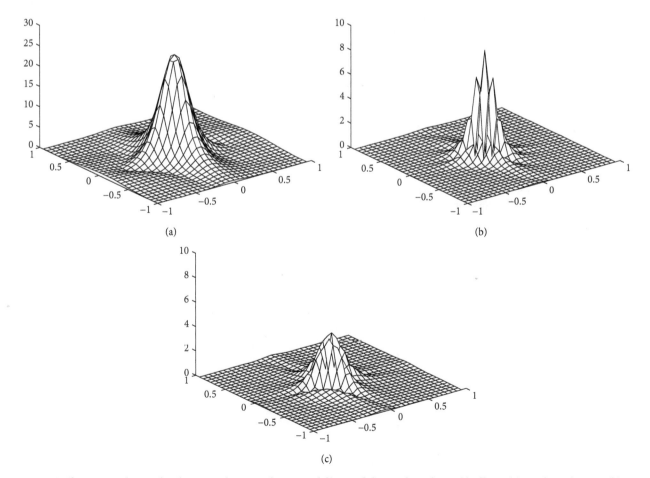

(a)

(b)

(c)

FIGURE 4: Differences in the amplitude spectra between the original filter and the resulting factorable filters: (a) Gradient descent. (b) CLA. (c) Proposed method.

between the original and cascade filters and using a flexible framework for incorporating additional information in the form of constraints, we obtained optimal stable solutions for nonfactorable filters.

References

[1] J. S. Lim, *Two-Dimensional Signal and Image Processing*, Prentice-Hall International, 1990.

[2] Z. Mou-Yan and R. Unbehauen, "On the approximate factorization of 2-D polynomials," *IEEE Transactions on Acoustics, Speech, and Signal Processing*, vol. 35, no. 4, pp. 577–579, 1987.

[3] N. E. Mastorakis, N. J. Theodorou, and S. G. Tzafestas, "A general factorization method for multivariable polynomials," *Multidimensional Systems and Signal Processing*, vol. 5, no. 2, pp. 151–178, 1994.

[4] P. Misra and R. V. Patel, "Simple factorizability of 2-D polynomials," in *Proceedings of the International Symposium on Circuits and Systems*, pp. 1207–1210, New Orleans, La, USA, 1990.

[5] B. C. Langand Frenzel, "Polynomial root finding," *IEEE Signal Processing Letters*, vol. 1, no. 10, pp. 141–143, 1994.

[6] L. Hoteit, "FFT-based fast polynomial rooting," in *Proceedings of the International Conference on Acoustics, Speech, and Signal Processing (ICASSP'00)*, vol. 6, pp. 3315–3318, Istanbul, Turkey, June 2000.

[7] S. Perantonis, N. Ampazis, S. Varoufakis, and G. Antoniou, "Constrained learning in Nneural networks: application to stable factorization of 2-D polynomials," *Neural Processing Letters*, vol. 7, no. 1, pp. 5–14, 1998.

[8] T. S. Huang, "Stability of two-dimensional recursive filters," *IEEE Transactions on Audio and Electroacoustics*, vol. 20, no. 2, pp. 158–163, 1972.

[9] D. S. Huang, H. H. S. Ip, and Z. Chi, "A neural root finder of polynomials based on root moments," *Neural Computation*, vol. 16, no. 8, pp. 1721–1762, 2004.

[10] D. S. Huang, H. S. I. Horace, C. K. L. Ken, Z. Chi, and H. S. Wong, "A new partitioning neural network model for recursively finding arbitrary roots of higher order arbitrary polynomials," *Applied Mathematics and Computation*, vol. 162, no. 3, pp. 1183–1200, 2005.

[11] D. S. Huang, "constructive approach for finding arbitrary roots of polynomials by neural networks," *AIEEE Transactions On Neural Networks*, vol. 15, no. 2, pp. 477–491, 2004.

[12] R. Hormis, G. Antoniou, and S. Mentzelopoulou, "Separation of two- dimensional polynomials via a sigma-pi neural net," in *Proceedings of the International Conference on Modelling and Simulation*, pp. 304–306, Pittsburg, Pa, USA, 1995.

4

Stem Control of a Sliding-Stem Pneumatic Control Valve Using a Recurrent Neural Network

Mohammad Heidari[1] and Hadi Homaei[2]

[1] Mechanical Engineering Group, Aligudarz Branch, Islamic Azad University, P.O. Box 159, Aligudarz, Iran
[2] Faculty of Engineering, Shahrekord University, P.O. Box 115, Shahrekord, Iran

Correspondence should be addressed to Mohammad Heidari; moh104337@yahoo.com

Academic Editor: Chao-Ton Su

This paper presents a neural scheme for controlling an actuator of pneumatic control valve system. Bondgraph method has been used to model the actuator of control valve, in order to compare the response characteristics of valve. The proposed controller is such that the system is always operating in a closed loop, which should lead to better performance characteristics. For comparison, minimum- and full-order observer controllers are also utilized to control the actuator of pneumatic control valve. Simulation results give superior performance of the proposed neural control scheme.

1. Introduction

Process plants consist of hundreds, or even thousands, of control loops all networked together to produce a product to be offered for sale. Each of these control loops is designed to keep some important process variables such as pressure, flow, level, and temperature within a required operating range to ensure the quality of the end product. Each of these loops receives and internally creates disturbances that detrimentally affect the process variable, and interaction from other loops in the network provides disturbances that influence the process variable. To reduce the effect of these load disturbances, sensors and transmitters collect information about the process variable and its relationship to some desired set points. A controller then processes this information and decides what must be done to get the process variable back to where it should be after a load disturbance occurs. When all the measuring, comparing, and calculating are done, some type of final control element must implement the strategy selected by the controller. The most common final control element in the process control industries is the control valve. The control valve manipulates a flowing fluid, such as gas, steam, water, or chemical compounds, to compensate for the load disturbance and keep the regulated process variable as close as possible to the desired set point. Control valves adjust the temperature, pressure, flow rate, and so forth by changing the flow rate. Figure 1 shows a reverse-acting diaphragm actuator of pneumatic control valve. Pneumatic control valves are still the most used valves in the process industries, due to their low cost and simplicity. Pneumatic valves are used extensively in various industries today. Industry standard has been established that details the vibration, humidity, thermal, salt spray, and temperature extremes that these valves must operate within. This makes the design of valve control systems a very challenging task. Control valves have two major components, valve body housing and the actuation unit. One factor in the quality of the final end product is the improvement of the control loop performance. A critical component in the loop is the final control element, the control valve package. Optimized actuator parameters play a vital role in the dynamic performance of the pneumatic control valve. Hägglund [1] presented a procedure that compensates for static friction (stiction) in pneumatic control valves.

The compensation is obtained by adding pulses to the control signal. The characteristics of the pulses are determined from the control action. The compensator is implemented in industrial controllers and control systems, and the industrial experiences show that the procedure reduces the control error during stick-slip motion significantly compared to standard control without stiction compensation.

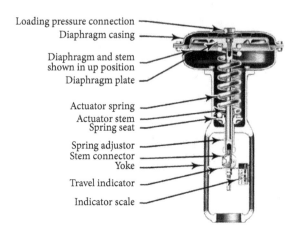

FIGURE 1: Reverse-acting diaphragm actuator of a pneumatic control valve.

The oscillations caused by static friction (stiction) in pneumatic control valves cause losses in quality and expense of raw materials. The input-output behavior of a pneumatic control valve is affected by stiction in valve. De Souza et al. [2] presented a well-known stiction compensation method that reduced variability both at process variable and pneumatic valve stem movement. The two-move method was revisited in their research and it was shown that assumptions on the knowledge of steady-state stem position of control valve that assured equality of set point and the controlled variable was not easily achievable.

Champagne and Boyle [3] reviewed the pneumatic actuator and positioner parameters that affect the control package performance. This was done through the use of a control valve package computer model to assess the dynamic performance. The attributes of spring return versus double-acting actuators were illustrated. The effects of supply pressure, step size, load margin, flow, actuator volume, and design style were investigated through the use of mathematical simulations of pneumatic control valve dynamic performance.

Bondgraph is a graphical representation of a physical dynamics system. It is similar to the better known block diagram and signal flow, with the major difference that the arcs in bondgraphs represent bidirectional exchange of physical energy, while those in block diagrams and signal-flow graphs represent unidirectional flow of information. Also, bondgraphs are multidomain and domain neutral. This means that a bondgraph can incorporate multiple domains simultaneously. The fundamental idea of a bondgraph is that power is transmitted between connected components by a combination of "effort" and "flow" (generalized effort & generalized flow). Bondgraphs were devised by Paynter [4] at MIT in April 1959 and subsequently developed into a methodology together with Karnopp et al. [5]. Early prominent promoters of bondgraph modeling techniques among others were Thoma [6], Dixhoorn, and Dransfield. They contributed substantially to the dissemination of bondgraph modeling in Europe, Australia, Japan, China and India. Athanasatos and Costopoulos [7] used the bondgraph method for finding the proactive fault in 4/3 way direction

control valve of a high-pressure hydraulic system. The accuracy of the bondgraph model was verified by comparing its response to the response of an actual hydraulic system. Zuccarini et al. [8] utilized the bondgraph as boundary condition for a detailed model of an idealized mitral valve. A specific application in cardiovascular modeling was demonstrated by focusing on a specific example, a 3D model of the mitral valve coupled to a lumped parameter model of the left ventricle. Ekren et al. [9] used three different control algorithms such as proportional, integral, differential (PID), fuzzy logic, and artificial neural network (ANN) for control of a variable speed compressor and electronic expansion valve in a chiller system. The results showed that ANN controller has lower power consumption of 8.1 percent and 6.6 percent than both PID and fuzzy controllers, respectively. Choi et al. [10] have modeled a system of position control which uses a single-rod cylinder activated by an electrorheological (ER) valve. From the state-space model for the governing equations, a neural network control scheme has been synthesized to achieve the position control of the cylinder system. The results showed the effectiveness of the proposed methodology.

In this paper, a control scheme was investigated to control a pneumatic control valve system. The robustness of the proposed scheme was presented through computer simulation and the efficacy of the scheme is shown both in the time and amplitude domains. A sliding-stem pneumatic control valve is modeled by bondgraph method. Then, several control schemes have been used for control of valve in order to compare the response characteristics of these different schemes.

This research is organized as follows. Section 2 recalls the bondgraph model of valve and proposes equations of motion of the valve. Section 3 develops the control schemes of the valve. Simulation results and discussion of the control schemes are given in Section 4. The paper is concluded with Section 5.

2. Bondgraph Model of Valve and Equations

The bondgraph model of the valve is shown in Figure 2. In this model, SE is the inlet pressure of the system. The pressure changes to force by multiplying in effect area of the diaphragm. In bondgraph, this transformer is modeled by TF. Element R is the friction of the system. Element I is the movable mass of valve and diaphragm Element C represents the spring of the valve actuator.

Also 1-junction is a common flow junction. 1-junctions have equality of flows and the efforts sum up to zero with the same power orientation. In fact, junctions can connect two or more bonds. The direction of the half arrows ($\rightarrow$) denotes the direction of power flow given by the product of the effort and flow variables associated with the power bond. The bonds in a bondgraph may be numbered sequentially using integers starting with 1. The two 1-junctions in the bondgraph shown can be uniquely identified as (S 1 2) and (S 4 5 6); similarly symbols like SE_1, R_6 can be used to identify a particular element. This system has two state variable P_4 and q_5. q_5 is

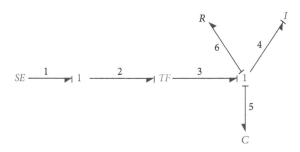

FIGURE 2: Bondgraph control valve actuator.

the displacement of valve stem and the variation of the spring length. Also $v_4 = P_4/I_4$ is the velocity of the valve stem. The equations of motion are derived using bondgraph method as below:

$$\dot{P}_4 = A \times SE_1 - K_3 q_5 - \frac{R_6}{I_4} P_4, \tag{1}$$

$$\dot{q}_5 = \frac{P_4}{I_4}. \tag{2}$$

Now, if the velocity and position of stem are zero in the initial condition, $X(0)$, then we have the following:

$$X(0) = \begin{bmatrix} P_4(0) \\ q_5(0) \end{bmatrix} = \begin{bmatrix} 0 \\ 0 \end{bmatrix}. \tag{3}$$

By derivation of relation (2) with respect to time we have the following:

$$\ddot{q}_5 = \frac{\dot{P}_4}{I_4}. \tag{4}$$

By substitution of $\dot{P}_4$ from (1) into (4) we have the following:

$$\ddot{q}_5 = \frac{A \times SE_1 - K_3 q_5 - (R_6/I_4) P_4}{I_4}. \tag{5}$$

By substitution of P_4 from (2) into (5) we have the following:

$$\ddot{q}_5 = \frac{1}{I_4} \left(A \times SE_1 - K_3 q_5 - R_6 \dot{q}_5 \right). \tag{6}$$

Using Laplace transformation of (6), we have the following:

$$\frac{q_5(s)}{SE_1(s)} = \frac{(A/I_4)}{s^2 + (R_6/I_4) s + (K_3/I_4)}. \tag{7}$$

Equation (7) is the transfer function of the valve. The results of bondgragh model of valve shows that the response of the system is identical with the result in [11].

3. Control Schemes

For completeness, this section briefly reviews the control schemes, which are the observer control and the NN control proposed in this paper.

3.1. State Observer.

The state observer estimates the state variables using the output and control input value. At this time, it can be configured only when the system is observable. $\tilde{x}$ is the observed state vector. Let us consider the system that is defined in form of a state-space representation as follows:

$$\dot{x} = Ax + Bu, \tag{8}$$

$$y = Cx + Du, \tag{9}$$

where x is called the state vector, $\dot{x}$ the derivative of the state vector with respect to time, y the output vector, and $u(t)$ the input or control vector. Also A is the system matrix, B the input matrix, C the output matrix, and D direct transmission matrix. Suppose that $\tilde{x}$ is an estimation for the state vector x. Then, we have the following:

$$\dot{\tilde{x}} = A\tilde{x} + Bu + K_e \left(y - C\tilde{x} \right). \tag{10}$$

Formula (10) indicates the state observer. y and u are inputs and $\tilde{x}$ is output. The term at the right end of (10) corrects the difference between the measured output y and the estimated output $\tilde{x}$. K_e works as the weighting matrix. Even though there is a difference between the matrix A and B of the actual system and the model, the influence is reduced by this correction. Deduct formula (10) from formula (8) to get the error of the observer. Then,

$$\dot{x} - \dot{\tilde{x}} = \left(A - K_e C \right) \left(x - \tilde{x} \right). \tag{11}$$

The result is formula (11). Suppose that the observer error $(x - \tilde{x})$ is e; that is to say, $e = (x - \tilde{x})$, formula (12) is arranged as follows:

$$\dot{e} = \left(A - K_e C \right) e. \tag{12}$$

From formula (12), we can recognize that the dynamic characteristics of the observer error are determined by the eigenvalue of $A - K_e C$. If $A - K_e C$ is a stable matrix, the error vector approaches zero related to any initial value $e(0)$. That is to say, $\tilde{x}(t)$ approaches $x(t)$ irrespective of the value of $x(0)$ and $\tilde{x}(0)$. If we select the eigenvalue of this matrix well, the error vector can approach to zero fast. If the given system is completely observable, we can make the eigenvalue of $A - K_e C$ as we want as selecting K_e well. That is to say, K_e is selected to make $A - K_e C$ as we want and this is the gain matrix of the state observer. The observer discussed thus far is designed to reconstruct all of the state variables. In practice, some of the state variables may be accurately measured. Such accurately measurable state variables need not to be estimated. An observer that estimates fewer than n state variables, where n is the dimension of the state vector, is called a reduced-order observer. The details of designing a minimum-order observer have been presented in [12].

3.2. Proposed Neural Controller.

The neural networks employed in this work were of the recurrent type. Recurrent networks have the advantage of being able to model dynamic systems accurately and in a compact form [13]. A recurrent network can be represented in a general diagrammatic form

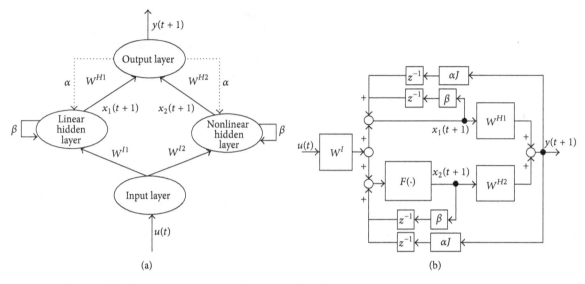

FIGURE 3: (a) Recurrent hybrid network structure. (b) Block diagram of recurrent hybrid network.

as illustrated in Figure 3(a). This diagram depicts the hybrid hidden layer as comprising a linear part and a nonlinear part and shows that, in addition to the usual feedforward connections, the networks also have feedback connections from the output layer to the hidden layer and self-feedback connections in the hidden layer. The reason for adopting a hybrid linear/non-linear structure for the hidden layer will be evident later.

At a given discrete time t, let $u(t)$ be the input to a recurrent hybrid network, $y(t)$ the output of the network, $x_1(t)$ the output of the linear part of the hidden layer, and $x_2(t)$ the output of the nonlinear part of the hidden layer. The operation of the network is summarized by the following equations (also see Figure 3(b)):

$$x_1(t+1) = W^{I1}u(t+1) + \beta x_1(t) + \alpha J_1 y(t),$$

$$x_2(t+1) = F\left\{W^{I2}u(t+1) + \beta x_2(t) + \alpha J_2 y(t)\right\}, \quad (13)$$

$$y(t+1) = W^{H1}x_1(t+1) + W^{H2}x_2(t+1),$$

where W^{I1} is the matrix of weights of connections between the input layer and the linear hidden layer, W^{I2} is the matrix of weights of connections between the input layer and the non-linear hidden layer, W^{H1} is the matrix of weights of connections between the linear hidden layer and the output layer, W^{H2} is the matrix of weights of connections between the non-linear hidden layer and the output layer, $F\{\}$ is the activation function of neurons in the non-linear hidden layer and α and β are the weights of the self-feedback and output feedback connections. J_1 and J_2 are, respectively, $(n_{H1} \times n_O)$ and $(n_{H2} \times n_O)$ matrices with all elements equal to 1, where n_{H1} and n_{H2} are the numbers of linear and non-linear hidden neurons, and n_O is the number of output neurons. If only

linear activation is adopted for the hidden neurons, the above equations are simplified to

$$y(t+1) = W^{H1}x(t+1), \quad (14)$$

$$x(t+1) = W^{I1}u(t+1) + \beta x(t) + \alpha J_1 y(t). \quad (15)$$

Replacing $y(t)$ by $W^{H1}x(t)$ in (15) gives

$$x(t+1) = W^{I1}u(t+1) + \left(\beta I + \alpha J_1 W^{H1}\right)x(t), \quad (16)$$

where I is a $(n_{H1} \times n_{H1})$ identity matrix.

Equation (16) is of the form

$$x(t+1) = Ax(t) + Bu(t+1), \quad (17)$$

where $A = \beta I + \alpha J_1 W^{H1}$ and $B = W^{I1}$. Equation (17) represents the state equation of a linear system of which x is the state vector. The elements of A and B can be adjusted through training so that any arbitrary linear system of order n_{H1} can be modelled by the given network. When non-linear neurons are adopted, this gives the network the ability to perform non-linear dynamic mapping and thus model non-linear dynamic systems [14, 15]. The existence in the recurrent network of a hidden layer with both linear and non-linear neurons facilitates the modeling of practical non-linear systems comprising linear and non-linear parts. Figure 4 shows the proposed control system for a pneumatic valve actuator. The system comprises a PD controller and an NN controller, which is a recurrent hybrid network used to model inverse dynamics of the valve. The NN is trained online during the control to make the system able to adapt to changes. The control architecture illustrated in Figure 3 was implemented on a personal computer using Neural Network Toolbox of MATLAB [16].

4. Results and Discussion

Table 1 shows the parameters of a sliding-stem pneumatic control valve.

TABLE 1: Valve parameters [11].

Name of variable	Parameter	Value
Effective area of diaphragm	A	$0.196\,\text{ft}^2$
Spring constant	K	6790
Movable mass	$I\,(M)$	0.03 slug
Resistance and friction coefficient	R	$1\,\text{lb}\cdot\text{s/ft}$
Air pressure	SE	$140\,\text{lb/ft}^2$

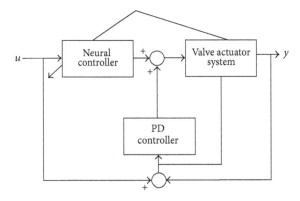

FIGURE 4: Block diagram of the proposed neural control system.

By substitution of Table 1 into (7), we have the following:

$$\frac{q_5(s)}{SE_1(s)} = \frac{6.53}{s^2 + 33.33s + 226333.3}. \tag{18}$$

Matrices of the state space equations of the valve are as follows:

$$A = \begin{bmatrix} 0 & 1 \\ -226333.33 & -33.33 \end{bmatrix}, \qquad B = \begin{bmatrix} 0 \\ 914.2 \end{bmatrix}, \tag{19}$$

$$C = \begin{bmatrix} 1 & 0 \end{bmatrix}, \qquad D = 0.$$

In this section, the design of control system with full- and minimum order observers is considered, when the system has reference inputs or command inputs. The output of the control system should follow the input. In following, the command input, the system should exhibit satisfactory performance (a reasonable rise time, overshoot, settling time, and so on). We consider control systems that are designed by use of the pole placement with observer approach. When a system has a reference input, several different block diagram configurations are conceivable, each having an observer controller. Two of these configurations are feedforward and feedback path. We would like to design the full- and minimum order observer controllers such that in the unit step response the maximum overshoot is less than 10% and settling time is about 0.5 sec. We first design the controller by finding the desired characteristic equation. A 10% overshoot and a settling time of 0.5 second yield $\xi = 0.591$ and $\omega_n = 13.53$; thus, the characteristic equation for dominant poles is $s^2 + 16s + 183.1 = 0$, where the dominant poles are located at $-8 \pm j10.91$ [17]. Hence, choose the desired closed-loop poles at $s = \mu_i$ $(i = 1, 2)$, where

$$\mu_1 = -8 + j10.91, \qquad \mu_2 = -8 - j10.91. \tag{20}$$

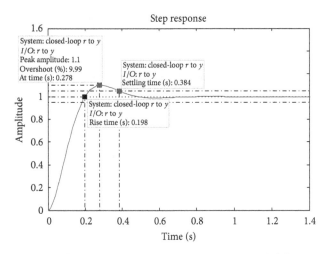

FIGURE 5: The unit step response of control system with full-order observer in feedforward path.

Also, we choose the desired observer poles at $s = -680$, $s = -680$. These poles create a stable controller. The state feedback gain matrix K and the observer gain matrix K_e can be obtained as follows:

$$K = \begin{bmatrix} -247.3389 & -0.019 \end{bmatrix},$$
$$K_e = \begin{bmatrix} 1326.67 & 191882.08 \end{bmatrix}^T. \tag{21}$$

The transfer function of the controller observer is obtained as follows:

$$G_s(s) = \frac{-331800s - 52710000}{s^2 + 1343s + 213300}. \tag{22}$$

If the full-order observer controller is placed in the feedforward path, from this block diagram, the closed-loop transfer function (CLTF) is obtained as follows:

$$\text{CLTF} = \frac{N\left(s^2 9.43e - 9 - 303300000s - 4.818e10\right)}{\left(s^4 + 1376s^3 + 484300s^2 + 7647000s + 84630000\right)}. \tag{23}$$

We can determine the value of the gain N, such that for a unit step input r, the output y is unity as time approaches infinity. Thus we choose the following:

$$N = \frac{84630000}{-4.818e10} = -1.7565e - 3. \tag{24}$$

The unit step response of the system is shown in Figure 5. Notice that the maximum overshoot is 9.99% and the settling and rise times are 0.384 and 0.198 second, respectively.

If we choose the full observer controller in the feedback path, then the closed-loop transfer function is obtained as follows:

$$\text{CLTF} = \frac{N\left(914.2s^2 + 1227000s + 1.95e8\right)}{\left(s^4 + 1376s^3 + 484300s^2 + 7647000s + 84630000\right)}. \tag{25}$$

TABLE 2: Structural and training parameters of neural controllers.

Controller	η	μ	α	β	n	N	A_F
NC	0.0001	0.01	0.9	0.8	$8+8$	30000	H_T

Note. η: learning term; μ: momentum term; α: feedback gain from output layer to hidden layer; β: feedback gain from hidden layer to itself; n: linear + nonlinear neurons in the hidden layer; N: iteration numbers; A_F: activation function for non-linear neurons; H_T: hyperbolic tangent.

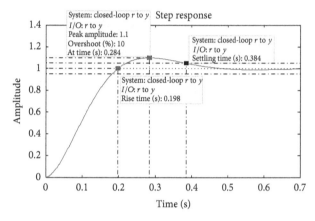

FIGURE 6: The unit step response of control system with full-order observer in feedback path.

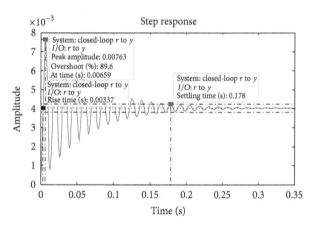

FIGURE 7: The unit step response of valve without any controller.

Thus, we can determine the value of the gain N as follows:

$$N = \frac{84630000}{1.95e8} = 0.434. \qquad (26)$$

The unit step response of control system with full-order observer in feedback path is shown in Figure 6. Notice that the maximum overshoot is 10% and the settling and rise times are 0.384 and 0.198 second, respectively.

Figure 7 shows the step response of valve stem without any controller. Here, the over shoot is too high and the settling time is also 0.178 second. The output has an overshoot less than 90% and rise time is 0.00337 second. But the design of full- and minimum order observer controller for valve led to the well unit step response characteristic.

The valve system was controlled using the proposed neural control system. Structural and learning parameters of the proposed neural network are given in Table 2.

If the learning rate is made too large, the algorithm becomes unstable. If the learning rate is set too small, the algorithm takes a long time to converge. Usually the learning rate is a constant real number between 0.1 and 1. It is not practical to determine the optimal setting for the learning rate before training and, in fact, the optimal learning rate changes during the training process, as the algorithm moves across the performance surface. The Mean square error (MSE) is defined as performance of the net. A backpropagation (BP) algorithm is designed to reduce error between the actual output and the desired output of the network in a gradient descent manner [13]. The hidden layer is responsible for internal representation of data and the information transformation between input and output layers. If there are too few neurons in the hidden layer, the network may not contain sufficient degrees of freedom to form a representation (i.e., in sufficient learning capacity). If too many neurons are defined, the network may become over trained (i.e., they classify training patterns well but lack the ability to generalize other independent data). Therefore, an interesting design for the number of neurons in the hidden layer, to determine the optimum network, will be important. Momentum can be added to backpropagation learning by making weight changes equal to the sum of a fraction of the last weight change and the new change suggested by the back propagation rule. The magnitude of the effect that the last weight change is allowed to have is mediated by a momentum constant, which can be any number between 0 and 1. So, here, different forms in the hidden layers are considered for the network. As a final result, the network with 16 neurons in hidden layer, learning, and momentum term in Table 2 has minimum performance with MSE = 0.02.

From Figure 8, the overshoot is initially very small. The output has an overshoot less than 7% and settling time shorter than 0.4 s.

5. Conclusion

Actuator valve systems are multivariable dynamic systems for which it is difficult to derive mathematical models. Therefore, analytical control schemes based on such models are complex to construct and generally do not perform well in practice. This paper has described a proposed neural control scheme for actuator of the pneumatic control valve. The aim of this study is the development of design procedure of an NN controller to meet transient response specifications of a sliding-stem pneumatic control valve. A type of actuator pneumatic control valve is modelled using bondgraph method. For comparison, full- and minimum order observer controllers are applied to the control of stem position in

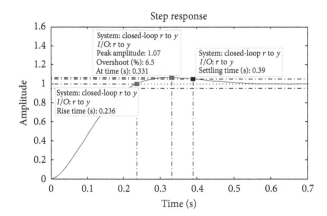

FIGURE 8: The unit step response of the valve using proposed neural controller.

a pneumatic control valve system. From this study, the following conclusions can be drawn.

(1) NN controller has smaller overshoot rather than minimum- and full-order observer.

(2) Minimum observer controller has smaller settling time and rise time respect to full-order observer.

(3) The full- and minimum order observers in feedback and feedforward path have the same overshoot, rise time, and settling time, if the normalization constants (N) are not the same.

References

[1] T. Hägglund, "A friction compensator for pneumatic control valves," *Journal of Process Control*, vol. 12, no. 8, pp. 897–904, 2002.

[2] M. A. De Souza L. Cuadros, C. J. Munaro, and S. Munareto, "Improved stiction compensation in pneumatic control valves," *Computers and Chemical Engineering*, vol. 38, pp. 106–114, 2012.

[3] R. P. Champagne and S. J. Boyle, "Optimizing valve actuator parameters to enhance control valve performance," *ISA Transactions*, vol. 35, no. 3, pp. 217–223, 1996.

[4] H. Paynter, *Analysis and Design of Engineering Systems*, MIT Press, Cambridge, Mass, USA, 1959.

[5] D. C. Karnopp, R. C. Rosenberg, and D. L. Margolis, *System Dynamics: Modeling, Simulation, and Control of Mechatronic Systems*, John Wiley & Sons, New York, NY, USA, 5th edition, 2012.

[6] J. U. Thoma, *Simulation by Bondgraphs: Introduction to a Graphical Method*, Springer, Berlin, Germany, 2012.

[7] P. Athanasatos and T. Costopoulos, "Proactive fault finding in a 4/3-way direction control valve of a high pressure hydraulic system using the bondgraph method with digital simulation," *Mechanism and Machine Theory*, vol. 50, pp. 64–89, 2012.

[8] V. D. Zuccarini, D. Rafirou, J. LeFevre, D. R. Hose, and P. V. Lawford, "Systemic modelling and computational physiology: the application of bondgraph boundary conditions for 3D cardiovascular models," *Simulation Modelling Practice and Theory*, vol. 17, no. 1, pp. 125–136, 2009.

[9] O. Ekren, S. Sahin, and Y. Isler, "Comparison of different controllers for variable speed compressor and electronic expansion valve," *International Journal of Refrigeration*, vol. 33, no. 6, pp. 1161–1168, 2010.

[10] S. B. Choi, C. C. Cheong, J. M. Jung, and Y. T. Choi, "Position control of an er valve-cylinder system via neural network controller," *Mechatronics*, vol. 7, no. 1, pp. 37–52, 1997.

[11] J. C. Mackanic, *Design, Construction and Evaluation of a Simulated Geothermal Flow System*, University of California, Berkeley, Calif, USA, 1980.

[12] K. Ogata, *Modern Control Engineering*, Prentice Hall, Upper Saddle River, NJ, USA, 5th edition, 2010.

[13] S. Zerkaoui, F. Druaux, E. Leclercq, and D. Lefebvre, "Stable adaptive control with recurrent neural networks for square MIMO non-linear systems," *Engineering Applications of Artificial Intelligence*, vol. 22, no. 4-5, pp. 702–717, 2009.

[14] M. Hernandez and Y. Tang, "Adaptive output-feedback decentralized control of a class of second order nonlinear systems using recurrent fuzzy neural networks," *Neurocomputing*, vol. 73, no. 1–3, pp. 461–467, 2009.

[15] H. W. Ge, W. L. Du, F. Qian, and Y. C. Liang, "Identification and control of nonlinear systems by a time-delay recurrent neural network," *Neurocomputing*, vol. 72, no. 13–15, pp. 2857–2864, 2009.

[16] H. Demuth and M. Beale, *Matlab Neural Networks Toolbox, User's Guide*, The MathWorks, Natick, Mass, USA, 2001, http://www.mathworks.com/.

[17] N. S. Nise, *Control System Engineering*, John Wiley & Sons, New York, NY, USA, 6th edition, 2010.

5

Using Ensemble of Neural Networks to Learn Stochastic Convection Parameterizations for Climate and Numerical Weather Prediction Models from Data Simulated by a Cloud Resolving Model

Vladimir M. Krasnopolsky,[1,2] Michael S. Fox-Rabinovitz,[2] and Alexei A. Belochitski[3,4]

[1] National Centers for Environmental Prediction, NOAA, College Park, MD 20740, USA
[2] Earth System Sciences Interdisciplinary Center, University of Maryland, College Park, MD 20740, USA
[3] Geophysical Fluid Dynamics Laboratory, NOAA, Princeton, NJ 08540, USA
[4] Brookhaven National Laboratory, Upton, NY 11973, USA

Correspondence should be addressed to Vladimir M. Krasnopolsky; vladimir.krasnopolsky@noaa.gov

Academic Editor: Ozgur Kisi

A novel approach based on the neural network (NN) ensemble technique is formulated and used for development of a NN stochastic convection parameterization for climate and numerical weather prediction (NWP) models. This fast parameterization is built based on learning from data simulated by a cloud-resolving model (CRM) initialized with and forced by the observed meteorological data available for 4-month boreal winter from November 1992 to February 1993. CRM-simulated data were averaged and processed to implicitly define a stochastic convection parameterization. This parameterization is learned from the data using an ensemble of NNs. The NN ensemble members are trained and tested. The inherent uncertainty of the stochastic convection parameterization derived following this approach is estimated. The newly developed NN convection parameterization has been tested in National Center of Atmospheric Research (NCAR) Community Atmospheric Model (CAM). It produced reasonable and promising decadal climate simulations for a large tropical Pacific region. The extent of the adaptive ability of the developed NN parameterization to the changes in the model environment is briefly discussed. This paper is devoted to a proof of concept and discusses methodology, initial results, and the major challenges of using the NN technique for developing convection parameterizations for climate and NWP models.

1. Introduction

Clouds and convection are among the most important and complex phenomena of the Earth's physical climate system. In spite of intense studies for centuries, clouds still provide an intellectual and computational challenge. Because of the vast range of time and space scales involved, researchers and models that they use typically focus on a particular component of a cloud system, with a narrow range of time and space scales, and prescribe features of the cloud that operate outside of that range. For example, microphysical models describing drop scale motions (e.g., drop coagulation) deal with the fine spatial and temporal scales (of order of millimeters (drop size) and seconds). For more detailed discussion of atmospheric moisture physics, see [1–4]. At the other end of the spectrum of representations of clouds is their representation in large-scale models, for example, in general circulation or global climate models (GCMs), which resolve atmospheric features with spatial scales of the order of 100 km, and temporal scales of the order of 10 minutes.

Numerical atmospheric and coupled atmospheric-oceanic-land models, or GCMs, used for climate and

Using Ensemble of Neural Networks to Learn Stochastic Convection Parameterizations for Climate and Numerical
Weather Prediction Models from Data Simulated by a Cloud Resolving Model

37

numerical weather predictions, are based on solving time-dependent 3-D geophysical fluid dynamics equations on the sphere. The governing equations of these complex models, based on conservation lows, can be written symbolically as

$$\frac{\partial \psi}{\partial t} + D(\psi, x) = P(\psi, x), \qquad (1)$$

where ψ is a 3-D-prognostic or -dependent variable (e.g., temperature, wind, pressure, and moisture); D is model dynamics (the set of 3-D partial differential equations of motion, thermodynamics, etc., approximated with a spectral or grid-point numerical scheme); x is a 3-D-independent variable (e.g., latitude, longitude, and height); P is model physics (e.g., long and short-wave atmospheric radiation, turbulence, convection and large-scale precipitation processes, clouds, interactions with land and ocean processes, etc.) and chemistry (constituency transport, chemical reactions, etc.). While scientific problems using these models are among the most complex and computationally intensive applications in the history of scientific exploration, the models employ drastic simplifications in their treatment of many physical processes important in climate and weather.

Physical and other processes included in model physics, P, are so complicated that it is practically possible to include them into GCMs only as 1-D (in the vertical direction) simplified or parameterized versions (usually called parameterizations). Thus, the model physics is composed of parameterizations as $P = \sum_k P_k$. These parameterizations constitute the right hand side forcing for the model dynamics equations (1). From the mathematical point of view, each parameterization can be considered as a mapping, which is a relationship between two vectors:

$$\mathbf{Y} = P_k(\mathbf{X}), \qquad (2)$$

where $\mathbf{X}$ is a vector consisting of profiles of atmospheric parameters describing the state of the atmosphere at a particular time at a particular location (a grid point) and $\mathbf{Y}$ is a vector of parameters providing an effective feedback to the atmosphere from the physical processes described by the parameterization P_k at the same location.

It is noteworthy that, after the very significant simplifications mentioned above and as it is formulated in (2), a parameterization does not depend on time and location explicitly. However, throughout model integration it is put in the environment, which changes in time and space when the parameterization is applied at different times and different horizontal locations (grid points) over the globe. The changes of the environment include temporal changes like diurnal, annual, other atmospheric and solar cycles, global climate changes, and spatial changes like the transition of the underlying surface from ocean to land and from one climate zone to another one (e.g., from the tropics to extra tropics). These internal changes constantly occurring throughout model integration reflect the actual external changes in the climate or weather system described by the model. In this paper, we investigate if our developed NN convection parameterization demonstrates the practically meaningful temporal and spatial generalization capability. The generalization capability allows

the NN convection parameterization to adapt to changing atmospheric states produced throughout climate model simulations.

A GCM does not resolve multiple subgrid processes that occur on temporal and spatial scales much finer than the GCM resolution. However, subgrid processes and scales are the processes and scales of which physics represents and is defined on. Because of that both $\mathbf{X}$ and $\mathbf{Y}$ in (2) have significant uncertainties and are actually stochastic variables. $\mathbf{X}$ and $\mathbf{Y}$ in (2) are defined on a GCM grid, and their uncertainties are due to and represent the subgrid scale variability, which is not resolved by GCM.

Thus, the mapping (2), which establishes the relationship between two stochastic variables $\mathbf{X}$ and $\mathbf{Y}$, is a stochastic mapping, and the parameterization P_k is a stochastic parameterization. Actually, the stochastic mapping is a family of mappings, each of which describes a relationship between two considered stochastic variables $\mathbf{X}$ and $\mathbf{Y}$ inside a range determined by the uncertainties of these variables with a probability determined by a joint probability distribution of these variables. The stochasticity of model physics parameterizations is a natural consequence of the finite model resolution, which leaves unresolved very important sub-grid scale processes [5]. Uncertainties of stochastic parameterization (2) carry important physical information about these subgrid (unresolved on a GCM grid) physical processes and should be properly taken into account in GCMs.

Usually, parameterizations, P_k, are formulated using relevant first principles and observational data and are based on solving deterministic equations (like radiative transfer equations). They also contain some secondary empirical components based on traditional statistical techniques like regression. As the result, for widely used the state-of-the-art GCMs, all major components of model physics and chemistry, are based on solving deterministic first principle physical or chemical equations. Thus, in the process of development of such a physically based parameterization, the family of mappings that represents the stochastic parameterization (2) is collapsed to one member of the family, completely neglecting the stochastic nature of the parameterization. Therefore, a physically based parameterization represents only one arbitrarily selected member of the family of mappings that represents the stochastic parameterization (2).

In this study, we develop a stochastic convection parameterization based on the learning from data approach, using a neural network (NN) technique. If sufficient amount of observations related to atmospheric convection, cloudiness, and precipitation was available, we could have attempted to learn the parameterization directly from observations. Unfortunately, in reality the available observations are sparse in space and time and not sufficient for such developments. To alleviate the problem, we use data simulated by models that explicitly resolve processes at the smaller temporal and spatial scales; that is, these models have resolution of a couple of orders of magnitude higher than that of GCMs. These models are capable of representing and resolving processes that are relevant to many major features of cloud systems with the spatial scales of the order of several kilometers and temporal scales of seconds to minutes. These are so called cloud resolving models (CRM), which simulate component aspects and evolution of cloud systems much more realistically than large-scale models. We employ the CRM [6–8] initialized and forced by observational data to simulate a limited (but more expanded, in terms of the spatial and temporal resolution and the number of variables, than available observational data) amount of data (they are called "pseudo-observations"). Then we use a NN technique to develop a stochastic convection parameterization (2) by learning from the simulated pseudo-observations.

In our previous works, we successfully applied a NN technique to develop accurate and fast emulations of complex physically based parameterizations. Because of the complexity of the physical processes involved and the complexity of their mathematical and numerical representations, some of these parameterizations are the most time-consuming components of GCMs. We have developed NN emulations for the most time-consuming part of model physics: model radiation [9–13]. Because, as it was mentioned above, a physically based parameterization is represented by a single mapping, we successfully used a single NN to emulate a physically based parameterization. However, a single NN is not an adequate tool for emulating a stochastic mapping (2), which is actually a family of mappings. An adequate tool in this case is an ensemble of NNs, which can effectively emulate the stochastic mapping (2) [4].

In this study, we use the CRM developed and provided by Khairoutdinov and Randall [7]. We also use the GCM developed by the National Center for Atmospheric Research (NCAR) that is called the Community Atmospheric Model (CAM). Thus, in this study we (a) apply a NN ensemble technique to learn a NN stochastic convection parameterization from the pseudo-observations simulated by the CRM, (b) introduce this NN stochastic convection parameterization into the NCAR CAM, and (c) run climate simulations to test the validity of the new NN stochastic convection parameterization. In Section 2, we formulate our approach and describe details of the training set creation and NN training. In Section 3, the results of validation of the developed NN ensemble convection parameterization are described. Section 4 presents discussion of results and Section 5 contains conclusions.

2. Formulation of the Approach: Development of a NN Ensemble Convection Parameterization from CRM Data

In this study, we develop an ensemble of NNs which emulates the behavior of fine-scale CRM simulations at larger GCM scales in a variety of regimes and initial conditions. The resulting ensemble NN parameterization can be used as a novel, and computationally viable convection parameterization in GCMs. This approach has a realistic potential of producing a parameterization of a similar or better quality to the existing physically based parameterizations that are used in GCMs, effectively taking into account subgrid scale (in terms of

a GCM) effects at a fraction of the computational cost of the existing approaches.

As we have shown in our previous works (e.g., [12]) any parameterization of model physics (2) can be emulated employing multilayer perceptron NNs using learning-from-data approach. This NN is an analytical approximation that uses a family of functions like

$$y_q = a_{q0} + \sum_{j=1}^{k} a_{qj} \cdot \phi \left(b_{j0} + \sum_{i=1}^{n} b_{ji} \cdot x_i \right); \quad q = 1, 2, \ldots, m,$$

$$(3)$$

where x_i and y_q are components of the input and output vectors X and Y, respectively, a and b are fitting parameters, and $\phi(b_{j0} + \sum_{i=1}^{n} b_{ji} \cdot x_i)$ is a "neuron." The activation function ϕ is usually a hyperbolic tangent, n and m are the numbers of inputs and outputs, respectively, and k is the number of neurons in (3). In the case of a stochastic parameterization, an ensemble of NNs (3) provides an adequate tool for representing a parameterization (2) [4].

2.1. Design and Development of NN Convection Parameterizations and Training Sets. Figure 1 summarizes the process of development of the NN parameterization. The CRM simulations use the TOGA-COARE (the international observational experiment in the tropics conducted for the 4-month period from November 1992 to February 1993) observational data for initialization and forcing and have the horizontal resolution ρ of 1 km, 64 or 96 vertical layers extending from the surface to ~30 km, and the time integration step of 5 s. We integrate the CRM over the domain of 256×256 km.

The development of the NN parameterization is a multi-step process. These steps are as follows.

(1) CRM simulated data: the CRM has been run for the 4-month period (from November 1992 to February 1993 or for 120 days of the TOGA-COARE observational experiment), and the high 1 km resolution output of the model has been obtained. The CRM-simulated temperature, wind, humidity, and other data are in a good agreement with those of the TOGA-COARE observational data. Also, the CRM produces additional prognostic and diagnostic fields not observed in the TOGA-COARE experiment.

(2) Reducing the horizontal resolution of the CRM simulated data: the CRM-simulated data are averaged in space and time. The data are averaged to a reduced horizontal resolution to r where $\rho < r \leq R$, and ρ and R are the CRM and GCM resolutions correspondingly. Also the data are interpolated/averaged onto the number of vertical layers $l = L$, where L is the number of vertical layers in the GCM.

(3) Projecting a CRM space of atmospheric states onto a GCM space of atmospheric states: the CRM has many variables that describe fine-scale processes not resolved by the GCM, for example, the condensed water in each CRM column. Such variables have no analogs in the GCM. From the point of view of

Using Ensemble of Neural Networks to Learn Stochastic Convection Parameterizations for Climate and Numerical Weather Prediction Models from Data Simulated by a Cloud Resolving Model

39

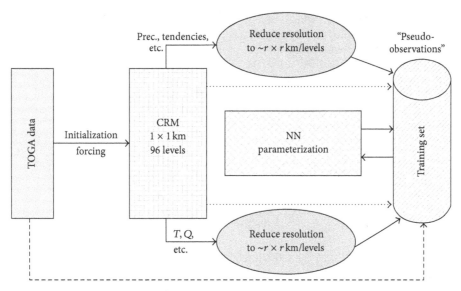

FIGURE 1: Development design of a NN convection parameterization. *T*, *Q*, and so forth refer to selected CRM-simulated fields used as inputs for NN parameterization; Prec., Tendencies, and so forth refer to selected CRM simulated variables used as NN outputs. The dotted and dashed lines indicate that observational and high-resolution simulated data can be added to the training data set if necessary.

a GCM "model reality" these variables are "hidden" variables responsible for sub-grid scale variability. The acknowledgement of this challenge requires development of the concept of uncertainty and "stochasticity"; it leads to recognition of a significant level of uncertainty in the pseudo-observations and of the stochasticity of the convection parameterization (2) learned from these data. The obtained set of "pseudo-observations" implicitly represents a stochastic convection parameterization with an uncertainty, which is an inherent feature of such a parameterization. Thus, only the variables that can be identified with the corresponding GCM variables or can be calculated from or converted to prognostic or diagnostic variables available in the GCM are selected to be included in the development set (called "pseudo-observations" in Figure 1; actually they are obtained from the averaged CRM simulated data). Only these variables are used as inputs and outputs of a NN convection parameterization. Thus, a subset of variables is selected from the reduced resolution CRM-simulated data created at the previous step (2), and this subset constitutes the NN development set. The dotted and dashed lines in Figure 1 show that, in principle, if it is found to be desirable, the high-resolution CRM-simulated data and/or even observed data can be added to the development set to enrich subgrid variability in the development data.

(4) The developed "pseudo-observations" are separated into two sets, one set being used for training and another independent set for testing/validation. Then the NN parameterization is trained using the training set. Due to the inherent uncertainty of pseudo-observations, the parameterization represented by these data is a stochastic parameterization; it should

be considered as a stochastic mapping. Thus, the NN parameterization is implemented as an ensemble of NNs.

All the aforementioned issues are discussed in detail in [4].

The validation procedure for the NN parameterization consists of two steps. First, the trained NN is applied to the test set and error statistics are calculated. Second, the tested NN parameterization is included into the GCM. This last step is the most important step of validation and of our approach.

2.2. NN Emulation of the Convection Parameterization and Estimation of Its Uncertainties

2.2.1. Data. The data set simulated for the NN development is limited by the length of the observational data set needed for forcing the CRM simulations (see Figure 1). The CRM was run for 120 days, using the TOGA-COARE forcing for the 256×256 km domain with 1 km resolution and 96 vertical layers (0–28 km). Then the simulated data were averaged at every hour of model integration to produce the simulation data set with an effective horizontal resolution of 256 km and 26 vertical levels. Finally, only variables that are available in the GCM (NCAR CAM) or can be calculated there have been selected. The final data set consists of 2,800 records of hourly mean data.

The simulation dataset was partitioned into two parts: a training set consisting of 2,240 records or 80% of data and a test set consisting of 560 records or 20% of data. Namely, first the 2,240 records are included in the training set and the last 560 records in the independent test set.

These two data sets have been used for the NN training and test/validation. As was noticed in the previous section, these data implicitly represent a stochastic parameterization and inherently contain an uncertainty, η, which is not a useless noise. However, in the process of learning the NN convection parameterization from pseudo-observations, from the point of view of a single NN trained using the data (both components X and Y of the data are stochastic variables), the situation is similar to the case when the data contain a significant level of noise.

Symbolically, the NN emulation of the stochastic parameterization (2) can be written as

$$Y = P_{NN}(X) + \eta + \varepsilon, \tag{4}$$

where P_{NN} is a NN emulation of the mapping P_k (2) and ε is a NN approximation error. Thus, in the case of the stochastic parameterization, the NN emulation task is different from the task of emulating a *deterministic* radiation parameterization in the GCM [9–11]. For example, in the GCM the radiation parameterization, which is a closed analytical expression or a computer code (mapping) is usually considered as an "exact" source of radiation information (it is not considered as a stochastic parameterization with an uncertainty); thus, for the NN emulation approach the goal is to emulate it as accurate as possible. This can be done because, in this case, the simulated data can be produced using the given parameterization (mapping), and considered as accurate data (with no noise greater than the round off errors).

In the current work, the situation is different. We do not have an expression (or computer code) for the mapping (2) that we want to emulate with NN (3). We can only assume that it exists and, in this case, it is a stochastic mapping, which is represented by pseudo-observations. Because we derive pseudo-observation, using a rather complex data processing described in the previous section, from the data simulated by the CRM, the pseudo-observations include a significant level of uncertainty. The uncertainty and stochasticity are the essential conceptual features of the NN parameterization that we are going to learn from the pseudo-observations. In a sense, emulating stochastic parameterization is closer to the task of learning from noisy empirical data [14]. This important difference should be taken into account when the NN approximation is trained, the approximation error statistics are analyzed and interpreted, and the NN architecture is selected. For example, in the case of training, the usually used criterion of minimum of the root mean square error should be substituted by the requirement that the root mean square error should not exceed the uncertainty η or

$$\frac{1}{N}\sum_{i=1}^{N}[Y_i - P_{NN}(X_i)]^2 < \eta^2, \tag{5}$$

where N is the number of records in the training set.

All NNs that satisfy the condition (5) are valid emulations of the stochastic parameterization (2). Actually, each of these NNs can be considered as an emulation of a member of the family of mappings that together represent the stochastic parameterization (2). Therefore, *all NNs satisfying (5) together—the entire ensemble of NNs—represent the stochastic parameterization (2).* It is clear now that any estimate of the magnitude of the uncertainty η is important for our

TABLE 1: NN architecture (inputs and outputs) investigated in the paper.

NN architecture	NN inputs		NN outputs			
In : out	T	QV	Q1C	Q2	PREC	CLD
36 : 55	18	18	18	18	1	18

T is temperature, QV is atmospheric moisture—vapor mixing ratio, Q1C: the "apparent heat source," Q2: the "apparent moist sink," PREC: precipitation rates, and CLD: cloudiness. Numbers in the table show the dimensionality of the corresponding input and output parameters. In : Out stand for NN inputs and outputs and show their corresponding numbers.

approach. We will attempt to derive such an estimate in the next sections.

2.2.2. NN Architectures, NN Training, and Validation. Selecting an emulating NN architecture includes two different aspects and types of decisions: (i) the selection of inputs and outputs and their numbers (n and m in (3)), which, as we have already mentioned, are determined by the availability of the variables in the GCM, and (ii) the selection of the number of hidden neurons (k in (3)) in the emulating NN, which is determined by many factors (the length of the training set, the level of uncertainty in the data, the characteristics of conversions of the training and test errors, etc.).

Table 1 shows (in terms of inputs and outputs) the architecture we have experimented with here. The major inputs are the vertical profiles of the following model prognostic and diagnostic fields: T—a profile of temperature—and QV—a profile of water vapor concentration. We experimented also with additional inputs: time, latitude, and longitude to take into account the changes in the data environment where the NN is applied; however, because in this particular case we work with data from a relatively small area and over a relatively short period of time (120 days), explicit introduction of the time and location dependencies does not make any difference and does not complement the indirect dependence on the time and location introduced by inputs T and QV. These inputs themselves depend on time and location. The major outputs for NN architecture shown in Table 1 are the vertical profiles (or vectors) of the following model prognostic and diagnostic fields: Q1C (a profile of the "apparent heat source"), Q2 (a profile of the "apparent moist sink"), PREC (precipitation rates, a scalar), and CLD (a profile of cloudiness).

The numbers in Table 1 show how many vertical levels of the corresponding profile (26 levels maximum as in the NCAR CAM) have been included as inputs in the NN. Many profiles have zeros, or constants, or values that are almost constant (their standard deviations are very small) for the entire data set at some levels (usually for the upper model levels in the stratosphere). Zeros and constants should not be included in inputs or outputs because (1) they carry no information about input/output functional dependence and (2) if not removed they introduce additional noise in training. As for small values that are almost constant, these small signals may be in some cases not a noise but very important signals; however, taking into account the level of uncertainty

Using Ensemble of Neural Networks to Learn Stochastic Convection Parameterizations for Climate and Numerical Weather Prediction Models from Data Simulated by a Cloud Resolving Model

41

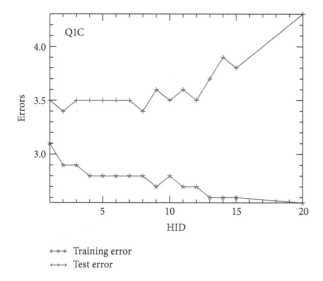

FIGURE 2: NN approximation errors on training (blue) and test (red) sets for Q1C. HID is the number of hidden neurons.

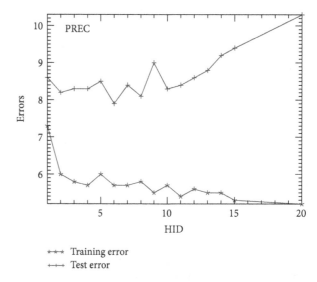

FIGURE 3: Same as in Figure 2 but for precipitation.

in the problem, information that these small signals may provide is well below the level of uncertainty and is practically useless. Moreover, some of these variables were included in training and no improvement was observed. In general, if they are important, they should be normalized differently or weighted.

Next, the number of hidden neurons (HID) has to be selected. We varied HID, trained a corresponding NN, and tested it. Figures 2 and 3 show the results of these experiments for two output parameters, Q1C and PREC.

It is noteworthy that the NN training (a least square minimization) attempts to minimize the total $(\eta + \varepsilon)^2$, that is, the sum of the approximation error and the uncertainty. Because of very different statistical properties of these components, they can be considered as independent random variables and approximately separated as

$$(\eta + \varepsilon)^2 \approx \eta^2 + \varepsilon^2. \tag{6}$$

Thus, η can be roughly estimated using detailed information about the training and test statistics. This issue is discussed in more detail below.

Figures 2 and 3 demonstrate a situation that is usually observed when NN is trained using data with a significant level of noise. The training error, after a sharp initial drop, stays almost constant and then decreases slowly. The test error, after an initial drop, stabilizes and then increases. The interpretation of this behavior is well known. After the initial improvement of the approximation of the data due to an increasing flexibility of an approximating NN, a short interval of stability is reached (at HID ~3 to 7) when NN fits the signal inside the corridor of errors. Then with the increase of the flexibility of the approximating NN, it starts fitting the noise; that is, the overfitting occurs. The training error is slowly decreasing; however, the test error quickly increases. Table 2 shows the number of fitting parameters (NN weights) in NNs with different HID, which were used for

Figures 2 and 3. Taking into account that the training set contains a limited number of records, 2240 records, it is not surprising that clearly pronounced overfitting is observed at HID > 10 when the number of NN weights, N_C, becomes comparable with the number of data records.

Thus, we can conclude that, for a particular simulated data set used, HID = 5 would be an acceptable choice for the number of hidden neurons in emulating NN. This value is inside of the intervals of stability of the training and test errors. Because for different NN outputs the interval of stability is slightly different, the choice of the optimal number of hidden neurons is hardly possible. The best solution of the problem, in our opinion, would be included in the NN ensemble members with various architectures (different numbers of hidden neurons and even with different inputs [4]).

The ensemble of ten NNs has been trained, and error statistics for seven of them that are significantly different are presented in Table 3. All NNs presented in Table 3 have the same number of inputs (36), outputs (55), and hidden neurons (5). They all have been initialized using the same initialization procedure [15] with different small random numbers. The ten different members of NN ensemble correspond to ten different local minima of the error function. Table 3 shows the comparison of NN ensemble member error statistics on the training set (Tr) and on the independent test set (Ts); both sets are described above in Section 2.2.1. For each NN output variable, three statistics were calculated (bias, RMSE, and correlation coefficient) by comparison of NN-generated output variables with the corresponding ones in the training or test set.

The *training errors* (Tr) for all output parameters are significantly closer to each other for different NN ensemble members and less sensitive to the selection of HID (not shown in Table 3) inside the interval of stability (see Figures 2 and 3) than the test errors (Ts). Thus, the training errors can be considered as a rough estimate of the noise in the

TABLE 2: The number of fitting parameters (NN weights), N_C, at different values of HID = k (see (3)).

			HID			
	1	2	5	10	15	20
N_C	166	273	594	1129	1667	2199

data, which is the inherent uncertainty η of the stochastic parameterization (2).

Following this assumption, we can approximately estimate the uncertainty η. For example, for Q1C the average training RMS error (calculated using Table 3) is about 2.4 K/day, which can be attributed to the uncertainty η. This estimate for the uncertainty for one of the model variable, which is introduced by taking into account sub-grid scale effects, is an important result per se. The quantitative information about the uncertainty is instrumental in evaluating the accuracy of the model forecast. Now, using (6) for the test error we can estimate the NN approximation error. For this example, the test error is 2.9 K/day and, following (6), only about 1.6 K/day of this error should be attributed to the NN approximation error. If we perform such a correction for all NN ensemble members presented in Table 3, we find out that, as in the aforementioned example, after the separation of the uncertainty (the training error), the NN approximation errors on the test set do not exceed (often they are smaller than) the uncertainty.

Figures 4, 5, and 6 illustrate performance of different members of the NN ensemble on the independent test set. Figure 4 demonstrates predictions of precipitation time series produced by different NN ensemble members in comparison with "pseudo-observations" (or "Data" in the figure legend). The NN ensemble members produce an envelope (with a rather measurable spread) which on average gives a very good prediction of precipitation on the test set. The spread of the envelope shows that there is still a measurable difference between NN ensemble members, and some of the members of the envelope (e.g., {9}) give results that are closer to the "pseudo-observations." The magnitude of the spread may serve as another measure of the uncertainty of the stochastic parameterization (2). It is in agreement with the measure we introduced above, with the magnitude of the training error for PREC shown in Table 3.

Figure 5 depicts mean profiles for one of the outputs of the NN parameterization, Q1C. As in the case of precipitation, different members of the NN ensemble create an envelope with a significant spread for the mean profiles, and the magnitude of the spread is close to the training error for Q1C shown in Table 3. The differences between members inside the envelope are small as compared with the uncertainty; however, these differences are significant. They give estimates of the differences between members of the family of mappings representing the stochastic parameterization (2) and implicitly available in pseudo-observations.

Figure 6 shows the Hovmöller diagrams (the time evolution of vertical profiles) for the time series of cloudiness (CLD) profiles for the NN ensemble mean as compared with the verification data. The upper panel shows the time

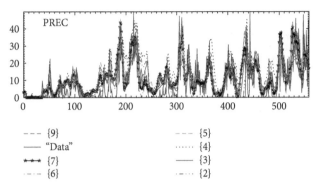

--- {9}	--- {5}
---- "Data"	...... {4}
✳✳✳ {7}	---- {3}
-·- {6}	-·-· {2}

FIGURE 4: NN simulations of precipitation on the test set. Different curves presented in the figure represent seven significantly different members of the NN ensemble (see the numbers in parentheses) and verification data. The NN ensemble member {9} is shown by the thick-dashed red line.

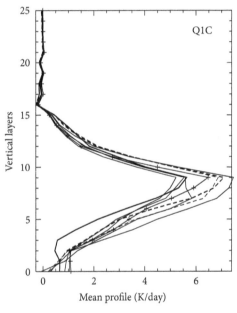

FIGURE 5: Q1C (the apparent heat source from convection) mean profiles on the test set produced by different NN ensemble members. The different curves presented in the figure correspond to different ensemble members; the thick solid line shows the verification data in the test set.

series of the pseudo-observation profiles, and the lower panel shows the time series of the profiles generated by NN ensemble. Each profile in the lower panel is the average of ten profiles generated by ten NN ensemble members. The patterns generated by the NN ensemble are a bit smoothed and diffused; they are not as sharp as the observed ones but are well recognizable. The NN ensemble mean represents the sequence of patterns well and without significant shifts.

As mentioned above, the NN errors on the raining set as well as the spread of the envelope created by different NN ensemble members represent the level of uncertainty in pseudo-observation data or the uncertainty of the stochastic parameterization (2). It means that, in the context of the current application (development of NN emulation for

Using Ensemble of Neural Networks to Learn Stochastic Convection Parameterizations for Climate and Numerical
Weather Prediction Models from Data Simulated by a Cloud Resolving Model

43

TABLE 3: NN ensemble member error statistics on training (Tr) and independent test (Ts) sets. CC is the correlation coefficient. HID = 5.

Data set	Ens. mem.	QlC (K/day)			Q2 (K/day)			Prec (mm/day)			CLD (fractions)		
		Bias	RMSE	CC	Bias	RMSE	CC	Bias	RMSE	CC	Bias	RMSE	CC
Tr	2	$1 \cdot 10^{-3}$	2.8	0.75	$2 \cdot 10^{-2}$	4.0	0.63	$1 \cdot 10^{-2}$	6.0	0.85	$1 \cdot 10^{-4}$	0.07	0.91
	3	$2 \cdot 10^{-3}$	2.4	0.78	$2 \cdot 10^{-2}$	3.7	0.66	$1 \cdot 10^{-2}$	5.7	0.86	$2 \cdot 10^{-6}$	0.07	0.92
	4	$1 \cdot 10^{-3}$	2.3	0.81	$2 \cdot 10^{-3}$	3.7	0.68	$4 \cdot 10^{-3}$	5.2	0.89	$1 \cdot 10^{-4}$	0.07	0.92
	5	$2 \cdot 10^{-3}$	2.3	0.80	$1 \cdot 10^{-3}$	3.8	0.66	$2 \cdot 10^{-2}$	5.3	0.88	$3 \cdot 10^{-5}$	0.07	0.91
	6	$4 \cdot 10^{-4}$	2.3	0.80	$1 \cdot 10^{-3}$	3.8	0.64	$1 \cdot 10^{-3}$	5.3	0.88	$6 \cdot 10^{-5}$	0.08	0.89
	7	$2 \cdot 10^{-4}$	2.3	0.81	$3 \cdot 10^{-4}$	3.7	0.67	$7 \cdot 10^{-3}$	5.2	0.89	$5 \cdot 10^{-5}$	0.06	0.93
	9	$1 \cdot 10^{-3}$	3.1	0.73	$4 \cdot 10^{-3}$	4.0	0.64	$2 \cdot 10^{-2}$	5.8	0.86	$1 \cdot 10^{-4}$	0.07	0.90
Ts	2	−0.1	3.5	0.62	0.02	4.7	0.49	−1.1	8.5	0.68	0.03	0.11	0.81
	3	−0.6	3.5	0.62	−0.8	5.0	0.44	−5.1	10.6	0.66	0.01	0.11	0.81
	4	−0.5	3.0	0.70	−0.6	4.5	0.53	−4.0	8.8	0.73	0.00	0.09	0.86
	5	−0.1	2.9	0.71	−0.1	3.9	0.52	−1.8	7.8	0.74	0.01	0.08	0.87
	6	−0.3	2.9	0.70	−0.1	3.9	0.51	−2.6	8.0	0.74	0.01	0.08	0.88
	7	−0.4	2.9	0.73	−0.5	4.3	0.58	−3.3	7.9	0.77	0.00	0.07	0.92
	9	−0.7	3.8	0.65	−0.8	4.7	0.51	−4.1	8.6	0.76	0.01	0.10	0.84

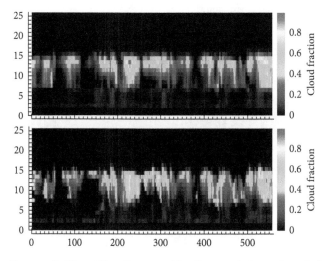

FIGURE 6: Hovmöller diagrams (the time evolution of vertical profiles) for the CLD profile time series: pseudo-observations, the upper panel and the NN ensemble mean, the lower panel. The x-axis shows time in hours for the test/validation set.

a stochastic convection parameterization (2)), selecting the best single emulating NN followed by the use of this "optimal" NN parameterization in the GCM is not the best approach.

All NNs presented here (as well as other NNs, for example, with different architectures, different number of neurons in the hidden layer evaluated in [4]) can be considered as valid emulations of the parameterization (2). These NNs should be considered as members of a NN ensemble realization of the stochastic parameterization (2) represented by a particular data set. The spread in the NN ensemble roughly reflects the skill (error) of the prediction that could be obtained using this NN ensemble.

3. Validation of the Stochastic NN Convection Parameterization in NCAR CAM

We consider the results presented in this section mostly as a proof of concept for our NN approach to developing NN convection parameterizations. Keeping this in mind, we present the results from the standpoint of their general quality with a clear understanding that more precise quantitative climatological results could be expected in our future efforts.

The NN stochastic convection parameterization described in the previous sections has been implemented as the ensemble of NNs, which are trained on the averaged CRM simulated data "pseudo-observations". In this section, we discuss the results of introduction of the NN stochastic parameterization into the NCAR CAM. Here our goal is to verify whether the NN ensemble, emulating the stochastic convection parameterization (2), provides meaningful/realistic outputs when using the CAM inputs. We performed the validation of our NN parameterization in the following two experiments.

(1) Over the TOGA-COARE location, the grid point (−2° S, 155° E) for the time period for which the TOGA-COARE data are available (the TOGA-COARE 4-month period from November 1992 to February 1993) we produced the grid-point time-mean profiles and time series.

(2) Over the large tropical Pacific region (with the area size of 120° × 30° and the following coordinates: 150°E < lon < 90° W; 15° S < lat < 15° N), we performed the parallel runs with the standard CAM and with the diagnostic CAM-NN run (see below) for the decadal (1990–2001) boreal winters, from November to February or NDJF, climate simulations. Throughout the CAM-NN run we applied at each grid point and at every time step the aforementioned ten

NN ensemble members and calculated the ensemble mean for each NN output (Q1C, Q2, and CLD profiles, and for PREC).

Note that the parallel decadal climate simulations have been actually performed for 11 years, but the decadal means (actually 11 boreal winters or NDJF) used below for validation have not included the TOGA-COARE period (see above). The TOGA-COARE data for the 4-month period from November 1992 to February 1993 were used for initializing and forcing CRM simulations, that is, for creating simulated data, which was converted into pseudo-observations used for the NN ensemble training. The validation of the parallel runs has been done for the independent decade.

For simple/initial testing and validation of the NN stochastic convection parameterization (2) in the CAM, we introduced a diagnostic mode of integration. For the diagnostic mode of integration, at every time step, the NN convection parameterization is applied, all ten NN ensemble members are evaluated, and averages of their outputs are calculated and used as NN ensemble convection parameterization outputs. Hereafter this diagnostic run is called CAM-NN. These outputs have been accumulated and the averaged fields have been calculated and compared with those produced by the original CAM convection parameterization and NCEP reanalysis data [16, 17], which provides verification data for climate simulations. Note that reanalysis data (an integrated set of global observations) is produced (every 10 years or so) using a data assimilation system (DAS) which employs a GCM and observational data for past several decades, for example, from 1948 to 2010. A DAS is a complicated procedure, which involves nonlinear optimization in the space of very high dimensionality, combining or blending observational data with the GCM simulations to produce the best possible estimates of atmospheric states for a reanalysis period.

3.1. Validation of the NN Convection Parameterization Using the NCAR CAM for the TOGA-COARE Location and 4-Month Period from November 1992 to February 1993.

At the first step of our validation, the outputs generated by the ensemble of ten NNs have been compared with CAM-simulated data for one grid point at the TOGA-COARE location ($-2°$ S, $155°$ E) during the TOGA-COARE period, from November 1992 to February 1993. Thus, the CAM-simulated data were collocated in space and time with the averaged CRM simulated data.

We used the CAM-simulated T and QV as inputs for the NN ensemble trained on the averaged CRM-simulated data (pseudo-observations). The major NN outputs (CLD and PREC) obtained in this experiment have been compared with CAM CLD and PREC and with pseudo-observations. Figure 7 shows mean CLD profiles for the aforementioned experiment. The CAM-NN profile deviates from the pseudo-observation profile because the NN ensemble has been trained for pseudo-observation inputs, not for the CAM ones. It is also different from the CAM profile, which suggests that our stochastic NN convection parameterization effectively introduces in the CAM-NN run the convection and cloud

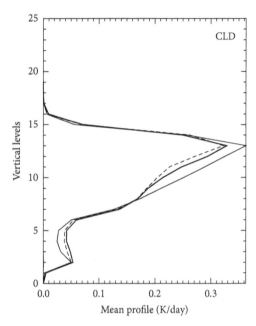

FIGURE 7: Three different mean cloud (CLD) profiles for the TOGA-COARE period: CAM-NN (thick solid), pseudo-observations (dashed), and CAM (solid).

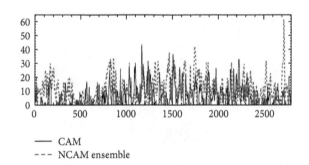

FIGURE 8: Precipitation (PREC, in mm/day) time series: CAM (black solid) and CAM-NN (or NCAM) ensemble mean (red dashed).

physics, which is different from that of introduced in the parallel CAM run employing an existing CAM convection parameterization.

Figure 8 shows the precipitation (PREC) time series produced by the original CAM run and the CAM-NN run using the NN ensemble mean. The scope, mean, and frequencies of the time series are quite similar for both models and look reasonable. Table 4 shows the bulk statistics for CLD and PREC variables for the CAM, CAM-NN runs and for pseudo-observations. Like in Figure 7 the statistics for the CAM-NN run are in between those of the CAM run and pseudo-observations; they are very reasonable and physically meaningful.

Let us stress that we should not expect full similarity here between CAM-NN and CAM statistics, profiles, and time series. The CAM-NN results are generated by our NN convection parameterization learned from CRM cloud physics, which is different from the cloud physics implemented currently in the CAM. Full similarity of the CAM and CAM-NN

Using Ensemble of Neural Networks to Learn Stochastic Convection Parameterizations for Climate and Numerical Weather Prediction Models from Data Simulated by a Cloud Resolving Model

45

TABLE 4: Bulk statistics for CLD and PREC outputs for CAM, CAM-NN, and pseudo-observations (PO).

	Mean	Standard deviation	Min	Max
PREC in mm/day				
PO	9.22	11.24	0.	80.8
CAM-NN	8.50	8.14	0.	63.6
CAM	6.41	7.23	0.	43.5
CLD in fraction				
PO	0.072	0.154	0.	1.00
CAM-NN	0.104	0.240	0.	1.00
CAM	0.159	0.256	0.	1.00

results would mean that our NN convection parameterization is not different form the convection parameterization used in the CAM and has no value in terms of introducing new physics in the CAM. Even in this case, it may still be valuable in terms of higher computational performance providing also a possibility of using NN ensembles.

3.2. Evaluating the NN Convection Parameterization Generalization Ability in Parallel Decadal Climate Simulations for a Large Tropical Pacific Region. Encouraged by the aforementioned success of our NN parameterization in the CAM-NN, we extended our diagnostic tests beyond the TOGA-COARE location and beyond the time interval covered by the CRM simulated data to test the NN parameterization generalization ability and its ability to adapt to the changing data environment. Namely, we performed the parallel decadal CAM and CAM-NN simulations and analyzed their results over a large tropical Pacific region.

We would like to emphasize that the NN convection parameterization has been developed for the TOGA-COARE location, which is represented by just one grid point in the CAM and which is actually a small area in the Equatorial Pacific (marked by a star in the middle panel of Figure 11). Also the TOGA-COARE data have been produced only over a short 4-month period (from November 1992 to February 1993 or NDJF). To evaluate the NN convection parameterization generalization and adaptive ability, we applied the NN ensemble convection parameterization in the CAM-NN run for the entire large tropical Pacific region (with the area size of $120° \times 30°$ and the following coordinates: $150°$ E $<$ lon $< 90°$ W; $15°$ S $<$ lat $< 15°$ N) during the decadal (1990–2001, with the TOGA-COARE 4-month period from November 1992 to February 1993 excluded) run. This is a very hard test for the generalization and adaptive ability of the NNs trained over a single location and a short 4-month period.

As described above, the developed NN convection parameterization has been introduced into the CAM-NN and run in the aforementioned diagnostic mode, for which CAM inputs have been used for calculating NN convection outputs. Below we compare the parallel decadal CAM-NN and CAM simulations and validate them against the NCEP reanalysis. Because NN convection was trained using simulated data

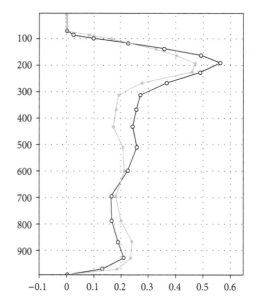

FIGURE 9: Vertical profiles of decadal boreal winter mean CLD for the TOGA-COARE location, in fractions, for the CAM-NN (open circles) and CAM (full circles) runs. Atmospheric pressure in hPa is the vertical coordinate.

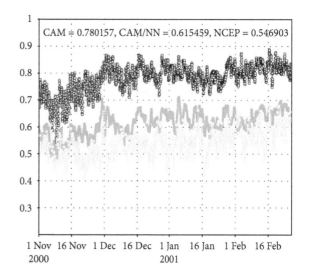

FIGURE 10: Time series of decadal boreal winter mean total cloudiness (CLD, in fractions) for the TOGA-COARE location for the CAM (black) and CAM-NN (green) runs, and for the NCEP reanalysis (yellow). Numbers in the figure show the mean values for the time series.

for the TOGA-COARE 4-month period (November 1992–February 1993), below we will analyze the decadal simulations for 4-month boreal winter seasons only.

The results of these decadal parallel climate simulations for the tropical Pacific region for decadal means of boreal winter (NDJF) distributions for total cloudiness (CLD) are shown in Figures 9, 10, and 11.

The decadal mean CLD profiles for the TOGA-COARE location for the CAM-NN and CAM runs shown in Figure 9

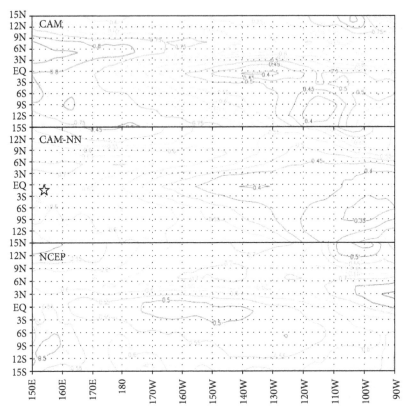

FIGURE 11: Decadal boreal winter mean cloudiness (CLD, in fractions) distribution for the CAM (upper panel) and CAM-NN (middle panel) runs over tropical Pacific region (with the area size of 120° × 30° and the following coordinates: 150° E < lon < 90° W shown with the 10° interval; 15° S < lat < 15° N shown with the 3° interval). The lower panel shows the corresponding NCEP reanalysis decadal mean distribution. The TOGA-COARE location, for which the pseudo-observations were generated and the NN ensemble was trained, is shown by a star in the middle panel. The contour interval is 0.05°C.

are close to each other. Note that the decadal mean profiles are consistent with those shown for the CAM-NN and CAM runs in Figure 7 for the TOGA-COARE period. When comparing these two figures, the difference in the vertical coordinates should be taken into account. In Figure 7 the model vertical level number is used as the vertical coordinate, whereas in Figure 9 the atmospheric pressure in hPa is used. The conversion from one coordinate to another one is essentially nonlinear. The pressure of about 200 hPa corresponds to the vertical level number 13.

The frequencies and magnitudes of the decadal mean CLD time series for the CAM and CAM-NN runs presented in Figure 10 are similar and consistent. The time series for the CAM run show measurably higher magnitudes, with the mean of 0.78, compared to those of the time series for the CAM-NN run, with the mean of 0.61. The time series of the NCEP reanalysis show lower magnitudes, with the mean of 0.54, which are significantly closer to those of the time series for CAM-NN. Note that the CLD results presented in Figure 6 have shown a close agreement of the CRM-simulated (and grid-box averaged) data and the NN ensemble mean, at the TOGA-COARE location. In our view, the improvement of the CLD time series for the decadal CAM-NN run for a large tropical region can be attributed to both a good quality of the CRM-simulated data, which implicitly represent a better

CRM cloud physics, and the positive impact from using the NN ensemble.

The horizontal distribution of total cloudiness for the large tropical Pacific Ocean region for the CAM-NN run versus the CAM control run and the NCEP reanalysis (Figure 11) have been produced and analyzed. For the region, the precipitation and cloudiness patterns for the parallel decadal CAM-NN and CAM simulations have been qualitatively and quantitatively compared.

The major result is that the regional CLD distributions for the decadal parallel runs presented in Figure 11 show a consistency and similarity, in terms of both the pattern and especially the magnitude, between the CAM-NN and CAM runs and, to some extent, with the NCEP reanalysis [17] used for validation. However, both the CAM and CAM-NN run patterns show some noticeable deviations from the NCEP reanalysis pattern. This is definitely the subject for the future improvements (see the future work outlined in Sections 4 and 5).

The CLD magnitudes for the CAM-NN run (Figure 11) are mostly closer to those of the NCEP reanalysis than the CLD magnitudes of the CAM run. However, such a positive feature should be mentioned cautiously because this is just an initial result. It is noteworthy that the CLD decadal time series for the TOGA-COARE location (Figure 10) and

Using Ensemble of Neural Networks to Learn Stochastic Convection Parameterizations for Climate and Numerical
Weather Prediction Models from Data Simulated by a Cloud Resolving Model

47

the CLD distribution for the tropical Pacific Ocean (Figure 11) are consistent in the sense that for both characteristics the CAM run shows measurably higher magnitudes compared to those of the CAM-NN run, the latter being closer to those of the NCEP reanalysis.

Similar results have been obtained for the decadal boreal winter precipitation distribution over the tropical Pacific Ocean region (see [4]).

4. Discussion

At this initial stage of our development of the stochastic NN convection parameterizations, which is mostly the proof of concept, it seems reasonable to compare the CAM and CAM-NN runs mostly in terms of their general consistency between themselves and with the NCEP reanalysis. A detailed climatological analysis of regional and global simulations for all seasons will be done at the next stage of our development. It will be based on using extended more representative CRM simulations with broader spatial and temporal coverage for developing stochastic NN convection parameterizations for the CAM, which could be applied globally and for all seasons.

The CAM-NN results are generated by our NN convection parameterization learned from CRM cloud physics, which is different from the cloud physics currently implemented in the CAM convection parameterization. The CAM and CAM-NN results are consistent and quite similar, with some differences discussed above.

In our view, the results presented above in Sections 2 and 3 demonstrate a realistic potential of the presented NN ensemble approach for developing stochastic NN convection parameterizations. Our first attempt in this direction led to meaningful results despite the fact that for our development we used for the NN training a limited amount of data available over a small area in the tropical Pacific Ocean (the TOGA-COARE site) and during only four month (the TOGA-COARE period from November 1992 to February 1993). We obtained physically meaningful results not only over this particular location and time interval, but our decadal climate simulation for cloudiness and precipitations over this location and over the extended large tropical Pacific Ocean region look meaningful even without introduction in NNs an explicit time and location dependencies. These results demonstrate: (1) a very good generalization ability of the NN ensemble in this application and (2) a good ability of the NN ensemble to adapt to a changing data environment using implicit dependencies of NN inputs on time and location without introducing these dependencies explicitly.

These two issues are extremely important for future development of this approach. Our final goal is to develop a global NN convection parameterization, which can be used in the CAM and other global GCMs. To achieve this goal, a representative global data set of pseudo-observations is required. However, data for initialization and forcing CRM are available only over a few sites (TOGA-COARE, ARM, etc.); thus, CRM simulations initialized and driven by a limited amount of observations are not representative in terms of different global geographical locations and different weather conditions. Hopefully, the aforementioned data

could be augmented by data simulated by the CRM, which is initialized and driven not only by observations but also by GCM-simulated data. In principle, the CRM could be run in such a way at each GCM grid point for a long period of time and supply a representative global set of pseudo-observations. However, since the CRM runs are very time consuming, this scenario is not practically feasible. In this context, good generalization and adaptation abilities of the stochastic NN convection parameterization demonstrated in this study become crucial; they will hopefully allow us to reduce the number of locations for generating pseudo-observations to a manageable and computationally affordable number of grid points.

It is noteworthy that the NN ensemble convection parameterization is very fast, contrary to any alternative approaches that have been developed to introduce new cloud and convective physics in GCMs (see [4], for details). These alternative approaches are very time consuming and barely affordable for climate simulations and weather prediction.

5. Conclusions

In this paper we introduce a novel approach to development of NN convection parameterizations based on applying the NN ensemble technique. This approach has been conceptually formulated and developed. Several very important notions are introduced which constitute the conceptual skeleton of the approach:

(1) pseudo-observations which are the result of averaging and projecting of high-dimensional and high-resolution CRM-simulated data. The pseudo-observations contain the uncertainty which is a result of averaging and projection of the original CRM simulated data,

(2) stochastic mapping/parameterization that is implicitly defined by pseudo-observations with uncertainties,

(3) NN ensemble emulation that is an adequate tool for emulating stochastic mappings/parameterizations,

(4) adaptation to temporal and spatial change in the environment, in which the NN ensemble parameterization performs through implicit time and location dependencies of NN inputs.

Our future plans include the following:

(1) running CRM simulations initialized and forced by GCM-simulated data and by reanalysis data to generate a more representative data set that will include a broader range of convection regimes, longer time periods, more locations, and more diverse weather conditions,

(2) using the representative global data set produced in this way to train a global NN convection parameterization,

(3) testing the NN convection parameterization trained using these new data in the CAM in diagnostic and prognostic modes,

(4) introducing tools allowing the NN parameterization to adapt to changes in the environment by: (1) using time and location as additional inputs in the NN parameterization and (2) using dynamically adjustable NN parameterization based on approaches developed in [18]. The approaches use various procedures to recognize new atmospheric states emerged due to the changes in the environment. These states are used for an online adjustment of the NN parameters.

Acknowledgments

The authors would like to thank Prof. Marat Khairoutdinov (SUNY) for providing the CRM (SAM), Dr. Peter Blossy for providing simulated data and consultations on SAM, and Dr. Philip J. Rasch (DOE PNNL) for multiple and fruitful discussions: MMAB Contribution no. 293.

References

[1] L. J. Donner and P. J. Rasch, "Cumulus initialization in a global model for numerical weather prediction," *Monthly Weather Review*, vol. 117, pp. 2654–2671, 1989.

[2] P. J. Rasch, J. Feichter, K. Law et al., "A comparison of scavenging and deposition processes in global models: results from the WCRP Cambridge workshop of 1995," *Tellus B*, vol. 52, no. 4, pp. 1025–1056, 2000.

[3] P. J. Rasch, M. J. Stevens, L. Ricciardulli et al., "A characterization of tropical transient activity in the CAM3 atmospheric hydrologic cycle," *Journal of Climate*, vol. 19, no. 11, pp. 2222–2242, 2006.

[4] V. Krasnopolsky, M. Fox-Rabinovitz, A. Belochitski, P. Rasch, P. Blossey, and Y. Kogan, "Development of neural network convection parameterizations for climate and NWP models using Cloud Resolving Model simulations," NCEP Office Note 469, 2011, http://www.emc.ncep.noaa.gov/officenotes/newernotes/on469.pdf.

[5] T. N. Palmer and P. D. Williams, "Introduction. Stochastic physics and climate modeling," *Philosophical Transactions of the Royal Society A*, vol. 366, pp. 2421–2427, 2008.

[6] M. F. Khairoutdinov and D. A. Randall, "A cloud resolving model as a cloud parameterization in the NCAR community climate system model: preliminary results," *Geophysical Research Letters*, vol. 28, no. 18, pp. 3617–3620, 2001.

[7] M. F. Khairoutdinov and D. A. Randall, "Cloud resolving modeling of the ARM summer 1997 IOP: model formulation, results, uncertainties, and sensitivities," *Journal of the Atmospheric Sciences*, vol. 60, no. 4, pp. 607–625, 2003.

[8] F. Guichard, J. C. Petch, J. L. Redelsperger et al., "Modelling the diurnal cycle of deep precipitating convection over land with cloud-resolving models and single-column models," *Quarterly Journal of the Royal Meteorological Society*, vol. 130, no. 604, pp. 3139–3172, 2004.

[9] V. M. Krasnopolsky, M. S. Fox-Rabinovitz, and D. V. Chalikov, "New approach to calculation of atmospheric model physics: accurate and fast neural network emulation of longwave radiation in a climate model," *Monthly Weather Review*, vol. 133, no. 5, pp. 1370–1383, 2005.

[10] V. M. Krasnopolsky, M. S. Fox-Rabinovitz, and A. A. Belochitski, "Decadal climate simulations using accurate and fast neural network emulation of full, long- and short wave, radiation," *Monthly Weather Review*, vol. 136, pp. 3683–3695, 2008.

[11] V. M. Krasnopolsky, M. S. Fox-Rabinovitz, Y. T. Hou, S. J. Lord, and A. A. Belochitski, "Accurate and fast neural network emulations of model radiation for the NCEP coupled climate forecast system: climate simulations and seasonal predictions," *Monthly Weather Review*, vol. 138, no. 5, pp. 1822–1842, 2010.

[12] V. M. Krasnopolsky, "Neural network emulations for complex multidimensional geophysical mappings: applications of neural network techniques to atmospheric and oceanic satellite retrievals and numerical modeling," *Reviews of Geophysics*, vol. 45, Article ID RG3009, 2007.

[13] V. Krasnopolsky, "Neural network applications to developing hybrid atmospheric and oceanic numerical models," in *Artificial Intelligence Methods in the Environmental Sciences*, S. E. Haupt, A. Pasini, and C. Marzban, Eds., pp. 217–234, Springer, 2009.

[14] V. Krasnopolsky, "Neural network applications to solve forward and inverse problems in atmospheric and oceanic satellite remote sensing," in *Artificial Intelligence Methods in the Environmental Sciences*, S. E. Haupt, A. Pasini, and C. Marzban, Eds., pp. 191–205, Springer, 2009.

[15] D. Nguyen and B. Widrow, "Improving the learning speed of 2-layer neural networks by choosing initial values of the adaptive weights," in *Proceedings of the International Joint Conference on Neural Networks (IJCNN '90)*, vol. 3, pp. 21–26, San Diego, Calif, USA, June 1990.

[16] E. Kalnay, M. Kanamitsu, R. Kistler et al., "The NCEP/NCAR 40-year reanalysis project," *Bulletin of the American Meteorological Society*, vol. 77, pp. 437–471, 1996.

[17] S. Saha, S. Moorthi, H.-L. Pan et al., "The NCEP climate forecast system reanalysis," *Bulletin of the American Meteorological Society*, vol. 91, pp. 1015–1057, 2010.

[18] V. M. Krasnopolsky, M. S. Fox-Rabinovitz, H. L. Tolman, and A. A. Belochitski, "Neural network approach for robust and fast calculation of physical processes in numerical environmental models: compound parameterization with a quality control of larger errors," *Neural Networks*, vol. 21, no. 2-3, pp. 535–543, 2008.

6

Methodological Triangulation Using Neural Networks for Business Research

Steven Walczak

The Business School, University of Colorado Denver, Denver, CO 80202, USA

Correspondence should be addressed to Steven Walczak, steven.walczak@ucdenver.edu

Academic Editor: Ping Feng Pai

Artificial neural network (ANN) modeling methods are becoming more widely used as both a research and application paradigm across a much wider variety of business, medical, engineering, and social science disciplines. The combination or triangulation of ANN methods with more traditional methods can facilitate the development of high-quality research models and also improve output performance for real world applications. Prior methodological triangulation that utilizes ANNs is reviewed and a new triangulation of ANNs with structural equation modeling and cluster analysis for predicting an individual's computer self-efficacy (CSE) is shown to empirically analyze the effect of methodological triangulation, at least for this specific information systems research case. A new construct, engagement, is identified as a necessary component of CSE models and the subsequent triangulated ANN models are able to achieve an 84% CSE group prediction accuracy.

1. Introduction

Artificial Neural networks (ANNs) have been used as a popular research and implementation paradigm in multiple domains for several decades now [1–9]. Recent literature is advocating the further usage of ANNs as a research methodology, especially in previously untried or underutilized domains [10, 11]. However, due to the early premise that ANNs are black boxes (i.e., it is difficult to evaluate the contribution of the independent variables) the demonstration of rigor and generalization of results from neural network research has been problematic.

Similarities between ANNs and various statistical methods (which have been shown to be both rigorous and generalizable) have been described for potential adopters [10, 12]. A common research paradigm for ANN researchers is to compare results obtained using an ANN to other more traditional statistical methods, including regression [13–16], discriminant analysis [17–21], other statistical methods [22–24], and multiple statistical methods [25–28]. Of the 16 articles just referenced, the majority of these results show ANNs being either similar to (with 2 being similar) or better than (with 12 outperforming) the compared statistical methods within the specific application domain.

While ANNs have a history, though short, their black box nature has led to adoption resistance by numerous-business related disciplines [29]. Methodological triangulation may help to overcome these adoption and usage reservations as well as providing a means for improving the overall efficacy of ANN applications. Methodological triangulation is the utilization of multiple methods on the same problem (empirical data) to gain confidence in the results obtained and to improve external validity [30, 31]. ANNs and traditional statistical methods are both quantitative in nature. A quantitative method is hereby defined as a specific tool, procedure, or technique that is used to analyze the data of a specific problem to produce a corresponding model or results to answer a business research question.

The comparative analysis of ANNs versus standard statistical methods previously mentioned is an example of concurrent or parallel methodological triangulation [32], which is performed extensively to demonstrate performance improvements obtained through the utilization of neural network modeling. This paper will focus on nonconcurrent methodological triangulation techniques. Nonconcurrent methodological triangulation occurs when a statistical or other machine learning method is used in combination with an ANN, but the other method is applied to data prior to the ANN to refine the input vector and gain confidence in the reliability of the independent variables or alternately after the ANN has produced its results to improve the overall performance and/or interpretation of those results. The definition of nonconcurrent methodological triangulation used in this paper is similar to the sequential and parallel development mixed method and the sequential elaboration mixed method described by Petter and Gallivan [32].

The research presented in this paper will assess the efficacy of utilizing nonconcurrent triangulation of method with ANNs, specifically the preselection of variables with recognized statistical techniques. The triangulated ANN will be applied to the case of estimating an individual's computer self-efficacy (CSE) without relying on self-evaluation, since self-evaluation may be subject to numerous biases [33, 34]. The next section provides a brief background on methodological triangulation that has been previously applied with ANNs followed by a section that describes the CSE estimation problem in more detail, which serves as a classification problem to demonstrate the results of the new methodology. The fourth section will present the triangulation methodology and describe the developed ANN models for CSE estimation. The penultimate section presents the results and a discussion of these results for CSE estimation utilizing the triangulated ANN.

2. Background

This section describes ANNs and the literature on triangulation with ANNs.

2.1. Brief Description of ANNs. Before describing previous research that has either advocated or demonstrated the triangulation of various statistical and other machine learning methods with ANNs, a brief description of ANNs is provided. The following description is best suited to backpropagation trained ANNs, but can be generalized for other types of ANNs as well, especially other supervised learning ANNs. An ANN is a collection of processing elements typically arranged in layers (see Figure 1). The input layer requires some type of numeric data value. These values are then multiplied by weights (another numeric value) and aggregated for each hidden layer processing element. Various aggregation functions may be used, but commonly either a standard summation or maximizing function is used, producing a value: $h_j = \sum_{i=1}^{n} x_i w_{i,j}$, which would be the aggregated input value for all input nodes (ranging over all possible i) for hidden processing node j. The hidden layer elements then transpose the aggregated input values using a nonlinear function, typically a sigmoid function, such that the output of each hidden node looks like: $g_j = (1 + e^{k * \text{Gain}})^{-1}$. The outputs of each hidden layer node are then aggregated to the next layer, which may be the output layer or another hidden layer.

Learning, and hence the development of an accurate model, may be performed in a supervised or unsupervised manner. Supervised learning will be emphasized in this paper and utilizes historic examples of the problem being modeled.

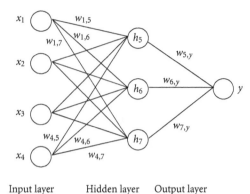

Not all weights are shown, in order to make the diagram easier to read/understand.

Figure 1: Sample supervised learning ANN architecture (e.g., backpropagation).

Examples of the independent variable sets are presented to the ANN, which then produces an output value or values as just described. The output value is compared to the known value from the historic training example and if an error above the error threshold exists, then the values of the weighted connections are adjusted to better approximate the observed output value. This type of learning is nonparametric and makes no assumptions about population distributions or the behavior of the error term [35].

ANNs have been shown to be able to accurately approximate almost any type of model for both classification and forecasting (regression), including both linear and nonlinear models [36–38]. Evaluation of supervised learning ANN models is performed by withholding a portion of the historic data sets and using this as an out-of-sample verification of the generalization of the ANN solution model to the real world. When comparing NNs against other methods, it should be the error on these out-of-sample or other out-of-sample results that is compared, where out of sample implies data that was not used for development of the ANN model.

2.2. Previous Work with Triangulating NNs. As already mentioned in the previous section, comparison of ANN classification or forecasting results to standard statistical methods following a model selection approach [35, 39] is a common method used by researchers to attempt to demonstrate both the validity of using an ANN model and also to demonstrate a methodological improvement gained from the use of the ANN modeling paradigm. However, the focus of the research reported in this paper is on nonconcurrent method triangulation and as such this section will focus on previous research that has utilized statistical and other methods in a nonconcurrent manner with ANNs.

A summary of prior research that implemented some form of triangulation that was not used for comparison of results is shown in Table 1. Very early work in improving ANN architecture design employed genetic algorithms (GAs) or genetic programming (GP) prior to instantiation of the ANN. ANNs have also been triangulated concurrently with

TABLE 1: Previous utilization of ANN triangulation.

Type of triangulation	Purpose	References
NC, prior	Faster development and optimization of ANN architecture, utilizing GA and GP	[40–44]
NC, prior	Reduce dependent variable set	[45]
NC, after	Reduction in output error using decision trees and parametric statistics	[46–49]
NC, after	Improved explanation of dependent variable effects	[50–52]
Concurrent	Improve classification for complex problems using ANN ensembles	[53–55]
NC, post	Integration of ensemble outputs	regression [56]; decision tree [57]; heuristic [58]

NC: nonconcurrent method triangulation.

other ANNs in an ensemble to improve classification performance for problems where a single classifier cannot perform adequately. All other existing work utilizing triangulation occurs following the production of results by the ANN model to reduce output error from the ANNs or to improve the explanation of the output results.

The proper selection of independent variables to utilize in the input vector for any ANN is required for performance optimization [45, 59–61]. Various techniques have been utilized in a nonconcurrent triangulation prior to training the ANN to eliminate correlated dependent variables and variables that have minimal or negative impact (noise) on the ANN results. These techniques include GAs to pre-select training data that will lead to faster convergence [43, 62], correlation matrices [60], regression [63], principal component analysis [29], and discriminant analysis [58].

An interesting example of the power of preprocessing of possible input data comes from a study by Durand et al. [64]. They develop two models concurrently with the first being a partial least squares (PLS) regression model that has data preprocessed with a GA and an ANN model that has data preprocessed with a mutual information algorithm. The original problem space contained 480 variables. The GA was able to reduce the number of variables down to 11 for the PLS regression model and the mutual information algorithm was able to reduce the number of variables down to 12 for the ANN model, thus utilizing only 2.5 percent of the total available variables. The ANN model ultimately produced the best generalization performance between the two compared models.

The preprocessing of input/training data or the postprocessing of ANN output data to improve its accuracy or understandability are advantageous techniques to improve ANN performance, at least within the limited domains where these techniques have been previously applied. A combination of both preprocessing and postprocessing is explored

in the remainder of this paper for the case of classifying individual CSE.

3. Methodology for ANN Triangulation

As described in the Background section, method triangulation is already widely used for neural network research. However, the triangulation is normally mentioned in passing and the effect of the triangulation is not typically evaluated.

One of the goals of the current research is to promote the ideal of utilizing method triangulation whenever ANNs are used in research or real world applications and to formalize to the extent possible a methodology for performing triangulation with ANNs. Another goal is to provide empirical evidence to demonstrate the efficacy of utilizing triangulation in ANN research.

A flowchart for implementing triangulation is shown in Figure 2. The methodology is focused on methodological triangulation that utilizes ANNs as one of 2 or more processes used nonconcurrently to develop robust research models or domain applications. The flowchart and proposed methodology does not include data preparation/cleansing, testing of multiple ANN architectures, or cross-comparison of different ANN learning methods; all of which are standard ANN model development practices [60, 61].

The alternate processes specified in the flowchart are meant to indicate that the researcher or developer has several choices here for which method to use in the triangulation process. Selection of a specific statistical method or other method is typically constrained by the from and qualities of the data to be analyzed.

The proposed methodology emphasizes two significant issues with ANN development: improving models through noise reduction and improving the interpretation of results (to overcome the black-box nature of ANNs). A side benefit of the methods advocated for triangulation prior to the ANN is that any reduction in the independent variable set will reduce the overall costs of the model [13, 35].

4. The CSE Problem: A Case Study for Evaluating Methodological Triangulation with ANNs

To demonstrate the benefit of the proposed triangulation method paradigm, a case study to predict CSE using ANNs is shown. The technology acceptance model (TAM) introduced by Davis [65] has long been used to predict the adoption of new technology by users. CSE is strongly linked, even as a determinant, with the perceived ease of use component of the TAM model. Prior research on CSE is highlighted in Table 2.

In a technology environment, determining CSE is important because low CSE may hinder learning [66, 67], while participants scoring high in CSE perform significantly better in computer software mastery [68–70]. However, CSE is difficult to measure rigorously. Contradictory CSE results from prior research may be due to weaknesses in existing measures of the construct as well as the need for control of antecedent and consequent factors directly associated with CSE [66].

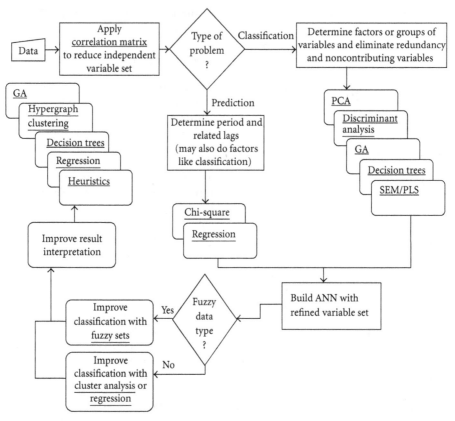

FIGURE 2: Flowchart for method triangulation with ANNs.

TABLE 2: Prior CSE research.

Purpose/findings	References
CSE shown to be determinant of PEU	[52, 71–74]
Definitions of CSE as ability to use computers	[66, 75]
Drior experience as antecedent of CSE	[66, 68, 76–80]
Computer anxiety as antecedent of CSE	[66, 73, 75, 77, 81]
Organizational support as antecedent of CSE	organization [74, 75, 78, 82] manager [83]
Engagement as antecedent of CSE (e.g., playfulness or innovativeness)	[73, 81, 84–87]

Variables that measure the four constructs shown in Table 2: prior experience; computer anxiety; organizational support; engagement, will make up the independent variable vector to the ANN.

Although computer anxiety has similar measurement problems to CSE, prior experience and organizational support are easier to measure than CSE because they are more objective, can be validated, and are less dependent on perceptions. Even when perceptual measures are used for organizational support, as in this study, they are probably less emotionally laden than CSE and anxiety, which are tied to ego and self-assessment. Engagement, although a perceptual measure, is also less emotionally laden than CSE and computer anxiety and is observable. The nonparametric and nonlinear nature of ANNs make them ideal for modeling

a problem that may have inaccurate or noisy data, such as in the evaluation of computer anxiety and engagement.

This section introduced the CSE problem, which is solved using triangulation in the next section.

5. Triangulation to Improve ANN Performance

CSE variables to measure the four constructs: prior experience (PE), computer anxiety (CA), organizational support (OS), and engagement (E) are collected using a survey that is administered to undergraduate and graduate students at a large southwestern state university in the United States. Students in both undergraduate classes and graduate classes were given the survey over a four-semester period. A total of 239 surveys were returned. Questions for the survey were derived from previously validated research and are shown in the appendix, Table 7. Three responses were dropped because of incomplete information on prior experience yielding 236 fully completed surveys.

The sample consisted of about 50% each of graduates and undergraduates and approximately two-thirds male. Almost 50% were of age 23 years or older. 93% had some work experience and 99% had more than one year of PC experience, thus minimizing differences in the prior experience variable values for the model.

Although considered to be more of a data cleansing operation as opposed to triangulation to improve performance through noise elimination by reducing the variable data set, outlier analysis using the box plot method was performed [88]. Two responses were identified as outliers, thus producing a working data set of 234 responses.

As shown in Table 7 in the appendix, a total of 14 independent variables were collected to predict an individual's CSE. As specified in the flowchart (see Figure 2), a correlation matrix of all independent variables was calculated [60] and high-correlation values indicated that all 4 of the prior experience variables were interdependent. Computer-based training and business application experience were dropped as having the highest correlation values. This is actually an interesting finding as a corollary result from the triangulation process, namely, that as prior work experience increases so does computer application experience. Eliminating the correlated variables reduced the independent variable set size from 14 variables down to 12 variables.

The next triangulation step to occur prior to the implementation of the ANN model is dependent on both the type of problem being solved (e.g., prediction or classification) and the variable data. The student population is a subset of and meant to be demonstrative of what could be achieved with the ERP training tool population at large and thus the distribution of the general population in unknown. Many of the parametric statistical models require the assumption of a normally distributed population of answers.

Structural equation modeling (SEM) is a methodology for analyzing latent variables, which cannot be measured directly. CSE and computer anxiety are examples of latent variables. However, SEM using LISREL, AMOS, and other similar packages makes assumptions of a normal distribution of the data and requires a relatively large sample size [89]. On the other hand, the partial least squares (PLS) method does not assume a normal distribution of the data and does not require as large a sample size as LISREL and similar statistical software packages. Therefore, PLS-based SEM serves as a triangulation statistical method to analyze the antecedent constructs for the CSE case study data.

PLS-SEM is used to analyze a measurement model and a structural model. The measurement model determines whether the measures used are reliable and whether the discriminant validity is adequate. The loading on its construct assesses the reliability of an indicator. Loading values should be at least 0.60 and ideally at 0.70 or above indicating that each measure is accounting for 50% or more of the variance of the underlying latent variable [89]. Two indicators for CSE were dropped because loadings on the construct were lower than the threshold. This helps to reduce the overall cost of the subsequent model through reduction in the number of variables required.

In Table 3, composite reliability scores show high reliability for the final constructs. All values for composite reliability are greater than 0.8 (except prior experience which is measured with unrelated formative indicators that are not expected to highly correlate with each other). The diagonal of the correlation matrix shows the square root of the average variance extracted (AVE). The AVE square root values are greater than the correlations among the constructs supporting convergent and discriminant validity. The means and standard deviations of the construct scales are also listed.

TABLE 3: Means, standard deviations, reliability, and correlations of constructs.

Construct	CSE	OS	PE	CA	Engage
μ	4.50	4.75	3.36	3.66	4.24
σ	1.43	1.45	0.86	1.58	1.49
Composite Reliability	0.853	0.807	0.717	0.894	0.947
CSE	**0.812**	0.317	−0.112	0.070	0.550
OS		**0.763**	0.025	0.005	0.415
PE			**0.751**	−0.066	−0.051
CA				**0.899**	0.097
Engage					0/865

Values on the correlations matrix diagonal (bold values) are square roots of the AVE.

TABLE 4: Variable loadings and cross-loadings.

	CSE	OS	PE	CA	Eng.
CSE1	**0.806**	0.217	−0.126	0.058	0.421
CSE2	**0.820**	0.269	−0.042	0.060	0.325
CSE3	**0.810**	0.241	−0.016	0.059	0.353
OS1	0.212	**0.779**	−0.055	−0.031	0.206
OS2	0.275	**0.745**	0.092	−0.001	0.340
OS3	0.171	**0.766**	−0.010	−0.024	0.223
Work Experience	−0.094	0.023	**0.845**	−0.044	−0.032
PC Experience	−0.072	0.013	**0.644**	−0.059	−0.050
CA1	0.031	−0.017	−0.127	**0.818**	−0.010
CA2	0.058	0.127	−0.019	**0.974**	0.171
E1	0.520	0.305	−0.061	0.053	**0.884**
E2	0.483	0.335	−0.142	0.129	**0.841**
E3	0.404	0.372	−0.018	0.167	**0.820**
E4	0.492	0.404	−0.027	0.043	**0.883**
E5	0.384	0.279	0.001	0.029	**0.855**
E6	0.485	0.391	−0.027	0.081	**0.905**

Table 4 shows the loadings and cross-loadings to the constructs of the measures, which had adequate reliability. All loadings are greater (in an absolute value) than 0.7, and are greater (in an absolute value) than cross-loadings showing again strong convergent and discriminant validity.

In the SEM model, (see Figure 3), the path coefficients produced by PLS show that engagement (0.492) and organizational support (0.112) are statistically significant ($P < 0.001$). Prior experience (−0.091) and computer anxiety (0.016) are not statistically significant. Demographic variables for age and gender were also evaluated in the original SEM model, but neither was statistically significant (0.012 and 0.029, resp.) and are subsequently removed from the model. The antecedents for the model shown in Figure 3 explained 32% (R^2) of the variance in CSE.

From the PLS-SEM model, it appears that either the engagement (E) construct variables or the organizational support (OS) variables or perhaps the combination of these

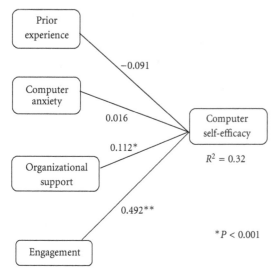

FIGURE 3: Results from PLS-SEM analysis.

two constructs will produce the best performing ANN model to predict an individual's CSE. As with most ANN research, various hidden node architectures are constructed for the three possible input vectors (E, OS, E, and OS combined) [35, 39]. Each ANN starts with a quantity of hidden nodes equal to half the number of input nodes and this value is incremented by one and the ANN retrained until the performance starts to decay, indicating overlearning. All architectures are trained utilizing the backpropagation (BP) learning algorithm and training is halted when a RMSE of less than 0.05 is reported by the training algorithm. Architectures with the number of hidden nodes equal to the number of input nodes almost universally outperformed the other architectures and samples of these architectures are shown in Figure 4.

Additional tests are performed evaluating ANNs trained using the radial basis function (RBF) training methodology, which should be more noise resistant and operates more efficiently in cases of extrapolation (versus interpolation) than BP [90]. As mentioned previously, comparing multiple ANN models and different supervised learning algorithms is a form of concurrent triangulation. The BP ANNs consistently outperformed the corresponding RBF ANNs and thus only the BP ANN results are reported.

Since the research is interested in investigating the improvement to ANN performance through the utilization of statistical method triangulation with ANNs, other combinations of constructs are also evaluated to determine if the E, OS, or E and OS input vectors do indeed produce the optimal prediction performance. All combinations of E, OS, and computer anxiety (CA) are developed as ANN models and an additional ANN model that includes prior experience (X) is also implemented. Each of the different construct combinations ANNs follow the same multiple architecture development and training protocol as that used for the three different ANN models recommended by the PLS-SEM method. Each construct combination uniformly used all of the construct variables from the survey which were not

eliminated by the correlation matrix, whenever that corresponding construct was part of the input vector.

Additionally, an ANN model that utilized all 14 variables is developed and compared with the other results to further examine the benefit gained from triangulation. Post-ANN result triangulation to increase ANN model performance and understanding is discussed in the next section.

6. Results

In this section, the results of the pre-ANN model specification triangulation are examined and post-ANN triangulation to improve and explain ANN results are demonstrated.

6.1. PLS-SME Triangulation Identifies Optimal Input Constructs. The prediction performance for the best performing architecture for each of the various ANNs evaluated is displayed highlighted in Table 5. Table 5 also shows the results of utilizing all variables, including the correlated variables eliminated earlier in the triangulation process. The evaluation is performed using a 12-fold cross-validation technique, which should approximate the obtainable results from utilizing a model that would have been trained on the full population set, but maintains the integrity of the data as all validation samples are withheld from the training data set for the 12 individual cross-validation ANN models [91]. Each ANN attempted to predict the composite CSE score, which was the summation of the three retained CSE variables (following the PLS analysis) and had a range from 3 to 21.

As shown in Table 5, the E only construct ANN, which was the most significant construct according to the PLS-SEM preprocessing, produced the smallest mean absolute error (MAE) term and also had the largest quantity of perfect predictions for predicting CSE. The combination of E and OS had the second smallest MAE. An additional column is presented in Table 5 that represents near misses for the ANN model CSE predictions. From the near-miss column, the E and CA combination model performs best on the near-miss evaluation, with the E only ANN model coming a close second (not statistically different) and the E and OS model in third place.

Additionally, it can be seen that utilizing all 14 of the collected variables to predict the PLS-SEM modified CSE-dependent variable has a much worse performance than any of the reduced variable set. This provides strong empirical evidence for the need to triangulate using correlation matrixes to reduce variables and consequent noise [45, 60, 61].

The question of how to evaluate this particular ANN prediction model arises from the various construct combinations shown in Table 5. Based on the MAE and also correct predictions, the PLS-SME preprocessing was able to correctly identify the best set of independent variables for the ANN input vector. Exact matches of the CSE value may not be necessary and near misses (predictions within one of the actual value) may be just as useful. Interpreting the data in this way by recalculating the results based on an approximate match is a form of post-ANN method triangulation based on a heuristic, which is conceptually similar to cluster analysis. Expanding the analysis with this posttriangulation heuristic,

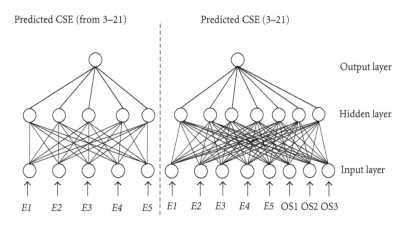

FIGURE 4: Backpropagation-trained ANN architectures for predicting CSE.

TABLE 5: Artificial neural network CSE prediction result for 234 evaluation cases.

Construct	MAE of predict of CSE	Perfect predict of CSE	Predict within 1 of CSE
E	**1.956**	**20.09%**	50.85%
OS	2.346	17.09%	45.73%
E, OS	2.022	14.96%	49.15%
CA	2.596	16.67%	42.74%
E, CA	2.029	17.95%	**51.28%**
OS, CA	2.419	15.81%	44.87%
E, OS, CA	2.088	13.68%	47.86%
E, OS, CA, X	2.235	16.67%	41.03%
Full model (all 14 var.)	3.650	10.26%	21.37%

[E: engagement, OS: organizational support, CA: computer anxiety, X: prior experience].

shows that the addition of the CA construct variables enables the ANN to achieve optimal performance for predicting CSE within 1, though the E only ANN model was a very close second.

Bansal et al. [13] make a strong case for simplifying ANN models to reduce cost and improve the interpretation and usability of the resulting model. Since the CA construct did not significantly improve the within one performance of the ANN, the reduced cost of the E only ANN may be sufficient to outweigh the small gains achieved through the addition of the CA construct. The utility of including the computer anxiety construct in an ANN CSE prediction model must be weighed against the cost of obtaining reliable measurements for this construct.

The preceding example empirically demonstrates that utilizing traditional statistical methods can significantly improve ANN performance through the identification of the optimal set of independent variables, or in this case optimal antecedent constructs. The correlation matrix was able to eliminate 2 variables from the dependent variable input set. Due to the population and data constraints, the selected PLS-SEM triangulation was able to further reduce the input vector size and accurately identified the optimal constructs for inclusion in the ANN model to predict the exact CSE value from 3 to 21.

6.2. Post ANN Triangulation to Improve Results and Interpretation. As noted earlier, another utilization of methodological triangulation is to improve the performance or interpretation of ANN output. The results from Table 5 already demonstrate that a posttriangulation heuristic method can improve results by 150 to 185 percent.

For the case of predicting an individual's CSE, an exact numeric value may not be necessary to utilize an ANN CSE prediction model's output, since CSE is generally more broadly classified into levels or groups such as very high CSE, high CSE, moderate CSE, low CSE, and very low CSE. A further analysis of the BP-trained ANN CSE prediction model's output is triangulated further to determine group identification and determine if this additional processing may improve the performance of the ANN CSE prediction models.

Values for delineating different levels of CSE are applied to the three aggregated CSE variables from the survey to distinguish five different CSE levels for the population from very low to very high (very low, low, moderate, high, and very high). For example, an individual with a CSE score between 3 and 7 inclusive is placed in the very low CSE group. This may be performed statistically using a k-means clustering algorithm with the number of clusters set to 5. The predicted CSE output values are also converted into a group classification using the same cutoffs that are applied to the user responses. The new five-group category classification results are displayed in Table 6 for each of the ANN construct models reported previously in Table 5, with the highest prediction accuracy values for each column highlighted.

The E-construct-only ANN CSE group classification prediction places the user in the correct CSE group 67.95% and within one group 93.59% of the time. The remaining predictions for all of the ANN CSE group classification models are within two groups of the correct classification (meaning that a very-low or low CSE user is never categorized as a very high CSE user and very high and high CSE users are never classified as very low CSE users). It should be noted that

TABLE 6: Group CSE classification triangulated from ANN output.

Constructs	Perfect group prediction	Within-1-group predictions	Perfect fuzzified group prediction
E	**67.95%**	93.59%	83.33%
OS	67.09%	75.21%	75.21%
E, OS	**67.95%**	88.89%	73.93%
CA	67.09%	92.74%	**84.19%**
E, CA	66.67%	**94.02%**	83.33%
OS, CA	**67.95%**	89.74%	76.92%
E, OS, CA	64.96%	**94.02%**	**84.19%**
E, OS, CA, X	61.54%	**94.02%**	79.19%

TABLE 7: Survey instrument measures.

Measure	Survey question	Source
CSE	I feel more comfortable using the tool on my own with the tool's Training Support Tool (TST)	[83]
CSE	I would be able to use the tool with the TST even if there was no one around to show me how to use it.	[75, 83]
CSE1	I expect to become very proficient with the tool by using the TST.	[86]
CSE2	I feel confident that I can use the tool with the TST.	[86]
CSE3	Using the TST probably helps me to be good with the tool	[86]
OS1	The business school has provided most of the necessary help and resources to get us used to the TST quickly	[74]
OS2	The business school realizes what benefits can be achieved with the use of the TST	[74]
OS3	I am always supported and encouraged by my professor to use the TST in my course	[74, 83]
CA1	I hesitate to use the tool without the TST for fear of making mistakes I cannot correct	[74]
CA2	I feel apprehensive about using the tool without the TST	[86]
E1	The TST keeps me totally absorbed in what I am doing.	[85, 86]
E2	The TST holds my attention.	[85]
E3	The TST is fun.	[85]
E4	The TST is interesting.	[85]
E5	The TST is engaging.	[85]

the traditional antecedents of CSE, CA and a combination of OS and CA also produce an identical perfect CSE group classification compared to the E-only construct ANN model.

The E-only ANN CSE prediction model with triangulated output did not produce the highest within-one-group predictions, similar to the case with the exact CSE value predictions, but had the second highest performance and again was not statistically different from the E and CA and also the E, OS and CA ANN models. As mentioned before, the additional cost associated with collected these variables versus the minimal performance increase needs to be evaluated to determine if the PLS-SEM constructs selection triangulation is merited.

CSE level classifications of individuals may also be viewed as fuzzy sets [92, 93], with the specific cutoffs for placement within a group (i.e., the boundary conditions) being indeterminate, but contained. For example, an individual with an aggregated CSE score of 17 working in a typical setting may be considered to belong to the very high CSE group, but that same individual employed at IBM, Texas Instruments, or Lockheed Martin might only be placed in the high or even medium CSE group. An overlap of 1 to 2 points between groups is enabled to simulate the application of a triangulated fuzzy algorithm that transforms the results into a more compatible fuzzy set notation, meaning that boundary members may be viewed as belonging to two possible groups, but still maintaining high homogeneity of members within a group [92]. The fuzzy group classification results are also displayed in Table 6, again with the highest classification accuracy highlighted. The fuzzy classification results compared to the perfect nonfuzzy classification results indicate a 10 to 15 percent increase in classification accuracy for most of the ANN models and may ultimately be a more realistic approach for organizations in trying to determine the CSE level of employees.

The fuzzy classification results displayed in Table 6 lend further empirical support for inclusion of the E construct in the CSE prediction model, with the E-only model performing second highest and not statistically different from the highest prediction percentage. The E, OS, and CA fuzzy interpretation model and the CA-only fuzzy interpretations are the highest. This lends partial support for the earlier findings that E and possibly OS are the two most significant

constructs. Another corollary finding is the potential for CA to be included as a required construct if optimal fuzzy model performance is desired. The PLS-SEM results displayed in Figure 3 show that CA is the only other construct to have a net positive impact on CSE, though this is fairly small.

7. Conclusion

This paper has presented evidence that triangulation of methods can improve the performance of ANN classification and prediction models. A case study of an ANN solution that predicts an individual's CSE was reported to provide further empirical evidence of the efficacy in utilizing methodological triangulation when employing ANNs.

The CSE prediction models utilized two different types of triangulation of methods: (1) preprocessing triangulation including both a correlation matrix and the statistical method (PLS_SEM) for sequential development [32] to identify the optimal set of independent variables for developing the ANN prediction model and (2) a post-ANN clustering heuristic and possibly an additional fuzzy set algorithm for sequential elaboration [32] to improve the classification performance of the ANN.

The preprocessing triangulation effectively reduced the independent variable set and also succeeded in identifying the most relevant construct, engagement, or E. The E-construct-only BP ANNs achieved either optimal performance for perfect predictions of the exact value or group value for an individual's CSE and had the lowest MAE. The triangulated clustering method may also help improve the understanding of the ANN's output by transforming it into a more meaningful representation of the classification strategies that would be followed by a human resources department to identify computer application training needs of employees [94].

The CSE prediction problem utilized to provide empirical results for the recommended triangulation methods is not a trivial case. Directly measuring CSE is problematic [66]. Utilizing antecedents to CSE that are measurable, such as engagement, provide reliable inputs to a CSE prediction model. This research has also demonstrated the need to include engagement in future research models of CSE. Subsequent output of a reliable CSE prediction may then be used as input to more complex models of technology acceptance and end-user training requirement models. Future research can investigate the use of ANN predicted CSE in the TAM and for more accurately predicting perceived ease of use.

From the review of the literature and the results presented here, future research involving the development of ANN classification or prediction models should utilize appropriate statistical methods to determine input variables for the ANN model. Additionally, when appropriate, the demystification of ANN output through posttriangulation methods can only serve to improve adoption of ANN methodologies.

While this paper has focused on how to triangulate statistical and other methods with ANN, where the ANN serves as the primary modeling paradigm, ANN themselves may also be utilized as a triangulating method to improve statistical and other modeling methods. Various researchers [95–97] have advocated the utilization of ANNs to assist in determining when a solution set has nonlinear properties and thus should not be modeled using strictly linear statistical modeling methods.

Additionally, ANNs may be used to estimate posterior probabilities in classification problems [98]. Rustum and Adeloye [99] claim that ANNs may also be used to fill in missing data from domains that typically have very low quantities of data and where data may be noisy or missing, thus ANNs may be used to fill in the missing data reliably. This would then enable other research modeling techniques to be applied to larger and cleaner sets of data.

The methodology proposed in this paper has been shown to be effective, at least for the domain of CSE and prior research has already utilized method triangulation, but without analyzing the effect of the triangulation. Some final precautions should be noted. The selection of both pre- and posttriangulation statistical tools and other methods to incorporate into any ANN research or development process is highly dependent on the type of data and goals of the research model. As noted in Figure 3, alternate processes are available and selection of the appropriate statistical method is reliant on the type and constraints of the data. However, as demonstrated, if appropriate statistical and other methods (e.g., heuristic) are implemented, the results of the corresponding ANN models can be improved 750 percent or greater (difference between the full variable basin BP ANN model (bottom row of Table 5) and the perfect fuzzified predictions (Table 6)).

Appendix

In Table 7, all survey questions are measured using a 7-point scale from 1 (highly disagree) to 7 (highly agree). Each question is adapted from the indicated sources to fit the experiment context (CSE = computer self-efficacy; OS = organizational support; CA = computer anxiety; and E = engagement).

Additional questions asked on the survey to determine prior experience (X), utilized a 4-point scale (1 = none; 2 = less than 1 year; 3 = 1 to 3 years; and 4 = more than 3 years).

How many years prior experience have you had with computer-based training?

How many years prior experience have you had with personal computers? $(X1)$

How many years prior experience have you had with business application software?

How many years prior work experience have you had? $(X2)$.

Acknowledgments

The author would like to thank the reviewers of *AANS* for their insights that helped make this work more understandable and valuable as a research methodology guide. Additional acknowledgement is given to Associate Professor Judy Scott at the University of Colorado Denver. She provided the initial idea for the case study presented in this paper as well as all of the data for the case study.

References

[1] R. Dybowski and V. Gant, "Artificial neural networks in pathology and medical laboratories," *The Lancet*, vol. 346, no. 8984, pp. 1203–1207, 1995.

[2] E. Y. Li, "Artificial neural networks and their business applications," *Information and Management*, vol. 27, no. 5, pp. 303–313, 1994.

[3] S. H. Liao and C. H. Wen, "Artificial neural networks classification and clustering of methodologies and applications—literature analysis from 1995 to 2005," *Expert Systems with Applications*, vol. 32, no. 1, pp. 1–11, 2007.

[4] G. Montague and J. Morris, "Neural-network contributions in biotechnology," *Trends in Biotechnology*, vol. 12, no. 8, pp. 312–324, 1994.

[5] K. A. Smith and J. N. D. Gupta, "Neural networks in business: techniques and applications for the operations researcher," *Computers and Operations Research*, vol. 27, no. 11-12, pp. 1023–1044, 2000.

[6] B. Widrow, D. E. Rumelhart, and M. A. Lehr, "Neural networks: applications in industry, business and science," *Communications of the ACM*, vol. 37, no. 3, pp. 93–105, 1994.

[7] B. K. Wong, T. A. Bodnovich, and Y. Selvi, "Neural network applications in business: a review and analysis of the literature

(1988-95)," *Decision Support Systems*, vol. 19, no. 4, pp. 301–320, 1997.

[8] B. K. Wong, V. S. Lai, and J. Lam, "A bibliography of neural network business applications research: 1994–1998," *Computers and Operations Research*, vol. 27, no. 11-12, pp. 1045–1076, 2000.

[9] F. Zahedi, "A meta-analysis of financial applications of neural networks," *International Journal of Computational Intelligence and Organization*, vol. 1, no. 3, pp. 164–178, 1996.

[10] K. B. DeTienne, D. H. DeTienne, and S. A. Joshi, "Neural Networks as Statistical Tools for Business Researchers," *Organizational Research Methods*, vol. 6, no. 2, pp. 236–265, 2003.

[11] G. P. Zhang, "Avoiding pitfalls in neural network research," *IEEE Transactions on Systems, Man and Cybernetics Part C: Applications and Reviews*, vol. 37, no. 1, pp. 3–16, 2007.

[12] B. Warner and M. Misra, "Understanding Neural Networks as Statistical Tools," *American Statistician*, vol. 50, no. 4, pp. 284–293, 1996.

[13] A. Bansal, R. J. Kauffman, and R. R. Weitz, "Comparing the modeling performance of regression and neural networks as data quality varies: a business value approach," *Journal of Management Information Systems*, vol. 10, no. 1, pp. 11–32, 1993.

[14] U. A. Kumar, "Comparison of neural networks and regression analysis: a new insight," *Expert Systems with Applications*, vol. 29, no. 2, pp. 424–430, 2005.

[15] S. W. Palocsay and M. M. White, "Neural network modeling in cross-cultural research: a comparison with multiple regression," *Organizational Research Methods*, vol. 7, no. 4, pp. 389–399, 2004.

[16] S. Sakai, K. Kobayashi, S. I. Toyabe, N. Mandai, T. Kanda, and K. Akazawa, "Comparison of the levels of accuracy of an artificial neural network model and a logistic regression model for the diagnosis of acute appendicitis," *Journal of Medical Systems*, vol. 31, no. 5, pp. 357–364, 2007.

[17] S. Ghosh-Dastidar, H. Adeli, and N. Dadmehr, "Mixed-band wavelet-chaos-neural network methodology for epilepsy and epileptic seizure detection," *IEEE Transactions on Biomedical Engineering*, vol. 54, no. 9, pp. 1545–1551, 2007.

[18] K. E. Graves and R. Nagarajah, "Uncertainty estimation using fuzzy measures for multiclass classification," *IEEE Transactions on Neural Networks*, vol. 18, no. 1, pp. 128–140, 2007.

[19] R. C. Lacher, P. K. Coats, S. C. Sharma, and L. F. Fant, "A neural network for classifying the financial health of a firm," *European Journal of Operational Research*, vol. 85, no. 1, pp. 53–65, 1995.

[20] R. Sharda, "Neural networks for the MS/OR analyst: an application bibliography," *Interfaces*, vol. 24, no. 2, pp. 116–130, 1994.

[21] V. Subramanian, M. S. Hung, and M. Y. Hu, "An experimental evaluation of neural networks for classification," *Computers and Operations Research*, vol. 20, no. 7, pp. 769–782, 1993.

[22] J. Farifteh, F. Van der Meer, C. Atzberger, and E. J. M. Carranza, "Quantitative analysis of salt-affected soil reflectance spectra: a comparison of two adaptive methods (PLSR and ANN)," *Remote Sensing of Environment*, vol. 110, no. 1, pp. 59–78, 2007.

[23] B. A. Jain and B. N. Nag, "Performance Evaluation of Neural Network Decision Models," *Journal of Management Information Systems*, vol. 14, no. 2, pp. 201–216, 1997.

[24] L. M. Salchenberger, E. M. Cinar, and N. A. Lash, "Neural networks: a new tool for predicting thrift failures," *Decision Sciences*, vol. 23, no. 4, pp. 899–916, 1992.

[25] I. Kurt, M. Ture, and A. T. Kurum, "Comparing performances of logistic regression, classification and regression tree, and

[26] T. S. Lim, W. Y. Loh, and Y. S. Shih, "Comparison of prediction accuracy, complexity, and training time of thirty-three old and new classification algorithms," *Machine Learning*, vol. 40, no. 3, pp. 203–228, 2000.

[27] K. Y. Tam and M. Y. Kiang, "Managerial applications of neural networks: the case of bank failure predictions," *Management Science*, vol. 38, no. 3, pp. 926–947, 1992.

[28] G. K. F. Tso and K. K. W. Yau, "Predicting electricity energy consumption: a comparison of regression analysis, decision tree and neural networks," *Energy*, vol. 32, no. 9, pp. 1761–1768, 2007.

[29] L. Yang, C. W. Dawson, M. R. Brown, and M. Gell, "Neural network and GA approaches for dwelling fire occurrence prediction," *Knowledge-Based Systems*, vol. 19, no. 4, pp. 213–219, 2006.

[30] J. Mingers, "Combining IS research methods: towards a pluralist methodology," *Information Systems Research*, vol. 12, no. 3, pp. 240–259, 2001.

[31] A. Tashakkori and C. Teddlie, *Mixed Methodology: Combining Qualitative and Quantitative Approaches*, Sage, London, UK, 1998.

[32] S. C. Petter and M. J. Gallivan, "Toward a framework for classifying and guiding mixed method research in information systems," in *Proceedings of the 37th Hawaii International Conference on System Sciences*, pp. 4061–4070, IEEE Computer Society, Los Alamitos, Calif, Usa, 2004.

[33] P. M. Podsakoff, S. B. MacKenzie, J. Y. Lee, and N. P. Podsakoff, "Common method biases in behavioral research: a critical review of the literature and recommended remedies," *Journal of Applied Psychology*, vol. 88, no. 5, pp. 879–903, 2003.

[34] P. M. Podsakoff and D. W. Organ, "Self-reports in organizational research: problems and prospects," *Journal of Management*, vol. 12, no. 4, pp. 531–554, 1986.

[35] S. Walczak, "Evaluating medical decision making heuristics and other business heuristics with neural networks," in *Intelligent Decision Making an AI Based Approach*, G. Phillips-Wren and L. C. Jain, Eds., chapter 10, Springer, New York, NY, USA, 2008.

[36] K. Hornik, "Approximation capabilities of multilayer feedforward networks," *Neural Networks*, vol. 4, no. 2, pp. 251–257, 1991.

[37] K. Hornik, M. Stinchcombe, and H. White, "Multilayer feedforward networks are universal approximators," *Neural Networks*, vol. 2, no. 5, pp. 359–366, 1989.

[38] H. White, "Connectionist nonparametric regression: multilayer feedforward networks can learn arbitrary mappings," *Neural Networks*, vol. 3, no. 5, pp. 535–549, 1990.

[39] N. R. Swanson and H. White, "A model-selection approach to assessing the information in the term structure using linear models and artificial neural networks," *Journal of Business & Economic Statistics*, vol. 13, no. 3, pp. 265–275, 1995.

[40] S. A. Billings and G. L. Zheng, "Radial basis function network configuration using genetic algorithms," *Neural Networks*, vol. 8, no. 6, pp. 877–890, 1995.

[41] J. N. D. Gupta, R. S. Sexton, and E. A. Tunc, "Selecting Scheduling Heuristics Using Neural Networks," *INFORMS Journal on Computing*, vol. 12, no. 2, pp. 150–162, 2000.

[42] M. Rocha, P. Cortez, and J. Neves, "Evolution of neural networks for classification and regression," *Neurocomputing*, vol. 70, no. 16-18, pp. 2809–2816, 2007.

[43] R. Sexton, "Identifying irrelevant variables in chaotic time series problems: using the genetic algorithm for training

neural networks," *Journal of Computational Intelligence in Finance*, vol. 6, no. 5, pp. 34–42, 1998.

[44] L. Yi-Hui, "Evolutionary neural network modeling for forecasting the field failure data of repairable systems," *Expert Systems with Applications*, vol. 33, no. 4, pp. 1090–1096, 2007.

[45] A. Tahai, S. Walczak, and J. T. Rigsby, "Improving artificial neural network performance through input variable selection," in *Applications of Fuzzy Sets and The Theory of Evidence to Accounting II*, P. Siegel, K. Omer, A. deKorvin, and A. Zebda, Eds., pp. 277–292, JAI Press, Stamford, Conn, USA, 1998.

[46] Z. Hua, Y. Wang, X. Xu, B. Zhang, and L. Liang, "Predicting corporate financial distress based on integration of support vector machine and logistic regression," *Expert Systems with Applications*, vol. 33, no. 2, pp. 434–440, 2007.

[47] R. J. Kuo, Y. L. An, H. S. Wang, and W. J. Chung, "Integration of self-organizing feature maps neural network and genetic K-means algorithm for market segmentation," *Expert Systems with Applications*, vol. 30, no. 2, pp. 313–324, 2006.

[48] R. J. Kuo, L. M. Ho, and C. M. Hu, "Integration of self-organizing feature map and K-means algorithm for market segmentation," *Computers and Operations Research*, vol. 29, no. 11, pp. 1475–1493, 2002.

[49] T. Marwala, "Bayesian training of neural networks using genetic programming," *Pattern Recognition Letters*, vol. 28, no. 12, pp. 1452–1458, 2007.

[50] D. Dancey, Z. A. Bandar, and D. McLean, "Logistic model tree extraction from artificial neural networks," *IEEE Transactions on Systems, Man, and Cybernetics B*, vol. 37, no. 4, pp. 794–802, 2007.

[51] K. L. Hsieh and Y. S. Lu, "Model construction and parameter effect for TFT-LCD process based on yield analysis by using ANNs and stepwise regression," *Expert Systems with Applications*, vol. 34, no. 1, pp. 717–724, 2008.

[52] R. Setiono, J. Y. L. Thong, and C. S. Yap, "Symbolic rule extraction from neural networks An application to identifying organizations adopting IT," *Information and Management*, vol. 34, no. 2, pp. 91–101, 1998.

[53] T. G. Diettrich, "Ensemble methods in machine learning," in *Proceedings of the 1st International Workshop Multiple Classifier Systems*, Lecture Notes in Computer Science, pp. 1–15, Springer Verlag, Cagliari, Italy, 2000.

[54] L. K. Hansen and P. Salamon, "Neural network ensembles," *IEEE Transactions on Pattern Analysis and Machine Intelligence*, vol. 12, no. 10, pp. 993–1001, 1990.

[55] G. P. Zhang and V. L. Berardi, "Time series forecasting with neural network ensembles: an application for exchange rate prediction," *Journal of the Operational Research Society*, vol. 52, no. 6, pp. 652–664, 2001.

[56] D. Chetchotsak and J. M. Twomey, "Combining neural networks for function approximation under conditions of sparse data: the biased regression approach," *International Journal of General Systems*, vol. 36, no. 4, pp. 479–499, 2007.

[57] Z. H. Zhou and Y. Jiang, "NeC4.5: neural ensemble based C4.5," *IEEE Transactions on Knowledge and Data Engineering*, vol. 16, no. 6, pp. 770–773, 2004.

[58] S. Walczak and M. Parthasarathy, "Modeling online service discontinuation with nonparametric agents," *Information Systems and e-Business Management*, vol. 4, no. 1, pp. 49–70, 2006.

[59] R. Pakath and J. S. Zaveri, "Specifying critical inputs in a genetic algorithm-driven decision support system: an automated facility," *Decision Sciences*, vol. 26, no. 6, pp. 749–771, 1995.

[60] M. Smith, *Neural Networks for Statistical Modeling*, Van Nostrand Reinhold, New York, NY, USA, 1993.

[61] S. Walczak and N. Cerpa, "Heuristic principles for the design of artificial neural networks," *Information and Software Technology*, vol. 41, no. 2, pp. 107–117, 1999.

[62] H. Z. Huang, R. Bo, and W. Chen, "An integrated computational intelligence approach to product concept generation and evaluation," *Mechanism and Machine Theory*, vol. 41, no. 5, pp. 567–583, 2006.

[63] S. Walczak, "An empirical analysis of data requirements for financial forecasting with neural networks," *Journal of Management Information Systems*, vol. 17, no. 4, pp. 203–222, 2001.

[64] A. Durand, O. Devos, C. Ruckebusch, and J. P. Huvenne, "Genetic algorithm optimisation combined with partial least squares regression and mutual information variable selection procedures in near-infrared quantitative analysis of cotton-viscose textiles," *Analytica Chimica Acta*, vol. 595, no. 1-2, pp. 72–79, 2007.

[65] F. D. Davis, "Perceived usefulness, perceived ease of use, and user acceptance of information technology," *MIS Quarterly: Management Information Systems*, vol. 13, no. 3, pp. 319–339, 1989.

[66] G. M. Marakas, M. Y. Yi, and R. D. Johnson, "The multilevel and multifaceted character of computer self-efficacy: toward clarification of the construct and an integrative framework for research," *Information Systems Research*, vol. 9, no. 2, pp. 126–163, 1998.

[67] J. J. Martocchio, "Effects of Conceptions of Ability on Anxiety, Self-Efficacy, and Learning in Training," *Journal of Applied Psychology*, vol. 79, no. 6, pp. 819–825, 1994.

[68] R. T. Christoph, G. A. Schoenfeld Jr, and J. W. Tansky, "Overcoming barriers to training utilizing technology: the influence of self-efficacy factors on multimedia-based training receptiveness," *Human Resource Development Quarterly*, vol. 9, no. 1, pp. 25–38, 1998.

[69] M. E. Gist, C. Schwoerer, and B. Rosen, "Effects of Alternative Training Methods on Self-Efficacy and Performance in Computer Software Training," *Journal of Applied Psychology*, vol. 74, no. 6, pp. 884–891, 1989.

[70] J. E. Mathieu, J. W. Martineau, and S. I. Tannenbaum, "Individual and situational influences on the development of self-efficacy: implications for training effectiveness," *Personnel Psychology*, vol. 46, no. 1, pp. 125–147, 1993.

[71] R. Agarwal, V. Sambamurthy, and R. M. Stair, "Research report: the evolving relationship between general and specific computer self-efficacy—an empirical assessment," *Information Systems Research*, vol. 11, no. 4, pp. 418–430, 2000.

[72] W. Hong, J. Y. L. Thong, W. M. Wong, and K. Y. Tam, "Determinants of user acceptance of digital libraries: an empirical examination of individual differences and system characteristics," *Journal of Management Information Systems*, vol. 18, no. 3, pp. 97–124, 2001.

[73] V. Venkatesh, "Determinants of perceived ease of use: integrating control, intrinsic motivation, and emotion into the technology acceptance model," *Information Systems Research*, vol. 11, no. 4, pp. 342–365, 2000.

[74] M. Igbaria and J. Iivari, "The effects of self-efficacy on computer usage," *Omega*, vol. 23, no. 6, pp. 587–605, 1995.

[75] D. R. Compeau and C. A. Higgins, "Computer self-efficacy: development of a measure and initial test," *MIS Quarterly: Management Information Systems*, vol. 19, no. 2, pp. 189–210, 1995.

[76] B. Hasan, "The influence of specific computer experiences on computer self-efficacy beliefs," *Computers in Human Behavior*, vol. 19, no. 4, pp. 443–450, 2003.

[77] R. D. Johnson and G. M. Marakas, "research report: the role of behavioral modeling in computer skills acquisition—toward refinement of the model," *Information Systems Research*, vol. 11, no. 4, pp. 402–417, 2000.

[78] R. W. Stone and J. W. Henry, "The roles of computer self-efficacy and outcome expectancy in influencing the computer end-user's organizational commitment," *Journal of End User Computing*, vol. 15, no. 1, pp. 38–53, 2003.

[79] S. Taylor and P. Todd, "Assessing IT usage: the role of prior experience," *MIS Quarterly: Management Information Systems*, vol. 19, no. 4, pp. 561–568, 1995.

[80] R. Torkzadeh, K. Pflughoeft, and L. Hall, "Computer self-efficacy, training effectiveness and user attitudes: an empirical study," *Behaviour and Information Technology*, vol. 18, no. 4, pp. 299–309, 1999.

[81] J. B. Thatcher and P. L. Perrewé, "An empirical examination of individual traits as antecedents to computer anxiety and computer self-efficacy," *MIS Quarterly: Management Information Systems*, vol. 26, no. 4, pp. 381–396, 2002.

[82] S. Taylor and P. A. Todd, "Understanding information technology usage: a test of competing models," *Information Systems Research*, vol. 6, no. 2, pp. 144–176, 1995.

[83] D. S. Staples, J. S. Hulland, and C. A. Higgins, "A Self-Efficacy Theory Explanation for the Management of Remote Workers in Virtual Organizations," *Organization Science*, vol. 10, no. 6, pp. 758–776, 1999.

[84] R. Agarwal and J. Prasad, "A Conceptual and Operational Definition of Personal Innovativeness in the Domain of Information Technology," *Information Systems Research*, vol. 9, no. 2, pp. 204–215, 1998.

[85] J. Webster and H. Ho, "Audience engagement in multimedia presentations," *Data Base for Advances in Information Systems*, vol. 28, no. 2, pp. 63–76, 1997.

[86] J. Webster and J. J. Martocchio, "Microcomputer playfulness: development of a measure with workplace implications," *MIS Quarterly: Management Information Systems*, vol. 16, no. 2, pp. 201–224, 1992.

[87] F. D. Davis, R. P. Bagozzi, and P. R. Warshaw, "Extrinsic and intrinsic motivation to use computers in the workplace," *Journal of Applied Social Psychology*, vol. 22, no. 14, pp. 1111–1132, 1992.

[88] J. F. Hair, W. C. Black, B. J. Babin, and R. E. Anderson, *Multivariate Data Analysis*, Prentice Hall, Upper Saddle River, NJ, USA, 7th edition, 2010.

[89] W. W. Chin, "The partial least squares approach for structural equation modeling," in *Modern Methods for Business Research*, G. A. Marcoulides, Ed., pp. 295–336, Lawrence Erlbaum Associates, Hillsdale, NJ, USA, 1998.

[90] E. Barnard and L. Wessels, "Extrapolation and interpolation in neural network classifiers," *IEEE Control Systems*, vol. 12, no. 5, pp. 50–53, 1992.

[91] B. Efron, *The Jackknife, the Bootstrap, and Other Resampling Plans*, SIAM, Philadelphia, Pa, USA, 1982.

[92] F. Höppner, F. Klawonn, R. Kruse, and T. Runkler, *Fuzzy Cluster Analysis*, Wiley, New York, NY, USA, 1999.

[93] L. A. Zadeh, "Fuzzy sets," *Information and Control*, vol. 8, no. 3, pp. 338–353, 1965.

[94] M. Gist, "Self-efficacy: implications for organizational behavior and human resource management," *Academy of Management Review*, vol. 12, no. 3, pp. 472–485, 1987.

[95] T. H. Lee, H. White, and C. W. J. Granger, "Testing for neglected nonlinearity in time series models. A comparison of neural network methods and alternative tests," *Journal of Econometrics*, vol. 56, no. 3, pp. 269–290, 1993.

[96] D. Scarborough and M. J. Somers, *Neural Networks in Organizational Research*, American Psychological Association, Washington, DC, USA, 2006.

[97] M. J. Somers, "Thinking differently: assessing nonlinearities in the relationship between work attitudes and job performance using a Bayesian neural network," *Journal of Occupational and Organizational Psychology*, vol. 74, no. 1, pp. 47–61, 2001.

[98] M. S. Hung, M. Y. Hu, M. S. Shanker, and B. E. Patuwo, "Estimating posterior probabilities in classification problems with neural networks," *International Journal of Computational Intelligence and Organization*, vol. 1, no. 1, pp. 49–60, 1996.

[99] R. Rustum and A. J. Adeloye, "Replacing outliers and missing values from activated sludge data using kohonen self-organizing map," *Journal of Environmental Engineering*, vol. 133, no. 9, pp. 909–916, 2007.

7

Intelligent Systems Developed for the Early Detection of Chronic Kidney Disease

Ruey Kei Chiu,[1] Renee Y. Chen,[1] Shin-An Wang,[1] Yen-Chun Chang,[2] and Li-Chien Chen[3]

[1] *Department of Information Management, Fu Jen Catholic University, Xinzhuang District, New Taipei City 24205, Taiwan*
[2] *Office of Computer Processing, En Chu Kong Hospital, Sanxia District, New Taipei City 23702, Taiwan*
[3] *Office of Information Processing, Cardinal Tien Hospital, Xindian District, New Taipei City 231, Taiwan*

Correspondence should be addressed to Ruey Kei Chiu; rkchiu@mail.fju.edu.tw

Academic Editor: Ping Feng Pai

This paper aims to construct intelligence models by applying the technologies of artificial neural networks including back-propagation network (BPN), generalized feedforward neural networks (GRNN), and modular neural network (MNN) that are developed, respectively, for the early detection of chronic kidney disease (CKD). The comparison of accuracy, sensitivity, and specificity among three models is subsequently performed. The model of best performance is chosen. By leveraging the aid of this system, CKD physicians can have an alternative way to detect chronic kidney diseases in early stage of a patient. Meanwhile, it may also be used by the public for self-detecting the risk of contracting CKD.

1. Introduction

According to the statistical data announced by the Department of Health of Taiwan's government in 2010 [1], the mortality caused by kidney disease has been ranked in the 10th place in all causes of death in Taiwan and thousands of others are at increased risk. The mortality caused from kidney disease is estimated as 12.5 in every 100,000 people. As a result, it costs as high as 35 percent of health insurance budget to treat the chronic kidney disease (CKD) patients with the age over 65 years old and end-stage kidney disease patients in all ages. It occupies a huge amount of expenditures in national insurance budget.

Regarding the measurement of serious levels of CKD, presently glomerular filtration rate (GFR) is the most commonly measuring indicator used in health institutions to estimate kidney health function. The physician in the health institution can calculate GFR from patient's blood creatinine, age, race, gender, and other factors depending upon the type of formal-recognized computation formulas [2, 3] employed. The GFR may indicate the health of a patent's kidney and can also be taken to determine the stage of severity of a patient with or without kidney disease.

In this paper, we aim to develop a feasible intelligent model for detecting CKD for evaluating the severity of a patient with or without CKD. The input data for model development and testing is collected from the health examination which is periodically carried out by the collaborative teaching hospital of this research.

2. The Major Methods for Measuring Chronic Kidney Disease

As it is mentioned in prior section, the GFR is the most common method used to measure kidney health function. It refers to the water filterability of glomerular of people's kidney. The normal value should be between 90 and 120 mL/min/1.73 m^2 (i.e., measured by mL per minute per 1.73 m^2). There are three common computation methods of GFR, which are (1) removing rate of 24-hour urine creatinine (i.e., Creatinine Clearance Rate, Ccr), (2) Cockcroft-Gault formula (also known as C-G formula), and (3) Modification of Diet in Renal Disease formula (also known as MDRD) [4]. The CKD is categorized into five stages by making use of GFR to measure kidney function. Although the course of the change from stage one to five may usually last for years, it

TABLE 1: Classification of CKD defined by KDOQI.

Stage	State of kidney function	Classification by severity by GFR
1	Kidney damage with normal or increasing in GFR	GFR ≥ 90
2	Kidney damage with mild decreasing in GFR	GFR of 60–89
3	Moderate with decreasing in GFR	GFR of 30–59
4	Severe with decreasing in GFR	GFR of 15–29
5	Kidney failure	GFR < 15 (or dialysis)

sometimes may enter into fifth stage pretty soon resulted in the necessity of dialysis or kidney transplant.

Again, National Kidney Foundation's Kidney Disease Outcomes Quality Initiative (KDOQI) [3] provides a conceptual framework for the diagnosis of the severity stages of CKD based on the different function levels of glomerular filtration rate (GFR). The new system represented a significant conceptual change, since kidney disease historically had been categorized mainly by causes. The diagnosis of CKD relies on markers of kidney damage and/or a reduction in GFR. Stages 1 and 2 define conditions of kidney damage in the presence of a GFR of at least 90 mL/min/1.73 m^2 or 60 to 89 mL/min/1.73 m^2, respectively, and stages 3 to 5 define conditions of moderately and severely reduced GFR irrespective of markers of kidney damage. The summary of this guideline is shown in Table 1 [3]. However, Levey et al. [5] especially mentioned that although this guideline was endorsed by the Kidney Disease: Improving Global Outcomes (KDIGO) in 2004 and this framework was constantly promoted to increase the attention to chronic kidney disease in clinical practice, research, and public health, it had also generated debate. It is the position of KDIGO and KDOQI that the definition and classification should reflect patient prognosis and that an analysis of outcomes would answer key questions underlying the debate. The common definition of CKD has facilitated comparisons between studies. Nevertheless, there are limitations to this classification system, which is by its nature simple and necessarily arbitrary in terms of specifying the thresholds for definition and different stages. When the classification system was developed in 2002 [3], the evidence base used for the development of this guideline was much smaller than the CKD evidence base today. Therefore, this guideline has been constantly revised from then on.

In Taiwan, the Taiwan Society of Nephrology (TSN) also presented the self-detecting method of kidney for the public. At present, the MDRD formula [3, 6] is recognized as a mostly common method adopted by kidney physicians to estimate GFR from serum creatinine level. Therefore, in this paper we take MDRD to calculate the GFR for the detection. The method of computational formula is shown in formula (1). The input data for the GFR calculation of each individual case in health examination are provided by the collaborative teaching hospital. We also used the calculated results as

the desired (targeted) value to develop our neural network models. One has

$$GFR = 186 \times creatinine^{-1.154} \times age^{-0.203} \left(\frac{mL/\min}{1.73\,m^2} \right). \quad (1)$$

Note: For female the result should be multiplied by a factor of 0.742.

It is specially worthy of note that the recent study from Matsushita et al. [7] indicates that although the Modification of Diet in Renal Disease (MDRD) study equation is recommended for estimating GFR, the Chronic Kidney Disease Epidemiology Collaboration (CKD-EPI) has proposed an alternative equation, which is known as CKD-EPI. The CKD-EPI applies different coefficients to the same 4 variables which include age, sex, race, and serum creatinine level, used in the MDRD study equation. The study takes the data from more than one million participant cases residing in 40 countries or regions. They find that the CKD-EPI equation estimates measured GFR more accurately than the MDRD study equation in most of the study areas. It shows approximately one-fourth of cases were reclassified to a higher estimated GFR category by the CKD-EPI equation compared with the MDRD study equation. In this one-fourth of cases are reclassified upward in GFR figure by CKD-EPI, 24.4% in the general population cohorts, 15.4% in the high risk cohorts, and 6.6% in the CKD cohorts. This improvement by CKD-EPI classification may lower the prevalence of CKD. Participant cases who are reclassified upward had lower risks of mortality and end-stage renal disease (ESRD) compared with those not reclassified [7].

3. Artificial Neural Network

The artificial neural network (ANN), usually simply called neural network (NN), is a mathematical model or computational model that is inspired by the structure and/or functional aspects of biological neural networks. Kriesel [6] indicated neural networks were a bioinspired mechanism of data processing that enables computers to learn technically similar to human-being brain. A neural network consists of an interconnected group of artificial neurons, and it processes information using a connectionist approach to computation. In most cases, an ANN is an adaptive system that changes its structure based on external (input) or internal information that flows through the network during the learning phase. It is properly the most prestigious and adoptable model in all application models in the field of artificial intelligence.

There are many different types of neural network models derived from the generic structure of ANN. In this paper's study, three neural network models employed for the experiment and comparison include the back-propagation neural network (BPNN) [6, 8], the generalized feedforward neural network (GFNN) [9, 10], and the modular neural network (MNN) [11]. The generic architectures of three-layer back-propagation neural network, generalized feedforward neural network and modular neural network are illustrated in Figures 1, 2, and 3, respectively.

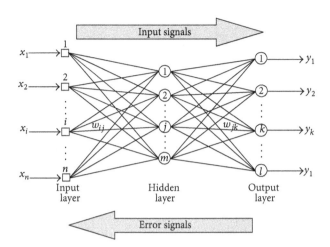

FIGURE 1: A generic model of three-layer back-propagation neural network.

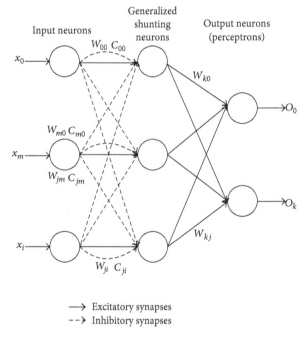

FIGURE 2: A generic architecture of generalized feedforward neural network.

4. Research Materials and Methods

Based on the literature reviews and expert interviews, this paper takes three neural network models including back-propagation neural network, feedforward neural network, and modular neural network, respectively, to generate the detection model for chronic kidney disease. The key influence input factors for each model are determined and verified from professional experts and physicians of kidney diseases. The set of influence factors derived from GFR computation formulas is shown in Table 2 and another set of key influence factors selected and determined in this paper as the input of neural networks is shown in Table 3, respectively. The classification performances of two input sets for model development are compared.

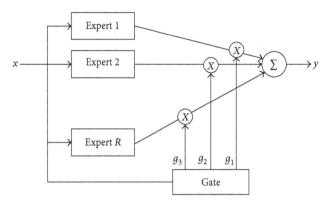

FIGURE 3: A generic architecture of modular neural network.

TABLE 2: The influence factors derived from the computation formula for GFR.

Factors	Description	Mean	Max.	Mini.
Sex	0 → Female 1 → Male	—	—	—
Age	Integer	77.38	93	67
Creatinine	Real	0.88	4.28	0.37
Weight	Real	60.719	98	32
GFR levels	0 → Negative 1, 2, 3, 4, 5 → Positive measured in levels	—	—	—

The input data set for developing neural networks are collected from the cases of health examination provided by the collaborative hospital of this study. 1161 heath examination cases covering past few years are selected. Before they are input for training and testing network models, a data preprocessing is processed to remove duplication and correct the error, inconsistency, and missing fields in each case record. Among these cases, there exit some unknown duplication cases which have unknown causes, they are identified and removed. Some cases have error in certain fields such as the figure being beyond its reasonable range or in a questionable high or low level. This is often seen in the figures for some physiological test. We try to confirm these figures with the authority of health examination center of hospital and try to correct it, otherwise they are removed. Some cases show postal code error or appear inconsistent with the personal contact address or vice versa, using different representation to refer the same meaning, which is commonly seen in gender filed and name field. More significantly, because not every subject conducts a complete health examination, certain fields used for risk measurement are missing. These cases are simply removed as well because they can not be used for model development. By this process, we can ensure the accuracy, completeness, and integrity of input data. After data preprocessing, only most accurate 430 patient cases remain for the development of intelligent models. Among these cases, 145 cases are prediagnosed as negative with CKD, and 285 cases are prediagnosed as positive. The details are shown in Table 4.

TABLE 3: The influence factors for the classification of neural networks for CKD detection.

Factors	Description	Mean	Max.	Min.
Creatinine	Real	0.88	4.28	0.37
Glucose (GLU)	Real	109.63	271	82
Systolic pressure (SP)	Real	135.78	195	88
Protein in urine (UP) or called proteinuria	$0 \rightarrow$ Negative $1 \rightarrow$ Trace $2 \rightarrow +$ $3 \rightarrow ++$ $4 \rightarrow +++$	—	—	—
Hematuria		—	—	—
Blood urea nitrogen (BUN)	Real	15.80	80.1	5.4
GFR-level	$0 \rightarrow$ Negative 1, 2, 3, 4, 5 $\rightarrow$ Positive measured in levels	—	—	—

TABLE 4: Data distribution for model training, testing, and cross-verification.

Input data for modeling	Number of records	Number of desired output
Training data	300	101 Negative 199 Positive in various levels
Testing data	100	34 Negative 66 Positive
Cross verification	30	10 Negative 20 Positive

TABLE 5: The best settings of network parameters for back-propagation network model.

Network parameters	Model FA	Model FB
Learning rule	Levenberg-Marquar	LevenbergMarquar
Transformation functions	Tanh Axon	Sigmoid Axon
No. of hiding layer	2	2
No. of neurons in hiding layer	5	8
Criterion for termination	MSE_{min}: 0.0001 $Epochs_{max}$: 3000	MSE_{min}: 0.0001 $Epochs_{max}$: 3000
Methods for weight update	Batch	Batch

5. Model Development

The development for a specific network model can be viewed as a series of modeling and simulation. We attempt to pursue the feasible model through the experiment of different combinations of modeling parameters selected for different network models. The parameters selected for experiment include the learning rules, the transform functions, the number of hiding layers, the number of neurons in each hidden layer, the weight update methods, and the criteria for the determination in model training and testing. The well-known NBuilder of neural solution is the tool adopted for model development. Among 430 cases, 300 cases are selected for training, 100 cases are used for testing, and the rest of 30 cases are taken for cross-verification during the model development. This data distribution is shown in Table 4. The desired output of classification for each case is formally identified beforehand by the professional physicians of chronic kidney disease from the collaborative teaching hospital by using GFR computation formula. The hybrid model of combining each individual neural network and genetic algorithm (GA) is also conducted in this research. In other words, GA will be taken to combine with back-propagation neural network, feedforward neural network, and modular neural network, respectively, in model development and comparison as well.

5.1. The Model Development of Back-Propagation Neural Network. Through a series of training and testing with the different sets of parameter combination selected, we gain the best model for back-propagation neural network in terms of its respective network parameters with respect to two different sets of input factors. One set is by adopting the key factors used in computation formula (simply called Model PA hereafter). The other set is by adopting the key factors selected in this paper (simply called Model FB hereafter). Table 5 shows these two best settings of parameters. The classification accuracy, sensitivity, and specificity with respect to Model FA and FB, respectively, are shown in Table 6. In Table 6, the metric of "accuracy" is used to measure the classification of accuracy with the proportion of the sum of the number of true positives and the number of true negatives. The metric of "sensitivity" is used to measure the proportion of actual positives which are correctly classified as such. The metric of "specificity" is used to measure the proportion of negatives which are correctly identified. From the results shown in Table 6, a pretty good classification result is gained with BPN both for Model FA and FB, while it shows a significant drop in classification performance in model testing stage both in BPN and BPN plus GA. By the results shown in Table 6, pure BPN model may gain better results in accuracy measure, while BPN plus GA may gain better results in sensitivity measure. The result also shows the model with the adoption of the key factors used in computation

TABLE 6: The performance gained from back-propagation neural network models.

BPN	Model FA		Model FB	
Pure BPN	Training	Test	Training	Test
Accuracy of classification	100%	94.75%	100%	72.42%
Sensitivity	100%	97.06%	100%	70.59%
Specificity	100%	92.42%	100%	74.24%
BPN + GA	Test		Test	
Accuracy of classification	91.71%		77.68%	
Sensitivity	97.06%		81.82%	
Specificity	86.36%		73.53%	

TABLE 7: The best settings of network parameters for generalized feedforward neural network.

Network parameters	Model FA	Model FB
Learning rule	LevenbergMarquar	LevenbergMarquar
Transformation functions	SigmoidAxon	TanhAxon
Number of hiding layer	2	2
Number of neurons in hiding layer	8	8
Criterion for termination	MSE_{min}: 0.0001 $Epochs_{max}$: 3000	MSE_{min}: 0.0001 $Epochs_{max}$: 3000
Methods for weight update	Batch	Batch

formula gains better results in all three measures. These results show that a hybrid model with the combination of BPN and GA seams does not improve the model performance in accuracy measure but it is helpful to improve sensitivity measure.

5.2. The Model Development of Generalized Feedforward Neural Network. Table 7 shows the best network parameters settings for the development of generalized feedforward neural network (GFNN). The classification accuracy, sensitivity, and specificity with respect to Model FA and FB, respectively, are shown in Table 8. As the results in Table 8 show, pure GFNN obtains a perfect classification percentage in three measures including accuracy, sensitivity, and specificity in training stage while GFNN plus GA apparently may gain better results in testing. However, they also show the results gained from GFNN are not so good in all three measures as those gained from BPN and BPN plus GA, respectively.

5.3. The Model Development of Modular Neural Network. Table 9 shows the parameters for the test of modular neural network (MNN). The classification accuracy, sensitivity, and specificity with respect to Model FA and FB, respectively, are shown in Table 10. As the testing results in Table 10 show, pure MNN is the same as prior two models which may obtain a perfect classification percentage in three measures in training stage, but MNN plus GA apparently may gain worse results in testing stage, which is different from the results shown in prior two models.

6. Performance Comparison of Models

The performances of three neural network models developed for comparison in this paper in terms of detection (i.e., classification) accuracy measure are summarized and shown

in Tables 11 and 12, respectively. Table 11 shows the detection accuracy in three pure neural network models while Table 12 shows the detection accuracy with GA model embedded in three respective pure models. We found BPN may gain the best accuracy regardless of in both Model FA and Model FB which are measured with 94.75% and 72.42% accuracy shown in Table 11, respectively in model testing. However, Model FA, which is the test by adopting the key factors used in computation formula, may gain much better performance than Model FB, which is the test by adopting the key factors selected in this paper. The same result is gained with the GA embedded in each fundamental model in test. As the results observed from Table 12, both BPN plus GA and GFNN plus GA gain close results in accuracy measure which is much better than MNN plus GA.

By further observation from the results of model test shown in Section 4, it is found that almost all models employed in test may gain near 100% accuracy in CKD detection in the training stage regardless of which sets of influence factors used in model training. However, if further model testing is conducted, it is found that the network models with the input of influence factors of CKD used by physicians employed in the computational formula always show better detection performance in all three aspects of measure including accuracy, sensitivity, and specificity measures. As we can see from Table 11, the BPN gains the highest 94.75% accuracy measure in the testing stage among three fundamental neural network models while GFNN gains only 86.63% in accuracy measure which is the lowest performance in three models.

Through further observations from test results as it is shown in Table 12, we find the hybrid network model of GFNN with GA embedded may significantly show improvement in detection performance in all three measures from its fundamental model in the testing stage although the reversed

TABLE 8: The performance gained from generalized feedforward neural network models.

GFNN	Model FA		Model FB	
Pure GFNN	Training	Test	Training	Test
Accuracy of classification	100%	86.63%	100%	86.63%
Sensitivity	100%	82.35%	100%	82.35%
Specificity	100%	90.91%	100%	90.91%
GFNN + GA	Test		Test	
Accuracy of classification	91.09%		78.39%	
Sensitivity	88.24%		76.47%	
Specificity	93.94%		80.30%	

TABLE 9: The best settings of network parameters for modular neural network.

Network parameters	Model FA	Model FB
Learning rule	LevenbergMarquar	LevenbergMarquar
Transformation functions	SigmoidAxon	SigmoidAxon
Number of hiding layer	2	2
Number of neurons in hiding layer	4	8
Criterion for termination	MSE_{min}: 0.0001 $Epochs_{max}$: 3000	MSE_{min}: 0.0001 $Epochs_{max}$: 3000
Methods for weight update	Batch	Batch

TABLE 10: The performance gained from modular neural network models.

MNN	Model FA		Model FB	
Pure MNN	Training	Test	Pure MNN	Training
Accuracy of classification	100%	93.23%	Accuracy of classification	100%
Sensitivity	100%	97.06%	Sensitivity	100%
Specificity	100%	89.39%	Specificity	100%
MNN + GA	Test		Test	
Accuracy of classification	88.82%		78.34%	
Sensitivity	89.39%		79.41%	
Specificity	88.24%		77.27%	

TABLE 11: Detection accuracy in three pure neural network models.

Network models	By adopting the key factors used in computation formula (Model FA)	By adopting the key factors selected in this paper (Model FB)
BPN	94.75%	72.42%
GFNN	86.63%	71.03%
MNN	93.23%	70.99%

enhancement is shown in BPN and MNN. Again, by the test figures shown in Section 4, although pure neural network models with GA show degraded performance improvement for Model FA in testing stage in terms of three measures in accuracy, sensitivity, and specificity, it shows significant improvement for Model FB. As a result, we conclude a hybrid model indeed may improve detection performance. This result may conclude that GA provides no benefit in the yield of better detection performance with the adoption of the key factors used in computation formula as the input to all models in testing.

According to the detection performance shown in Tables 11 and 12, we conclude that BPN might be the best-fitting

Model FA among three fundamental neural network models employed in detecting CKD while the models BPN and GFNN with GA embedded, respectively, might be the best hybrid models for CKD detection but only GFNN plus GA can gain enhancement in detection performance in both sets of influence factors as input. These conclusions should be further verified and compared with other models selected for test in later studies before they can be assured.

7. Conclusion

We conclude that neural network models developed for CKD detection may effectively and feasibly equip medical staff with

TABLE 12: Detection accuracy in three neural network models with GA.

Network models	Model FA	Model FB
BPN + GA	91.71%	77.68%
GFNN + GA	91.09%	78.39%
MNN + GA	88.82%	78.34%

the ability to make precise diagnosis and treatment to the patient.

In the future study, further model modification and testing for the intelligence models developed in this paper should be conducted to enhance the accuracy in detection performance and to ensure they are sufficiently good for being truly employed in medical practice. In the meantime, different intelligence models can be widely and persistently applied for system development in this domain application as well in order to search for a best one model to be adopted. In the future system development, it is worthwhile to deploy the system to the cloud platform so that the public users can also use this system to conduct a self-detection of having had CKD.

References

[1] Department of Health (DOH), "The statistical data of the causes of civilian mortality," Taiwan, 2010, http://www.doh.gov.tw/CHT2006/DM/DM2_2.aspx?now_fod_list_no=11122&class_no=440&level_no=3.

[2] A. S. Levey, P. E. De Jong, J. Coresh et al., "The definition, classification, and prognosis of chronic kidney disease: a KDIGO controversies conference report," Kidney International, vol. 80, no. 1, pp. 17–28, 2011.

[3] National Kidney Foundation (NKF), "KDOQI clinical practice guidelines for chronic kidney disease: evaluation, classification and stratification," American Journal of Kidney Diseases, vol. 39, pp. S1–S266, 2002.

[4] A. S. Levey, T. Greene, J. W. Kusek, and G. L. Beck, "A simplified equation to predict glomerular filtration rate from serum creatinine," Journal American Society for Nephrology, vol. 11, article 155A, 2000.

[5] A. S. Levey, K. U. Eckardt, Y. Tsukamoto et al., "Definition and classification of chronic kidney disease: a position statement from KIidney Disease: Improving Global Outcomes (KDIGO)," Kidney International, vol. 67, no. 6, pp. 2089–2100, 2005.

[6] D. Kriesel, "A brief introduction to neural networks," 2011, http://www.dkriesel.com.

[7] K. Matsushita, B. K. Mahmoodi, M. Woodward et al., "Comparison of risk prediction using the CKD-EPI equation and the MDRD study equation for estimated Glomerular filtration rate," The Journal of the American Medical Association, vol. 307, no. 18, pp. 1941–1951, 2012.

[8] R. K. Chiu, C. I. Huang, and Y. C. Chang, "The study on the construction of intelligence-based decision support system for diabetes diagnosis and risk evaluation," Journal of Medical Informatics, vol. 19, no. 3, pp. 1–24, 2010.

[9] G. Arulampalam and A. Bouzerdoum, "Training shunting inhibitory artificial neural networks as classifiers," Neural Network World, vol. 10, no. 3, pp. 333–350, 2000.

[10] G. Arulampalam and A. Bouzerdoum, "A generalized feedforward neural network classifier," in Proceedings of the International Joint Conference on Neural Networks, pp. 1429–1434, July 2003.

[11] R. Jacobs, M. Jordan, S. Nowlan, and G. Hinton, "Adaptive mixtures of local experts," Neural Computation, vol. 3, no. 1, pp. 79–87, 1991.

8

Modelling Biological Systems with Competitive Coherence

Vic Norris, Maurice Engel, and Maurice Demarty

Theoretical Biology Unit, EA 3829, Department of Biology, University of Rouen, 76821 Mont-Saint-Aignan, France

Correspondence should be addressed to Vic Norris, victor.norris@univ-rouen.fr

Academic Editor: Olivier Bastien

Many living systems, from cells to brains to governments, are controlled by the activity of a small subset of their constituents. It has been argued that coherence is of evolutionary advantage and that this active subset of constituents results from competition between two processes, a Next process that brings about coherence over time, and a Now process that brings about coherence between the interior and the exterior of the system at a particular time. This competition has been termed competitive coherence and has been implemented in a toy-learning program in order to clarify the concept and to generate—and ultimately test—new hypotheses covering subjects as diverse as complexity, emergence, DNA replication, global mutations, dreaming, bioputing (computing using either the parts of biological system or the entire biological system), and equilibrium and nonequilibrium structures. Here, we show that a program using competitive coherence, Coco, can learn to respond to a simple input sequence 1, 2, 3, 2, 3, with responses to inputs that differ according to the position of the input in the sequence and hence require competition between both Next and Now processes.

1. Introduction

The quest for universal laws in biology and other sciences has led to the development—and sometimes the acceptance—of concepts such as tensegrity [1], edge of chaos [2, 3], small worlds [4], and self-organised criticality [5]. This quest has also led to the pioneering (N, k) model developed by Kauffman in which N is the number of nodes in an arbitrarily defined Boolean network and k is the fixed degree of connectivity between them [6]. The actual use of the (N, k) model to the microbiologist, for example, is that it might help explain how a bacterium negotiates the enormity of phenotype space so as to generate a limited number of reproducible phenotypes on which natural selection can act. Although the (N, k) model successfully generates a small number of short state cycles from an inexplorable vast number of combinations—which might be equated to generating a few phenotypes from the vast number apparently available to the cell—the model has its limitations for the microbiologist as, for example, it has a fixed connectivity, it does not evolve, and it does not actually do anything.

In a different attempt to find a universal law in biology, one of us began working on the idea of network coherence in the seventies. This idea is related to neural networks (though the idea was developed with no knowledge of them) which have indeed been proposed as important in generating phenotypes [7]. The network coherence idea turned out to be scale-free and to address one of the most important problems that confronts bacteria, eukaryotic cells, collections of cells (including brains), and even social organisations. This problem is how a system can behave in (1) a coherent way over time so as to maintain historical continuity and (2) a coherent way at a particular time that makes sense in terms of both internal and environmental conditions. A possible solution would be for these systems to operate using the principle of *competitive coherence* [8, 9]. Competitive coherence can be used to describe the way that a key subset of constituents—the Active Set—are chosen to determine the behaviour of an organisation at a particular level. This choice results from a competition for inclusion in the Active Set between elements with connections that confer coherence over time (i.e., continuity) and connections that confer internal and external coherence at the present time. Given that living systems are complex or rather *hypercomplex* systems, characterised by emergent properties, we have speculated that competitive coherence has parameters useful for clarifying emergent properties and, perhaps, for classifying and quantifying types of complexity

[10]. We have further argued that competitive coherence might even be considered as the hallmark of life itself.

One of the objections to universal laws such as competitive coherence is that without testing they are mere handwaving. To try to overcome this objection and to make the central idea and related ideas clear, we have implemented competitive coherence into a toy-learning program in which the competitive coherence part, Coco, learns or fails to learn when playing against an environment that rewards or punishes Coco by changing connections between elements. In what follows, we describe the structure of the program, results from this toy version, and optional extras that could be added to or manipulated within the program. Some of these optional extras are wildly speculative but they are included to show that Coco might be useful as a generator, editor, and test-bed for new and/or woolly concepts including those that might find a home in biology-based computing [11].

2. Principle of the Program

The central idea is that an *active* subset of elements determines the behaviour of a system: the majority of elements are inactive. The members of this active subset, the size of which is fixed, are chosen by a competition between two processes, *Next* and *Now* (Figure 1). The active subset corresponds to those elements that have their addresses in the current line of the Activity Register. The subset of elements that are active at the same time constitutes the state of the system at that time and each line in the Activity Register says what state is at a particular time; consecutive lines correspond to consecutive states of the system. How is this state obtained? An overview of the program is given in Figure 2 to show the order of the essential subroutines, which are explained in detail in the following subsections. COMPUTE is the cyclical core of the system. INITIALISE sets up the initial conditions by filling at random the Now and Next fields (two separate sets of weightings) of each element with the addresses of other elements, and by filling at random the first line (which corresponds to the state of the system) of the Activity Register with addresses. INPUT provides one input at a time (by loading the address into the Activity Register of a specific element); these inputs are taken in order from a defined sequence. DOWNTIME prevents an element whose address has been loaded into the Activity Register from having its address loaded again within a brief time. MUTATE changes at random the contents of the Now and Next fields (in a sense, the weightings). LOAD is responsible for extracting and ranking the scores of the elements' Now and Next fields and then comparing these scores so as to decide which address to load to the Activity Register. LOAD is helped by REVERSE DOWNTIME, which stops an element likely to be useful later from being used too soon, and by COMPATIBILITY-EMERGENCE, which increases the probability that some groups of elements have their addresses loaded at the same time (corresponding to these elements being active together). REWARD-PUNISH routines detect and evaluate outputs and reward or punish

the elements involved by strengthening or weakening the Now/Next links between them. The results are displayed every loop of the COMPUTE routine, which corresponds to a line in the Activity Register being filled (see the following).

2.1. The Biological Elements. An individual gene or neurone or another biological building block is represented in the program as an element. In the version presented here, there are a thousand elements. Only ten elements (again in the version presented here) can be active—that is, determine the state of the system—at any one time. The composition of this subset of active elements determines whether this active subset is successful or not.

Each element contains, in the version presented here, two fields: Now and Next (Figure 3). Each element has an address. Each field contains the addresses of other elements with which the element has been associated successfully during learning (see the following). The Now field contains the addresses of those elements that have been successful in the same time step in which the element itself was successful whilst the Next field contains the addresses of those elements that have been successful in the time step following the step in which the element was active. A time step corresponds to a single line in the Activity Register, hence the active subset of elements corresponds to those elements that have their addresses in the current line of the Activity Register. In other words, each line says what the state of the system is in terms of *activity* in that particular time step.

2.2. The Activity Register. Each line in the Activity Register contains the addresses of the small subset of elements that are active at a particular time (Figure 4). Each line is filled according to a set of rules (see the following), and when the register is full, the first line is filled again (so the register operates cyclically). A line is set to zero before it is filled.

2.3. Coherence via the Now Process. Biological systems are characterised by coherence. At the level of human society, the composition of a successful football team reflects the importance of coherence in the manager's choice of players: the team must contain players who can take on the roles of goalkeeper, defenders, midfield players and attackers. Choosing the players is a progressive process: the choice of the goalkeeper influences the choice of the defenders which then influences the choice of the defenders. At the level of a bacterium, the composition of a bacterium reflects its growth strategy: if *Escherichia coli* is to grow rapidly, it needs to express the genes that encode ribosomes, tRNA synthetases, RNA polymerases, and the proteins that drive the cell cycle whereas if it is to survive in harsh conditions and in the absence of nutrients, it needs to express the genes that, for example, encode proteins that compact and protect its genome such as Dps [12]. Biological systems from sports' teams and brains to bacteria that fail to achieve this *internal* coherence risk elimination in a world in which natural selection operates. The coherence that a biological system must achieve also has an *external* component. The football manager may choose his team as a function of the

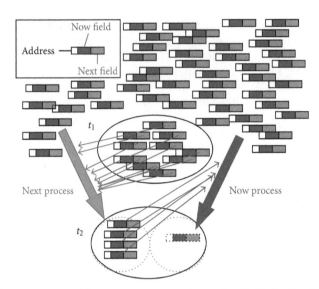

FIGURE 1: The principle of Now-Next competition. The elements active at time t_1 (inside black ellipse) are used to select the elements to be active at time t_2. This selection uses the Next fields of the elements active at time t_1 (red arrows). As the new elements are activated at time t_2 (inside the red dotted circle), the Now fields of these new elements are also used to select and activate more elements (blue arrows) such as the element inside the dotted blue circle. The elements to be activated are selected from a large set of inactive elements by a competition between the Now and Next processes. The inset shows an element which has an address and two fields.

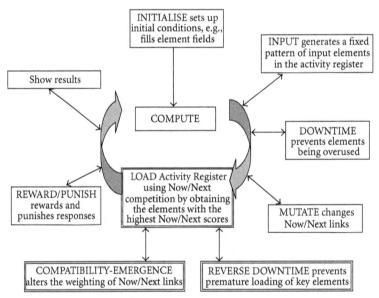

FIGURE 2: Overview of essential modules. A single cycle of the COMPUTE routine results in the addresses of a subset of the elements being loaded into a line of the Activity Register; this corresponds to *activating* these elements. Certain elements are inputs and others are outputs. The INPUT routine creates an input by loading the address of an input element into the Activity Register. The learning part of the program, Coco, eventually responds to an input by loading the address of an output element into the Activity Register; this corresponds to an output. The actual loading of addresses results from a competition between Now and Next links; the scores obtained from counting these links may be modified by an EMERGENCE routine. The DOWNTIME and REVERSE DOWNTIME routines may make certain elements ineligible for loading, depending on the history of these elements. Outputs are detected, evaluated, and rewarded or punished by REWARD/PUNISH routines. Each time a line of the Activity Register has been filled, the results are displayed.

pitch, the weather, their position in a league table, and the opposing team (which may contain players known for their "physical" approach). The bacterium should not express the full complement of genes needed for fast growth if it is in conditions in which there are few nutrients and in which physical conditions such as temperature and humidity require stress responses. The Now process is intended to represent the way biological systems achieve both internal and external coherence. For example, suppose that at high temperatures, phospholipids with long, saturated fatty acids

Address	Now field					Next field				
1	878	63	50	533	119	43	227	136	19	256
2	13	218	516	923	121	724	447	225	134	15
3	611	577	488	818	63	70	337	722	297	98
4	437	316	218	726	413	124	126	117	747	299
...										
999	165	534	183	612	626	667	879	355	649	220
1000	388	431	566	435	924	654	255	818	921	33

FIGURE 3: The Elements table. The Now and Next fields of an element contain the addresses of the elements with which the element in question has been successfully active (for convenience of representation each field here contains only 5 addresses).

Present state t	10	5	18	11	6	4	23
Developing state $t+1$	7	22	16				

FIGURE 4: The Activity Register. Two lines are shown (corresponding to two successive active states), one full and the other (italics) in the process of being filled (for convenience, only 7 entries and only two lines are shown).

are needed to confer stability to the membrane; suppose that genes 7, 19, and 23 encode membrane proteins with an affinity for such phospholipids (Figure 5); the expression of one of these genes (e.g., 23) may help to create a domain on the membrane enriched in both the protein encoded by 23 and the long chain phospholipid; the existence of this domain then helps the expression of 19 which has a protein product that also contributes to the size and stability of the domain; this in turn helps the expression of 7 (for the possible biological significance see [13]).

2.4. Coherence via the Next Process. The Now process on its own is not enough to allow a biological system to adapt effectively to its environment. This is because these environments often require different responses to the same stimulus because the historical contexts are different. One may not respond in the same way to an invitation from Human Resources following a successful sales campaign as following the news that the company is about to go out of business. A Next process is required to take account of the dependency of a correct response on the history of the system. This is made easier by the fact that environments are often unchanging for long periods and, when they do change, change in predictable ways; rules in sport, for example, do not change very often. And even when different environments exist at the same time, it would not be advisable for a sports' team that wants to compete at a good level for it to play football one week, switch to hockey the next, then rugby, and so forth. It would not be a winning strategy for a bacterium to switch phenotypes either (we ignore here events at the level of the population of bacteria which needs to explore phenotypic heterogeneity). For example, three genes that are active in one time step, 7, 19, and 23, may have connections via their Next fields to the same subset of genes, 22, 24, and 33 (Figure 6) with 7

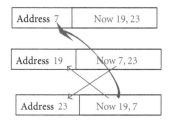

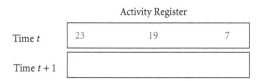

	Activity Register		
Time t	23	19	7
Time $t+1$			

FIGURE 5: The Now Process. Out of a large set of elements (genes), a few, well-connected ones are chosen (positioned) to be active (expressed) at a particular time. For example, if gene 23 encodes a protein with the same lipid preferences as the proteins encoded by genes 19 and 7 the expression of these genes may be synergistic (for convenience, only two addresses are shown in the Now field).

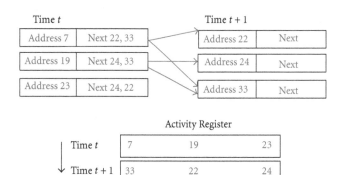

	Activity Register		
Time t	7	19	23
Time $t+1$	33	22	24

FIGURE 6: The Next Process. The elements (genes) active in time step t determine the elements that will be active in time step $t+1$.

encoding a transcriptional activator being produced in one time step and 22 and 23 being the genes under its control and hence expressed in the following time step.

2.5. Competition between the Now and Next Processes. Modelling competitive coherence in the program consists of the competition between the Now and Next processes for choosing the subset of elements that are to be active (i.e., determine the state of the system). This activation takes the form of loading the addresses of elements into the new line of the Activity Register. The competition is on the basis of the scores of the elements. To load a new line, first, the Next fields of the elements present in the current line are consulted and the number of occurrences of the addresses in these fields is counted to give Next Scores (Figure 7). These Next Scores are then ranked in HighestNext to give, in Figure 7, element 7 with the highest score (of 8).

Once the address of this first element has been loaded into the new line, the following highest score in the

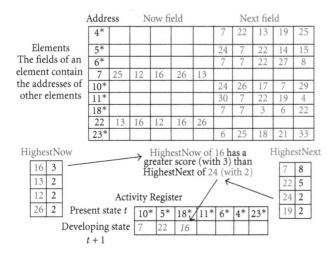

FIGURE 7: Competition between Now and Next Processes. The diagram shows the operation of filling the third position in the new line of the Activity Register (corresponding to the developing state of the system). The elements in the current line of the Activity Register are labelled with an asterisk and only their Next fields are shown. The two elements loaded into the new line at the start of the competition for third position have their Now fields in bold; their Next fields are not shown. The Now and Next scores are in the second column of HighestNow and HighestNext, respectively. See text for full explanation.

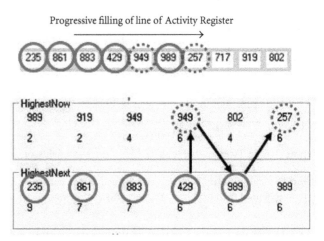

FIGURE 8: Differential Contributions of the Next and Now processes. A line of the Activity Register that has just been filled is shown along with part of the contents of the HighestNext and HighestNow counters at this time. The addresses in these counters are on the top and the corresponding scores on the bottom. The red circles show the addresses of elements contributed by the Next process and the dotted blue circles show those contributed by the Now process. The arrows show where there is a clear change in the contributions of the processes to filling the Activity Register.

HighestNext list is consulted: this is 22 with a score of 5. It is not, however, loaded straightaway because 7 has been loaded and 7 has a Now field. The addresses of the elements in 7's Now field are counted and ranked in HighestNow; in this example, the ranking is at random because the scores of these addresses are all the same (here, 1). The highest scores in HighestNext and HighestNow are then compared and the address of the element with the higher score is then loaded into the Activity Register (if they have the same score, the Now element is preferred).

There are now two addresses in the Activity Register, 7 and 22. The addresses in the Now fields of both 7 and 22 are counted and ranked to give at the top of HighestNow 16 with a score of 3. The address at the top of HighestNext is 24 with a score of 2. Comparison of the two scores shows that the address of element 16 has the greater score and this address is therefore loaded to the Activity Register. Once an address has been loaded, its score is set to zero to prevent it from being loaded a second time.

This competition between Next and Now processes continues until the line of the Activity Register has been filled. Note that, during the determination of the new state of the system, the relative contribution of the two processes changes since, first, the number of Now fields increases as addresses are progressively loaded into the Activity Register (i.e., as more and more elements become active), and, second, each time an element is chosen from the HighestNext, the following one has a lower score. In other words, the Next process dominates at the beginning and the Now process at the end (Figure 8).

2.6. Inputs and Outputs. Both inputs and outputs correspond to specific elements each of which has a Now and a Next field. In this version, there are three inputs, 1, 2, and 3, and three outputs, 998, 999, and 1000. An input is generated when the INPUT subroutine inserts one (and only one) of the three inputs into the new line of the Activity Register. An output is generated when Coco loads an output element into the new line of the Activity Register. The lines between the input line and the output line constitute an *input-output module*.

A new input is generated in the line immediately following an output. A new output must occur in the four lines following an input; if an output is not generated in these time steps, an arbitrarily chosen output is inserted into the fourth line. A maximum number of lines before forcing an output is needed if the program is to run rapidly when the proportion of output elements to the total number of elements becomes small (since the initial probability of generating an output is similarly low). The choice of four lines as a maximum is also arbitrary.

Inputs are not related to outputs: it does not matter whether the output is right or wrong. The sequence of inputs is fixed: $(1, 2, 3, 2, 3)_n$. Elements in lines containing outputs that correspond to inputs are rewarded—or punished if the outputs are wrong (see the following). Coco is considered to have succeeded when it has learnt to generate $(1000, 999, 999, 1000, 998)_n$ in response to the input sequence (Figure 9). This simple input-output relationship was chosen because neither the Now nor the Next process alone is sufficient to lead to Coco learning. The Now process fails because two different outputs—999 and 1000—are required when 2 is the input (and also because two different outputs—999 and 998—are required when 3 is the input).

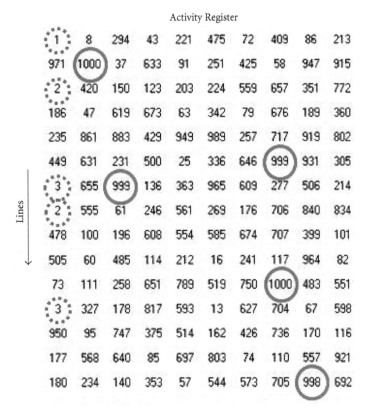

FIGURE 9: Contents of Activity Register after learning. The screen print shows consecutive lines in the Activity Register. Inputs are circled with dotted blue lines and outputs with continuous red lines.

The Next process fails because two different outputs—999 and 998—are required when 3 follows 2.

2.7. Downtime. An element that has been active (i.e., its address has been loaded into a line of the Activity Register) cannot be activated again for ten more timesteps. Inputs that are generated by the environment subroutine are not affected by downtimes (artefactual inputs generated by the dynamics of Coco do have downtimes). Outputs do not have downtimes. Downtimes are taken into account when the Now and Next scores are worked out. Downtime can be problem when the size of the Activity Register is increased since Coco can run out of elements to load; for example, if there are only 1000 elements, if the Activity Register has a line containing 100 elements, and if Downtime is set to 10, there are not enough elements to load. There is an echo here of the *E. coli* cell cycle in which, after initiation of chromosome replication, the constituents of the initiation hyperstructure are inactivated or sequestered to prevent a second initiation event [14], whilst after cell division, the constituents of the division hyperstructure are presumably also disabled to prevent repeated divisions in the bacterial poles [15].

2.8. Rewarding and Punishing. Rewarding entails strengthening the connections between successful states (and series of successful states). Briefly, this is achieved by (1) taking an element with its address in a line of the Activity Register between and including the input and output lines, which we term a module (see the previous part) and (2) writing this address into the Now or Next fields of other elements in the same or in the preceding lines of the Activity Register (Figure 10). First, the environmental part of the program detects whether there is an output in the new line and, if so, decides whether there is more than one output (more than one output is punished, see the following). Then, if the output is correct, two addresses are chosen from the same line in the successful module and the second address is written into the Now field of the first element. This is done for every element in the entire module (i.e., each line is treated). These connections are not made when it would entail connecting an element to itself (i.e., self-referral) or overwriting the address of another element that is actually already in the same line. The Next connections are rewarded in much the same way except that elements are taken from one line of the module and the addresses that are written into their Next fields are taken from the following line. Self-referral and overwriting of successful elements is avoided as in the case of rewarding via the Now connections. It should be noted that a connection is made between the previous module and the rewarded module insofar as the Next fields of the last line of the previous module are connected to the first line of the rewarded module (note too that the Next rewarding has to stop at the penultimate line of the rewarded module because the future line is not

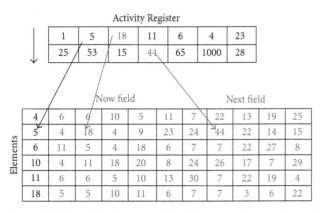

FIGURE 10: Rewarding by overwriting. The connections of element 5, whose address is in a line of a successful module in the Activity Register, are strengthened (black arrow). A randomly chosen address in the Now field of 5 is overwritten with 18, which is another address present in the same line as 5 (blue arrow), whilst a randomly chosen address in the Next field of 5 is overwritten with 44, which is an address present in the following line (red arrow).

known!). A small section of the elements, along with a couple of lines of the Activity Register and the HighestNow and HighestNext registers (Figure 11) shows the pattern of connectivity resulting from learning to couple an input with the appropriate output for Coco with a 1000 elements, Anumber of 10 (size of Active Set) and Knumber of 7 (size of Now and Next fields).

Punishing entails taking a *single* Activity Register line at random from the failed input-output module or taking the last line of the previous module. The Now fields of the elements whose addresses are in this line are then consulted. A randomly chosen address is then used to overwrite one of these Now addresses. The Next fields of these elements (which helped determine the following line) are altered in a similar way. There is a mutation aspect to punishment (Section 4.3).

2.9. Synchrony. There is a synchrony in the program that results from it being based on successive lines in the Activity Register, each of which is examined in a time step. Reward and punish decisions are then made in this time step to change the connections between the elements by altering the contents of their Now and Next fields; these alterations are made together in a synchronous fashion. The actual loading of addresses into a new line is a mixture of synchronous and asynchronous events: the Next scores are obtained together at the end of one time step (and the process exhibits synchrony) whilst the Now scores are obtained progressively during the loading of the Activity Register (and the process exhibits asynchrony).

3. Results

3.1. With Next Alone. The relative contributions of Now and Next scores to the loading of addresses into the Activity Register can be altered by a constant factor, NowNextWeighting.

If this factor is set very low or very high, it switches the program so that it operates with either just Nexts or just Nows. Generally, this factor equals 1. By setting NowNextWeighting to 1/100, the Next scores dominate. The graphs show the fraction (total outputs-correct outputs)/total outputs, so a line towards the top of the figure corresponds to a failure to learn effectively. When the Nexts alone determine the loading of the Activity Register (red circles), learning does not occur (Figure 12). Note that only a truncated part of HighestNext and HighestNow is shown and that the scores shown in the bottom row are before scaling by NowNextWeighting.

3.2. With Now Alone. Setting NowNextWeighting to 100 allows the Now scores to dominate. The graphs in Figure 13 show the proportion of incorrect outputs (failures to learn) to total outputs, so a series of successful outputs corresponds to a negative slope. In one case, learning has not occurred after 20000 timesteps (Figure 13(a)). In another case, learning has actually occurred at a late stage (Figure 13(b)). The explanation is that the Next scores are still operating even with this NowNextWeighting because the first address chosen for the NewLine of the Activity Register is chosen from the Next element with the HighestNext score (unless an input is loaded). This initial choice does not depend on the NowNextWeighting. The Activity Register corresponding to this surprising learning confirms that the Nows have contributed the addresses (compare contents of last line of Activity Register and with contents of HighestNow and HighestNext in Figure 13(c)).

3.3. Without Downtime. The address of an element that has loaded into the Activity Register cannot be loaded again within the next ten timesteps. In the absence of DOWNTIME, Coco does not learn (Figure 14(a)). One evident reason for this is that false inputs can be loaded into the Activity Register (Figure 14(b)).

3.4. With Now, Next, and Downtime. Three independent runs of the program show that Coco learns the task albeit sometimes with difficulty (Figure 15). Inspection of the Activity Register and the HighestNext and HighestNow confirms that the initial contribution to the last line in the register comes first from the Next (red circles) and then from the Now (blue circles). Note that only a truncated part of HighestNext and HighestNow is shown. Note too the limited size of the Activity Register (Section 4.14). What might DOWNTIME correspond to in a biological system? In a bacterium, it might correspond to the state of a gene x in an operon which requires an activator but which also encodes an unstable repressor Y of this operon; activating the gene would then lead to both production of X and of Y; Y would then switch off the operon for a Downtime until it was degraded. A more interesting possible example is that of the sequestration of newly replicated, hemimethylated DNA in *E. coli* (which occurs when the SeqA protein recognises that a GATC sequence in the old strand is methylated whilst its complement in the new strand has yet to be replicated); since a gene may have a greater chance of being expressed when

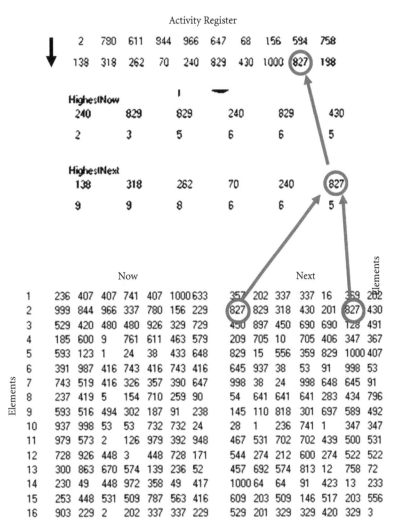

FIGURE 11: The connectivity after successful learning. An input line and the following, correct, output line in the Activity Register are shown. The total scores of some of the elements whose addresses are in the Next fields of the elements in the top line of the Activity Register can be seen in the bottom row of HighestNext. If the Next field of element 2 is inspected, two references to element 827 are found; these two references are part of the total of five references to element 827; this score of five is sufficient for the address of element 827 to be loaded into the new line of the Activity Register (so activating element 827). Note the presence of the output itself, 1000.

the region within which it lies is being replicating (perhaps due to greater accessibility to RNA polymerase), some genes with GATC sequences may be both switched on and switched off by the act of replication. This latter possibility might be modelled specifically by confining DOWNTIME to those elements that are activated by the CYCLE subroutine, as mentioned in Section 4.2. What then might the inputs and outputs correspond to in a biological system? As shown here, Coco readily learns to give the same output to different inputs. It also learns to give a different output to the same input depending on the history of the inputs; this could correspond to a low concentration of nutrients having a different meaning for a bacterium if this concentration follows a period of starvation or a period of plenty; in the former case it means that conditions are improving and in the latter case it means that they are getting worse, and the appropriate response of the bacterium would be to grow or to sporulate, respectively.

3.5. An Oscillatory Input Gives an Oscillatory Output. The environment gives the inputs $(1, 2, 3)$ in a cycle $(1, 2, 3, 2, 3)_n$ and immediately Coco responds with an output the environment gives the next input. Hence, Coco learns to respond to an oscillating input pattern with an oscillating output pattern. This can be confirmed after learning has occurred by removing inputs and following the pattern active elements (i.e., the addresses in the Activity Register). It does indeed maintain the output pattern in the absence of inputs and absence of changes to connectivity normally caused by rewarding, punishing, and noise (data not shown). This shows the extent to which the state of the system reflects the interdependency of the elements loaded to the Activity Register. Note though that if the Activity register is small (low Anumber) and the connections are weak (low Knumber), inputs must be continued (along with rewarding) to maintain the oscillating output pattern. We discuss further the significance of

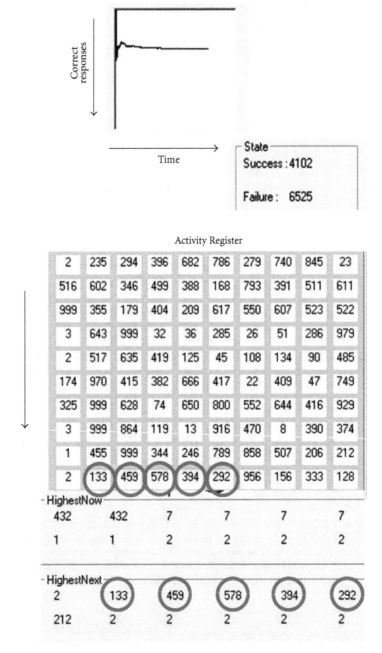

FIGURE 12: Running the program depending on the Nexts. No learning has occurred after 20000 time steps (the time taken to fill, analyse, and respond to a single line in the Activity Register); the contents of the Activity Register and the HighestNow and HighestNext confirm the Next contribution (red circles). Correct responses is (total number of responses–correct responses)/total number of responses. Note that the total number of successes and failures (10627) would only equal the number of timesteps or lines (here 20000) if the program were constrained to give an output in the same line as it had received an input (rather than up to four lines later).

a noncyclical input-output pattern—and how to achieve this—in Section 4.18.

4. Optional Extras

4.1. Positive and Negative Links. Biological systems generally have both activators and repressors. Simulation suggests that the ratio between them is a major influence on the dynamics

[16]. In the program, elements can be connected positively and negatively. When the Now and Next scores are calculated, each address present in a field with a positive link counts as +1 whilst an address with a negative link counts as −1. The positive or negative nature of a link is defined at random at the start of the program and is not modified afterwards. In the present version, 10% of the signs are negative (though it learns when none of them are negative).

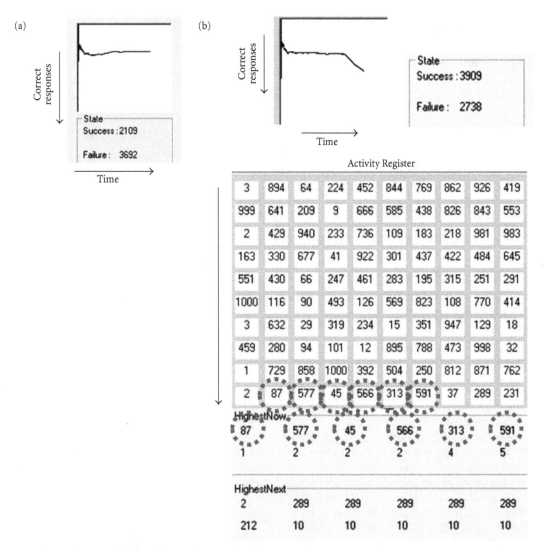

FIGURE 13: Running the program depending on the Nows. (a) No learning has occurred after 20000 timesteps, and (b) Learning has been delayed in this case after 20000 timesteps and the contents of the Activity Register and the HighestNow and HighestNext confirm the Now contribution (dotted blue circles).

4.2. DNA Replication. Growing bacteria replicate their DNA. It has been proposed that the replication of a gene affects the probability that the gene and its physical neighbours may have an altered probability of transcription [17, 18]. One consequence of this could be to enable the bacterium to avoid getting trapped in a very limited state cycle of phenotypes. In other words, DNA replication itself might constitute a way of exploring phenotype space. Such exploration could even constitute a coherent exploration of phenotype space if the position of the gene on the chromosome were close to those of other genes with related functions (and far from those with opposed functions). To introduce this parameter into the program, a CYCLE subroutine allows an element to be loaded into the Activity Register irrespective of the Now and Next connections. This element is chosen in order from the elements (e.g., first 17 is inserted, then 18, then 19, etc.). It is not inserted into the Activity Register if Coco has just given the correct output (which corresponds in this version of the program to CyclePermission = 0).

4.3. Mutations and Noise. Mutations occur as part of the PUNISH subroutines. In fact, the overwriting of the Now and Next fields (of the elements with addresses in the line to be punished) is a mutation process insofar as the new addresses that are written into these fields are chosen at random. This overwriting is done at a frequency determined by the MutationThreshold which, in the version presented here, is set so that overwriting occurs on one out of ten occasions.

There is more to the mutation story than this though. After the program has run for 200 timesteps, a RunningScore is kept of how many of the last ten outputs have been correct (this involves a sliding window, RunningScoreWindow, set to ten). Depending on this RunningScore, mutations are either made at different frequencies or not made at all. A mutation is made by taking an element with an address that is rarely found in the fields of the other elements (i.e., a lonely element) and writing it into a field of any one of the other elements chosen at random. This is done ten

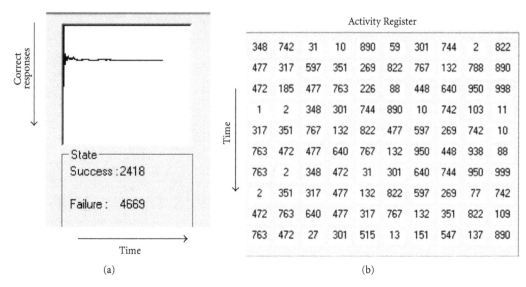

Activity Register

348	742	31	10	890	59	301	744	2	822
477	317	597	351	269	822	767	132	788	890
472	185	477	763	226	88	448	640	950	998
1	2	348	301	744	890	10	742	103	11
317	351	767	132	822	477	597	269	742	10
763	472	477	640	767	132	950	448	938	88
763	2	348	472	31	301	640	744	950	999
2	351	317	477	132	822	597	269	77	742
472	763	640	477	317	767	132	351	822	109
763	472	27	301	515	13	151	547	137	890

State
Success : 2418

Failure :   4669

(a)   (b)

FIGURE 14: No learning without DOWNTIME. (a) After 20000 timesteps, Coco shows no sign of learning. (b) The Activity Register shows that inputs are being generated inappropriately.

times per output if the RunningScore is low. If the last ten outputs were all correct, no mutations are made. Clearly, RunningScoreWindow is a parameter that the program itself could modify during running but, in the version presented here, it is held constant at ten.

Noise is not present in the basic version of the program presented here but is easy to introduce. For example, in Figure 16 the NoiseLevel has been set to insert a random address for every twenty or so (on average) addresses loaded into the Activity Register (i.e., around every three lines). The results show that the learning displayed by Coco is fairly robust and, even when it is forced to *forget*, it can relearn rapidly.

Finally, a SCRAMBLE subroutine may be a source of *mutations*. This routine operates in a democratic way to ensure that when elements have the same score, they are chosen at random to be ranked in HighestNow and HighestNext. This may result in an address being loaded into a position in the Activity Register that it had not occupied previously and bring to an end a winning streak, at least, temporarily. The fact that learning is often stable despite scrambling is again indicative of the robustness of this learning.

4.4. Reverse Downtime. Input-output modules can readily become compressed so that, for example, an input in line n of the Activity Register followed by an output in line $n + 4$ can be shortened such that the output occurs in line $n + 2$ or indeed in line n itself (Figure 17). The idea behind REVERSE DOWNTIME is to avoid this compression by preventing the addresses of elements in line $t + 1$ from being loaded into the previous line t. This entails using the REVERSE DOWN-TIME subroutine to examine progressively the elements of addresses loaded into the NewLine and ensuring that the addresses in their Nexts, which may correspond to elements often active in the following line, are not loaded via the Now

process. Preventing such addresses from being loaded is done via the NOW EXTRACTION subroutine which sets their scores to zero (in this version, it is not done by the NEXT EXTRACTION subroutine too—but could be). Although it is not clear to us that the REVERSE DOWNTIME subroutine has an equivalent in cells, it might be argued that REVERSE DOWNTIME resembles checkpoints, which prevent late cell cycle events from occurring until earlier ones have been completed [19].

4.5. Uptime. It would be easy to introduce an uptime in which an element that had already participated successfully would have a greater chance of being loaded again. This would be a variant of the Matthew effect in which the rich get richer (and the poor, poorer), which has been explored in connectivity studies [20].

4.6. Emergence. One of the characteristics of an emergent property is that it resists attempts to predict or deduce it [21]. An emergent property could be, for example, the affinity of certain membrane proteins for the phospholipid, cardiolipin, so that they assemble into a membrane domain enriched in cardiolipin where these proteins then function together. In the framework of competitive coherence, emergence is related to the formation of the new state, the subset of elements that are active together because their addresses are loaded together into the Activity Register [10]. Suppose that a subset of the elements (e.g., 27, 37, 47, 57, 67, and 77) correspond to proteins with a strong affinity for cardiolipin. Similarly, another subset of elements (e.g., 23, 33, 43, 53, 63, and 73) might correspond to proteins with an affinity for another phospholipid, phosphatidylethanolamine. This could be done for a hundred different phospholipids. In the program, these affinities could correspond to a hardwiring done in the INITIALISE subroutine such that the probability that 27 and 37 and so forth are loaded into the Activity

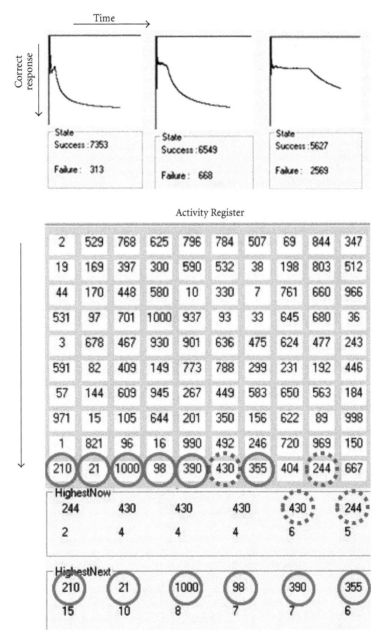

FIGURE 15: Successful learning with Now, Next, and Downtime processes working. Three, consecutive, independent examples are shown after 20000 timesteps. The contents of the Activity Register, HighestNext, and HighestNow of one of them are shown (now addresses are circled with a dotted blue line and Next addresses with a red line).

Register is greater if one of them is already present. If this combination of elements turns out to be a successful one, this might be considered as the emergence of the property of an affinity for cardiolipin.

The aforementioned approach to emergence can be modelled to some extent in the program via a Compatibility Table, which is a 2D matrix of the elements in which the Compatibility of Element(i) × Element(j) is a factor. During the loading of the Activity Register, this factor is used to multiply the Now and Next scores of the elements so as to help determine which is the highest. The factor in (i, j) is determined once and for all at the start of the program (i.e., it

is hardwired). It would be possible to have a large number of sets of factors (e.g., a hundred sets of factors each linking ten elements) and then explore the effect—for example, it might significantly reduce the combinatorial space. In the present version, all the factors in the Compatibility Table are set to 1 (so they have no effect) with the exception of the inputs with one another which are set to zero (e.g., Compatibility(2,3) = 0).

4.7. *Global Changes via Yin-Yang.* A bacterium like *E. coli* can be exposed suddenly to an environmental change that

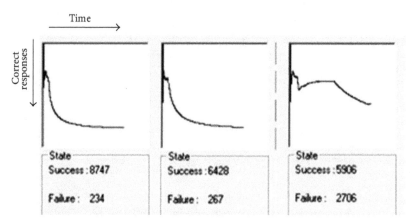

FIGURE 16: Robustness to noise. Three separate runs of the program, each for 20000 timesteps, show how allowing noise has in the third run perturbed Coco twice and caused it to forget a previously learnt sequence.

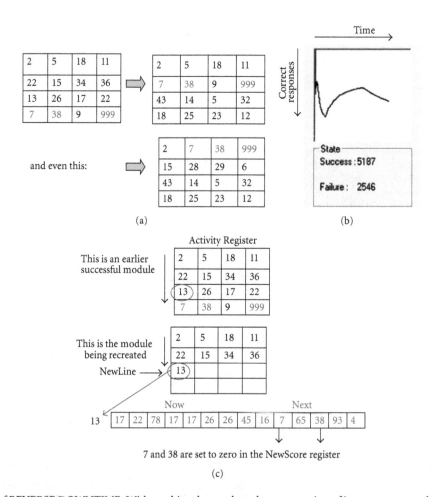

FIGURE 17: Principle of REVERSE DOWNTIME. Without this rule to reduce the compression of input-output modules, addresses can move from one line to another line closer to the input line. (a) The Activity Register is shown here with only four elements (for simplicity) and initially has addresses of certain elements (red) in a successful output line; these addresses can become displaced towards the input line. (b) The results of 20000 timesteps without REVERSE DOWNTIME. (c) Implementing REVERSE DOWNTIME during the loading of a NewLine requires the Next field of 13 to be consulted; this shows that 7 and 38 often follow 13, so, to avoid compression by 7 and 38 being loaded into the NewLine, the NowScore register for 7 and 38 is set to zero.

affects a great many of its systems. Typically, such global changes might include those in temperature or calcium concentration. Global changes can also result from internal changes such as those resulting from alterations in DNA supercoiling, mediated by topoisomerases like DNA gyrase, which then affect the expression of many genes [22]. Such changes distort the entire phenotype but in a way that is related to the original phenotype. It seems reasonable to imagine that mutations that affect the activity of enzymes like gyrase have a different role in evolution from those that affect enzymes involved in the metabolism of lactose. One way to explore this in the program is to choose two elements (e.g., 6 and 7) to represent two different global conditions (such as a high calcium level and a low calcium level alias Yin and Yang). When a 6 is loaded into the Activity Register, the Compatibility Table is modified temporarily such that different addresses may be loaded into the Activity Register under these Yin conditions. The effect of loading a 6 can be carried over several time steps before the Compatibility Table is reset. When a 7 is loaded into the Activity Register, the Compatibility Table is modified in a different way to take into account the Yang conditions. In the present version, no such changes are allowed to the Compatibility Table.

4.8. Equilibrium and Nonequilibrium Structures. It has been proposed that bacteria and other cells are confronted with the task of reconciling surviving harsh conditions, which requires quasi-equilibrium structures (thick, cross-linked walls, and liquid crystalline DNA), with growing in favourable conditions, which requires nonequilibrium structures (such as those formed by the dynamic, ATP/GTP consuming, dynamically coupled processes of transcription and translation) [23–26]. To put it picturesquely, cells are confronted with life on the scales of equilibria and, conceivably, use the cell cycle in their balancing act [23, 27]. It might therefore be interesting to explore what happens when the equivalent of the energy currencies of the cell, ATP, GTP, and polyphosphate, is introduced into the program. This might be achieved by attributing the role of ATP to an element and giving this element special properties. For example, this element (e.g., element 77) might have to be present in the Activity Register for a subset of other nonequilibrium elements to be loaded (which could be done via the Compatibility Table); if 77 were absent from the Activity Register, this subset could not be loaded although another subset of equilibrium structures could be; the probability with which 77 could be loaded might depend on a combination in a line of the Activity Register of an input element (corresponding to glucose) and other elements (corresponding to glycolytic enzymes).

4.9. Several Activity Registers. The Yin-Yang approach (Section 4.7) could be adapted to study some of the underappreciated implications of DNA being double stranded [28, 29]. This might be done by employing two Activity Registers running in parallel, one using the odd numbers and the other the even numbers. Loading one Activity Register (corresponding to creating a nonequilibrium hyperstructure) would require ATP whilst loading the other Activity Register (corresponding to creating an equilibrium hyperstructure) would require the absence of ATP (Section 4.8). This might allow two phenotypes to be selected simultaneously so as to balance the scales of equilibria (Section 4.8). More interesting still would be to create a hierarchy of Activity Registers or to allow Coco itself to create them during learning.

4.10. Free-Running, Dreaming, and Looking Ahead. If Coco's environment were partially disconnected, Coco can continue running—more exactly, free-running—in the absence of inputs. Such free-running would occur if the environment were not to respond immediately to an output. Periods of free-running could be used to play in a sandbox or to dream. A sandbox is a concept that refers to a software environment where potentially dangerous operations can be tested in isolation, thus reducing the chances of damaging the primary program. Using a sandbox allows risk-free exploratory behaviour and, in a sense, corresponds to Coco operating in a look-ahead mode. In this mode, Coco might be disconnected from the environment and run through different combinations of stored input and output modules (where modules are sequential lines of the Activity Register). These modules might be associated with special elements 12 and 13 to represent pleasure and pain, respectively, depending on whether they have been rewarded or punished. Starting from the present state, Coco might load the Activity Register with different addresses for different runs (e.g., 20 timesteps) and compare the pleasure index (e.g., sum of $12/(12 + 13)$) for these runs (in which inputs from the environment are replaced by those stored in the modules). The initial loading of the Activity Register corresponding to the most successful run would then be adopted and environmental inputs once again were allowed.

Hypotheses about the function of dreaming might be explored via the creation of a parallel set of objects copied from the normal ones, namely, a DreamActivity Register running in dream time with DreamElements, DreamNow, and DreamNext. Perhaps this could be used to discover and remedy pathogenic connectivities that lead the system to get stuck in deep basins of attraction and so forth. Such action might be based on a characterisation of the states in the Activity Register. For example, for each line in the Activity Register, the ten addresses have elements where each contains seven Now addresses and seven Next addresses, hence a total for the line of 70 Now addresses and 70 Next addresses. Each line, alias the state of the system at that time, can therefore be characterised by a pair of coordinates (different Now addresses, different Next addresses). Intuitively, a successful state should tend towards (length of line, length of line)—here (10, 10)—whilst an unsuccessful state should tend towards (length of line × size of Now field, length of line × size of Next field)—here (70, 70). (This is not strictly speaking correct, but it gives the flavour.) The sequence of these coordinates then constitutes a function that might be recognised and used during dreaming.

A different approach would be to use dreaming to make a landscape of the connection space by loading the Activity Register with different elements and then letting it run so as to determine state cycles and basins of attraction; when the program has done, it might be possible to modify the connections so as to maximise the use of the landscape and connect basins. One attractive possibility is that Coco acts during free-running to minimise conflict between the Next and Now processes. This would take the form of changing the connections so that in loading addresses into a line of the Activity Register the same elements are scored highly by both processes. It amounts to making the Next and Now processes coherent with one another. Indeed, insofar as incoherence results in unhappiness, it could even be argued that this would create a state of happiness in systems as different as men, bacteria, and machines!

How far away is all this from real biology? Is the dreaming envisaged here only relevant to higher organisms or does it extend, for example, to bacteria? If that were the case, related questions include how we would know that a bacterium was dreaming and what it would mean for the bacterium. Showing that dreaming had a role in the learning of Coco might cast some light on its potential evolutionary value for all organisms.

4.11. Varying the Size of the Now and Next Fields. In the version presented here, the Now and Next fields are of constant size (each contains 7 addresses). This is far from biological reality where networks generally contain nodes with very different connectivities, including hubs and "driver" nodes [30–32]. These connectivities can take the form of protein activators and repressors of gene expression [33], small molecules acting on functioning-dependent structures [34], ions travelling along charged filaments such as microtubules or DNA [35], ions and molecules moving along and through pili and nanotubes [36, 37], convergence on common frequencies of oscillation [38, 39], joining a hyperstructure [25], and so forth. Coco would be much closer to modelling reality if the size of the fields were to vary as a function of learning (one reason for this is that increasing the size of a field permits element X to have stronger connections to element Y because X's field can hold more copies of Y's address). This may prove relatively easy to implement: for example, rewarding and punishing might entail increasing and decreasing the fields, respectively (as well as overwriting).

The relative strengths of the Now and Next connections can also be modified via the NowNextWeighting. As shown in Sections 3.1 and 3.2, setting NowNextWeighting very low or very high makes Coco run with either just Nexts or just Nows. Insofar as Next connections can be equated with local connections and Now connections with global connections, changing the value of NowNextWeighting can result in a phase transition in connectivity with similarity perhaps to the great deluge algorithm [40] or to Dual-Phase Evolution [41] or even, in the world of microbiology, to maintaining the right ratio of nonequilibrium to equilibrium hyperstructures within cells [23].

4.12. An Interactive Environment. An output is immediately followed by an environmental input that does not depend on the nature of the output. There is no possibility therefore for the present version of the program to influence the environment. This excludes the richness of connections that may emerge from dialogues between a learning system such as Coco and its environment. Two-way connections between a biological system such as a bacterium and its environment are fundamental and trying to understand them using Coco might take the form of Coco learning to play a simple game such as Noughts and Crosses (Tic-Tac-Toe).

4.13. Three or More Fields: from, Now, and Next and So Forth. The addition of a From field might add a new dimension to Coco. A From field would record the addresses of elements which preceded successful states in which the element was active. This would allow Coco to run backwards during Dreamtime (Section 4.10), analogous perhaps to the way humans mull over the day's events. In this speculation, such running might then allow input-output modules with similar characteristics to be identified (Section 4.10) and eventually connected via yet another, higher-level field involving a higher-level Activity Register. This, we would like to think, might be the equivalent of generating concepts.

4.14. Size of the Active Set. The size of the Active Set is an important parameter that can be changed and, in particular, increased, to take into account biological systems in which many elements can be active at the same time. In the present version of the program, the maximum size of the Activity Register is limited by the number of elements and by DOWNTIME (Section 2.7). This limits the size of the Active Set to around 80. An example of results obtained with an Activity Register containing 60 addresses is shown in Figure 18. Increasing the number of elements to, for example, 4000, allows learning with an Activity Register containing 100 addresses (Figure 18). It may prove important under some circumstances for Coco itself to modify the size of the Active Set. This might be the case if an input were to arrive "out of the blue" when Coco is in free-running mode; if an input were to trigger a sudden change in the size of the Activity Register, this could have a major effect, perhaps similar to that reported for the effects of a stimulus on connectivity in the cortex (for references see [41]) and perhaps similar too to the greater receptivity of bacteria to their environment when conditions start to worsen [42].

4.15. Collaborative Coherence. It will not have escaped the attention of the reader that, instead of separating the scores of the elements in competition for inclusion in the Active Set into Next and Now scores, these scores could be added together or even be combined synergistically to yield a kind of collaborative coherence. Philosophically, it would be nice to escape competition but we have no preliminary evidence that collaborative coherence leads to learning.

4.16. Pain and Pleasure. The present version punishes incorrect responses by randomly overwriting connections.

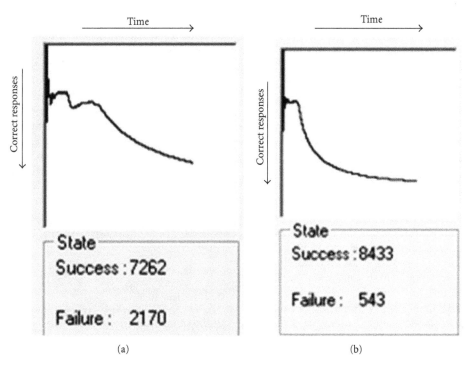

FIGURE 18: Examples of successful learning with (a) 1000 elements and an Activity Register containing 60 addresses. (b) 4000 elements and an Activity Register containing 100 addresses.

This squanders a lot of information. A potentially better approach would be to retain and reuse information about mistakes by, for example, making use of specific elements such as 12 and 13 to represent pleasure and pain, respectively, in combination with a LOOK AHEAD subroutine (Section 4.10). Rewarding successful states might then entail writing a 12 into the Now and Next fields of the elements whose addresses are in the rewarded line of the Activity Register and, reciprocally, punishing might entail writing a 13 into them. This information could then be exploited using the LOOK AHEAD subroutine sketched out before that would count and compare the total of the addresses of these two elements when looking into possible futures (Section 4.10). An interesting question here is what would end up in the Now and Next fields of elements 12 and 13 themselves. Presumably, these fields would reflect connections to common, strong sources of pleasure and pain; these connections might then be used to drive the system towards or away from these sources.

4.17. Long-Term Memory. One way to obtain a long-term memory would be via a connections' matrix (number of elements × number of elements) that would record Now connections between elements that had participated in the same successful state (there could be similar ones for Next connections and, perhaps, further two matrices for unsuccessful states). A SUCCESSFUL CONNECTIONS subroutine could then be used to prevent overwriting successful connections or, at least, to alter the probability of overwriting these connections.

4.18. Noncyclical Input Sequences. Cycles are of major importance in biology. A primary example is the cell cycle which still remains to be fully understood [43]. The learning task presented here is based on an input sequence that is presented cyclically. Each output is immediately followed by a new input; at no time does Coco "run on its own" or run freely (Section 4.10). In responding to an input that "comes out of nowhere," as in the case of the first input in a linear series of inputs, the size of the Activity Register may be important (Section 4.14). One might envisage that during free-running the Activity Register would be small but would increase greatly on receiving an input; such increase might enable an input to make a decisive contribution to the composition of the Activity Register, particularly in the case of a variable K number since in such conditions, and when learning has occurred, the Now and Next fields of inputs become large (Section 4.11, unpublished data). It would also be interesting to explore the effects (on responding to an unannounced input) of changes to connectivity made during free-running (Section 4.10), changes that might even include modification of the weights associated with the Now and Next fields of inputs; such temporary modifications could be made during looking ahead.

Free-running whilst waiting for an input would entail Coco filling the Activity Register and wandering through the enormity of the combinatorial space in a state cycle [6]. The nature and length of such cycles may prove an important parameter in learning to respond to inputs that are given at random intervals from one another and from the outputs. This is because it is of little value in learning to connect (via the Next process) an active state containing an input to the active state that immediately precedes it if this preceding state is hardly ever repeated. A possible solution would be for Coco to enter a short state cycle whilst waiting for the next input such that each input in the sequence was accessible from its own preceding state cycle. It is conceivable that these cycles might again be generated by the changes in connectivity occurring during dreaming (Section 4.10).

5. Relationship to Existing Systems

Hopfield's network model [44] uses the same learning rule as used by Hebb in which learning occurs as a result of the strengthening of the weights of the links between nodes [45]; this resembles the strengthening of links in Coco by the writing of addresses into the Now and Next fields of elements. In the Hopfield model it is assumed that the individual units preserve their individual states until they are selected at random for a new update; in Coco, the elements also preserve their identity until they are selected, but this selection is confined to members of the Active Set and occurs during rewarding and punishing. In a Hopfield network, each unit is connected to all other units (except itself); in Coco, each element can only be connected to a few others (the Knumber) via the Now and Next fields. A Hopfield network is symmetric because the weight of the link between unit i and unit j equals that between unit j and unit i; the network in Coco is asymmetric. In a Hopfield network, all the nodes contribute to the change in the activation of any single node at any one time; in Coco, only the elements (nodes/units) in the previous Active Set and in the developing Active Set contribute to the activation of an element (node/unit). In a Hopfield network, there is one type of connection between the nodes; in Coco, there are two types of connection—Next and Now. In a Hopfield network, the units can be in a state of either 1 or 0; similarly, in Coco, the elements can be either active or inactive.

It might be argued that a Hopfield network is a type of the Coco program. For example, if an attempt were to be made to turn Coco into a Hopfield network, (1) the size of the Knumber would be set similar to the size of the Enumber (i.e., the total number of elements) to make it closer to a weighting factor that takes into account all elements, (2) the activity of an element would be determined by its absolute score (using a threshold) rather than by its score relative to a limited number of competing elements, (3) the Anumber (the size of the Active Set) would therefore become a variable whose size would vary with the number of elements deemed to be active, (4) the Next links would correspond to the links between nodes but the Now links would have no equivalent, (5) the asymmetrical Coco network would tend towards symmetry if changes in the links to element i in the Next field of element j were accompanied by reciprocal changes in the links to element j in the Next field of element i (of course, Coco would then no longer run in the same way), and (6) some of the biologically relevant developments of Coco would have to be implemented in a Hopfield network which would be hard since Coco lends itself to the study of types of links with different properties; see Sections 4.6

and 4.7. In this context, it should be stressed that the weights in Coco are discrete, transparent, and easy to study and to manipulate.

Boolean networks have been extensively used to model biological systems. Thomas and collaborators have developed logical analysis which they have used both to study specific systems [46] and to derive general principles [47]. From such analyses, predictions can be made for experimental biologists to test. Logical analysis is not, however, a learning system like Coco. Reciprocally, Coco is not designed at present to model specific biological systems. As mentioned in Section 1, the (N, k) Boolean network of Kauffman [6] has given insight into the dynamics of biological systems and, in particular, into the concept of cells as living on the "edge of chaos" [2, 3]. But again, it is not a learning system like Coco.

6. Discussion

Few would deny that living systems are rich, complicated, and (hyper)complex. Such systems are often, almost necessarily, modelled and simulated by invoking Occam's Razor and adopting a reductionist approach. Life may, however, have originated as a rich, complicated, and diverse system, as, in other words, a prebiotic ecology [48]. In attempting to capture some of the characteristics of living system in a program, we have therefore adopted the holist approach of putting everything in and seeing what, if anything, emerges. To try to create a test-bed for concepts and to ensure that these concepts have some substance, we have written a program with a learning part, Coco. Coco contains parameters that may have very loose equivalents in aspects of evolution via global (as opposed to local) mutation, DNA replication, emergence, life on the scales of equilibria, and even the generation of concepts and dreaming. Most importantly, Coco is based on coherence.

Coherence characterises living systems. Coherence mechanisms operating—or suspected by some to operate—at the level of cells include tensegrity, ion condensation, DNA supercoiling, and a variety of oscillations [25, 48–52] plus, of course, mechanisms based on the usual activators and repressors of transcription along with DNA packaging proteins. Competitive coherence is an attempt to describe how bacterial phenotypes are created by a competition between maintaining a consistent story over time and creating a response that is coherent with respect to both internal and external conditions. Previously, it has been proposed that the bacterium *E. coli* can be considered as passing through a series of states in which a distinct set of its constituent molecules or "elements" are active [8]. The activity of these elements is determined by a competition between two processes. One of these processes depends on the previous cell state whilst the other depends on the internal coherence of the developing state. The simultaneous operation of these two processes is competitive coherence. Competitive coherence is in fact a scale-free concept. It can be applied to a population of bacteria such as a colony in which each cell is an element with its own Now and Next fields. In this case, a typical Now process might involve global connections via a sonic vibration created by the combined metabolic activity of all the growing cells in the colony (which constitute the Active Set) [38] whilst the Next process might involve essentially local connections via diffusible molecules, sex pili, and lipid nanotubes [37]. We have invoked competitive coherence at higher levels to explain, for example, how a football team is selected. It is perhaps no longer original in computer science since the idea of two competing processes staggered in time can be found elsewhere in Simple Recurrent Networks [53]. What may be new is the possibility that the implementation of competitive coherence into a learning program could give rise to parameters suitable for describing the rich form of complexity found in living systems which depends on the interaction between many types of connection and which we have termed hypercomplexity [10]. The preliminary results from the toy program presented here encourage us to think that this may be the case.

One of these preliminary results is on the maximum size of the Activity Register that can result in Coco learning (Section 4.14). In Section 1, we mentioned the problem of how cells manage to negotiate the enormity of phenotype space in a reproducible and selectable way [6]; if, for example, a phenotype were determined by a simple combination of on-off expression of genes, a bacterium like *E. coli* with over 4000 genes would have the difficult task of exploring 2^{4000} combinations. (It should be noted though that no one knows how many genes are expressed at one time in an individual cell, let alone how many of these expressed genes are actually determining the phenotype, that is, form part of the Active Set.) However, if the phenotype were determined not directly by genes but at a higher level by a hundred or so extended macromolecular assemblies or *hyperstructures* comprising many different macromolecules—for which there is good evidence [25, 54, 55]—the number of on-off combinations would fall to 2^{100}. As we show here, a system with 4000 elements, of which a hundred form an Active Set, can learn via competitive coherence.

Finally, if there is any substance to our claim that competitive coherence is a fundamental to life, perhaps even its defining characteristic [56], the concept should be of value in novel approaches to computing inspired by and reliant on the way real cells behave [11].

7. Conclusion

Competitive coherence is a concept used to describe how a subset of elements out of a large set is activated to determine behaviour. It has been proposed as operating at many levels in biology. The results of the toy version of a type of neural network, based on competitive coherence, are presented here and show that it can learn. This is consistent with competitive coherence playing a central role in living systems. The parameters responsible for the functioning of the competitive coherence part of the program, which, for example, are related to complexity and emergence, may be of interest to biologists and others.

Acknowledgments

For helpful discussions, the authors thank Abdallah Zemirline, Alex Grossman, Francois Kepes, Jacques Ninio, and Michel Thellier. They also thank the anonymous referees for many valuable comments. For support they thank the Epigenomics Project, Evry, and the University of Brest. This paper is dedicated to the memory of Maurice Demarty.

References

[1] D. E. Ingber, "The origin of cellular life," *Bioessays*, vol. 22, no. 12, pp. 1160–1170, 2000.

[2] J. P. Crutchfield and K. Young, "Computation at the edge of chaos," in *Complexity, Entropy and the Physics of Information: SFI Studies in the Sciences of Complexity*, W. H. Zurek, Ed., pp. 223–269, Addison-Wesley, Reading, Mass, USA, 1990.

[3] C. G. Langton, "Computation at the edge of chaos: phase transitions and emergent computation," *Physica D*, vol. 42, no. 1–3, pp. 12–37, 1990.

[4] D. J. Watts and S. H. Strogatz, "Collective dynamics of 'small-world9 networks," *Nature*, vol. 393, no. 6684, pp. 440–442, 1998.

[5] P. Bak, *How Nature Works: The Science of Self-Organized Criticality*, Copernicus, New York, NY, USA, 1996.

[6] S. Kauffman, *At Home in the Universe, the Search for the Laws of Complexity*, Penguin, London, UK, 1996.

[7] D. Bray, "Intracellular signalling as a parallel distributed process," *Journal of Theoretical Biology*, vol. 143, no. 2, pp. 215–231, 1990.

[8] V. Norris, "Modelling *Escherichia coli* The concept of competitive coherence," *Comptes Rendus de l'Academie des Sciences*, vol. 321, no. 9, pp. 777–787, 1998.

[9] V. Norris, "Competitive coherence," in *Encyclopedia of Sciences and Religions*, N. P. Azari, A. Runehov, and L. Oviedo, Eds., Springer, New York, NY, USA, 2012.

[10] V. Norris, A. Cabin, and A. Zemirline, "Hypercomplexity," *Acta Biotheoretica*, vol. 53, no. 4, pp. 313–330, 2005.

[11] V. Norris, A. Zemirline, P. Amar et al., "Computing with bacterial constituents, cells and populations: from bioputing to bactoputing," *Theory in Biosciences*, pp. 1–18, 2011.

[12] S. G. Wolf, D. Frenkiel, T. Arad, S. E. Finkeil, R. Kolter, and A. Minsky, "DNA protection by stress-induced biocrystallization," *Nature*, vol. 400, no. 6739, pp. 83–85, 1999.

[13] V. Norris and M. S. Madsen, "Autocatalytic gene expression occurs via transertion and membrane domain formation and underlies differentiation in bacteria: a model," *Journal of Molecular Biology*, vol. 253, no. 5, pp. 739–748, 1995.

[14] T. Katayama, S. Ozaki, K. Keyamura, and K. Fujimitsu, "Regulation of the replication cycle: conserved and diverse regulatory systems for DnaA and oriC," *Nature Reviews Microbiology*, vol. 8, no. 3, pp. 163–170, 2010.

[15] V. Norris, C. Woldringh, and E. Mileykovskaya, "A hypothesis to explain division site selection in *Escherichia coli* by combining nucleoid occlusion and Min," *FEBS Letters*, vol. 561, no. 1–3, pp. 3–10, 2004.

[16] Y. Grondin, D. J. Raine, and V. Norris, "The correlation between architecture and mRNA abundance in the genetic regulatory network of *Escherichia coli*," *BMC Systems Biology*, vol. 1, p. 30, 2007.

[17] C. L. Woldrinh and N. Nanninga, "Structure of the nucleoid and cytoplasm in the intact cell," in *Molecular Cytology of*

Escherichia coli, N. Nanninga, Ed., pp. 161–197, Academic Press, London, UK, 1985.

[18] V. Norris, L. Janniere, and P. Amar, "Hypothesis: variations in the rate of DNA replication determine the phenotype of daughter cells," in *Modelling Complex Biological Systems in the Context of Genomics*, EDP Sciences, Evry, France, 2007.

[19] L. H. Hartwell and T. A. Weinert, "Checkpoints: controls that ensure the order of cell cycle events," *Science*, vol. 246, no. 4930, pp. 629–634, 1989.

[20] A. L. Barabási and R. Albert, "Emergence of scaling in random networks," *Science*, vol. 286, no. 5439, pp. 509–512, 1999.

[21] M. H. V. Van Regenmortel, "Emergence in Biology," in *Modelling and Simulation of Biological Processes in the Context of Genomics*, P. Amar, V. Norris, G. Bernot et al., Eds., pp. 123–132, Genopole, Evry, France, 2004.

[22] K. S. Jeong, Y. Xie, H. Hiasa, and A. B. Khodursky, "Analysis of pleiotropic transcriptional profiles: a case study of DNA gyrase inhibition.," *PLoS Genetics*, vol. 2, no. 9, p. e152, 2006.

[23] V. Norris, M. Demarty, D. Raine, A. Cabin-Flaman, and L. Le Sceller, "Hypothesis: hyperstructures regulate initiation in *Escherichia coli* and other bacteria," *Biochimie*, vol. 84, no. 4, pp. 341–347, 2002.

[24] A. Minsky, E. Shimoni, and D. Frenkiel-Krispin, "Stress, order and survival," *Nature Reviews Molecular Cell Biology*, vol. 3, no. 1, pp. 50–60, 2002.

[25] V. Norris, T. Den Blaauwen, R. H. Doi et al., "Toward a hyperstructure taxonomy," *Annual Review of Microbiology*, vol. 61, pp. 309–329, 2007.

[26] V. Norris, "Speculations on the initiation of chromosome replication in *Escherichia coli*: the dualism hypothesis," *Medical Hypotheses*, vol. 76, no. 5, pp. 706–716, 2011.

[27] V. Norris and P. Amar, "Life on the scales: initiation of replication in *Escherichia coli*," in *Modelling Complex Biological Systems in the Context of Genomics*, EDF Sciences, Evry, France, 2012.

[28] E. P. C. Rocha, J. Fralick, G. Vediyappan, A. Danchin, and V. Norris, "A strand-specific model for chromosome segregation in bacteria," *Molecular Microbiology*, vol. 49, no. 4, pp. 895–903, 2003.

[29] M. A. White, J. K. Eykelenboom, M. A. Lopez-Vernaza, E. Wilson, and D. R. F. Leach, "Non-random segregation of sister chromosomes in *Escherichia coli*," *Nature*, vol. 455, no. 7217, pp. 1248–1250, 2008.

[30] D. J. Raine and V. Norris, *Metabolic cycles and self-organised criticality*. Interjournal of complex systems, Paper 361, http://www.interjournal.org/, 2000.

[31] A. L. Barabási and Z. N. Oltvai, "Network biology: understanding the cell's functional organization," *Nature Reviews Genetics*, vol. 5, no. 2, pp. 101–113, 2004.

[32] Y. Y. Liu, J. J. Slotine, and A. L. Barabási, "Controllability of complex networks," *Nature*, vol. 473, no. 7346, pp. 167–173, 2011.

[33] N. Guelzim, S. Bottani, P. Bourgine, and F. Képès, "Topological and causal structure of the yeast transcriptional regulatory network," *Nature Genetics*, vol. 31, no. 1, pp. 60–63, 2002.

[34] M. Thellier, G. Legent, P. Amar, V. Norris, and C. Ripoll, "Steady-state kinetic behaviour of functioning-dependent structures," *FEBS Journal*, vol. 273, no. 18, pp. 4287–4299, 2006.

[35] C. Ripoll, V. Norris, and M. Thellier, "Ion condensation and signal transduction," *BioEssays*, vol. 26, no. 5, pp. 549–557, 2004.

[36] G. Reguera, K. D. McCarthy, T. Mehta, J. S. Nicoll, M. T. Tuominen, and D. R. Lovley, "Extracellular electron transfer via microbial nanowires," *Nature*, vol. 435, no. 7045, pp. 1098–1101, 2005.

[37] G. P. Dubey and S. Ben-Yehuda, "Intercellular nanotubes mediate bacterial communication," *Cell*, vol. 144, no. 4, pp. 590–600, 2011.

[38] M. Matsuhashi, A. N. Pankrushina, K. Endoh et al., "Bacillus carboniphilus cells respond to growth-promoting physical signals from cells of homologous and heterologous bacteria," *Journal of General and Applied Microbiology*, vol. 42, no. 4, pp. 315–323, 1996.

[39] G. Reguera, "When microbial conversations get physical," *Trends in Microbiology*, vol. 19, no. 3, pp. 105–113, 2011.

[40] G. Dueck, "New optimization heuristics; The great deluge algorithm and the record-to-record travel," *Journal of Computational Physics*, vol. 104, no. 1, pp. 86–92, 1993.

[41] G. Paperin, D. G. Green, and S. Sadedin, "Dual-phase evolution in complex adaptive systems," *Journal of the Royal Society Interface*, vol. 8, no. 58, pp. 609–629, 2011.

[42] J. Vohradský and J. J. Ramsden, "Genome resource utilization during prokaryotic development," *The FASEB Journal*, vol. 15, no. 11, pp. 2054–2056, 2001.

[43] X. Wang, C. Lesterlin, R. Reyes-Lamothe, G. Ball, and D. J. Sherratt, "Replication and segregation of an *Escherichia coli* chromosome with two replication origins," *Proceedings of the National Academy of Sciences of the United States of America*, vol. 108, no. 26, pp. E243–E250, 2011.

[44] J. J. Hopfield, "Neural networks and physical systems with emergent collective computational abilities," *Proceedings of the National Academy of Sciences of the United States of America*, vol. 79, no. 8, pp. 2554–2558, 1982.

[45] D. O. Hebb, *The Organization of Behavior*, Wiley and Sons, New York, NY, USA, 1949.

[46] M. Kaufman, J. Urbain, and R. Thomas, "Towards a logical analysis of the immune response," *Journal of Theoretical Biology*, vol. 114, no. 4, pp. 527–561, 1985.

[47] R. Thomas, D. Thieffry, and M. Kaufman, "Dynamical behaviour of biological regulatory networks I. Biological role of feedback loops and practical use of the concept of the loop-characteristic state," *Bulletin of Mathematical Biology*, vol. 57, no. 2, pp. 247–276, 1995.

[48] A. Hunding, F. Kepes, D. Lancet et al., "Compositional complementarity and prebiotic ecology in the origin of life," *BioEssays*, vol. 28, no. 4, pp. 399–412, 2006.

[49] H. Fröhlich, "Long range coherence and energy storage in biological systems," *International Journal of Quantum Chemistry*, vol. 42, no. 5, pp. 641–649, 1968.

[50] V. Norris and G. J. Hyland, "Do bacteria sing? Sonic intercellular communication between bacteria may reflect electromagnetic intracellular communication involving coherent collective vibrational modes that could integrate enzyme activities and gene expression," *Molecular Microbiology*, vol. 24, no. 4, pp. 879–880, 1997.

[51] D. E. Ingber, "The architecture of life," *Scientific American*, vol. 278, no. 1, pp. 48–57, 1998.

[52] A. Travers and G. Muskhelishvili, "DNA supercoiling—a global transcriptional regulator for enterobacterial growth?" *Nature Reviews Microbiology*, vol. 3, no. 2, pp. 157–169, 2005.

[53] J. L. Elman, "An alternative view of the mental lexicon," *Trends in Cognitive Sciences*, vol. 8, no. 7, pp. 301–306, 2004.

[54] R. Narayanaswamy, M. Levy, M. Tsechansky et al., "Widespread reorganization of metabolic enzymes into reversible assemblies upon nutrient starvation," *Proceedings of the National Academy of Sciences of the United States of America*, vol. 106, no. 25, pp. 10147–10152, 2009.

[55] P. M. Llopis, A. F. Jackson, O. Sliusarenko et al., "Spatial organization of the flow of genetic information in bacteria," *Nature*, vol. 466, no. 7302, pp. 77–81, 2010.

[56] V. Norris, P. Amar, G. Bernot et al., "Questions for cell cyclists," *Journal of Biological Physics and Chemistry*, vol. 4, pp. 124–130, 2004.

9

Hemodialysis Key Features Mining and Patients Clustering Technologies

Tzu-Chuen Lu and Chun-Ya Tseng

Department of Information Management, Chaoyang University of Technology, Wufeng District, Taichung 41349, Taiwan

Correspondence should be addressed to Tzu-Chuen Lu, tclu@cyut.edu.tw

Academic Editor: Anke Meyer-Baese

The kidneys are very vital organs. Failing kidneys lose their ability to filter out waste products, resulting in kidney disease. To extend or save the lives of patients with impaired kidney function, kidney replacement is typically utilized, such as hemodialysis. This work uses an entropy function to identify key features related to hemodialysis. By identifying these key features, one can determine whether a patient requires hemodialysis. This work uses these key features as dimensions in cluster analysis. The key features can effectively determine whether a patient requires hemodialysis. The proposed data mining scheme finds association rules of each cluster. Hidden rules for causing any kidney disease can therefore be identified. The contributions and key points of this paper are as follows. (1) This paper finds some key features that can be used to predict the patient who may has high probability to perform hemodialysis. (2) The proposed scheme applies k-means clustering algorithm with the key features to category the patients. (3) A data mining technique is used to find the association rules from each cluster. (4) The mined rules can be used to determine whether a patient requires hemodialysis.

1. Introduction

The human kidney is located on the posterior abdominal wall on both sides of the spinal column. The main functions of the kidney include metabolism control, waste and toxin excretion, regulation of blood pressure, and maintaining the body's fluid balance. All blood in the body passes through the kidney 20 times per hour. When renal function is impaired, the body's waste cannot be metabolized, which can result in back pain, edema, uremia, high blood pressure, inflammation of the urethra, lethargy, insomnia, tinnitus, hair loss, blurred vision, slow reaction time, depression, fear, mental disorders, and other adverse consequences. Furthermore, an impaired kidney will produce and secrete erythropoietin. When secretion of red blood cells is insufficient, patients will have the anemia. The kidney also helps maintain the calcium and phosphate balance in blood, such that a patient with renal failure may develop bone lesions.

When renal function is abnormal, toxins can be produced, damaging organs and possibly leading to death. To extend or save the lives of patients with impaired kidney function, kidney replacement is typically utilized, including kidney transplantation, hemodialysis (HD), and peritoneal dialysis (PD). Although kidney transplantation is the most clinically effective method, few donor kidneys are available and transplantation can be limited by the physical conditions of patients. Notably, HD can extend the lives of kidney patients.

Although medical technology is mature, factors causing diseases are changing due to changing environments. Any factor may potentially lead to disease. When the detection index of a patient exceeds the standard and kidney disease has been diagnosed, patients must go the hospital for kidney replacement therapy. For instance, a doctor may recommend that high-risk patients adjust their habits by, say, stopping smoking, controlling blood pressure, maintaining normal urination, controlling urinary protein levels, maintaining normal sleeping patterns, controlling blood sugar levels, reducing the use of medications, avoiding reductions in the body's resistance, maintaining low body fat levels, and reducing the burden on the kidneys.

However, improving one's physical condition and diet are insufficient. To control one's physical condition, periodic health examinations at a hospital have become a common disease-prevention strategy. Doctors may offer advice to patients based on health examination results to reduce disease risk.

Many scholars have applied data mining techniques for disease prediction. These techniques include clustering, association rules, and time-series analysis. Different analyses may require different mining techniques. Selection of an appropriate mining technique is the key to obtaining valuable data. However, choosing a data mining technique is very difficult for general hospitals, especially when dealing with different forms of original data. Therefore, to help medical professionals identify hidden factors that cause kidney diseases, this work applies a novel hemodialysis system (HD system). The HD system may identify factors not previously known.

General medical staff may perform routine examinations for particular factors associated with a particular disease and ignore other factors that may be associated with other diseases, such as kidney diseases. For example, staff may only assess blood urea nitrogen (BUN) and creatinine (CRE) levels and CRE clearance (CC). However, increasing amounts of data indicate that some hidden rules and relationships may exist. Therefore, this work uses an entropy function to identify key features related to HD. By identifying these key features, one can determine whether a patient requires HD. This work uses these key features as dimensions in cluster analysis. When patients requiring HD are classified into the same group, and the other patients are classified into the other group, the key features can effectively determine whether a patient requires HD. The proposed data mining scheme finds association rules of each cluster. Hidden rules for causing any kidney disease can therefore be identified.

2. Literature Review

2.1. Hemodialysis. Hemodialysis is also called dialysis. An artificial kidney discharges uremic toxins and water to eliminate uremic symptoms. In an HD system, a semipermeable membrane separates the blood and dialysate. The human blood continues passing through on one side of an artificial kidney and the dialysate carries away uremic toxins on the other side. Finally, the cleaned blood will back into the body. This continuous cycle eventually purifies blood.

A doctor may recommend that patient undergo dialysis according to the difference between acute and chronic. If kidney failure is acute, the doctor will recommend that the patient undergo dialysis before the occurrence of uremic

toxins accumulate. For chronic kidney failure, medical treatment is first utilized and HD may be initiated after uremia occurs. Additionally, a doctor may assess according to the causes of kidney failure, kidney size, anemic state, degradation of kidney function, and recovery. Moreover, each examination indicator will be assessed. The most commonly used indicators are BUN concentration, CRE concentration, CC, urine-specific gravity, and osmotic pressure [1, 2].

2.1.1. Blood Urea Nitrogen (BUN). Blood urea nitrogen is the metabolite of proteins and amino acids excreted by the kidneys. The BUN concentration in blood can be used to determine whether kidney function is normal. The normal BUN range is 10–20 mg/dL. If the BUN concentration exceeds 20 mg/dL, this is called high azotemia. However, the BUN concentration may increase temporarily because of dehydration, eating large amounts of high-protein foods, upper gastrointestinal bleeding, severe liver disease, infection, steroid use, and impaired kidney blood flow. When the BUN concentration is high and the CRE concentration is normal, kidney function is normal. Although the BUN concentration can be used as an indicator of kidney function, it is not as accurate as the CRE concentration and CC.

2.1.2. Creatinine (CRE). Creatinine is mainly a metabolite of muscle activity and daily production is excreted through the kidneys. Daily CRE production cannot be fully excreted and the CRE concentration increases when TRY kidney function is impaired. As the CRE concentration increases, kidney function decreases. Because CRE is a waste generated by muscle metabolism, the CRE concentration is associated with the total amount of muscle or weight but is not related to diet or water intake. The CRE concentration may reflect kidney function more accurately than the BUN concentration. When the CRE concentration is in the normal range, it does mean that kidney function is normal; that is, CC is a better tool when assessing kidney function. The compensatory capacity of the kidney is large. For example, although the CRE concentration may increase from 1.4 mg/dL to 1.5 mg/dL, kidney function may have declined by more than 50%.

2.1.3. Creatinine Clearance (CC). Creatinine clearance is widely used and is an accurate estimation of kidney function. Creatinine Clearance is the amount of CRE cleared per minute. The CC for a healthy person is 80–120 mL/min; the average is 100 mL/min. Kidney failure is minor when the CC is 50–70 mL/min and moderate when CC is only 30–50 mL/min. If CC is <30 mL/min, kidney failure is severe and uremic symptoms will develop gradually. When CC is <10 gradually, a patient must start dialysis. By collecting all the urine produced within 24 hours, CC can be determined easily. Notably, CC is derived as follows:

$$CC = \frac{\text{Urine } CRE_{concentration} \ (mg\%) \times 24 \text{ hours urine volume (c.c.)}}{\text{Blood } CRE_{concentration} \ (mg\%) \times 1440 \ (minutes)}. \tag{1}$$

2.1.4. Urine-Specific Gravity and Osmotic Pressure. Urine-specific gravity and osmotic pressure reflects the ability of the kidney to concentrate urine. If the specific gravity of urine is ≤1.018 or each urine-specific gravity gap is ≤0.008, the ability of the kidney to concentrate urine is impaired. Moreover, the ratio of osmolality to blood osmotic pressure must exceed 1.0; otherwise, the ability of the kidney to concentrate urine is impaired. If the ratio of urine to blood osmotic pressure is ≤3 after water fasting for 12 hours, the ability of the kidney to concentrate urine is impaired. Abnormal urine concentration function usually occurs in patients with analgesic nephropathy.

Doctors recommend patients undergo dialysis when their BUN concentration exceeds 90 mg/dL, the CRE concentration exceeds 9 mg/dL, and CC is <0.17 mL/sec, or the CRE concentration exceeds 707.2 mg/dL. However, when the BUN concentration begins increasing, the kidney is very fragile. That is, the kidney that has been damaged exceeds 1/3 when HD is required [3]. Thus, indexes such as the albumin globulin ratio (A/G ratio) of kidney function (Table 1), red blood cell (RBC) count in blood tests (Table 2), or white blood cell (WBC) count by urinalysis (Table 3) are related to kidney function [1]. This work proposes an effective scheme that identifies unknown key features to predict HD. This work uses the entropy function to identify key features that are strongly related to HD and applies the k-means clustering algorithm to these key features to group patients.

Hung proposed an association rule mining with multiple minimum supports for predicting hospitalization of HD patients [4]. Hung used this association rule to analyze factors that may lead to HD to reduce the number of patients hospitalized for kidney impairment.

Hung relied on routinely examined HD indexes for patients per month, including BUN, CRE, uric acid (UA), natrium (Na), potassium (K), calcium (Ca), phosphate (IP), and alkaline phosphatase levels and analyzed 667 derived variables, such as protein ratio, to determine whether monocytes infected or a patient was undernourished. Hung obtained 9 rules from 5,793 records. For instance, diabetic patients with high cholesterol levels were hospitalized most. Inadequate dialysis was a high risk factor for hospitalization. If patient is female, aged 40–49, infected with monocytes, and had a recent hemoglobin (Hb/Ht) test value that was too low, the frequency of hospitalization was high. If hematocrit (Ht) was abnormal twice in the last three months, average platelet volume (MPV) was abnormal twice, and total protein (TP) was abnormal once, the probability of hospitalization was 93%. If TP, glutamic oxaloacetic transaminase (GOT), and glutamic pyruvic transaminase (GPT) of patients were abnormal twice in the last three months and uric acid was also abnormal, hospitalization risk was 100%.

Huang analyzed risk of mortality for patients on long-term HD in 2009 [5]. Huang used the Classification and Regression Tree, Mann-Whitney *U* Test, Chi-square Test, Pearson Correlation, and the Nomogram to analyze 992 patients on long-term HD. Albumin level and age were the factors most strongly related to mortality. Huang clustered and analyzed patients. If a patient had good nutrition and was young, mortality of diabetic patients was 5.45 times

TABLE 1: Kidney function test features.

Kidney function test items		Reference	Units
Blood urea nitrogen	BUN	5–25	mg/dL
Creatinine	CRE	0.3–1.4	mg/dL
Uric acid	UA	2.5–7.0	mg/dL
Albumin-globulin in ratio	A/G ratio	1.0–1.8	
Creatinine clearance/24 hrs urine	CC	M: 71–135 F: 78–116	mL/min
Renin	Penin	0.15–3.95	pg/mL/hr
Creatinine urine	Creatinine urine	60–250	mg/dL
Natrium	Na	135–145	meq/L
Potassium	K	3.4–4.5	meq/L
Calcium	Ca	8.4–10.6	mg/dL
Phosphorus	IP	2.1–4.7	mg/dL
Alkaline phosphatase	ALP	27–110	U/L

TABLE 2: Blood test features.

Blood test items		Reference	Units
Hemoglobin	Hb	M: 14–18 F: 12–16	g/dL
Red blood cell	RBC	M: 450–600 F: 400–550	mil/mm^3
White blood cell	WBC	5000–10000	mm^3
Hematocrit	Hct	M: 40–55 F: 37–50	%
Platelets	PLT	15–40.0	10^3/uL
Mean corpuscular volume	MCV	83–100	u^3
Mean corpuscular hemoglobin	MCH	27–32.5	uug
Mean corpuscular hemoglobin concentration	MCHC	32–36	%
Reticulocyte	Reticulocyte	0.5–2.0	%
Malaria	Malaria	(−)	
Erythrocyte sedimentation Rate.	ESR	M: 1–15 F: 1–20	mm/hr
Differential count	DC		
Band	Band	0–2	%
Neutrophils	Neutrophils	50–70	%
Lymphocytes	Lymphocytes	20–40	%
Monocytes	Monocytes	2–6	%
Eosinophils	Eosinophils	1–4	%
Basophils	Basophils	0–1	%
Bleeding times	BT	0–3	Minute
Coagulation times	CT	2–6	Minute
Blood type	Blood type		
Rhesus factor	Rh Factor	(+)	
Blood pressure	BP		mm/Hg
Height	Height		cm
Weight	Weight		kg

that of nondiabetic patients. However, if a patient was malnourished and older, albumin and CRE levels were the factors most strongly related to mortality. Thus, albumin

TABLE 3: Urine test features.

Urine test items		Reference	Units
Color/appearance	Color/appearance		
Reaction pH	Reaction PH	5.5–8.5	
Protein	Protein	<(+)	mg/mL
Sugar	Sugar	(−)	g/dL
Bilirubin	BIL	(−)	
Urobilinogen	URO	≤1; 4	umol/L
Urine red blood cells	RBC	0–3	/HPF
Urine white blood cells	WBC	0–5	/HPF
Pus cell	Pus cell	0-1	/HPF
Epith cell	Epith cell	M: 0–3 F: 0–15	/HPF
Casts	Casts	Not found	/LPF
Ketones	Ketones	(−)	mmol/L
Crystals	Crystals	− ~ (±)	/LPF
Bacteria and other	Bacteria and other	−	/HPF

level, age, diabetes status, and CRE level can help predict risk of mortality.

Yeh et al. used a data mining technique to predict hospitalization of HD patients in 2011 [6]. The availability of medical resources and dialysis quality may decline when too many patients are admitted to a hospital. Therefore, Yeh et al. used analysis of the C4.5 decision tree and the multiple minimum support (MS) association rule mining technology for analysis. The C4.5 decision tree was used to eliminate null values and association rule mining was used to identify hospitalization of HD patients. According to the records of hospitalized patients, hospitalized patients seldom have a chronic disease or may not have a chronic disease, but doctors only determine whether a patient should be hospitalized during an examination.

Lin used hospital records of patients combined with the association rule and the time-series analysis to establish a health-management information system for chronic diseases [7]. Lin found that occluded cerebral arteries may lead to cerebral thrombosis and a cerebral embolism. After examination by a doctor, the rule is effective in avoiding a second stroke. Additionally, ill-defined heart diseases still require improvement. Lin used data mining to provide the chronic disease patients' family members and medical staffs for controlling their disease.

These scholars usually used well-known blood tests as mining rules. This work uses an effective and novel scheme to identify some previously unknown features to predict HD. The entropy function is applied to identify features that are strongly related to HD, and the k-means clustering algorithm is applied with these key features to group patients.

2.2. Entropy Function. Information gain, proposed by Quinlan in 1979 [8], is a basis of the decision tree constructed by Interactive Dichotomiser 3 (ID3). Information gain can also be utilized to determine differences in feature attributes and other classification attributes. Further, it is usually used to select the split point of ID3.

We assume a classification problem that includes N data records, m feature dimensions, and k clusters. The measurement of a single feature's information gain must be determined based on two correlated values, called entropy; the difference between two correlated values is called information entropy

$$\text{Entropy}(N) = \sum P_t \times \log\left(\frac{1}{P_t}\right) = -\sum p_t \times \log(p_t), \quad (2)$$

$$\text{Entropy}\left(D_j\right) = \sum_{v=1}^{|D_j|} \frac{D_{jv}}{N} \times \text{Entropy}\left(D_{jv}\right), \quad (3)$$

$$\text{Gain}\left(D_j\right) = \text{Entropy}(N) - \text{Entropy}\left(D_j\right). \quad (4)$$

In (2), Entropy (N) is the total information content of whole problems, and this total information content is taken as a basis of single feature information gain, in which P_t is the probability of occurrence of t classification in N dataset.

In (3), Entropy (D_{jv}) is the information content of the j feature dimension, the v value, and classification and information quantity, D_{jv} is the j feature dimension, including v kinds of values, and the j feature dimension has $|D_j|$ values.

In (4), Gain (D_j) is a classification problem, the information gain received by the j feature dimension. Through (2)–(4), the information gain of each feature for a classification problem is found. This work then evaluates all threshold settings and collects the features with the greatest information gain to form a feature set for classification. Entropy is used to identify key features and cluster HD patients to determine the accuracy of key features.

2.3. Clustering Algorithm. Although many clustering techniques have been proposed, the k-means algorithm is the most representative and widely applied [9]. The k-means algorithm is also called the generalized Lloyd algorithm (GLA) [10]. The k-means algorithm transforms each data record into a data point and random numbers are utilized to generate the initial cluster center to determine which data point belongs to which cluster point. The divided data points are used to calculate the distance between a data point and the cluster center, such that a data point will belong to one cluster center when the data point is closer to one cluster center than another cluster center. The newly recomputed cluster center is the average among all data points in a cluster, and the new cluster center is taken as a basis for the next iteration. This process is repeated until no change occurs. The steps of the k-means algorithm are as follows.

(1) Use random numbers to generate the initial cluster centers $C_i = \{1, 2, \ldots, k\}$.

(2) Calculate the Euclidean distance $d(X, C_i)$ for each data point $X = \{x_1, x_2, \ldots, x_m\}$ and each cluster center C_i. The point with the shortest distance is classified in to C_i, and the distance formula is as follows:

$$d(X, C_i) = \sqrt{\sum_{j=1}^{m} \left(x_j - c_{ij}\right)^2}. \quad (5)$$

(3) Recompute the new cluster center C_i. If the movement of all data points in a cluster stop moving, all clustering work stops; otherwise, steps (1) and (2) are repeated for clustering.

2.4. Association Rule. An association rule is a widely used technique. It progressively scans a database to identify rules for the relationships between items. For instance, the probability that people will buy bread after buying milk is milk $\rightarrow$ bread (support = 50% and confidence = 100%); support means that the probability of a consumer buying both milk and bread is 50%, and confidence means that the probability of a consumer buying bread after buying milk is 100%.

Agrawal et al. developed the Apriori algorithm in 1994 [11]. The Apriori algorithm is one of the most popular data mining methods, where I is all itemsets, each data record is $X = \{x_1, x_2, \ldots, x_m\}$, and $X \subseteq I$. The expression of the association rule is $x_1 \rightarrow x_2$ (support, confidence), where $x_1 \subseteq I$, $x_2 \subseteq I$, and $x_1 \cap x_2 = \varphi$. Support and confidence affect mining results most. Support is the occupied percentage for N data records and the probability of occurrence of both x_1 and x_2 is $(x_1 \cup x_2)/N$. Confidence is the probability of x_1 and x_2 and is called a strong association rule.

First, set the threshold of minimum support and minimum confidence to generate frequently occurring items, where L_b represents frequently occurring b-itemsets, and all generated L_b frequent itemsets are combined to generate candidate itemsets. Only the support and confidence values that are greater than the minimum support and minimum confidence thresholds are retained. This process is repeated until all L_b frequent itemsets are identified.

3. Proposed Algorithms

This work applies a novel and effective scheme to find key features that predict HD. This work uses the entropy function to find the key features that are strongly related to HD and applies the k-means clustering algorithm with these key features to group patients. Furthermore, the proposed scheme applies the data mining technique to identify association rules from each cluster. These rules can be used to warn patients who may require HD. Figure 1 shows the system architecture, which is divided into four procedures.

These procedures are as follows.

(1) The input procedure, which should be handled very carefully, can determine the disease target and input various sources and formats into a database. This procedure has a marked impact on the subsequent procedure.

(2) The preprocess procedure is divided into two subprocedures. For quantitative processing, one subprocedure, data are converted into an appropriate analytical form; for example, a string form is converted into a numeric form, or a numeric form is converted into a similar spacing. For selecting features, the other subprocedure, this work uses the entropy function to find the key features that are strongly related to diseases.

(3) The mining procedure is also divided in two subprocedures. For clustering analysis, one subprocedure, the clustering algorithm is applied to these key features to group patients. For the association rule, the other subprocedure, the Apriori algorithm is applied to find the association rule in each cluster.

(4) The output procedure may express the entire mining result, and a medical professional will explain the mining result, and find any factor that may cause a disease.

3.1. Input Procedure. Examination information is from many sources, such as a hospital information system (HIS), laboratory information system (LIS), or Excel report. These different systems may have different data storage formats. For example, in the A database, gender is 1 for male and 2 for female, but in the B database, M is for male and F is for female. Thus, an error may occur while collecting data. Therefore, one should apply the preprocess process to ensure that information is correct, complete, and sufficient. The preprocess process is divided into five steps.

(1) Unified data storage format: to simplify mining, all information must be in the same format.

(2) Irrelevant data: if one does not specify the mining topic, mining efficiency and even accuracy will be adversely affected.

(3) Incorrect data: incorrect data may be caused by a source error or login error; thus, one should modify or remove.

(4) Formats do not match: to smooth information mining, information must be converted into an appropriate format when necessary.

(5) Incomplete data: incomplete data is a common problem; for example, some information may be lost, lacking for a certain period.

3.2. Preprocess Procedure. Data are standardized to improve analytical accuracy. A standard value may be applied to an item such as triglycerides (TG). If the TG level is ≥ 201 mg/dL, it exceeds and the standard is 100; if TG is normal it is in the range of 20–200 and the standard is 50; if TG is smaller than <19 mg/dL, it is lower than the standard and the standard is 0. If data are consecutive, a packing normalization method is used; its formula is as follows:

$$v'_j = \left\lfloor \left(\frac{v_j - \min_j}{\max_j - \min_j} \right) \times Q_j \right\rfloor, \qquad (6)$$

where v_j represents raw data, $\min_j$ is the minimum value of j, $\max_j$ is the maximum value of j, v'_j is the packing normalized value, and Q_j is quantified distance. Table 4 shows example data after quantization.

Table 4 is a normalized form used to derive information gain and in association rule analysis, and it can effectively

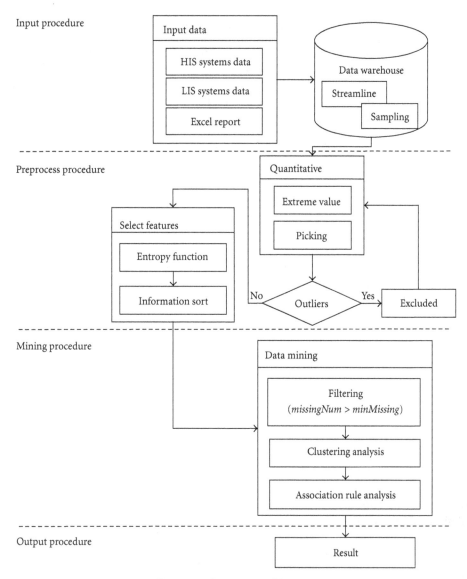

FIGURE 1: The system architecture.

differentiate between patients. This work simultaneously uses extreme value normalization; its formula is

$$v''_j = \frac{v_j - \min_j}{\max_j - \min_j} \times 100, \tag{7}$$

where v_j represents raw data, $\min_j$ is the minimum value of j, $\max_j$ is the maximum value of j, and v''_j is the packing normalized value. For instance, if the WBC value is 1, max = 10.7, and min = 3.5, then $v'' = [(1 - 3.5)/(10.7 - 3.5)] \times 100 = 38.89\%$ can be derived by applying (7).

In the entire database, the maximum and minimum values of each item markedly affect the quantification result, and the values are called outliers. If outliers exist, anomalies will also exist; for example, suppose that Q of CRE is 80, and CRE values are generally 0.37–2.99; however, a polarization datum may occur when a record is 6990. After quantization, values in the range of 0.37–2.99 will be quantified as 1, and the value recorded as 6990 will be assigned 80. Therefore, this work creates a mechanism to remove outliers. To avoid

the influence of outlier values, this work sets a minNum threshold for each record. For example, assume minNum = 3 is the threshold. The total number of hemoglobin (HB), which is quantified as 2 (HB = 2), is 9; however, that of HB, which is quantified as 0 (HB = 0), is 1. This means that most data are assigned to HB = 2, and only 1 datum is assigned to HB = 0. The total number of quantified values that are smaller than minNum is the extreme value. This scheme replaces the extreme value with the average value.

3.3. Information Gain Analysis. This work uses dialysis item to identify information gain. For example, 6 patients are on dialysis (Dialysis = 1) (Table 4), the occurrence probability is $P_1 = 6/15$, and information gain is $P_1 \times \log(1/P_1) = (6/15) \times \log(6/15) = 0.528771$. When 9 patients are nondialysis (Dialysis = 0), occurrence probability is $P_0 = 9/15$, information gain is $P_0 \times \log(1/P_0) = (9/15) \times \log(9/15) = 0.442179$, and total information gain of P_0 and P_1 is 0.970951.

TABLE 4: Packing method normalized data.

Q_j	Sex 2	Age 5	WBC 4	RBC 3	HB 3	BUN 4	CRE 2	UA 2	GOT 4	GPT 5	TP 2	ALB 2	GLO 2	A/G 2	TG 3	Dialysis 2
1	1	3	1	1	1	3	1	0	0	0	0	0	0	0	1	1
2	0	1	3	1	0	0	0	0	0	1	1	0	1	0	1	1
3	0	1	1	0	0	1	0	0	1	1	0	0	0	0	1	1
4	0	2	0	1	0	0	0	0	2	0	0	0	0	0	2	0
5	1	3	1	1	1	2	1	0	3	4	1	1	1	0	1	0
6	1	1	1	1	2	1	1	1	0	0	0	0	0	0	1	1
7	0	4	2	0	0	1	1	0	0	0	1	0	1	0	1	0
8	1	1	1	1	2	3	1	0	2	4	0	0	0	1	2	1
9	1	2	0	1	2	2	1	1	1	2	0	0	0	1	1	0
10	0	2	3	1	0	2	0	1	2	1	0	0	1	0	2	0
11	1	0	1	2	2	1	0	0	1	1	1	1	1	0	1	0
12	0	0	1	1	0	3	0	0	0	0	0	0	0	0	1	0
13	0	2	1	2	0	0	0	0	0	1	1	0	1	0	1	1
14	1	2	2	0	1	1	1	1	1	0	0	1	0	1	1	0
15	1	2	3	1	2	3	1	1	1	1	0	1	0	1	1	0

TABLE 5: Calculation information gain of sex relative to dialysis.

Sex j	Dialysis	Count (D_{jv})	$P_{D_{jv}}$	$P_{D_{jv}} \times \log(1/P_{D_{jv}})$	Entropy (D_{jv})	Entropy (D_j)
0	0	4	4/7	0.46	0.99	0.459773
	1	3	3/7	0.52		
1	0	5	5/8	0.42	0.95	0.509031
	1	3	3/8	0.53		
		Sum				0.968804

Next, this work calculates the information gain of each item relative to dialysis item. Take Sex (Table 5) as an example. The Sex of 7 women is 0 (Sex = 0) and only 4 records with non-dialysis (Dialysis = 0), the probability is $P_{D_{jv}} = 4/7$ of Sex = 0 and Dialysis = 0, and information gain is 0.46. Three records have Sex = 0 and Dialysis = 1; thus, the probability $P_{D_{jv}} = 3/7$, and information gain is 0.52. Total information gain of 0.46 and 0.52 is 0.99. Information gain of the women is $0.99 \times (7/16) = 0.459773$ because the probability of Sex = 0 is 7/16. After summing the information gain of the women (Sex = 0) and men (Sex = 1), total information gain is 0.968804, where 0.968804 = 0.459773 + 0.509031. Next, via (3), which is Entropy (N) − Entropy (D_j), Gain $(D_j) = 0.970951 − 0.968804 = 0.002147$.

The information gain of each item related to dialysis can be obtained and ranked, and the association rule can be mined using the top few items as key features. Take Table 6 as an example. Assume that the top three items are chosen. Thus, Age, WBC, and BUN are taken as key features.

3.4. Data Mining Procedure

3.4.1. Missing Values.
Some patients may have missing values. If their records are removed directly, some import information may be lost. Thus, this work applies a second filter before data mining analysis. This research sets minMissing as the threshold and takes missingNum as a null value of each record. If missingNum > minMissing, then the record is removed. Otherwise, missingNum $\leqq$ minMissing, the record will be retained and the missing null values will be replaced by the mean value. For instance, Age, WBC, and BUN are the top three key features when records are missing records. Assume minMissing is 1. When a record for which missingNum > 1, the record is removed; otherwise, the record is retained and the missing null values are replaced by the mean value.

3.4.2. Clustering.
This work uses key features for clustering, where $x_1, x_2, \ldots, x_m$ as m key features, $X = \{x_1, x_2, \ldots, x_m\}$ are patient records, x_j is a key feature in X, $1 \leq j \leq m$, and k is the cluster number. The k-means process is as follows.

(1) First, randomly generate k initial cluster centers $C_i = \{c_1, c_2, \ldots, c_m\}$. Figure 2(a) has ten solid circles, $N = 10$, which are the locations of each record, and three triangles, $k = 3$, which are the locations of cluster centers C_i.

(2) Apply (5), $d(X, C_i) = \sqrt{\sum_{j=1}^m (x_j - c_{ij})^2}$, to calculate the distance between each patient's data point X and the cluster center C_i. When some X distance d_1 is less than d_i, X will be classified to C_1.

(3) Let $\hat{C}_i = \{X_{c_i1}, X_{c_i2}, \ldots, X_{c_iS}\}$ be a cluster center membership, where S is the total number of members in C_i, and X_{c_iu} is u patient's data point in C_i. Thus,

TABLE 6: Information gain of each item.

Items	Sex	Age	WBC	RBC	HB	BUN	CRE	UA	GOT	GPT	TP	ALB	GLO	A/G	TG
Gain	0.002	0.577	0.329	0.14	0.06	0.28	0.05	0.09	0.18	0.2	0.05	0.24	0.02	0.06	0.03

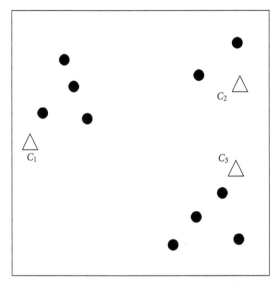

(a) Initial dataset and cluster center (Before)

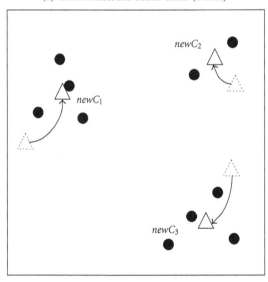

(b) Center displacement (After)

FIGURE 2: The diagram of clustering algorithm.

$newC_l$ will be added to the sum of $X_{c_i S}$ in each $\hat{C}_i$, and $newC_i = \{(\sum_{u=1}^{s} x_{u1}/S), (\sum_{u=2}^{s} x_{u2}/S), \ldots, (\sum_{u=1}^{s} x_{uj}/S)\}$ can then be obtained. This function can also be taken as a new cluster center.

(4) Repeat steps (2) and (3) until each C_i remains the same.

3.4.3. Association Rule. Next, the proposed scheme finds each clustering characteristic rule using Apriori association rule analysis. We assume that the total number of records

in cluster C_i is S, and each cluster membership is $\hat{C}_i = \{X_{c_i 1}, X_{c_i 2}, \ldots, X_{c_i S}\}$; thus, the u patient's data point $X_{c,u}$ is in the $\hat{C}_i$, and the j key features x_{uj} are in $X_{c_i u} = \{x_{u1}, x_{u2}, \ldots, x_{um}\}$. Next, the association rule is used to analyze each cluster C_i.

(1) First, set the values of minimum support minSup and minimum confidence minConf.

(2) Convert the normalization table into an extreme values table.

(3) Find the candidate set. We assume $\alpha = item_{jp}^i$, where $item_{jp}^i$ is the p quantified value of the j key feature in $\hat{C}_i$, $1 \leq p \leq Q$, and $Sup(\alpha)$ denotes the occurrence probability of $item_{jp}^i$ in $\hat{C}_i$. If $Sup(\alpha) \geq minSup$, then $item_{jp}^i$ becomes a candidate itemset L_Z and proceed to the next step.

(4) Through candidate set $L_z = \{\alpha_1, \alpha_2, \ldots, \alpha_y\}$, generate a set of two items, $\hat{L}_y = \{\alpha_1 \cup \alpha_2, \alpha_1 \cup \alpha_3, \ldots, \alpha_1 \cup \alpha_y, \alpha_2 \cup \alpha_3, \ldots, \alpha_{y-1} \cup \alpha_y\}$; however, α_A and α_B cannot be the same item. Calculate the occurrence probability of each group, $Sup(\alpha_A \cup \alpha_B)$. If $Sup(\alpha_A \cup \alpha_B) > minSup$, it becomes a member of frequent itemset L_{Z+1}.

(5) Take L_Z as a candidate set and repeat step (4) until the candidate set is null.

(6) Generate the association rule of the frequent itemset. If the confidence of the rule exceeds minConf, the rule is set up and the process is as follows.

    (i) Let α^* be one of the frequent itemsets L_f, $\alpha^* = (R_A \cup R_B)$.

    (ii) Generate rules $R_A \rightarrow R_B$ and $R_B \rightarrow R_A$.

In the case of A clustering C_A, where minSup = 2 and minConf = 0.5, the key features are $item_1$ = Age, $item_2$ = WBC, and $item_3$ = BUN, and $S = 7$ is the total number of records in C_A. Thus, this work finds the frequent itemsets L_1 using the minSup and minConf thresholds. The proposed scheme merges two items by L_1 as a candidate set, where j = Age, $p = 3$ in α_1, and j = WBC and $p = 1$ in α_3, and then calculates $Sup(\alpha_1 \cup \alpha_3)$. If $Sup(\alpha_1 \cup \alpha_3) \geq minSup$, then let α_1 and α_3 be the two frequent itemsets until no more frequent itemsets are found.

Next, the quantified values are converted back into their original values if all rules are found; the formula is

$$v_j = \frac{v_j'}{Q_j} \times \left(\max_j - \min_j\right) + \min_j, \qquad (8)$$

where v_j' is a quantified value, $\min_j$ is the minimum value of j, $\max_j$ is the maximum value of j, v_j is the original value, and Q_j is a quantified interval. Take WBC = 1 → Age = 3 as an example rule. If the $\max_j$ of WBC is 10.7, the $\min_j$ value is 3.5, and Q_j is 4; then the original value of WBC = 1 is WBC = $1/4 \times (10.7 - 3.5) + 3.5 = 5.3$. If the $\max_j$ value of Age is 68, the $\min_j$ value is 30, and Q_j is 5; then the original value of Age = 3 is Age = $3/5 \times (68 - 30) + 30 = 52.8$. Through (8), the association rule WBC = 1 → Age = 3 can be transformed into WBC = 5.3 → Age = 52.8.

4. Experimental Results

This experiment uses health examination records provided by hospitals. The data are mainly for outpatient dialysis and general outpatients. The hospital has 105 records with many values missing. This is because each patient does not undergo all examinations. Therefore, data must first be filtered to eliminate records with missing values. This work adopts BUN and CRE, which are related to kidney function, as the first filter. If any null value occurs in BUN or CRE, the record is removed. In total, 18,166 records are retained after the first filtering.

The purpose of quantification in the preprocess procedure is to convert values into a continuity value or significant difference value from a finite interval. This work sets interval Q_j for each item based on recommendations by medical staff. Table 7 shows the intervals.

4.1. Choose Key Features. The mining result does not make sense when too many items are used. The proposed scheme uses the Entropy function to identify the top 4 key features between each item and dialysis; these features are are UA, AST (GOT), TG, and K (Blood).

4.2. Mining Procedure

4.2.1. Clustering Analysis. Based upon the above clustering algorithm, this work applies the k-means clustering algorithm with these key features to group patients. Before the experiment, records with many missing values were filtered out, leaving 7118 records. Table 8 shows the cluster grouping result. For example, 1169 patients are classified into the first group. The average indicator values are UA = 6.54, AST (GOT) = 24.48, TG = 119.79, and K (Blood) = 5.10, and the average density of the first group is 13.26. The average difference among all groups is 27.02, which is the best result of 100 random trial runs.

4.2.2. Association Rule Analysis. This work identifies the top four items related to dialysis as TG, AST (GOT), UA, and K (Blood); AST (GOT) is the main indicator of liver function. These four items are adopted as key features and the association rule technique is applied to analyze each group rule after clustering, where minSup = 35% and minConf = 65%. The association rules of the four clusters are shown in Table 9.

4.3. Summary. This work uses the clustering algorithm and the association rule algorithm to identify some previously unknown features of HD patients and possible association rules. This work then evaluates all threshold settings and

TABLE 7: Each interval of item.

ID	Item	Interval
1	TG	50
2	AST (GOT)	20
3	Ch	50
4	ALT (GPT)	20
5	UA	2
6	K (Boold)	2
7	BUN	5
8	Amylase (B)	50
...	...	...

TABLE 8: Clustering results.

Cluster	UA	AST (GOT)	TG	K (Blood)	Density
Cluster-1	6.54	24.48	119.72	5.10	14.14
Cluster-2	6.16	30.12	138.92	3.92	11.59
Cluster-3	4.47	24.72	112.33	4.07	11.22
Cluster-4	8.40	28.03	228.72	4.20	20.91

collects the features with the greatest information gained to form a feature set for classification. Entropy is used to identify key features and cluster HD patients to determine the accuracy of key features. During the clustering process, the clustering algorithm is applied on these key features to group patients, and the entropy function can effectively determine clustering analysis with the key features. Furthermore, this work applies the apriori algorithm to find the association rules of each cluster. Hidden rules for causing any kidney disease can therefore be identified.

This experiment adopts the health examination records provided by one general hospital of Taiwan. During the experiment process, the experimental results will be discussed with medical staffs. From the experimental results, we can find that if BUN is in the range of 58.5–61.5 (60 ± 1.5) and Na (Blood) is in the range of 137.5–140.25 (140 ± 2.5), patients have a high risk of receiving a dialysis. The BUN is reported to be a reliable indicator of high risk, but the Na (Blood) is not clearly defined. Therefore, the Na (Blood) needs for further analysis and clarification. Conversely, if UA is in the range of 6.25–6.75 (6.5 ± 0.25), TG is in the range of 134.75–184.75 (159.75 ± 25), and K (Blood) is in the range of 3.89–4.39 (4.14 ± 0.25), or AC-GLU is in the range of 111–161 (136 ± 25), patients have a low risk of receiving a dialysis.

The medical staffs express that the UA, TG, and AC-GLU will definitely affect the possibility of patients to receive a dialysis, but K (Blood) is not clearly defined to create an influence on patients. The factor should be further analysis. At last, there is one more special feature, AST (GOT) because it appears both in the groups of high risk and low risk. The medical staffs express, actually AST (GOT) is not directly related to HD. Thus, AST (GOT) is not a key factor to determine whether a patient requires HD.

TABLE 9: Association rule of each cluster-k.

α^*	Sup (α^*)	Conf.
Cluster-1 ($k = 1$)		
BUN = 60 ± 1.5 → Dialysis = Yes	487	91%
Dialysis = Yes → AST (GOT) = 24.5 ± 10	708	74%
AST (GOT) = 24.5 ± 10 → Dialysis = Yes	523	73%
Na (Blood) =140 ± 2.5 → Dialysis = Yes	455	70%
Dialysis = Yes → BUN = 60 ± 1.5	487	69%
Na (Blood) = 140 ± 2.5 → AST (GOT) = 24.5 ± 10	434	66%
Cluster-2 ($k = 2$)		
CRE = 0.85 ± 0.15 → Dialysis = No	487	91%
UA = 6.5 ± 0.25 TG = 159.75 ± 25 → Dialysis = No	1341	97%
AC-GLU = 136 ± 25 → Dialysis = No	1265	94%
TG = 159.75 ± 25 → Dialysis = No	1696	93%
UA = 6.5 ± 0.25 → Dialysis = No	1920	93%
AST (GOT) = 45 ±10 → Dialysis = No	1479	92%
K (Boold) = 4.14 ± 0.25 → Dialysis = No	1938	91%
TG = 159.75 ± 25 Dialysis = No → UA = 6.5 ± 0.25	1341	79%
TG = 159.75 ± 25 → UA = 6.5 ± 0.25	1378	76%
TG =159.75 ± 25 → UA = 6.5 ± 0.25 Dialysis = No	1341	74%
UA = 6.5 ± 0.25 Dialysis = No → TG = 159.75 ± 25	1341	70%
UA = 6.5 ± 0.25 → TG = 159.75 ± 25	1378	67%
UA = 6.5 ± 0.25 → TG = 159.75 ± 25 Dialysis = No	1341	65%
CRE = 0.85 ± 0.15 → Dialysis = No	487	91%
UA = 6.5 ± 0.25 TG = 159.75 ± 25 → Dialysis = No	1341	97%
Cluster-3 ($k = 3$)		
CRE = 0.85 ± 0.15 → Dialysis = No	732	100%
CRE = 0.85 ± 0.15 K (Boold) = 5 ± 0.25 → Dialysis = No	560	100%
K (Boold) = 4.14 ± 0.25 → Dialysis = No	910	95%
AST (GOT) = 24.5 ± 10 K (Boold) = 4.14 ± 0.25 → Dialysis = No	507	94%
AST (GOT) = 24.5 ± 10 → Dialysis = No	505	92%
AST (GOT) = 24.5 ± 10 → Dialysis = No	679	86%
CRE = 0.85 ± 0.15 → K (Boold) = 4.14 ± 0.25	560	77%
CRE = 0.85 ± 0.15 Dialysis = No → K (Boold) = 4.14 ± 0.25	560	77%
CRE = 0.85 ± 0.15 → K (Boold) = 4.14 ± 0.25 Dialysis = No	560	77%
AST (GOT) = 24.5 ± 10 Dialysis = No → K (Boold) = 4.14 ± 0.25	507	75%
Dialysis = No → K (Boold) = 4.14 ± 0.25	910	74%
AST (GOT) = 24.5 ± 10 → K (Boold) = 4.14 ± 0.25	539	68%
Cluster-4 ($k = 4$)		
AST (GOT) = 45 ± 10 K (Boold) = 4.14 ± 0.25 → Dialysis = No	364	98%
K (Boold) = 4.14 ± 0.25 → Dialysis = No	503	91%
AST (GOT) = 45 + 10 → Dialysis = No	537	90%
K (Boold) = 4.14 ± 0.25 Dialysis = No → AST (GOT) = 45 ± 10	364	72%
Dialysis = No → AST (GOT) = 45 ± 10	537	71%
AST (GOT) = 45 ± 10 Dialysis = No → K (Boold) = 4.14 ± 0.25	364	68%
K (Boold) = 4.14 ± 0.25 → AST (GOT) = 45 ± 10	372	68%
Dialysis = No → K (Boold) = 4.14 ± 0.25	503	67%
K (Boold) = 4.14 ± 0.25 → AST (GOT) = 45 ± 10 Dialysis = No	364	66%

5. Conclusion

Medical staffs try to find some information from patient's health examination records to reduce the occurrence of disease. However, some hidden information may be ignored because of the human observation or the restriction of book. Although there are many data mining techniques that have been proposed, most of them are focused on some known items. Seldom techniques in regard with searching for hidden key features are proposed. The reason is because the examination items are too many but incomplete. It is hard to find out the association rule by using system.

This research will help medical staffs to find some unknown key features to predict the hemodialysis. We apply k-means clustering algorithm with these key features to group the patients. Furthermore, the proposed scheme applies data mining technique to find the association rule from each cluster. The rules can help the patients to detect any occurrence possibility of disease.

Acknowledgment

The authors would like to thank the National Science Council of the Republic of China, Taiwan, for financially supporting this paper under Contract no. NSC 99-2622-E-324-006-CC3.

References

[1] DrKao, "Normal Test Values," 2010, http://www.drkao.com/1st_site/health_wap/normal_main.htm.

[2] Green Cross, "How to Detect Renal Function," 2010, http://www.greencross.org.tw/kidney/symptom_sign/kid_func.html.

[3] Shin Kong Wu Ho-Su Memorial Hospital, 2010, http://www.skh.org.tw/mnews/178/4-2.htm.

[4] K. C. Hung, *Multiple minimum support association rule mining for hospitalization prediction of hemodialysis patients [M.S. thesis]*, Computer Science and Information Engineering, 2004.

[5] S. Y. Huang, *The evaluation & analysis of the risk of mortality for patients receiving long-term hemodialysis proposal [M.S. thesis]*, Graduate Institute of Biomedical Informatics, 2009.

[6] J. Y. Yeh, T. H. Wu, and C. W. Tsao, "Using data mining techniques to predict hospitalization of hemodialysis patients," *Decision Support Systems*, vol. 50, no. 2, pp. 439–448, 2011.

[7] Y. J. Lin, *Applying data mining in health management information system for chronic desease [M.S. thesis]*, Department of Computer Science and Information Management, 2008.

[8] J. R. Quinlan, "Induction of decision trees," *Machine Learning*, vol. 1, no. 1, pp. 81–106, 1986.

[9] T. Kanungo, D. M. Mount, N. S. Netanyahu, C. D. Piatko, R. Silverman, and A. Y. Wu, "An efficient k-means clustering algorithms: analysis and implementation," *IEEE Transactions on Pattern Analysis and Machine Intelligence*, vol. 24, no. 7, pp. 881–892, 2002.

[10] J. Z. C. Lai, T. J. Huang, and Y. C. Liaw, "A fast k-means clustering algorithm using cluster center displacement," *Pattern Recognition*, vol. 42, no. 11, pp. 2551–2556, 2009.

[11] R. Agrawal, R. Srikant, H. Mannila et al., "Fast discovery of association rules," in *Advances in Knowledge Discovery and Data Mining*, pp. 307–328, 1996.

10

Selection of Spatiotemporal Features in Breast MRI to Differentiate between Malignant and Benign Small Lesions Using Computer-Aided Diagnosis

F. Steinbruecker,[1] **A. Meyer-Baese,**[2] **C. Plant,**[2] **T. Schlossbauer,**[3] **and U. Meyer-Baese**[4]

[1] *Department of Computer Science, Technical University of Munich, 8574 Garching, Germany*
[2] *Department of Scientific Computing, Florida State University, Tallahassee, FL 32306-4120, USA*
[3] *Institute for Clinical Radiology, University of Munich, 81377 Munich, Germany*
[4] *Department of Electrical and Computer Engineering, FAMU/FSU College of Engineering, Tallahassee, FL 32310-6046, USA*

Correspondence should be addressed to A. Meyer-Baese, ameyerbaese@fsu.edu

Academic Editor: Juan Manuel Gorriz Saez

Automated detection and diagnosis of small lesions in breast MRI represents a challenge for the traditional computer-aided diagnosis (CAD) systems. The goal of the present research was to compare and determine the optimal feature sets describing the morphology and the enhancement kinetic features for a set of small lesions and to determine their diagnostic performance. For each of the small lesions, we extracted morphological and dynamical features describing both global and local shape, and kinetics behavior. In this paper, we compare the performance of each extracted feature set for the differential diagnosis of enhancing lesions in breast MRI. Based on several simulation results, we determined the optimal feature number and tested different classification techniques. The results suggest that the computerized analysis system based on spatiotemporal features has the potential to increase the diagnostic accuracy of MRI mammography for small lesions and can be used as a basis for computer-aided diagnosis of breast cancer with MR mammography.

1. Introduction

Breast cancer is one of the most common cancers among women. Contrast-enhanced MR imaging of the breast was reported to be a highly sensitive method for the detection of invasive breast cancer [1]. Different investigators described that certain dynamic signal intensity (SI) characteristics (rapid and intense contrast enhancement followed by a wash out phase) obtained in dynamic studies are a strong indicator for malignancy [2]. Morphologic criteria have also been identified as valuable diagnostic tools [3]. Recently, combinations of different dynamic and morphologic characteristics have been reported [4] that can reach diagnostic sensitivities up to 97% and specificities up to 76.5%.

As an important aspect remains the fact that many of these techniques were applied on a database of predominantly tumors of a size larger than 2 cm. In these cases, MRI reaches a very high sensitivity in the detection of invasive breast cancer due to both morphological criteria as well as characteristic time-signal intensity curves. However, the value of dynamic MRI and of automatic identification and classification of characteristic kinetic curves is not well established in small lesions when clinical findings, mammography, and ultrasound are unclear. Recent clinical research has shown that DCIS with small invasive carcinoma can be adequately visualized in MRI [5] and that MRI provides an accurate estimation of invasive breast cancer tumor size, especially in tumors of 2 cm or smaller [6].

Visual assessment of morphological properties is highly interobserver variable [7], while automated computation of features leads to more reproducible indices and thus to a more standardized and objective diagnosis. In this sense, we present novel mathematical descriptors for both morphology and dynamics and will compare their performance regarding small lesion classification based on novel feature selection algorithms.

More than 40% of the false-negative MR diagnosis are associated with pure ductal carcinoma in situ (DCIS) and with small lesion size and thus indicating a lower sensitivity of MRI for these cases. It has been shown that double reading achieves a higher sensitivity but is time-consuming and as an alternative a computer-assisted system was suggested [8]. The success of CAD in conventional X-ray mammography [9–13] motivates further the research of similar automated diagnosis techniques in breast MRI.

In the present study, we design and evaluate a computerized analysis system for the diagnosis of small breast masses with an average diameter of <1 cm.

The automated evaluation is a multistep system which includes global and local features such as shape descriptors, dynamical features, and spatiotemporal features combining both morphology and dynamics aspects. Different classification techniques are employed to test the performance of the complete system. Summarizing, in the present paper, a multifactorial protocol, including image registration, and morphologic and dynamic criteria are evaluated in predominantly small lesions of 1.0 cm or less as shown in Figure 1.

2. Material and Methods

2.1. Patients. A total of 40 patients, all females having an age range 42–73, with indeterminate small mammographic breast lesions were examined. All patients were consecutively selected after clinical examinations, mammography in standard projections (craniocaudal and oblique mediolateral projections) and ultrasound. Only lesions BIRADS 3 and 4 were selected where at least one of the following criteria was present: nonpalpable lesion, previous surgery with intense scarring, or location difficult for biopsy (close to chest wall). All patients had histopathologically confirmed diagnosis from needle aspiration/excision biopsy and surgical removal. Breast cancer was diagnosed in 17 out of the total 31 cases. The average size of both benign and malignant tumors was less than 1.1 cm.

2.2. MR Imaging. MRI was performed with a 1.5 T system (Magnetom Vision, Siemens, Erlangen, Germany) with two different protocols equipped with a dedicated surface coil to enable simultaneous imaging of both breasts. The patients were placed in a prone position. First, transversal images were acquired with a STIR (short TI inversion recovery) sequence (TR = 5600 ms, TE = 60 ms, FA = 90°, IT = 150 ms, matrix size 256 × 256 pixels, slice thickness 4 mm). Then a dynamic T1 weighted gradient echo sequence (3D fast low angle shot sequence) was performed (TR = 12 ms, TE = 5 ms, FA = 25°) in transversal slice orientation with a matrix size of 256 × 256 pixels and an effective slice thickness of 4 mm or 2 mm.

The dynamic study consisted of 6 measurements with an interval of 83 s. The first frame was acquired before injection of paramagnetic contrast agent (gadopentetate dimeglumine, 0.1 mmol/kg body weight, Magnevist, Schering, Berlin, Germany) immediately followed by the 5 other measurements. The initial localization of suspicious breast lesions was performed by computing difference images, that is, subtracting the image data of the first from the fourth acquisition. As a preprocessing step to clustering, each raw gray level time-series $S(\tau)$, $\tau \in \{1, \ldots, 6\}$ was transformed into a signal time-series of relative signal enhancement $x(\tau)$ for each voxel, the precontrast scan at $\tau = 1$ serving as reference, in other words $x(\tau) = (x(\tau) - x(1))/x(1)$. Thus, we ensure that the proposed method is less sensitive to changing between different MR scanners and/or protocols.

Automatic motion correction represents an important prerequisite to a correct automated small lesion evaluation [14]. Especially for small lesions, the assumption of correct spatial alignment often leads to misinterpretation of the diagnostic significance of enhancing lesions [15]. Therefore, we performed an elastic image registration method based on the optical flow method [16]. The employed motion compensation algorithm is based on the Horn and Schunck method [17] and represents a variational method for computing the displacement field, the so-called optical flow, in an image sequence. In contrast to optical flow, we do not want to compute the displacement field in a projected image of our data, but the actual displacement in 3D space. In our work, however, we favor the original quadratic formulation, since we explicitly need the filling-in effect of a nonrobust regularizer to fill in the information in masked regions. To overcome the problem of having a nonconvex energy in the energy functional, we use the coarse-to-fine warping scheme detailed in [16], which linearizes the data term as in [17] and computes incremental solutions on different image scales.

We tested motion compensation for two and three directions and found the optimal motion compensation results in two directions [18]. Segmentation of the tumor is semiautomatic and we define an ROI including all voxels of a lesion with an initial contrast enhancement of ≥50%. The center of the lesion was interactively marked on one slice of the subtraction images and then a region growing algorithm included all adjacent contrast-enhancing voxels and also those from neighboring slices. Thus a 3-D form of the lesion was determined. An interactive ROI was necessary whenever the lesion was connected with diffuse contrast enhancement, as it is the case in mastopathic tissue.

3. Computer-Aided Diagnosis (CAD) System

The small lesion evaluation is based on a multi-step system that includes a reduction of motion artifacts based on a novel nonrigid registration method, an extraction of morphologic features, dynamic enhancement patterns as well as mixed features for diagnostic feature selection and performance of lesion evaluation. Figure 1 visualizes the proposed automated system for small lesion detection.

3.1. Feature Extraction. The complexity of the spatio-temporal tumor representation requires specific morphology and/or kinetic descriptors. We analyzed geometric and

Selection of Spatiotemporal Features in Breast MRI to Differentiate between Malignant
and Benign Small Lesions Using Computer-Aided Diagnosis

101

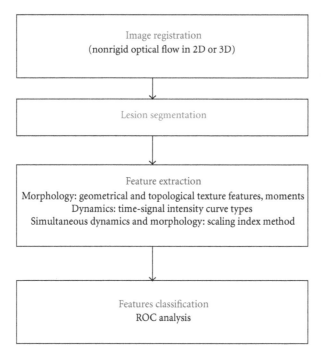

FIGURE 1: Diagram of a computer-assisted system for the evaluation of small contrast enhancing lesions.

Krawtchouk moments and geometrical features as shape descriptors, provided a temporal enhancement modeling for kinetic feature extraction and the scaling index method for the simultaneous morphological and dynamics representation.

3.1.1. Contour Features. To represent the shape of the tumor contour, the tumor voxels having nontumor voxel as a neighbor were extracted to represent the contour of the tumor. In this context, neighbor voxels include diagonally adjacent voxels, but not voxels from a different transverse slice. Due to the different grid sizes in the three directions of the MR images and possible gaps between transverse slices, the tumor contour in one transverse slice does not necessarily continue smoothly into the next transverse slice. Considering tumor contours between transverse slices therefore introduces contour voxels that are completely in the tumor interior in one slice. This is illustrated in Figure 2: the dark voxels are contour voxels and the arrows indicate the computed contour chain. If voxels in the tumor having at least one non-tumor voxel as a neighbor on an adjacent transverse slice were considered part of the contour, in this example, the crossed-out voxels would belong to the contour.

Figure 3 shows an example for a tumor where the contour shifts considerably from one transverse slice to another.

The contour in each slice was stored as an 1D chain of the 3D position of each contour voxel, constituting a "walk" along the contour. The chains of several slices were spliced together end to end to form a chain of 3D vectors representing the contour of the tumor.

Next, the center of mass of the tumor was computed as

$$\overline{v} := \frac{1}{n} \sum_{i=1}^{n} v_i, \tag{1}$$

where n is the number of voxels belonging to the tumor, and v_i is location of the ith tumor voxel. Since the center of mass was computed from the binary image of the tumor, irregularities in the voxel gray values of the tumor were not taken into account.

Knowing the center of mass, for each contour voxel c_i, the radius r_i and the azimuth ω_i (i.e., the angle between the vector from the center of mass to the voxel c_i and the sagittal plane) were computed the following way:

$$r_i := \|c_i - \overline{v}\|_2,$$

$$\omega_i := \arcsin\left(\frac{c_{ix} - \overline{v}_x}{\sqrt{\left(c_{ix} - \overline{v}_x\right)^2 + \left(c_{iy} - \overline{v}_y\right)^2}}\right), \tag{2}$$

where the subscripts x and y denote the position of the voxel in sagittal and coronal direction, respectively. ω_i was also extended to the range from $-\pi$ to π by taking into account the sign of $(c_{iy} - \overline{v}_y)$.

From the chain of floating point values $r_1, \ldots, r_m$, the minimum value $r_{\min}$ and the maximum value $r_{\max}$ were computed, as well as

$$\text{the mean value } \overline{r} := \frac{1}{m} \sum_{i=1}^{m} r_i, \tag{3}$$

$$\text{the standard deviation } \sigma_r := \sqrt{\frac{1}{m} \sum_{i=1}^{m} (r_i - \overline{r})^2}, \tag{4}$$

$$\text{the entropy } h_r := -\sum_{i=1}^{100} p_i \cdot \log_2(p_i). \tag{5}$$

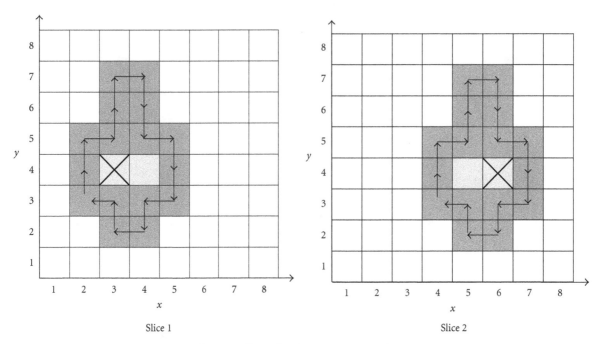

Slice 1   Slice 2

FIGURE 2: Example of contour computation.

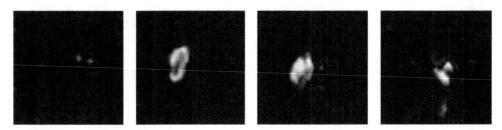

FIGURE 3: Left to right: tumor in adjacent transverse slices of a $512 \times 512 \times 32$ voxel MR image.

The entropy h_r was computed from the normalized distribution of the values into 100 "buckets", where p_i is defined as follows:

For $0 \le i \le 99$:

$$p_i := \frac{\left| \left\{ r_j \mid i \le \left(r_j - r_{\min} \right) / \left(r_{\max} - r_{\min} \right) \cdot 100 < i + 1 \right\} \right|}{m}. \tag{6}$$

From the radius, $r_{\min}$, $r_{\max}$, $\bar{r}$, σ_r, and h_r were used as morphological features of the tumor. From the azimuth, only the entropy h_ω (computed for ω as in (5) and (6)) was used as a feature, since the values $\omega_{\min}$ and $\omega_{\max}$ are always around π and $-\pi$, respectively, and the value σ_ω is not invariant under rotation of the tumor image.

An additional measurement describing the compactness of the tumor, which was also used as a feature, is the number of contour voxels, divided by the number of all voxels belonging to the tumor.

3.1.2. Morphological Features. The spatial and morphological variations of a tumor can be easily captured by shape descriptors. We analyze two modalities as shape descriptors based on moments: the geometric and Krawtchouk moments.

Geometrical Moments. We will employ low-order three-dimensional geometrical moment invariants as described in [19] because they have a low computation time and the results are stable to noise and distortion. We will utilize the 6 low-order finite-term three-dimensional moment invariants as described in [19]. There are one second-order and fourth-order, two third-order and three fourth-order moment invariants.

Krawtchouk Moments. Global and local shape description represents an important field in 3D medical image analysis. For breast lesion classification, there is a stringent need to describe properly the huge data volumes stemming from 3D images by a small set of parameters which captures the morphology (shape) well. However, very few techniques have been proposed for both global and local shape description. We employed Krawtchouk moments [20] as shape descriptors for both malignant and benign lesions. Weighted 3-D

Selection of Spatiotemporal Features in Breast MRI to Differentiate between Malignant
and Benign Small Lesions Using Computer-Aided Diagnosis

103

Krawtchouk moments have several advantages compared to other known methods: (1) they are defined in the discrete field and thus do not introduce any discretization error like Spherical Harmonics defined in a continuous field and (2) low-order moments can capture abrupt changes in the shape of an object. The weighted 3D Krawtchouk moments [20] form a very compact descriptor of a tumor, achieved in a very short computational time. Every tumor can be represented by Krawtchouk moments since it is expressed as a function $f(x, y, z)$ in a discrete grid $[0 \cdots N - 1] \times [0 \cdots M - 1] \times [0 \cdots L - 1]$.

Krawtchouk moments represent a set of orthonormal polynomials associated with the binomial distribution [21]. The nth order Krawtchouk classical polynomials can be expressed as a hypergeometric function:

$$K_n(x; p, N) = \sum_{k=0}^{N} a_{k,n,p} x^k = {}_2F_1\left(-n, -x; -N; \frac{1}{p}\right) \quad (7)$$

with $x, n = 0, 1 \cdots N$; $N > 0$; $p \in (0, 1)$ and the hypergeometric function ${}_2F_1$ is defined as

$$ {}_2F_1(a, b; c; z) = \sum_{k=0}^{\infty} \frac{(a)_k (b)_k}{(c)_k} \frac{z^k}{k!}, \quad (8)$$

and with $(a)_k$ being the Pochhammer symbol

$$(a)_k = a(a+1) \cdots (a+k-1) = \frac{\Gamma(a+k)}{\Gamma(a)}. \quad (9)$$

The set of the Krawtchouk polynomials $S = \{K_n(x; p, N), n = 0 \cdots N\}$ has $N + 1$ elements. This corresponds to a set of discrete basis functions with the weight function

$$w(x; p, N) = \binom{N}{x} p^x (1-p)^{N-x},$$

$$\rho(n; p, N) = (-1)^n \left(\frac{1-p}{p}\right)^n \frac{n!}{(-N)_n}. \quad (10)$$

We assume that $f(x, y, z)$ is a 3-dimensional function defined in a discrete field $A = \{(x, y, z) : x, y, z \in N, x = [0 \cdots N - 1], y = [0 \cdots M - 1], z = [0 \cdots L - 1]\}$. The weighted three-dimensional moments of order $(n + m + l)$ of f are given as

$$\widetilde{Q}_{mnl} = \sum_{x=0}^{N-1} \sum_{y=0}^{M-1} \sum_{z=0}^{L-1} \overline{K}_n(x; p_x, N - 1)$$

$$\cdot \overline{K}_m\left(y; p_y, M - 1\right) \overline{K}_l(z; p_z, L - 1)$$

$$\cdot f(x, y, z), \quad (11)$$

with $p_x, p_y, p_z \in (0, 1)$. Local features can be extracted by the appropriate selection of low-order Krawtchouk moments. $\overline{K}_n(x; p, N)$ is given as

$$\overline{K}_n(x; p, N) = K_n(x; p, N) \sqrt{\frac{w(x; p, N)}{\rho(n; p, N)}}. \quad (12)$$

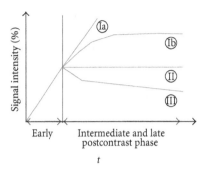

FIGURE 4: Schematic drawing of the time-signal intensity (SI) curve types [2]. Type I corresponds to a straight (Ia) or curved (Ib) line; enhancement continues over the entire dynamic study. Type II is a plateau curve with a sharp bend after the initial upstroke. Type III is a washout time course. In breast cancer, plateau or washout-time courses (type II or III) prevail. Steadily progressive signal intensity time courses (type I) are exhibited by benign enhancing lesions.

$\overline{K}_m(y; p_y, M - 1)$ and $\overline{K}_l(z; p_z, L - 1)$ are defined correspondingly. Thus, every 3-dimensional function $f(x, y, z)$ in a 3-dimensional field can be decomposed into weighted 3-dimensional Krawtchouk moments $\widetilde{Q}_{nml}$.

The tumor can be represented by Krawtchouk moments since it is expressed as a function $f(x, y, z)$ in a discrete space $[0 \cdots N - 1] \times [0 \cdots M - 1] \times [0 \cdots L - 1]$.

3.1.3. Dynamical Features. Lesion differential diagnosis in dynamic protocols is based on the assumption that benign and malignant lesions exhibit different enhancement kinetics. In [2], it was shown that the shape of the time-signal intensity curve represents an important criterion in differentiating benign and malignant enhancing lesions in dynamic breast MR imaging. The results indicate that the enhancement kinetics, as represented by the time-signal intensity curves visualized in Figure 4, differ significantly for benign and malignant enhancing lesions and thus represent a basis for differential diagnosis. In breast cancer, plateau or washout-time courses (type II or III) prevail. Steadily progressive signal intensity time courses (type I) are exhibited by benign enhancing lesions. Also, these enhancement kinetics are not only present in benign tumors but also in fybrocystic changes [2].

Computing the average signal intensity of the tumor before contrast agent administration (SI) and after contrast agent administration (SI$_C$), the relative enhancement can be computed as

$$\Delta SI(t) := \frac{SI_C(t) - SI(t)}{SI(t)} \cdot 100\%. \quad (13)$$

To capture the slope of the curve of relative signal intensity enhancement (RSIE) versus time in the late postcontrast time, we computed the line ($s = a \cdot t + b$) that approximates the curve of the RSIE for the last three time scans. The values a and b are the least square solutions of the overdetermined system of equations $a \cdot t_i + b = s_{i,j}$ for the three last points in time ($i \in \{3, 4, 5\}$), as well as for all tumor voxels j, with $s_{i,j}$ being the RSIE in voxel j at time scan i.

The solutions to these equations are given by

$$a = \frac{3n \sum t_i s_{i,j} - \sum t_i \sum s_{i,j}}{3n \cdot \sum t_i^2 - \left(\sum t_i\right)^2},$$

$$b = \frac{\sum s_{i,j} \sum t_i^2 - \sum t_i \sum t_i s_{i,j}}{3n \cdot \sum t_i^2 - \left(\sum t_i\right)^2},$$

(14)

where n is the number of voxels in the tumor, and $\sum$ is an abbreviation for $\sum_{j=1}^{3} \sum_{i=1}^{n}$. The slope a was used as a feature to describe the dynamics.

3.1.4. Simultaneous Morphology and Dynamics Representations.
The scaling index method [22] is a technique that is based on both morphology and kinetics. It represents the local structure around a given point. In the context of breast MRI, such a point consists of the sagittal, coronal, and transverse position of a tumor voxel and its third time scan gray value, and the scaling index serves as an approximation of the dimension of local point distributions.

Mathematically, the scaling index represents the 2-D image as a set of points in a three-dimensional state space defined by the coordinates x, y, z and the gray value $f(x, y, z)$. For every point P_i with coordinates (x_i, y_i, z_i) the number of points in a sphere with radius r_1 and a sphere with radius r_2 is determined and the scaling index α_i is computed based on the following equation:

$$\alpha_i = \frac{\left(\log N(P_i, r_2) - \log N(P_i, r_1)\right)}{\left(\log r_2 - \log r_1\right)},$$

(15)

where $N(P_i, r)$ is the number of points located within an n-dimensional sphere of radius r centered at P_i. As radii, we choose the bounds of the tumor shape. Thus, the obtained scaling-index is a measure for the local dimensionality of the tumor and thus quantifies its morphological and dynamical features. There is a correlation between the scaling index and the structural nature: $\alpha = 0$ for clumpy structures, $\alpha = 1$ for points embedded in straight lines, and $\alpha = 2$ for points in a flat distribution.

For each of the three time scans ($i \in \{1, 3, 5\}$), the standard deviation and entropy were determined and used as a feature to capture the heterogeneous behavior of the enhancement in a tumor.

3.2. Classification Techniques.
The following section gives a description of classification methods applied to evaluate the effect of spatiotemporal features in breast MR images.

Discriminant analysis represents an important area of multivariate statistics and finds a wide application in medical imaging problems. The most known approaches are linear discriminant analysis (LDA), quadratic discriminant analysis (QDA), and Fisher's canonical discriminant analysis.

Let us assume that $\mathbf{x}$ describes a K-dimensional feature vector that is, there are J classes and there are N_j samples available in group j. The mean in group j is given by μ_j and the covariance matrix is given by Σ_j.

3.2.1. Bayes Classification Based on LDA and QDA.
The Bayes classification [23] is based on estimating the prior probabilities π_i for each class which describe the prior estimates about how probable a class is.

This classification method assigns each new sample to the group with the highest a posterior probability. Thus, the classification rule becomes

$$C_j = \left(\mathbf{x}_i - \mu_j\right)^T \left(\Sigma_j\right)^{-1} \left(\mathbf{x}_i - \mu_j\right) + \log\left|\Sigma_j\right| - 2\log \pi_j,$$

(16)

where μ_j represent the means of the classes and Σ_j the corresponding covariance matrix. The assignment to a certain class j for a certain pattern is made based on the smallest determined value of C_j.

There are two cases to be distinguished regarding the covariance matrices: if the covariance matrices are different for each class, then we have a QDA (quadratic discriminant analysis) classifier, while if they are identical for the different classes, it becomes an LDA (linear discriminant analysis) classifier.

3.2.2. Fisher's Linear Discriminant Analysis.
The underlying idea of Fisher's linear discriminant analysis (FLDA) is to determine the directions in the multivariate space which allow the best discrimination between the sample classes. FLDA is based on a common covariance estimate and finds the most dominant direction and afterwards searches for "orthogonal" directions with the same property. The technique can extract at most $J - 1$ components.

This technique identifies the first discriminating component based on finding the vector $\mathbf{a}$ that maximizes the discrimination index given as

$$\frac{\mathbf{a}^T \mathbf{B} \mathbf{a}}{\mathbf{a}^T \mathbf{W} \mathbf{a}}$$

(17)

with $\mathbf{B}$ denoting the interclass sum-of-squares matrix and $\mathbf{W}$ the intraclass sum-of-squares matrix.

4. Results

In the following, we will explore the results of the previously described features' sets from different classification techniques. The results will elucidate the descriptive power of several tumor features for small lesion detection and diagnosis.

4.1. Effectiveness of Krawtchouk Moments.
The Krawtchouk moments describe a representation of local shape parameters and can thus describe the differences in morphology between benign and malignant tumors. Since the obtained number of Krawtchouk moments is very high (>200), we reduced their dimension based on principal component analysis (PCA). Table 1 shows the results for the Krawtchouk moments for different classifiers and number of principal components. In general, the quadratic discriminant analysis shows the best results and for PC >10 they tend to deteriorate.

Selection of Spatiotemporal Features in Breast MRI to Differentiate between Malignant
and Benign Small Lesions Using Computer-Aided Diagnosis

105

TABLE 1: Classification results based on Krawtchouk moments for different principal components (PC). Abbreviations: linear discriminant analysis (LDA), naive Bayes linear discriminant analysis (N.B.LDA), quadratic discriminant analysis (QDA), naive Bayes quadratic discriminant analysis (N.B.QDA), and Fisher's linear discriminant (FLDA).

PC	Correctly classified (%)				
	LDA	N.B.LDA	QDA	N.B.QDA	FLDA
1	71.0	71.0	64.5	64.5	71.0
2	71.0	74.2	58.1	64.5	74.2
3	64.5	67.7	67.7	58.1	67.7
4	64.5	64.5	74.2	71.0	64.5
5	64.5	64.5	74.2	64.5	64.5
6	61.3	64.5	**77.4**	64.5	61.3
7	67.7	74.2	74.2	67.7	71.0
8	71.0	74.2	74.2	67.7	71.0
9	61.3	74.2	71.0	67.7	61.3
10	61.3	74.2	74.2	67.7	61.3
11	58.1	67.7	71.0	67.7	58.1

TABLE 2: Combined classification of the feature groups and different classification methods. Abbreviations: linear discriminant analysis (LDA), naive Bayes linear discriminant analysis (N.B.LDA), quadratic discriminant analysis (QDA), naive Bayes quadratic discriminant analysis (N.B.QDA), and Fisher's linear discriminant (FLDA).

Features	Correctly classified (%)				
	LDA	N.B.LDA	QDA	N.B.QDA	FLDA
Contour features	64.5	74.2	67.7	77.4	64.5
Scaling index features	67.7	71.0	61.3	51.6	67.7
Tumor RSIE features	64.5	74.2	74.2	77.4	64.5
Contour RSIE features	64.5	74.2	54.8	54.8	64.5
Geometric moments	51.6	54.8	51.6	64.5	51.6
Krawtchouk moments	71.0	74.2	**77.4**	71.0	74.2

TABLE 3: Sensitivity and specificity for specific features alone and in combination based on linear naive Bayes classification.

Features	True positive (%)	True negative (%)
Contour feature (radius standard deviation)	70.5	85.7
Scaling index features (entropy)	**82.3**	57.1
Tumor RSIE features (entropy (time scan 4))	76.4	71.4
Contour RSIE features (entropy (time scan 4))	76.4	71.4
Slope of RSIE	76.4	64.3
Geometric 5th moment	71.6	**100**
Bayes classification without geometric moments	76.4	78.5
Bayes classification with geometric moments	88.2	78.5

TABLE 4: AUC values for selected single features and all features combined based on an FLDA classification.

Features	AUC (%)
Contour feature (radius mean)	**82.6**
Scaling index features (mean)	79.6
Tumor RSIE features (entropy (time scan 3))	81.5
Contour RSIE features (entropy (time scan 4))	81.3
Slope of RSIE	72.7
FLDA classification with all features	**84.7**

4.2. Effectiveness of Combined Feature Groups. We now examine not anymore every single feature but group the features together in specific classes that contain the features described in the previous sections. Table 2 shows the results for five distinct classifiers assuming motion compensation in 2 directions. The Krawtchouk moments (reduced to a six-dimensional vector by PCA) yield the best results since they capture both local and global shape properties.

We perform receiver operating characteristic (ROC) analysis to determine the sensitivity, specificity, and area under the curve (AUC) of the CAD system. The results of the sensitivity and specificity for the current data set based on specific features selected based on their discrimination capability and also in combination are shown in Table 3. The scaling index entropy yields the highest sensitivity and the 5th geometric moment the highest specificity. This finding is not surprising since the scaling index is a spatio-temporal feature while the geometric moment is averaging over the tumor's shape. Since benign lesions tend to have smoother surfaces than malignant, this feature can be used as a first-step discriminator between those lesions. The inclusion of geometric moments in the feature set increases the sensitivity but leaves the specificity unchanged.

The best AUC-values for single features as well as for all features combined can be found in Table 4.

The AUC-values demonstrate that the contour features are very powerful descriptors and are able to capture the spatio-temporal behavior of small lesions.

5. Conclusion

The goal of the presented study was the introduction of new techniques for the automatic evaluation of dynamic MR mammography in *small lesions* and is motivated to increase specificity in MRI and thus improve the quality of breast MRI postprocessing, reduce the number of missed or misinterpreted cases leading to false-negative diagnosis.

Several novel lesion descriptors such as morphological, kinetic and spatio-temporal are applied and evaluated in context with benign and malignant lesion discrimination. Different classification techniques were applied to the classification of the lesions. A surprisingly low number of eight features proved to contain relevant information and achieved for both Fisher's LDA and LDA good classification results. Krawtchouk moments proved to capture both the local and global shape features and represent thus in term of classification the best shape descriptors. In terms of spatio-temporal features, the scaling index entropy yields the highest sensitivity demonstrating that the enhancement pattern in small lesions has to be analyzed both in terms of spatial and temporal information. The benign characteristics are best described by geometric moments. The AUC-values demonstrate that the contour features can capture very well the spatio-temporal behavior of these small lesions.

The results suggest that quantitative diagnostic features can be employed for developing automated CAD for small lesions to achieve a high detection and diagnosis performance. The performed ROC-analysis shows the potential of increasing the diagnostic accuracy of MR mammography by improving the sensitivity without reduction of specificity for the data sets examined.

Acknowledgments

The research was supported by NIH Grant 5K25CA106799-05 and by an Alexander von Humboldt Fellowship.

References

[1] S. G. Orel, M. D. Schnall, C. M. Powell et al., "Staging of suspected breast cancer: effect of MR imaging and MR-guided biopsy," *Radiology*, vol. 196, no. 1, pp. 115–122, 1995.

[2] C. K. Kuhl, P. Mielcareck, S. Klaschik et al., "Dynamic breast MR imaging: are signal intensity time course data useful for differential diagnosis of enhancing lesions?" *Radiology*, vol. 211, no. 1, pp. 101–110, 1999.

[3] M. D. Schnall, S. Rosten, S. Englander, S. G. Orel, and L. W. Nunes, "A combined architectural and kinetic interpretation model for breast MR images," *Academic Radiology*, vol. 8, no. 7, pp. 591–597, 2001.

[4] B. K. Szabó, P. Aspelin, M. Wiberg, and B. Bone, "Dynamic MR imaging of the breast. Analysis of kinetic and morphologic diagnostic criteria," *Acta Radiologica*, vol. 44, no. 4, pp. 379–386, 2003.

[5] A. P. Schouten van der Velden, C. Boetes, P. Bult, and T. Wobbes, "The value of magnetic resonance imaging in diagnosis and size assessment of in situ and small invasive breast carcinoma," *American Journal of Surgery*, vol. 192, no. 2, pp. 172–178, 2006.

[6] G. M. Grimsby, R. Gray, A. Dueck et al., "Is there concordance of invasive breast cancer pathologic tumor size with magnetic resonance imaging?" *The American Journal of Surgery*, vol. 198, no. 4, pp. 500–504, 2009.

[7] M. J. Stoutjesdijk, J. J. Fütterer, C. Boetes, L. E. Van Die, G. Jager, and J. O. Barentsz, "Variability in the description of morphologic and contrast enhancement characteristics of breast lesions on magnetic resonance imaging," *Investigative Radiology*, vol. 40, no. 6, pp. 355–362, 2005.

[8] I. M. A. Obdeijn, C. E. Loo, A. J. Rijnsburger et al., "Assessment of false-negative cases of breast MR imaging in women with a familial or genetic predisposition," *Breast Cancer Research and Treatment*, vol. 119, no. 2, pp. 399–407, 2010.

[9] G. D. Tourassi, R. Vargas-Voracek, D. M. Catarious, and C. E. Floyd, "Computer-assisted detection of mammographic masses: a template matching scheme based on mutual information," *Medical Physics*, vol. 30, no. 8, pp. 2123–2130, 2003.

[10] G. D. Tourassi, B. Harrawood, S. Singh, and J. Y. Lo, "Information-theoretic CAD system in mammography: entropy-based indexing for computational efficiency and robust performance," *Medical Physics*, vol. 34, no. 8, pp. 3193–3204, 2007.

[11] G. D. Tourassi, R. Ike, S. Singh, and B. Harrawood, "Evaluating the effect of image preprocessing on an information-theoretic CAD system in mammography," *Academic Radiology*, vol. 15, no. 5, pp. 626–634, 2008.

[12] L. Hadjiiski, B. Sahiner, and H. Chan, "Evaluating the effect of image preprocessing on an information-theoretic cad system in mammography.," *Current Opinion in Obstetrics and Gynecology*, vol. 18, no. 7, pp. 64–70, 2006.

[13] M. A. Kupinski and M. L. Giger, "Automated seeded lesion segmentation on digital mammograms," *IEEE Transactions on Medical Imaging*, vol. 17, no. 4, pp. 510–517, 1998.

[14] S. Behrens, H. Laue, M. Althaus et al., "Computer assistance for MR based diagnosis of breast cancer: present and future challenges," *Computerized Medical Imaging and Graphics*, vol. 31, no. 4-5, pp. 236–247, 2007.

[15] A. Hill, A. Mehnert, S. Crozier, and K. McMahon, "Evaluating the accuracy and impact of registration in dynamic contrast-enhanced breast MRI," *Concepts in Magnetic Resonance B*, vol. 35, no. 2, pp. 106–120, 2009.

[16] N. Papenberg, A. Bruhn, T. Brox, S. Didas, and J. Weickert, "Highly accurate optic flow computation with theoretically justified warping," *International Journal of Computer Vision*, vol. 67, no. 2, pp. 141–158, 2006.

[17] B. Horn and B. Schunck, *Determining optical flow*, 1981.

[18] F. Steinbruecker, A. Meyer-Baese, A. Wismueller, and T. Schlossbauer, "Application and evaluation of motion compensation technique to breast mri," in *Proceedings of the Evolutionary and Bio-Inspired Computation: Theory and Applications III*, vol. 7347 of *Proceedings of SPIE*, pp. 73470J–73470J-8, 2009.

[19] D. Xu and H. Li, "Geometric moment invariants," *Pattern Recognition*, vol. 41, no. 1, pp. 240–249, 2008.

[20] A. Mademlis, A. Axenopoulos, P. Daras, D. Tzovaras, and M. G. Strintzis, "3D content-based search based on 3D Krawtchouk moments," in *Proceedings of the 3rd International Symposium on 3D Data Processing, Visualization, and Transmission (3DPVT '06)*, pp. 743–749, June 2006.

[21] P. T. Yap, R. Paramesran, and S. H. Ong, "Image analysis by Krawtchouk moments," *IEEE Transactions on Image Processing*, vol. 12, no. 11, pp. 1367–1377, 2003.

[22] F. Jamitzky, R. W. Stark, W. Bunk et al., "Scaling-index method as an image processing tool in scanning-probe microscopy," *Ultramicroscopy*, vol. 86, no. 1-2, pp. 241–246, 2001.

[23] S. Theodoridis and K. Koutroumbas, *Pattern Recognition*, Academic Press, 1998.

11

Fuzzified Data Based Neural Network Modeling for Health Assessment of Multistorey Shear Buildings

Deepti Moyi Sahoo and S. Chakraverty

Department of Mathematics, National Institute of Technology Rourkela, Rourkela, Odisha 769 008, India

Correspondence should be addressed to S. Chakraverty; sne_chak@yahoo.com

Academic Editor: Matt Aitkenhead

The present study intends to propose identification methodologies for multistorey shear buildings using the powerful technique of Artificial Neural Network (ANN) models which can handle fuzzified data. Identification with crisp data is known, and also neural network method has already been used by various researchers for this case. Here, the input and output data may be in fuzzified form. This is because in general we may not get the corresponding input and output values exactly (in crisp form), but we have only the uncertain information of the data. This uncertain data is assumed in terms of fuzzy number, and the corresponding problem of system identification is investigated.

1. Introduction

System identification methods in structural dynamics, in general, solve inverse vibration problems to identify properties of a structure from measured data. The rapid progress in the field of computer science and computational mathematics during recent decades has led to an increasing use of process computers and models to analyze, supervise, and control technical processes. The use of computers and efficient mathematical tools allows identification of the process dynamics by evaluating the input and output signals of the system. The result of such a process identification is usually a mathematical model by which the dynamic behaviour can be estimated or predicted. The system identification problem has been nicely explained in a recent paper [1]. The same statements from [1] are reproduced below for the benefit of the readers.

The study of structures dynamic behaviour may be categorized into two distinct activities: analytical and/or numerical modelling (e.g., finite element models) and vibration tests (e.g., experimental modal models). Due to different limitations and assumptions, each approach has its advantages and shortcomings. Therefore, in order to determine the dynamic properties of the structure, reconciliation processes including model correlation and/or model updating should be performed. Model updating can be defined as the adjustment of an existing analytical/numerical model in the light of measured vibration test. After adjustment, the updated model is expected to represent the dynamic behaviour of the structure more accurately as proposed by Friswell et al. [2]. With the recent advances in computing technology for data acquisition, signal processing, and analysis, the parameters of structural models may be updated from the measured responses under excitation of the structure. This procedure is achieved using system identification techniques as an inverse problem. The inverse problem may be defined as determination of the internal structure of a physical system from the system's measured behaviour, or estimation of an unknown input that gives rise to a measured output signal according to Tanaka and Bui [3].

Comprehensive literature surveys have been provided on the subject of model updating of the structural systems by Alvin et al. [4], and Time series methods for fault detection and identification in vibrating structures were presented by Fassois and Sakellariou [5]. Shear buildings are among the most widely studied structural systems. Previous works on model updating of shear buildings rely mostly on using modal parameter identification and physical or structural parameter

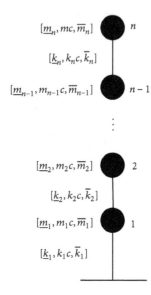

FIGURE 1: Multistorey shear structure with n-levels having fuzzy structural parameters.

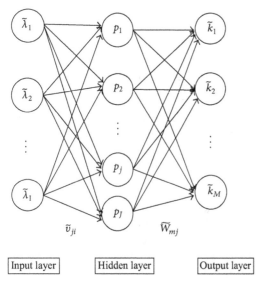

FIGURE 2: Layered feed-forward fuzzy neural network.

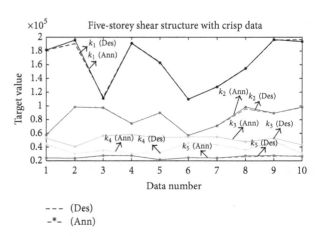

--- (Des)
-*- (Ann)

FIGURE 3: Comparison between the desired and the ANN values of $\widetilde{K}$ for a single-storey shear structure.

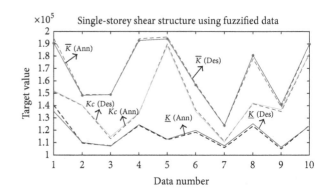

FIGURE 4: Comparison between the desired and the ANN values of $\widetilde{K}$ for a single-storey shear structure.

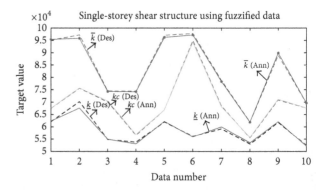

FIGURE 5: Comparison between the desired and the ANN values of $\widetilde{K}$ for a single-storey shear.

identification to drive the corresponding update procedures. As regards the publications, Marsi et al. [6] gave various methodologies for different types of problems in system identification. Various techniques for improving structural dynamic models were reviewed in a review paper by Ibanez [7], and studies made by Datta et al. [8] related to system identification of buildings done until that date were also surveyed. Some of the related publications may be mentioned as those of Loh and Tou [9] and Yuan et al. [10].

It is known that, the systems which may be modeled as linear, the identification problem often turns in to a non-linear optimization problem. This requires an intelligent iterative scheme to have the required solution. There exists various online and offline methods, namely, the Gauss-Newton, Kalman filtering and probabilistic methods such

as maximum likelihood estimation, and so forth. However, the identification problem for a large number of parameters, following two basic difficulties are faced often:

(i) objective function surface may have multiple maxima and minima, and the convergence to the correct parameters is possible only if the initial guess is considered as close to the parameters to be identified;

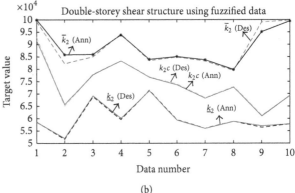

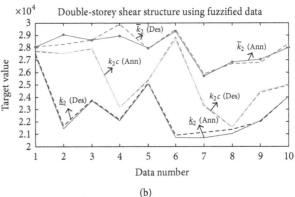

FIGURE 6: (a) Comparison between the desired and the ANN values of $\widetilde{k}_1$ for a double-storey shear structure. (b) Comparison between the desired and the ANN values of $\widetilde{k}_2$ for a double-storey shear structure.

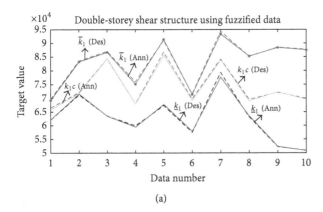

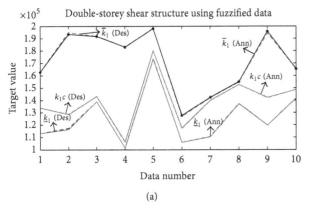

FIGURE 7: (a) Comparison between the desired and the ANN values of $\widetilde{k}_1$ for a double-storey shear structure. (b) Comparison between the desired and the ANN values of $\widetilde{k}_2$ for a double-storey shear structure.

(ii) inverse problem in general gives nonunique parameter estimates.

To overcome these difficulties, researchers have developed various identification methodologies for the said problem by using powerful technique of Artificial Neural Network (ANN). Chen [11] presented a neural network based method for determining the modal parameters of structures from field measurement. Using the observed dynamic responses, he trained the neural network based on back-propagation technique. He then directly identified the modal parameters of the structure using the weight matrices of the neural network. In particular, Huang et al. [12] presented a novel procedure for identifying the dynamic characteristics of a building using a back-propagation neural network technique. Another novel neural network based approach has been presented by Kao and Hung [13] for detecting structural damage. A decentralized stiffness identification method with neural networks for a multidegree of freedom structure has been developed by Wu et al. [14]. Localized damage detection and parametric identification method with direct use of earthquake responses for large-scale infrastructures has also been proposed by Xu et al. [15]. A neural network

based strategy by Xu et al. [16] was developed for direct identification of structural parameters from the time domain dynamic responses of an object structure without anyeigen value analysis.

System identification on the other hand tries to identify structural matrices of mass, damping and stiffness directly. Among various methodologies in this regard Chakraverty [17], Perry et al. [18], Wang [19], Yoshitomi and Takewaki [20], and Lu and Tu [21] developed different techniques to handle the system identification problems. Yuan et al. [10] developed a methodology that identifies the mass and stiffness matrices of a shear building from the first two orders of structural mode measurement. Koh et al. [22] proposed several Ga-based substructural identification methods, which work by solving parts of the structure at a time to improve the convergence of mass and stiffness estimates particularly for large systems. Chakraverty [17] proposed procedures to refine the methods of Yuan et al. [10] to identify the structural mass and stiffness matrices of shear buildings from the modal test data. The refinement was obtained using Holzer criteria. Tang et al. [23] utilized a differential evolution (DE) strategy for parameter estimation of the structural systems with limited output data, noise polluted signals, and no prior

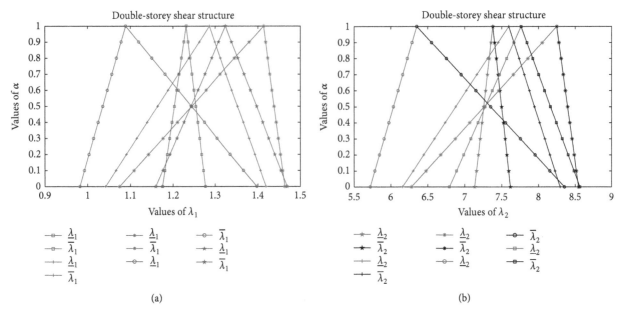

FIGURE 8: (a) Comparison of $\underline{\lambda_1}$ and $\overline{\lambda_1}$ with respect to α. (b) Comparison of $\underline{\lambda_2}$ and $\overline{\lambda_2}$ with respect to α.

knowledge of mass, damping, or stiffness matrices. Recent works on model updating of multistory shear buildings for simultaneous identification of mass, stiffness, and damping matrices using two different soft-computing methods have been developed by Khanmirza et al. [1]. It may be seen from above that Artificial Neural Networks (ANNs) provide a fundamentally different approach to system identification. They have been successfully applied for identification and control of dynamics systems in various fields of engineering because of excellent learning capacity and high tolerance to partially inaccurate data.

It is revealed from the above literature review that various authors developed different identification methodologies using ANN. They supposed that the data obtained are in exact or crisp form. But in actual practice the experimental data obtained from equipments are with errors that may be due to human or equipment error, thereby giving uncertain form of the data. Although one may also use probabilistic methods to handle such problems. Then, the probabilistic method requires huge quantity of data which may not be easy or feasible. Thus in this paper, a minimum number of data are taken in fuzzified form to have the essence of the uncertainty. Accordingly, in this paper, identification methodologies for multistorey shear buildings have been proposed using the powerful technique of Artificial Neural Network (ANN) models which can handle fuzzified data. It is already mentioned that identification with crisp data is known and also neural network method has already been used by various researchers for this case. Here, the input and output data may be in fuzzified form. This is because in general we may not get the corresponding input and output values exactly (in crisp form), but we have only the uncertain information of the data. This uncertain data has been assumed to be in terms of fuzzy numbers.

In this paper, the initial design parameters, namely, stiffness and mass and so the frequency of the said problem is known. But after a large span of time, the structure may be subjected to various manmade and natural calamities. Then, the engineers want to know the present health of the structure by system identification methods. It is assumed that only the stiffness is changed and the mass remains the same. As such equipments are available to get the present values of the frequencies and using these one may get the present parameter values by ANN. But while doing the experiment, one may not get the exact values of the parameters. But we may get those values as uncertain, namely, in fuzzy form. So if sensors are placed to capture the frequency of the floors in fuzzy (uncertain) form, then those may be fed into the proposed new ANN model to get the present stiffness parameters in fuzzified form. In order to train the new ANN model, set of data are generated numerically beforehand. As such, converged ANN model gives the present stiffness parameter values in interval form for each floor. Thus, one may predict the health of the uncertain structure. Corresponding example problems have been solved, and related results are reported to show the reliability and powerfulness of the model.

2. Analysis and Modelling

System identification refers to the branch of numerical analysis which uses the experimental input and output data to develop mathematical models of systems which finally identify the parameters. The floor masses for this methodology are assumed to be $[\underline{m_1}, m_1 c, \overline{m_1}]$, $[\underline{m_2}, m_2 c, \overline{m_2}], \ldots, [\underline{m_n}, m_n c, \overline{m_n}]$, and the stiffness $[\underline{k_1}, k_1 c, \overline{k_1}], [\underline{k_2}, k_2 c, \overline{k_2}], \ldots, [\underline{k_n}, k_n c, \overline{k_n}]$ are the structural parameters which are to be identified. It may be seen that all the mass and stiffness parameters are taken in fuzzy form. As such here for each mass m_i, we have $\underline{m_i}$ as the left value, $m_i c$ as the centre value, and $\overline{m_i}$ as the right value. Similarly for the stiffness parameter for each mass k_i, we have $\underline{k_i}$ as the left value, $k_i c$ as the centre value, and $\overline{k_i}$ as the right value. The n-storey shear structure is shown in Figure 1. Corresponding dynamic equation of motion for n-storey (supposed as n degrees of freedom) shear structure without damping may be written as

$$\{\widetilde{M}\}\{\ddot{\widetilde{X}}\} + \{\widetilde{K}\}\{\widetilde{X}\} = \{\widetilde{0}\}, \tag{1}$$

where $\{\ddot{\widetilde{x}}\} = \{\underline{\ddot{x}}, \ddot{x}c, \overline{\ddot{x}}\}$, $\{\widetilde{x}\} = [\underline{x}, xc, \overline{x}]$.

$\{\widetilde{M}\} = [\underline{M}, Mc, \overline{M}]$ is $n \times n$ mass matrix of the structure and is given by

$$\{\widetilde{M}\} = \begin{bmatrix} [\underline{m_1}, m_1 c, \overline{m_1}] & 0 & \cdots & \cdots & 0 \\ 0 & [\underline{m_2}, m_2 c, \overline{m_2}] & 0 & \cdots & 0 \\ \cdots & \cdots & \cdots & \cdots & \cdots \\ \cdots & \cdots & 0 & [\underline{m_{n-1}}, m_{n-1}c, \overline{m_{n-1}}] & [\underline{m_n}, m_n c, \overline{m_n}] \\ 0 & \cdots & \cdots & 0 & 0 \end{bmatrix}. \tag{2}$$

$\{\widetilde{K}\} = [\underline{K}, Kc, \overline{K}]$ is $n \times n$ stiffness matrix of the structure and may be written as

$$\{\widetilde{K}\} = \begin{bmatrix} \widetilde{k_1} + \widetilde{k_2} & \widetilde{k_2} & 0 & \cdots & 0 \\ -\widetilde{k_2} & \widetilde{k_2} + \widetilde{k_3} & -\widetilde{k_3} & \cdots & 0 \\ \cdots & \cdots & & & \cdots \\ 0 & \cdots & -\widetilde{k_{n-1}} & \widetilde{k_{n-1}} + \widetilde{k_n} & \widetilde{k_n} \\ 0 & \cdots & & -\widetilde{k_n} & \widetilde{k_n} \end{bmatrix}, \tag{3}$$

and $\{\widetilde{X}\} = \{\widetilde{x_1}, \widetilde{x_2}, \ldots, \widetilde{x_n}\}^T$ are the vectors of displacement.

We will first solve the above free vibration equation for vibration characteristics, namely, for frequency and mode shapes of the said structural system in order to get the stiffness parameters in fuzzified form. Accordingly putting $\{\widetilde{X}\} = \{\widetilde{\phi}\}e^{i(\widetilde{\omega})t}$ in free vibration equation (1), we get

$$\left(\{\widetilde{K}\} - \{\widetilde{M}\}[\widetilde{\omega}]^2\right)\{\widetilde{\phi}\} = \{\widetilde{0}\}, \tag{4}$$

where $\{\widetilde{\omega}\}^2 = [\underline{\omega}, \omega c, \overline{\omega}]^2 = [\underline{\lambda}, \lambda c, \overline{\lambda}]$ are eigenvalues or the natural frequency and $\{\widetilde{\phi}\}$ are mode shapes of the structure, respectively.

3. Basic Concept of Fuzzy Set Theory

Definition 1. Let X be a universal set. Then, the fuzzy subset A of X is defined by its membership function

$$\mu_A : X \longrightarrow [0,1], \tag{5}$$

which assigns a real number $\mu_A(x)$ in the interval $[0, 1]$, to each element $x \in X$, where the value of $\mu_A(x)$ at x shows the grade of membership of x in A.

Definition 2. Given a fuzzy set A in X and any real number $\alpha \in [0, 1]$, then, the α-cut or α-level or cut worthy set of A, denoted by A_α, is the crisp set

$$A_\alpha = \{x \in X \mid \mu_A(x) \geq \alpha\}. \tag{6}$$

The strong α-cut, denoted by $A_{\alpha+}$, is the crisp set

$$A_{\alpha+} = \{x \in X \mid \mu_A(x) \geq \alpha\}. \tag{7}$$

Definition 3. A fuzzy number is a convex normalized fuzzy set of the real line R whose membership function is piecewise continuous.

Definition 4. A triangular fuzzy number A can be defined as a triplet $[a_1, a_2, a_3]$. Its membership function is defined as

$$\mu_A(x) = \begin{cases} 0, & x < a_1 \\ \dfrac{x - a_1}{a_2 - a_1}, & a_1 \leq x \leq a_2 \\ \dfrac{a_3 - x}{a_3 - a_2}, & a_2 \leq x \leq a_3 \\ 0, & x > a_3. \end{cases} \tag{8}$$

Above TFN may be transformed to an interval form A_α by α-cut as

$$A_\alpha = \left[a_1^{(\alpha)}, a_3^{(\alpha)}\right] = \left[(a_2 - a_1)\alpha + a_1, -(a_3 - a_2)\alpha + a_3\right]. \tag{9}$$

4. Operation of Fuzzy Number

In this section, we consider arithmetic operation on fuzzy numbers and the result is expressed in membership function:

$$\forall x, y, z \in R. \tag{10}$$

(1) Addition: $A(+)B$

$$\mu_{A(+)B}(z) = \bigvee_{z=x+y} (\mu_A(x) \wedge \mu_B(y)). \tag{11}$$

(2) Subtraction: $A(-)B$

$$\mu_{A(-)B}(z) = \bigvee_{z=x-y} (\mu_A(x) \wedge \mu_B(y)). \tag{12}$$

(3) Multiplication: $A(\cdot)B$

$$\mu_{A(\cdot)B}(z) = \bigvee_{z=x\cdot y} (\mu_A(x) \wedge \mu_B(y)). \tag{13}$$

TABLE 1: Comparison between the desired and the ANN values of k_1, k_2, k_3, k_4, and k_5 for a five-storey shear structure.

Data number	k_1 (Ann)	k_1 (Des)	k_2 (Ann)	k_2 (Des)	k_3 (Ann)	k_3 (Des)	k_4 (Ann)	k_4 (Des)	k_5 (Ann)	k_5 (Des)
1	181277.7318	181472.3686	57722.68	57880.6541	53111.561	53114.814	44531.8138	44120.9218	24304.5301	24387.4436
2	195883.7223	190579.1937	98497.3362	98529.6391	40890.7789	40714.2336	30510.5884	30636.6569	24013.4116	23815.5846
3	110889.324	112698.6816	97540.2878	97858.3474	56939.1333	56982.5861	35467.0709	35538.4597	27905.0723	27655.1679
4	191334.6369	191337.5856	74367.0906	74268.7824	58151.3678	58679.865	30921.7444	30923.4278	27758.983	27951.999
5	162671.148	163235.9246	90080.9291	90014.0234	53507.0758	53574.7031	31851.263	31942.6356	21775.0509	21868.726
6	109757.8778	109754.0405	57034.3391	57094.3169	55073.904	55154.8026	46360.9403	46469.1566	24899.5619	24897.644
7	127671.411	127849.8219	71003.1282	71088.0641	54999.758	54862.6494	43688.9611	43896.5725	24554.2598	24455.862
8	154429.3614	154688.1519	98500.0073	95786.7763	48031.3148	47844.5404	36250.0047	36341.9896	27719.1389	26463.1301
9	196399.16	195750.6835	89751.9025	89610.3665	53100.0372	53109.5578	48498.0106	49004.441	27950.5364	27093.6483
10	193722.4668	196488.8535	98520.881	97974.6213	43228.929	43423.7338	30822.0268	30688.9216	26813.9637	27546.8668

(4) Division: $A(/)B$

$$\mu_{A(/)B}(z) = \bigvee_{z=x/y} (\mu_A(x) \wedge \mu_B(y)). \qquad (14)$$

(5) Minimum: $A(\wedge)B$

$$\mu_{A(\wedge)B}(z) = \bigvee_{z=x\wedge y} (\mu_A(x) \wedge \mu_B(y)). \qquad (15)$$

(6) Maximum: $A(\vee)B$

$$\mu_{A(\vee)B}(z) = \bigvee_{z=x\vee y} (\mu_A(x) \wedge \mu_B(y)). \qquad (16)$$

5. Artificial Neural Network (ANN) and Error-Back Propagation Training Algorithm (EBPTA) for Fuzzified Data

Traditional ANN and EBPTA are well known, but here for the sake of completeness, those are developed for fuzzy case. In ANN, the first layer is considered to be input layer and the last layer is the output layer. Between the input and output layers, there may be more than one hidden layer. Each layer will contain number of neurons or nodes (processing elements) depending upon the problem. These processing elements operate in parallel and are arranged in patterns similar to the patterns found in biological neural nets. The processing elements are connected to each other by adjustable weights. The input/output behavior of the network changes if the weights are changed. So, the weights of the net may be chosen in such a way so as to achieve a desired output. To satisfy this goal, systematic ways of adjusting the weights have to be developed to handle the fuzzified data which are known as training or learning algorithm. Neural network basically depends upon the type of processing elements or nodes, the network topology, and the learning algorithm. Here, error back-propagation training algorithm and feedforward recall have been used but to handle the uncertain system. The typical network is given in Figure 2.

In this Figure, Z_i, P_j, and O_m are input, hidden, and output layers, respectively. The weights between input and hidden layers are denoted by v_{ji}, and the weights between hidden and output layers are denoted by W_{kj}. Here, $\widetilde{Z}_i = [\underline{\lambda_i} \ \lambda_i c \ \overline{\lambda_i}]$ and $\widetilde{O}_k = [\underline{k_m} \ k_m c \ \overline{k_m}]$.

Given R training pairs $\{\widetilde{Z}_1, \tilde{d}_1; \widetilde{Z}_2, \tilde{d}_2; \ldots, \widetilde{Z}_R, \tilde{d}_R\}$ where $\widetilde{Z}_i(I \times 1)$ are input and $\tilde{d}_i(M \times 1)$ are desired values for the given inputs, the error value is computed as

$$\widetilde{E} = \frac{1}{2}\left(\tilde{d}_m - \widetilde{O}_m\right)^2, \quad m = 1, 2, \ldots M, \qquad (17)$$

for the present neural network as shown in Figure 2. The error signal terms of the output $(\tilde{\delta}_{Om})$ and hidden layers $(\tilde{\delta}_{pj})$ are written, respectively, as

$$\tilde{\delta}_{Om} = 0.5 * \left(\tilde{d}_m - \widetilde{O}_m\right)\left(1 - \widetilde{O}_m^2\right), \quad m = 1, 2, \ldots M,$$

$$\tilde{\delta}_{Pj} = 0.5 * \left(1 - \widetilde{P}_j^2\right)\sum_{m=1}^{M} \tilde{\delta}_{Om}\widetilde{W}_{Pj}, \quad j = 1, 2, \ldots J. \qquad (18)$$

Consequently, output layer weights $(\widetilde{W}_{mj})$ and hidden layer weights $(\tilde{v}_{ji})$ are adjusted as

$$\widetilde{W}_{mj}^{(New)} = \widetilde{W}_{mj}^{(Old)} + \eta\tilde{\delta}_{Om}P_j, \quad m = 1, 2, \ldots M, \ j = 1, 2, \ldots J,$$

$$\tilde{v}_{ji}^{(New)} = \tilde{v}_{ji}^{(Old)} + \eta\tilde{\delta}_{Pj}Z_i, \quad j = 1, 2, \ldots J, \ i = 1, 2, \ldots I, \qquad (19)$$

where η is the learning constant.

6. Results and Discussion

To investigate the present method here, examples of one- and two-storey shear structures are considered. So, for example, the floor masses for two-storey shear structure are $[\underline{m_1}, m_1 c, \overline{m_1}]$, $[\underline{m_2}, m_2 c, \overline{m_2}]$ and the stiffnesses $[\underline{k_1}, k_1 c, \overline{k_1}]$, $[\underline{k_2}, k_2 c, \overline{k_2}]$ are the structural parameters. Here,

TABLE 2: (a) Comparison between the desired and the ANN values of k_1, k_2, k_3, k_4, and k_5 for a ten-storey shear structure. (b) Comparison between the desired and the ANN values of k_6, k_7, k_8, k_9, and k_{10} for a ten-storey shear structure.

(a)

Data number	k_1 (Ann)	k_1 (Des)	k_2 (Ann)	k_2 (Des)	k_3 (Ann)	k_3 (Des)	k_4 (Ann)	k_4 (Des)	k_5 (Ann)	k_5 (Des)
1	116900.6563	114999.7254	23626.293	23947.0748	25255.905	24299.2141	29078.6982	29493.0391	27766.1413	28842.8102
2	137413.4659	135922.821	22400.1311	21970.538	22076.7651	22160.1892	28671.6078	29898.7215	23928.6799	23185.2425
3	174166.5579	171165.6706	26751.8243	27587.6627	28439.4836	28089.9027	28056.19	27636.7332	28909.5075	29349.7909
4	185745.6345	187147.6518	28203.5977	29952.1598	23288.5994	23565.0893	25414.2964	25588.2055	24175.8385	24794.8455
5	131376.8088	132868.9612	22531.4396	21865.7144	20887.9013	20732.4343	22490.5032	21838.4294	21747.4496	22317.9161
6	174687.251	165011.8025	25813.5863	27811.4527	25015.1015	25909.9146	25615.7328	24979.4882	24612.1573	23962.9025
7	185115.3655	197483.6148	24841.291	21957.9798	27352.9705	29101.8783	25184.1779	25178.456	27414.6225	27050.7748
8	107439.5782	107596.7361	28408.1614	29923.5897	22079.0745	21937.6594	29361.5732	29942.4301	25283.6014	25585.5903
9	164872.2954	158701.9167	25498.9862	28022.6157	26269.1879	24323.6779	28505.5766	28548.5168	27421.7863	27566.307
10	134496.3197	136428.6869	23984.6699	23091.3643	26528.5422	27288.6387	20735.4877	20391.8449	26590.0291	26789.4101

(b)

Data number	k_6 (Ann)	k_6 (Des)	k_7 (Ann)	k_7 (Des)	k_8 (Ann)	k_8 (Des)	k_9 (Ann)	k_9 (Des)	k_{10} (Ann)	k_{10} (Des)
1	21170.0974	20899.5068	25777.6655	25605.5953	28204.3487	29899.5021	27503.4171	25859.8704	27163.5463	25814.4649
2	22417.1364	20549.7415	27621.6492	28654.3859	27612.505	28451.7819	28303.9996	29823.0322	22093.3505	22094.0508
3	29672.9685	29638.7013	25998.8211	27124.1481	22438.2305	21982.2179	26315.5549	26153.251	27684.8546	29019.9081
4	19962.2582	19656.5635	21156.2588	20166.7471	22269.5196	21950.7153	23818.7821	23766.1108	27240.5745	27020.6645
5	20161.805	20514.4829	25387.6098	28009.2088	23922.4631	23268.3965	27519.8427	28771.8175	23219.6412	23774.551
6	22307.0935	23043.4895	21527.1166	21425.0932	27311.6444	28803.3786	27670.7454	27848.5243	27234.7985	27349.5593
7	27804.4452	25801.9183	24442.8169	24784.7447	25319.1653	24711.0187	25870.6554	24649.5428	27640.8021	29541.0279
8	25509.2344	25309.6445	22738.1369	22568.3535	23936.8813	24039.6937	28924.1116	28139.7693	25172.6749	25428.1311
9	28341.8519	29012.0809	25380.1928	23690.9169	23071.1828	21792.3148	28034.5751	28984.4414	26519.4395	25401.0583
10	27911.2912	29624.314	26475.8553	24319.8061	21306.3632	21696.0881	25327.5363	24074.5574	24485.2563	23343.2942

TABLE 3: Comparison between the desired and the ANN values of $\widetilde{K}$ for a single-storey shear structure.

Data number	$\underline{K}$ (Ann)	$\underline{K}$ (Des)	Kc (Ann)	Kc (Des)	$\overline{K}$ (Ann)	$\overline{K}$ (Des)
1	124932.9319	124189.1286	135932.8213	135095.2381	191905.7285	190281.611
2	135763.4956	140411.2146	152464.2896	151324.954	191726.9669	194488.719
3	110291.5736	109665.4525	141591.1084	140180.8034	148514.9196	149096.4092
4	107394.0584	107596.6692	115134.7117	113217.3293	149119.797	148935.2638
5	124430.5911	123991.6154	134455.7107	133781.941	192947.0787	194225.0591
6	112574.5401	112331.8935	188853.0283	190015.3846	194542.4439	195633.454
7	120988.7913	118390.7788	138166.8698	136934.6781	157619.3944	157540.8595
8	108960.7756	105997.9543	113526.3083	111130.2755	126504.2017	123995.2526
9	124700.9011	123497.9913	143556.5197	141726.7069	179985.5092	178035.2068
10	105227.009	104965.443	135988.057	135335.8571	140612.991	138983.8837

masses are assumed to be constant (as mentioned earlier). So, we will identify the stiffness parameter in fuzzy form using the fuzzy form of the frequency where frequency may be obtained from some experiments. In the following paragraphs, we have used the proposed method to identify the stiffness parameter for one-, two-, five-, and ten-storey frame structures. Here, we have considered the cases with crisp data for five- and ten-storeys and then fuzzified data for one- and two-storeys. The training data are also considered with the influence of noise, namely, in terms of triangular fuzzy number data. Accordingly we have considered the following four cases:

TABLE 4: Comparison between the desired and the ANN values of $\widetilde{K}$ for a single-storey shear structure.

Data number	$\underline{k}$ (Ann)	$\underline{k}$ (Des)	kc (Ann)	kc (Des)	$\overline{k}$ (Ann)	$\overline{k}$ (Des)
1	62365.0341	62104.5643	67644.4378	67547.619	95458.8463	95145.8055
2	67613.8959	70215.6073	75826.931	75662.477	95893.1612	97249.3595
3	55005.0087	54842.7263	70556.3936	70090.4017	74368.7997	74553.2046
4	53128.7186	53798.3346	56947.542	56618.6646	74261.1768	74472.6319
5	62246.1626	61995.8077	66881.2194	66895.9705	96278.4523	97122.5295
6	55957.2602	56165.9467	94391.1219	95012.6923	97271.6645	97826.727
7	60056.7259	59195.3894	68223.7328	68472.3391	78385.7211	78780.4298
8	53587.3374	53008.9771	55747.5298	55570.1378	61968.3882	61997.6263
9	62126.6388	61758.9957	71196.546	70863.3535	89991.9346	89022.6034
10	52238.7913	52482.7215	67702.5259	67677.9286	69679.1387	69496.9418

TABLE 5: (a) Comparison between the desired and the ANN values of $\widetilde{k}_1$ for a double-storey shear structure. (b) Comparison between the desired and the ANN values of $\widetilde{k}_2$ for a double-storey shear structure.

(a)

Data number	$\underline{k_1}$ (Ann)	$\underline{k_1}$ (Des)	k_1c (Ann)	k_1c (Des)	$\overline{k_1}$ (Ann)	$\overline{k_1}$ (Des)
1	113258.5422	113317.1008	133858.2555	133969.3413	162741.2326	162807.3359
2	116526.66	117338.8613	128622.4646	129208.408	193447.2534	195183.0465
3	139119.0131	139093.7802	143501.0894	143175.117	191801.5675	192053.204
4	101316.7594	101558.7126	106512.8803	105287.6998	183040.5812	183137.9743
5	173554.7972	173805.8096	180269.037	180336.4392	198199.4731	198416.3724
6	105985.8857	106047.1179	117592.2043	116726.841	127688.8972	126931.9426
7	110472.1362	110631.6345	140132.9188	139925.7771	142461.6007	142303.5615
8	137120.3743	137250.974	152856.9037	152687.5831	155005.6994	154807.0901
9	119783.849	119821.8403	142480.6438	141679.9468	195824.6624	194293.6984
10	141708.5217	141794.4104	148654.6797	148978.7638	165370.4902	165685.9891

(b)

Data number	$\underline{k_2}$ (Ann)	$\underline{k_2}$ (Des)	k_2c (Ann)	k_2c (Des)	$\overline{k_2}$ (Ann)	$\overline{k_2}$ (Des)
1	58488.0205	58566.0533	91472.5908	92796.1403	99954.016	99152.6233
2	51977.6459	51640.041	65679.199	65072.7474	85856.2114	82258.2268
3	69213.7504	68833.6105	77764.8854	78069.9896	85939.2478	85054.9378
4	60124.2902	59566.1848	83319.0924	83316.9426	93794.9834	94103.325
5	71317.3378	71432.6496	76748.5343	76956.3233	83930.3883	83468.7652
6	59384.591	59531.6634	73687.8221	74121.1031	85087.5853	84905.276
7	56031.7629	56050.5807	68215.603	68455.8273	83728.3652	83326.3957
8	58849.1438	58906.6227	72741.8224	73046.2969	79796.3231	79495.3742
9	57077.8681	56400.72	61035.9761	61329.384	95110.8992	99091.8975
10	57858.7023	57830.2476	69404.8867	69250.9562	99433.354	99954.0197

Case(i): Five-storey shear structure with crisp data,

Case(ii): Ten-storey shear structure with crisp data,

Case(iii): Single-storey shear structure with fuzzified data,

Case(iv): Double-storey shear structure with fuzzified data.

Computer programs have been written and tested for variety of experiments for the above cases. For the first two cases, namely, Case(i) and Case(ii), the inputs are taken as the crisp

TABLE 6: (a) Comparison between the desired and the ANN values of $\tilde{k}_1$ for a double-storey shear structure. (b) Comparison between the desired and the ANN values of $\tilde{k}_2$ for a double-storey shear structure.

(a)

Data number	$\underline{k_1}$ (Ann)	$\underline{k_1}$ (Des)	$k_1 c$ (Ann)	$k_1 c$ (Des)	$\overline{k_1}$ (Ann)	$\overline{k_1}$ (Des)
1	62193.4503	62149.2679	65871.2249	66562.894	69219.2648	69672.8181
2	71578.6175	71235.4748	71816.4848	72130.1157	83311.5254	83571.557
3	63514.5116	63533.5212	84447.6191	84399.8043	86708.0123	87062.8972
4	59459.7849	59872.6899	67907.0231	67971.4105	75148.6421	76002.6234
5	67809.323	67385.6336	85655.9802	86827.0037	91460.6917	91106.0592
6	57879.7498	57499.8627	69206.8111	69745.3738	71387.5577	71516.0705
7	77679.4222	79304.6034	83870.4195	84180.7933	93380.175	94408.5477
8	63484.2106	63107.2659	69028.8134	69579.1498	85313.0398	85212.3715
9	52329.6174	52222.7046	72316.9085	72125.2707	88399.7894	88475.7194
10	50895.5951	50988.8812	69532.938	69859.5759	87547.575	87746.6634

(b)

Data number	$\underline{k_2}$ (Ann)	$\underline{k_2}$ (Des)	$k_2 c$ (Ann)	$k_2 c$ (Des)	$\overline{k_2}$ (Ann)	$\overline{k_2}$ (Des)
1	27396.6322	27507.0572	27776.8241	27698.5425	28078.4211	28085.141
2	21439.7109	21682.5355	27548.5904	27550.771	29081.9724	28275.8382
3	23717.5546	23773.9554	27948.7301	27919.6303	28617.4807	28629.8048
4	22090.0439	22160.1892	23180.7111	23205.2425	28962.7934	29908.7215
5	25086.5697	25154.2346	25465.6455	25360.6413	27961.1253	27904.0722
6	20724.6386	20919.5068	28645.592	28852.8102	29353.9707	29493.0391
7	20706.4881	21137.0574	23381.0249	23275.6543	25716.8788	25890.2606
8	21056.3736	21382.9255	21574.7879	21557.5235	26851.9289	26712.6437
9	22075.9397	22008.6282	24479.3131	24386.4498	27062.0237	26806.523
10	24070.1411	24079.5484	25009.5776	24971.7702	28009.5803	28335.006

frequency values and the outputs are the stiffness parameters which are also in crisp form. On the other hand, for Cases(iii) and (iv), the inputs are taken as the fuzzified frequency values and the outputs are the stiffness parameters again in fuzzified form in the developed Fuzzy Neural Network (FNN) algorithm.

For the first case, an example of a storey shear structure is taken where the masses are $m_1 = m_2 = m_3 = m_4 = m_5 = 36000$ and the stiffness parameters are within the range $k_1 = [100000 \ 200000]$, $k_2 = [50000 \ 100000]$, $k_3 = [40000 \ 60000]$, $k_4 = [30000 \ 50000]$, and $k_5 = [20000 \ 30000]$. A comparison between the desired and ANN values has been presented in Table 1. This table has been plotted in Figure 3.

In Case(ii), an example for a ten-storey shear structure has been considered with constant masses similar to Case(i) and the stiffness parameters are in the range $k_1 = [100000 \ 200000]$, $k_2 = k_3 = k_4 = k_5 = k_6 = k_7 = k_8 = k_9 = k_{10} = [20000 \ 30000]$. The desired and ANN values for k_1 to k_5 and k_6 to k_{10} are compared in Tables 2(a) and 2(b), respectively.

For Case(iii), the first example is that of a single-storey shear structure with masses $\widetilde{M} = 36000$ and the stiffness

parameters lie within the range $\underline{K} = [100000 \ 200000]$, $Kc = [100010 \ 200010]$, and $\overline{K} = [100020 \ 200020]$. A comparison between desired and the ANN values has been incorporated in Table 3. This table has been plotted in Figure 4. In the second example, a single-storey shear structure is considered with masses $\widetilde{M} = 36000$ and the stiffness parameter varying within the range $\underline{K} = [50000 \ 100000]$, $Kc = [50010 \ 100010]$, and $\overline{K} = [50020 \ 100020]$. Comparison between the desired and the ANN values is tabulated in Table 4 and is plotted in Figure 5.

In Case(iv), the first example of a double-storey shear structure is considered where the masses are $\widetilde{m}_1 = \widetilde{m}_2 = 36000$ and the stiffness parameters varying within the range $\underline{k_1} = [100000 \ 200000]$, $k_1 c = [100010 \ 200010]$, $\overline{k_1} = [100020 \ 200020]$ and $\underline{k_2} = [20000 \ 30000]$, $k_2 c = [20010 \ 30010]$, and $\overline{k_2} = [20020 \ 30020]$. The desired and ANN values have been compared in Tables 5(a) and 5(b). This table has also been shown in Figures 6(a) and 6(b). In the second example, a double-storey shear structure is implemented with masses $\widetilde{m}_1 = \widetilde{m}_2 = 36000$ and the stiffness parameters having the range $\underline{k_1} = [50000 \ 100000]$, $k_1 c = [50010 \ 100010]$, $\overline{k_1} = [50020 \ 100020]$ and

TABLE 7: (a) Comparison between the desired and the ANN values of $\underline{k_1}$, $\overline{k_1}$ and $\underline{k_2}$, $\overline{k_2}$ for a double-storey shear structure for $\alpha = 0.3$. (b) Comparison between the desired and the ANN values of $\underline{k_1}$, $\overline{k_1}$ and $\underline{k_2}$, $\overline{k_2}$ for a double-storey shear structure for $\alpha = 0.5$. (c) Comparison between the desired and the ANN values of $\underline{k_1}$, $\overline{k_1}$ and $\underline{k_2}$, $\overline{\overline{k_2}}$ for a double-storey shear structure for $\alpha = 0.8$.

(a)

Data number	$\underline{k_1}$ (Ann)	$\underline{k_1}$ (Des)	$\overline{k_1}$ (Ann)	$\overline{k_1}$ (Des)	$\underline{k_2}$ (Ann)	$\underline{k_1}$ (Des)	$\overline{k_2}$ (Ann)	$\overline{k_2}$ (Des)
1	109470	109250	124660	123870	63676	63908	81668	81670
2	119370	119420	141760	141590	59687	59772	79075	78865
3	141840	141880	154360	154170	63017	63149	77680	77561
4	126590	126380	179820	178510	58265	57879	84888	87763
5	143790	143950	160360	160670	61323	61256	90425	90743

(b)

Data number	$\underline{k_1}$ (Ann)	$\underline{k_1}$ (Des)	$\overline{k_1}$ (Ann)	$\overline{k_1}$ (Des)	$\underline{k_2}$ (Ann)	$\underline{k_1}$ (Des)	$\overline{k_2}$ (Ann)	$\overline{k_2}$ (Des)
1	111790	111390	122640	121830	66536	66826	79388	79513
2	125300	125280	141300	141110	62124	62253	75972	75891
3	144990	144970	153930	153750	65795	65976	76269	76271
4	131130	130750	169150	167990	59057	58865	78073	80211
5	145180	145390	157010	157330	63632	63541	84419	84602

(c)

Data number	$\underline{k_1}$ (Ann)	$\underline{k_1}$ (Des)	$\overline{k_1}$ (Ann)	$\overline{k_1}$ (Des)	$\underline{k_2}$ (Ann)	$\underline{k_1}$ (Des)	$\overline{k_2}$ (Ann)	$\overline{k_2}$ (Des)
1	115270	114590	119610	118770	70827	71203	75968	76278
2	134200	134070	140600	140400	65779	65975	71318	71430
3	149710	149600	153290	153110	69963	70218	74153	74336
4	137940	137310	153150	152200	60244	60344	67851	68882
5	147270	147540	152000	152320	67096	66967	75411	75392

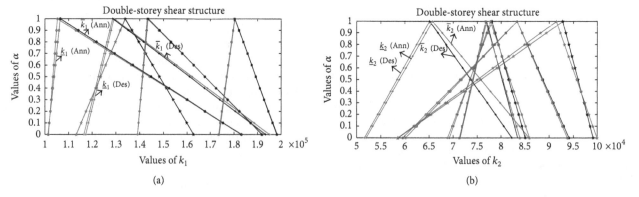

FIGURE 9: (a) Comparison of $\underline{k_1}$ and $\overline{k_1}$ with respect to α. (b) Comparison of $\underline{k_2}$ and $\overline{k_2}$ with respect to α.

$\underline{k_2}$ = [20000 30000], k_2c = [20010 30010], and $\overline{k_2}$ = [20020 30020]. Comparison between the desired and ANN values are again incorporated in Tables 6(a) and 6(b). This table is plotted in Figures 7(a) and 7(b).

The training data with the influence of noise for two-storey shear structure in TFN form for five sets of data have been presented here. Accordingly, Figures 8(a) and 8(b) refer the fuzzy plot of frequency. Moreover, the Triangular

Fuzzy Number (TFN) plots of identified stiffness are cited in Figures 9(a) and 9(b). Also for different alpha values such as $\alpha = 0.3$, $\alpha = 0.5$, and $\alpha = 0.8$, the comparison between the desired and ANN values with another five sets of data has been given in Tables 7(a), and 7(b), and 7(c).

7. Conclusion

Here, the procedure is demonstrated to identify stiffness parameters for multistorey shear structure using fuzzified data in ANN. The present study considers example problems of one-, two-, , and ten-storey shear structures. Identification study for and ten-storey shear structures has been done with crisp data. Then, fuzzified data has been considered for one- and two-storey shear structures for the present identification procedure. Initial design parameters, namely, stiffness and mass and so the frequency of the said problem is known in term of fuzzy numbers. The engineers want to know the present health of the structure by system identification methods. It is assumed that only the stiffness is changed and the mass remains the same. The present values of the frequencies may be obtained by available equipments, and using these, one may get the present parameter values by ANN. So, if sensors are placed to capture the frequency of the floors in fuzzy (uncertain) form, then, those may be fed into the proposed new ANN model to get the present stiffness parameters. The methods of one- and two-storey shear structures with fuzzified data may very well be extended for higher storey structures following the present procedure. As regards the influence of noise, it may be seen that the input and output data for two-storey shear structure are actually in terms of Triangular Fuzzy Number (TFN) which themselves dictate the noise in both monotonic increasing and decreasing senses. In order to train the new ANN model, set of data are generated numerically beforehand. As such, converged ANN model gives the present stiffness parameter values in fuzzified form for each floor. Thus, one may predict the health of the structure. Corresponding example problems (as mentioned) have been solved, and related results are reported to show the reliability and powerfulness of the model.

Acknowledgments

The authors would like to acknowledge funding from the Ministry of Earth Sciences, New Delhi, India. They are also thankful to the anonymous reviewers for their valuable suggestion to improve the paper.

References

[1] E. Khanmirza, N. Khaji, and V. J. Majd, "Model updating of multistory shear buildings for simultaneous identification of mass, stiffness and damping matrices using two different soft-computing methods," *Expert Systems with Applications*, vol. 38, no. 5, pp. 5320–5329, 2011.

[2] M. I. Friswell, D. J. Inman, and D. F. Pilkey, "The direct updating of damping and stiffness matrices," *AIAA Journal*, vol. 36, no. 3, pp. 491–493, 1998.

[3] M. Tanaka and H. D. Bui, *Inverse Problems in Engineering Mechanics*, Balkema, Rotterdam, The Netherlands, 1994.

[4] K. F. Alvin, A. N. Robertson, G. W. Reich, and K. C. Park, "Structural system identification: from reality to models," *Computers and Structures*, vol. 81, no. 12, pp. 1149–1176, 2003.

[5] S. D. Fassois and J. S. Sakellariou, "Time-series methods for fault detection and identification in vibrating structures," *Philosophical Transactions of the Royal Society A*, vol. 365, no. 1851, pp. 411–448, 2007.

[6] S. F. Marsi, G. A. Bekey, H. Sassi, and T. K. Caughey, "Non-parametric identification of a class of non-linear multidegree dynamic systems," *Earthquake Engineering & Structural Dynamics*, vol. 10, no. 1, pp. 1–30, 1982.

[7] P. Ibanez, "Review of analytical and experimental techniques for improving structural dynamic models," *Welding Research Council Bulletin*, no. 249, 1979.

[8] A. K. Datta, M. Shrikhande, and D. K. Paul, "System identification of buildings: a review," in *Proceedings of 11th Symposium on Earthquake Engineering*, University of Roorkee, Roorkee, India.

[9] C.-H Loh and I.-C Tou, "A system identification approach to the detection of changes in both linear and non-linear structural parameters," *Earthquake Engineering & Structural Dynamics*, vol. 24, no. 1, pp. 85–97, 1995.

[10] P. Yuan, Z. Wu, and X. Ma, "Estimated mass and stiffness matrices of shear building from modal test data," *Earthquake Engineering and Structural Dynamics*, vol. 27, no. 5, pp. 415–421, 1998.

[11] C. H. Chen, "Structural identification from field measurement data using a neural network," *Smart Materials and Structures*, vol. 14, no. 3, pp. S104–S115, 2005.

[12] C. S. Huang, S. L. Hung, C. M. Wen, and T. T. Tu, "A neural network approach for structural identification and diagnosis of a building from seismic response data," *Earthquake Engineering and Structural Dynamics*, vol. 32, no. 2, pp. 187–206, 2003.

[13] C. Y. Kao and S. L. Hung, "Detection of structural damage via free vibration responses generated by approximating artificial neural networks," *Computers and Structures*, vol. 81, no. 28-29, pp. 2631–2644, 2003.

[14] Z. Wu, B. Xu, and K. Yokoyama, "Decentralized parametric damage detection based on neural networks," *Computer-Aided Civil and Infrastructure Engineering*, vol. 17, no. 3, pp. 175–184, 2002.

[15] B. Xu, Z. Wu, G. Chen, and K. Yokoyama, "A localized identification method with neural networks and its application to structural health monitoring," *Journal of Structural Engineering A*, vol. 48, pp. 419–427, 2002.

[16] B. Xu, Z. Wu, G. Chen, and K. Yokoyama, "Direct identification of structural parameters from dynamic responses with neural networks," *Engineering Applications of Artificial Intelligence*, vol. 17, no. 8, pp. 931–943, 2004.

[17] S. Chakraverty, "Identification of structural parameters of multistorey shear buildings from modal data," *Earthquake Engineering and Structural Dynamics*, vol. 34, no. 6, pp. 543–554, 2005.

[18] M. J. Perry, C. G. Koh, and Y. S. Choo, "Modified genetic algorithm strategy for structural identification," *Computers and Structures*, vol. 84, no. 8-9, pp. 529–540, 2006.

[19] G. S. Wang, "Application of hybrid genetic algorithm to system identification," *Structural Control and Health Monitoring*, vol. 16, no. 2, pp. 125–153, 2009.

[20] S. Yoshitomi and I. Takewaki, "Noise-bias compensation in physical-parameter system identification under microtremor input," *Engineering Structures*, vol. 31, no. 2, pp. 580–590, 2009.

[21] Y. Lu and Z. Tu, "A two-level neural network approach for dynamic FE model updating including damping," *Journal of Sound and Vibration*, vol. 275, no. 3–5, pp. 931–952, 2004.

[22] C. G. Koh, Y. F. Chen, and C. Y. Liaw, "A hybrid computational strategy for identification of structural parameters," *Computers and Structures*, vol. 81, no. 2, pp. 107–117, 2003.

[23] H. Tang, S. Xue, and C. Fan, "Differential evolution strategy for structural system identification," *Computers and Structures*, vol. 86, no. 21-22, pp. 2004–2012, 2008.

12

Measuring Non-Gaussianity by Phi-Transformed and Fuzzy Histograms

Claudia Plant,[1] **Son Mai Thai,**[2] **Junming Shao,**[3] **Fabian J. Theis,**[4] **Anke Meyer-Baese,**[1] **and Christian Böhm**[2]

[1] *400 Dirac Science Library, Florida State University, Tallahassee, FL 32306-4120, USA*
[2] *Department for Informatics, Research Unit for Database Systems, University of Munich, Oettingenstraße 67, 80538 Munich, Germany*
[3] *Klinikum rechts der Isar der TUM, Ismaninger Straße 22, 81675 Munich, Germany*
[4] *Helmholtz Zentrum München, Ingolstädter Landstraße 1, 85764 Neuherberg, Germany*

Correspondence should be addressed to Claudia Plant, cplant@fsu.edu

Academic Editor: Juan Manuel Gorriz Saez

Independent component analysis (ICA) is an essential building block for data analysis in many applications. Selecting the truly meaningful components from the result of an ICA algorithm, or comparing the results of different algorithms, however, is nontrivial problems. We introduce a very general technique for evaluating ICA results rooted in information-theoretic model selection. The basic idea is to exploit the natural link between non-Gaussianity and data compression: the better the data transformation represented by one or several ICs improves the effectiveness of data compression, the higher is the relevance of the ICs. We propose two different methods which allow an efficient data compression of non-Gaussian signals: Phi-transformed histograms and fuzzy histograms. In an extensive experimental evaluation, we demonstrate that our novel information-theoretic measures robustly select non-Gaussian components from data in a fully automatic way, that is, without requiring any restrictive assumptions or thresholds.

1. Introduction

Independent component analysis (ICA) is a powerful technique for signal demixing and data analysis in numerous applications. For example, in neuroscience, ICA is essential for the analysis of functional magnetic resonance imaging (fMRI) data and electroencephalograms (EEGs). The function of the human brain is very complex and can be only imaged at a very coarse spatial resolution. Millions of nerve cells are contained in a single voxel of fMRI data. The neural activity is indirectly measured by the so-called BOLD-effect, that is, by the increased supply of active regions with oxygenated blood. In EEG, the brain function can be directly measured by the voltage fluctuations resulting from ionic current flows within the neurons. The spacial resolution of EEG, however, is even much lower than that of fMRI. Usually, an EEG is recorded using an array of 64 electrodes distributed over the scalp. Often, the purpose of acquiring fMRI or EEG data is obtaining a better understanding of brain function while

the subject is performing some task. An example for such an experiment is to show subjects images while they are in the scanner to study the processing of visual stimuli, see Section 4.1.4. Recent results in neuroscience, for example [1], confirm the organization of the human brain into distinct functional modules. During task processing, some functional modules are actively contributing to the task. However, many other modules are also active but not involved into task-specific activities. Due to the low resolution of fMRI and EEG data, we observe a partial volume effect: the signal at one particular voxel or electrode consists of task-related activities, nontask-related activities, and a lot of noise. ICA is a powerful tool for signal demixing and, therefore, in principle very suitable to reconstruct the interesting task-related activity.

Many ICA algorithms use the non-Gaussianity as implicit or explicit optimization goal. The rationale behind this decision is due to a reversion of the central limit theorem: the sum of a sufficiently large number of independent random variables, each with finite mean and variance, will approximate a normal distribution. Therefore, an algorithm for the demixing of signals has to optimize for non-Gaussianity in order to obtain the original signals. We adopt this idea in this paper and define a data compression method which yields a high compression rate exactly if the data distribution is far away from Gaussianity and no compression in the data distribution is exactly gaussian.

However, the evaluation and interpretation of the result of ICA is often difficult for two major reasons. First, most ICA algorithms always yield a result, even if the underlying assumption (e.g., non-Gaussianity for the algorithm FastICA [2]) is unfulfilled. Thus, many ICA algorithms extract as many independent sources as there are mixed signals in the dataset, no matter how many of them really fulfill the underlying assumption. Second, ICA has no unique and natural evaluation criterion to assess the relevance or strength of the detected result (like, e.g., the variance criterion for principle component analysis (PCA)). Different ICA algorithms use different objective functions, and to select one of them as an *overall objective*, or *neutral* criterion would give unjustified preference to the result of that specific algorithm. Moreover, if the user is interested in comparing an ICA result to completely different modeling techniques like PCA, regression, mixture models, and so forth, these ICA-internal criteria are obviously unsuitable. Depending on the actual intension of the user, different model selection criteria for ICA might be appropriate. In this paper, we investigate the *compressibility* of the data as a more neutral criterion for the quality of single component or the overall ICA result.

2. Related Work

2.1. Model Selection for ICA. Model selection for ICA or automatically identifying the most interesting components is an active research question. Perhaps the most widely used options for model selection are measures like Kurtosis, Skewness, and approximations of neg-entropy [3]. However, these measures are also applied as optimization criteria by some ICA algorithms. Thus, a comparison of the results across algorithms is impossible. Moreover, these measures are very sensitive with respect to noise points and single outliers.

In [4], Rasmussen et al. propose an approach for model selection of epoched EEG signals. In their model order selection procedure, the data set is split into two sets, training- and test set, to ensure an unbiased measure of generalization. With each model hypothesis, the negative logarithm of the likelihood function is then calculated using a probabilistic framework on the training and test set. The model having minimal generalization error is selected. This approach, however, is based on certain assumptions about source autocorrelation and tends to be sensitive to noise.

The most common method for model order selection is based on principal component analysis (PCA) of the data covariance matrix, which is proposed by Hyvärinen et al. [3]. The choice of number of sources to be selected is based on the number of dominant eigenvalues which significantly contribute to the total variance. This approach is fast and

simple to implement, however, it suffers from a number of problems, for example, an inaccurate eigenvalue decomposition of the data covariance matrix in the noise-free case with fewer numbers of sources than sensors and sensitivity to noise. Moreover, there are no reasons to say that the subspace spanned by dominant principal components contains the source of interest [5]. Another approach proposed by James and Hesse [5] is to do the step-wise extraction of the sources until it reaches a predefined accuracy. However, the choice of reasonable accuracy level is also one drawback of this algorithm.

Related to model selection but still a different problem is the reliability of ICA results. The widely used iterative fix-point algorithm FastIca [6] converges towards different local optima of the optimization surface. The technique Icasso [7] combines Bootstrapping with a visualization to allow the user to investigate the relationship between different ICA results. Reliable results can be easily identified as dense clusters in the visualization. However, no information on the quality of the results is provided, which is the major focus of our work. Similar to Icasso, Meinecke et al. [8] proposed a resampling method to assess the quality ICA results by computing the stability of the independent subspaces. First, they create surrogate datasets by randomly selecting independent components from an ICA decomposition and apply the ICA algorithm for each of the surrogate data sets. Then, they separate the data space into one or multidimensional subspaces by their block structure and compute the uncertainty for each subspace. This proposed reliability estimation can be used to choose the appropriate BSS-model, to enhance the separation performance and, most importantly, to flag components which have a physical meaning.

2.2. Minimum Description Length for Model Selection. The minimum description length (MDL) principle is based on the simple idea that the best model to describe the data is one with the overall shortest description of the data and model itself, and it is essentially the same as Occam's razor.

The MDL principle has been successfully applied for model selection for a large variety of tasks, ranging from linear regression [9], image segmentation [10] to polyhedral surface models [11].

In data mining, the MDL principle has recently attracted some attention enabling parameter-free algorithms to graph mining [12], clustering, for example [13–15], and outlier detection [16]. Sun et al. [12] proposed GraphScope, a parameter-free technique to mine information from streams of graphs. This technique used MDL to decide how and when to form and modify communities automatically. Böhm et al. [15] proposed OCI, a novel fully automatic algorithm to clustering non-Gaussian data with outliers, based on MDL to control the splitting, filtering, and merging phase in a parameter-free and very efficient top-down clustering approach. CoCo [16], a technique for parameter-free outlier detection, is based on the ideas of data compression and coding costs. CoCo used MDL to define an intuitive outlier factor together with a novel algorithm for outlier detection.

This technique is parameter free and can be applied to a wide range of data distributions. OCI combines local ICA with clustering and outlier filtering. Related to this idea, in [17], Gruber et al. propose an approach for automated image denoising combining local PCA or ICA with model selection by MDL.

In this paper, we propose a model selection criterion based on the MDL principle suitable for measuring the quality of single components as well as complete ICA results.

3. Independent Component Analysis and Data Compression

One of the fundamental assumptions of many important ICA algorithms is that independent sources can be found by searching for maximal non-Gaussian directions in the data space. Non-Gaussianity leads to a decrease in entropy, and therefore, to a potential improvement of the efficiency of data compression. In principle, the achievable compression rate of a dataset, after ICA, is higher compared to the original dataset. The principle of minimum description length (MDL) uses the probability $P(x)$ of a data object x to represent it according to Huffman coding. Huffman coding gives a lower bound for the compression rate of a data set D achievable by any concrete coding scheme, as follows: $\sum_{x \in D} -\log_2(P(x))$. If x is taken from a continuous domain (e.g., the vector space $\mathcal{R}^d$ for the blind source separation of a number d of signals), the relative probability given by a probability density function $p(x)$ is applied instead of the absolute probability. The relative and absolute log-likelihoods (which could be obtained by discretizing x) are identical up to a constant value which can be safely ignored, as we discuss in detail in Section 3.1. For a complete description of the dataset (allowing decompression), the parameters of the probability density function (PDF) such as mean and variance for Gaussian PDFs need to be coded and their code lengths added to the negative log-likelihood of the data. We call this term the code book. For each parameter, a number of bits equal to $(1/2)\log_2(n)$ where n is the number of objects in D, is required, as fundamental results from information theory have proven [18]. Intuitively, the term $(1/2)\log_2(n)$ reflects the fact that the parameters need to be coded more precisely when a higher number n of data objects is modeled by the PDF. The MDL principle is often applied for model selection of parametric models like Gaussians, or Gaussian mixture models (GMMs). Gaussian mixture models vary in the model complexity, that is, the number of parameters needed for modeling. MDL-based techniques are well able to compare models of different complexity. The main purpose of the code book is to punish complexity in order to avoid overly complex, over-fitted models (like a GMM having one component exactly at the position of each data object: such a model would yield a minimal Huffman coding, but also a maximal code-book length). By the two concepts, Huffman coding using the negative log-likelihood of a PDF and the code-book for the parameters of the PDF, the principle of MDL provides a very general framework which allows the comparison of

very different modeling techniques like principal component analysis (based on a Gaussian PDF model), clustering [13], regression [19] for continuous domains, but, in principle, also for discrete or mixed domains. At the same time, model complexity is punished and, therefore, overfitting avoided. Related criteria for general model selection include, for example, the Bayesian information criterion and the Aikake information criterion. However, these criteria are not adapted to the ICA model. In the following section, we discuss how to apply the MDL principle in the context of ICA.

3.1. General Idea of the Minimum Description Length Principle. The minimum description length (MDL) principle is a well-established technique for selecting the best model out of a finite or infinite number of possible models for a given data set D (in our case, a signal). The model is usually given in terms of a probability function $f(x)$ which assigns to every element $x \in D$ a probability that this element occurs in the dataset. For continuous domains, $f(x)$ is a probability density function satisfying $\int_{-\infty}^{+\infty} f(x)\mathbf{d}x = 1$. The idea of MDL is that $f(x)$ can be used as a basis to compress the data set D using Huffman coding and to exploit that this coding becomes the more efficient (w.r.t. the achievable compression rate, or more precisely the code length after compression) the better $f(x)$ represents the true data distribution. According to Huffman coding, the minimum code length corresponds to the negative log-likelihood of the data set, that is,

$$\text{NLLH}_f(D) = -\sum_{x \in D} \log_2 f(x). \tag{1}$$

While only for discrete domains the values of $f(x)$ are scaled between 0 and 1, this negative log-likelihood is also applied for continuous domains, but then some caveats apply. Basically, we can always reduce the continuous case to the noncontinuous case by discretizing the data (e.g., by a regular grid with a fixed resolution g). In this case,

$$F_g(x) = \int_{g \cdot \lfloor x/g \rfloor}^{g \cdot \lfloor x/g+1 \rfloor} f(\xi)\mathbf{d}\xi \tag{2}$$

is a probability function scaled between 0 and 1 with

$$\lim_{g \to 0} \frac{F_g(x)}{g} = f(x). \tag{3}$$

For the negative log-likelihood of the so-discretized dataset D_g, we get

$$\begin{aligned}
\text{NLLH}_f\left(D_g\right) &= -\sum_{x \in D} \log_2 F_g(x) \\
&\approx -\sum_{x \in D} \log_2 g \cdot f(x) \\
&= \text{NLLH}_f(D) - n\log_2 g,
\end{aligned} \tag{4}$$

where in the case $g \to 0$ we have exact equality and also $-n\log_2 g \to \infty$, corresponding to the obvious fact that we need an infinite number of bits to represent a real number with infinite precision. However, when comparing different models of the data (i.e., different probability functions $f_1(x)$ and $f_2(x)$), we simply have to ensure that all data are basically discretized with the same (and sufficiently high) resolution g in the original data space and then ignore the term $-n\log_2 g$ which is equal in all compared models of the data (note that data in a computer is always represented with finite precision, and, therefore, always implicitly discretized):

$$
\begin{aligned}
\lim_{g \to 0} & \left(\text{NLLH}_{f_2}\left(D_g\right) - \text{NLLH}_{f_1}\left(D_g\right) \right) \\
&= \lim_{g \to 0} \left(\left(\text{NLLH}_{f_2}(D) - n\log_2 g \right) \right. \\
&\qquad \left. - \left(\text{NLLH}_{f_1}(D) - n\log_2 g \right) \right) \\
&= \text{NLLH}_{f_2}(D) - \text{NLLH}_{f_1}(D).
\end{aligned}
\tag{5}
$$

We simply have to observe that (1) the resolution is not implicitly changed by any transformations of the dataset (like, e.g., a linear scaling $\alpha \cdot x$ of the data objects) and (2) that ignoring the term might lead to negative values of $\text{NLLH}_f(D)$ (so we partly lose the nice intuition of a number of bits encoding the data objects, and particularly that 0 is a lower limit of this amount of information).

The principle of coding a signal with a pdf $f(x)$ is visualized in Figure 1 where a signal (a superposition of three sinuses) is coded. To represent one given point of the signal (at $t = 15.5$), we should actually use a discretization of x as indicated in the right part of the diagram to obtain an actual code length for the value x. However, we can also directly use the negative log-likelihood of the value x with the above-mentioned implications.

In addition to the amount of information which is caused by the negative log-likelihood of the data, we need also to code the function f. From an information-coding perspective, we need this information in order to be able to decode the data again after transferring it through a communication channel. The function f tells us which code words translate back to what original data objects, so it serves as a code book. From a statistical perspective, the coding of f is needed to avoid overfitting. The intention of f is to generalize the data, and not to anticipate it, as a weird function would do which has simply a peak at every position where a data object is available. For both purposes, the representation of the code book must require considerably less information than the data itself. In this paper, we will propose two different methods to represent the function f. In Figure 1, a kernel density estimator (KDE) was used. However, KDE needs a number of parameters which is the same as the number of points, and, therefore, it is not suitable for our purpose. The classical (parametric) method is to use a class of model functions (like a Gaussian pdf) and to code the parameters (for Gaussian, μ and σ) with an amount of information corresponding to $(1/2)\log_2 n$ per parameter. This number can be derived by an optimization process which takes into account that a small error in the parameters does not lead to a serious deterioration of the NLLH, particularly if n is small and only a few data objects are modeled by f. The number of $(1/2)\log_2 n$ bits represents an optimal trade-off (and includes this deterioration of NLLH already). Throughout this paper,

we will use the minimum description length of a dataset as goal for minimization:

$$
\text{MDL}_f(D) = \text{NLLH}_f(D) + \frac{1}{2}\#\text{PAR}(f) \cdot \log_2 n.
\tag{6}
$$

We will in the following sections propose nonparametric methods which are both related to histograms. Therefore, the number of parameters in principle corresponds to the number of bins. We do not use histograms directly since our goal is to code the signals in a way that punishes the Gaussianity and rewards the non-Gaussianity. Thus, we propose two different methods which modify the histogram concept in a suitable way.

3.2. Phi-Transformed Histograms. Techniques like [15] or [20] successfully use the exponential power distribution (EPD), a generalized distribution function including Gaussian, Laplacian, uniform, and many other distribution functions for assessing the ICA result using MDL. The reduced entropy of non-Gaussian projections in the data allows a higher compression rate and thus favors a good ICA result. However, the selection of EPD is overly restrictive. For instance, multimodal and asymmetric distributions cannot be well represented by EPD but are highly relevant to ICA. In the following, we describe an alternative representation of the PDF which is efficient if (and only if) the data is considerably different from Gaussian. Besides the non-Gaussianity, we have no additional assumption (like for instance EPD) on the data. To achieve this, we tentatively assume Gaussianity in each signal of length n and transform the assumed Gaussian distribution into a uniform distribution in the interval $(0, 1)$ by applying the Gaussian cumulative distribution function $\Phi((x - \mu)/\sigma)$ (the Φ-transformation) to each signal of the data representation to be tested (e.g., after projection on the independent components). Then, the resulting distribution is represented by a histogram $(H_1, \ldots, H_b)$ with a number b of equidistant bins where b is optimized as we will show later. $H_j (1 \le j \le b)$ is the number of objects falling in the corresponding half open interval $[(j-1)/b, \ j/b)$. If the signal is Gaussian indeed, then the signals after Φ-transformation will be uniform and the histogram bins will be (more or less) uniformly filled. Therefore, a trivial histogram with only one bin will in this case yield the best coding cost (and thus, no real data compression comes into effect). The Φ-transformation itself causes a change of the coding cost which is equivalent to the entropy of the Gaussian distribution function, as we show in as follows.

The negative log-likelihood of the signal before the Φ-transformation with the tentative assumption that the signals are compressed by the Gaussian pdf correspond to

$$
\begin{aligned}
\text{NLLH}_{\text{before}} &= \sum_{x \in D} -\log_2\left(\frac{1}{\sqrt{2\pi\sigma^2}} e^{-(x-\mu)^2/2\sigma^2} \right) \\
&= n \cdot \log_2\left(\sqrt{2\pi\sigma^2} \right) + \frac{1}{2\sigma^2 \ln 2} \sum_{x \in D} (x - \mu)^2,
\end{aligned}
\tag{7}
$$

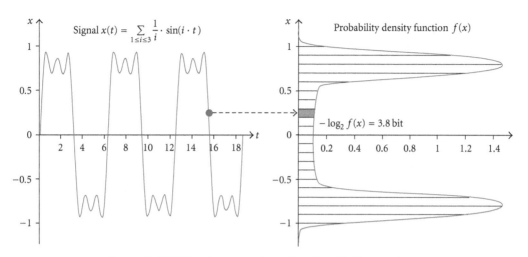

FIGURE 1: MDL-based compression of signals by Huffman coding.

and since $(1/n) \sum (x - \mu)^2$ is exactly the definition of the variance σ^2, we have

$$\text{NLLH}_{\text{before}} = n \cdot \log_2\left(\sqrt{2\pi e \sigma^2}\right), \qquad (8)$$

which is independent from the distribution which the signal x actually has. After the Φ-transformation, we code the signal under the assumption that it is uniformly distributed in $(0, 1)$. Thus, we obtain

$$\text{NLLH}_{\text{after}} = \sum_{x \in D} - \log_2(1) = 0, \qquad (9)$$

and again, we do not worry that it appears as if no information is necessary to code the signals after the Φ-transformation. But the difference between coding of the signals before and after the Φ-transformation corresponds to

$$\text{PRE} = \text{NLLH}_{\text{before}} - \text{NLLH}_{\text{after}} = n \cdot \log_2\left(\sqrt{2\pi e \sigma^2}\right). \quad (10)$$

Representing the histogram $(H_1, \ldots, H_b)$ as a probability density function (integrating to 1) leads to

$$f_H(x) = H_{\lfloor b \cdot x + 1 \rfloor} \cdot \frac{b}{n}. \qquad (11)$$

The negative log-likelihood of this Φ-transformed signal corresponds to

$$\begin{aligned}
\text{NLLH}_{f_H}(D) &= \sum_{x \in D} - \log_2\left(H_{\lfloor b \cdot x + 1 \rfloor} \cdot \frac{b}{n}\right) \\
&= \sum_{x \in D} \log_2 \frac{n}{H_{\lfloor b \cdot x + 1 \rfloor}} - \sum_{x \in D} \log_2 b,
\end{aligned} \qquad (12)$$

and since we have H_i objects in histogram bin i, we can change the first sum into the entropy of the histogram:

$$\text{NLLH}_{f_H}(D) = \sum_{1 \le i \le b}\left(H_i \cdot \log_2 \frac{n}{H_i}\right) - n \cdot \log_2 b. \qquad (13)$$

Using this coding scheme, the overall code length ($\text{CLRG}(D, b)$, code length relative to Gaussianity) of the signal is provided by

$$\text{CLRG}(D, b) = \overbrace{\sum_{1 \le j \le b} H_j \cdot \log_2 \frac{n}{H_j}}^{\text{histogram entropy}}$$
$$\overbrace{- n \cdot \log_2 b}^{\text{offset cost}} \qquad (14)$$
$$\overbrace{+ \frac{b-1}{2}\log_2 n}^{\text{code book}}$$
$$\overbrace{+ \text{PRE}}^{\text{preproc}}.$$

As introduced in Section 3, the first two terms represent the negative log-likelihood of the data given the histogram. The first corresponds to the entropy of the histogram, and the second term, stemming from casting the histogram into a PDF, has also the following intuition: when coding the same data with a varying number of histogram bins, the resulting log-likelihoods are based on different basic resolutions of the data space (a grid with a number b of partitions). Although the choice of a particular basic resolution is irrelevant for the end-result, for comparability, all alternative solutions must be based on a common resolution. We choose $g = 1$ as basic resolution, and subtract for each object the number of bits by which we know the position of the object more precisely than in the basic resolution. The trivial histogram having $b = 1$ represents the case where the data is assumed to be Gaussian: since the Gaussian cumulative distribution function $\Phi((x - \mu)/\sigma)$ has been applied to the data, Gaussian data are transformed into uniform data, and our histograms have an implicit assumption of uniformity *inside* each bin. Therefore, we call it *offset cost* because it stands for coding the position of a value *inside* a histogram bin. If some choice of $b \ne 1$ leads to smaller $\text{CLRG}(D, b)$, we have evidence that the signal is different from Gaussian. It is easy to see that in

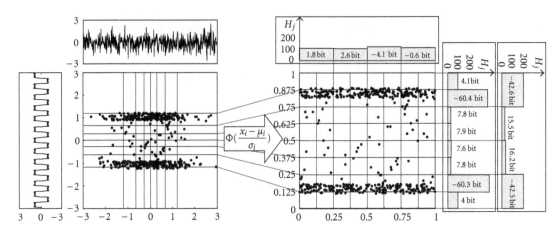

FIGURE 2: Overview of the computation of $CLRG(D, b)$: left: scatter plot of two signals in original space. On the x-axis: Gaussian noise signal. On the y-axis: signal with a rectangular pattern. The lines represent the quantiles assuming a Gaussian distribution; right: the scatter plot after applying the Gaussian CDF. The quantiles now form an equidistant grid. On the axes: histograms and compression costs using Huffman coding. Since the Gaussian signal does not contain any pattern beyond Gaussianity, it cannot be compressed in CDF-space.

the case $b = 1$ the code length is $CLRG(D, b) = PRE$, which is a consequence of our definition of the offset cost. Therefore, we call our cost function code length relative to Gaussianity, (CLRG). If no choice that $b \neq 1$ leads to $CLRG(D, b) < PRE$, then either the data is truly Gaussian or the number of data objects is not high enough to give evidence for non-Gaussianity. In the latter case, we use Gaussianity as the safe default-assumption. The third term is the cost required for the code book: to completely describe b histogram bins it is sufficient to use $b - 1$ codewords since the remaining probability is implicitly specified. The last term, PRE is for preprocessing, that is, taking the Φ-transform into account.

Figure 2 gives an overview and example of our method. On the left side, the result of an ICA run is depicted which has successfully separated a number $d = 2$ of signals (each having $n = 500$ points). The corresponding scatter-plot shows a Gaussian signal on the x-axis, a rectangular signal on the y-axis (note that the corresponding signal plots on the axes are actually transposed for better visibility). On the right side, we see the result after applying the Gaussian CDF. Some histograms with different resolutions are also shown. On the x-axis, the histogram with $b = 4$ bins is approximately uniformly filled (like also most other histograms with a different selection of b). Consequently, only a very small number of bits is saved compared to Gaussianity (e.g., only 4.1 bits for the complete signal part falling in the third bin H_3) by applying this histogram as PDF in Huffman coding (here, the cost per bin are reported including log-likelihood and offset-cost). The overall saving of 0.29 bit are contrasted by a code-book length of $(3/2)\log_2 n = 13.4$, so the histogram representation does not pay off. In contrast, the two histograms on the y-axis do pay off, since for $b = 8$, we have overall savings over Gaussianity of 81.3 bit by Huffman coding, but only $(7/2)\log_2 n = 31.4$ bits of codebook.

3.2.1. An Optimization Heuristic for the Histogram Resolution.

We need to optimize b individually for each signal such that the overall coding cost $CLRG(D, b)$ is minimized. As an efficient and effective heuristic, we propose to only consider histogram resolutions where b is a power of 2. This is time efficient since the number of alternative results is logarithmic in n (as we will show), and the next coarser histogram can be intelligently gained from the previous. In addition, the strategy is effective since a sufficient number of alternative results is examined.

We start with a histogram resolution based on the worst-case assumption that (almost) all objects fall into the same histogram bin of a histogram of very high resolution b_m. That means that the log-likelihood approaches 0. The offset cost corresponds to $-n\log_2 b_m$ but the parameter cost are very high: $((b_m - 1)/2)\log_2 n$. The other extreme case is the model with the lowest possible resolution $b = 1$ having no log-likelihood, no offset-cost, and no parameter cost. The histogram with resolution b_m can pay off only if the following condition holds:

$$n \log_2 b_m \geq \frac{b_m - 1}{2} \log_2 n, \qquad (15)$$

which is certainly true if $b_m \leq n/2$. We use $b_m = 2^{\lfloor \log_2 n \rfloor}$, the first power of two less or equal n as starting resolution. Then, in each step, the algorithm generates a new histogram $H' = (H'_1, \ldots, H'_{b/2})$ from the previous histogram $H = (H_1, \ldots, H_b)$ by merging each pair of adjacent bins using $H'_j = H_{2j-1} + H_{2j}$ for all j having $1 \leq j \leq b/2$. The overall number of adding operations for histogram bins starting from the histogram $H^{\text{start}} = (H^{\text{start}}_1, \ldots, H^{\text{start}}_{b_m})$ to the final histogram $H^{\text{end}} = (H^{\text{end}}_1)$ corresponds to

$$\sum_{1 \leq i \leq b_m/2} i = b_m - 1 = 2^{\lfloor \log_2 n \rfloor} - 1 \in O(n). \qquad (16)$$

The coding cost of the data with respect to each alternative histogram is evaluated as described in Section 3.2 and the histogram with resolution b_{opt} providing the best compression is reported as result for dimension i. In the case of $b_{\text{opt}} = 1$, no compression was achieved by assuming non-Gaussianity. After having optimized b_{opt} for each signal separately, $CLRG(D, b)$, the coding costs of the data are provided as in Section 3.2 applying b_{opt}. To measure the overall improvement in compression achieved by ICA $CLRG(D, b)$ is summed up across all dimensions i:

$$CLRG(D) = \sum_{1 \leq i \leq d} \left(\min_{0 \leq \log_2 b \leq \lfloor \log_2 n \rfloor} CLRG(D, b) \right). \quad (17)$$

3.3. Fuzzy Histograms. Often histograms are not a good description of data since they define a discontinuous function whereas the original data distribution often corresponds to a continuous function. Since we want to focus on non-Gaussianity without any other assumption on the underlying distribution function, a good alternative to histograms is fuzzy histograms. In statistics, often kernel density estimators (KDEs) are applied in cases where a continuous representation of the distribution function is needed. However, KDEs require a number of parameters which is higher than the number of objects, and, therefore, KDEs are not suitable for our philosophy of compressing the dataset according to the defined distribution function (although other information-theoretic KDEs exist). Therefore, we apply the simpler fuzzy histograms which extend histograms as follows.

We have a kernel function $\kappa_{\mu_i, \sigma}(x)$ which is assigned to each fuzzy histogram bin i. Like with ordinary histograms, the location parameters μ_i are equidistant, that is,

$$\mu_i = m \cdot i + t, \quad (18)$$

and the scale parameter σ is uniform for all bins (and also called bandwidth). In this paper, we use the normal distribution:

$$\kappa_{\mu_i, \sigma}(x) = n_{\mu_i, \sigma}(x) = \frac{1}{\sqrt{2\pi\sigma^2}} \exp\left(-\frac{(x - \mu_i)^2}{\sigma^2}\right) \quad (19)$$

since it allows an elegant way to express the coding cost relatively to Gaussianity without explicitly transforming the dataset using the cumulative standard normal distribution $\Phi(x)$. To every histogram bin, a weight w_i, which indicates to which extent the bin is filled, is assigned. The sum over all w_i, is unity. The fuzzy histogram then defines the probability density function:

$$f(x) = \sum_{1 \leq i \leq b} w_i \cdot \kappa_{\mu_i, \sigma}(x), \quad (20)$$

which is continuous (as it is a sum of continuous functions) and integrates to 1 (as all w_i sum up to one and each kernel function integrates to 1).

We determine the positions $\mu_1, \ldots, \mu_b$ (or, actually the parameters m and t to determine all μ_i in an equidistant way) as well as the bandwidth σ in an iterative learning algorithm. We initialize the parameters such that

$$\mu_1 = \min_{x \in D}(x), \qquad \mu_b = \max_{x \in D}(x),$$
$$w_i = \frac{1}{b}, \quad (\forall i, 1 \leq i \leq b), \qquad \sigma = \frac{\mu_b - \mu_1}{b}. \quad (21)$$

That means that we set the initial slope $m = (\mu_b - \mu_1)/b$ and $t = \mu_1 - m$.

Each point $x \in D$ may be assigned to more than one bin. It is gradually assigned and the sum of all assignments equals 1. The assignment is based on Bayes' theorem:

$$p(i \mid x) = \frac{w_i \cdot \kappa_{\mu_i, \sigma}(x)}{\sum_{1 \leq j \leq b} w_j \cdot \kappa_{\mu_j, \sigma}(x)}, \quad (22)$$

and the weights can be determined as

$$w_i = \frac{1}{|D|} \sum_{x \in D} p(i \mid x). \quad (23)$$

Then, we assign the points according to (22). We then determine each μ_i (calling it $\hat{\mu}_i$) individually (temporarily omitting the requirement that they are equi-distant) as

$$\hat{\mu}_i = \frac{1}{|D| \cdot w_i} \sum_{x \in D} p(i \mid x) \cdot x \quad (24)$$

and determine m and t as a weighted linear regression of the $\hat{\mu}_i$. Let $\bar{\mu} = \sum_{1 \leq i \leq b} w_i \cdot \hat{\mu}_i$ be the weighted average of all $\hat{\mu}_i$ and $\bar{i} = \sum_{1 \leq i \leq b} w_i \cdot i$ the weighted average of all i. Then, we obtain

$$m = \frac{\sum_{1 \leq i \leq b} w_i \cdot (i - \bar{i}) \cdot (\hat{\mu}_i - \bar{\mu})}{\sum_{1 \leq i \leq b} w_i \cdot (i - \bar{i})^2}, \qquad t = \bar{\mu} - m\bar{i}. \quad (25)$$

Finally, we determine the bandwidth parameter σ by the average variance which is caused by D in every bin:

$$\sigma^2 = \frac{1}{|D|} \sum_{x \in D} \sum_{1 \leq i \leq b} p(i \mid x) \cdot (x - \mu_i)^2. \quad (26)$$

These steps starting from evaluation (22) are repeated until convergence.

4. Experiments

This section contains an extensive experimental evaluation. We start by a proof of concept demonstrating the benefits of information-theoretic model selection for ICA over established model selection criteria such as kurtosis in Section 4.1. Since in these experiments phi-transformed histograms and equidistant Gaussian Mixture Models perform very similar, for space limitations, we only show the results of phi-transformed histograms. In Section 4.2, we discuss the two possibilities of estimating the code length relative to Gaussianity.

4.1. Proof of Concept: Information-Theoretic Model Selection for ICA

4.1.1. Selection of the Relevant Dimensions. Which ICs truly represent meaningful signals? Measures like kurtosis, skewness, and other approximations of neg-entropy are often used for selecting the relevant ICs but need to be suitably thresholded, which is a nontrivial task. Figures 3(a) and 3(b)

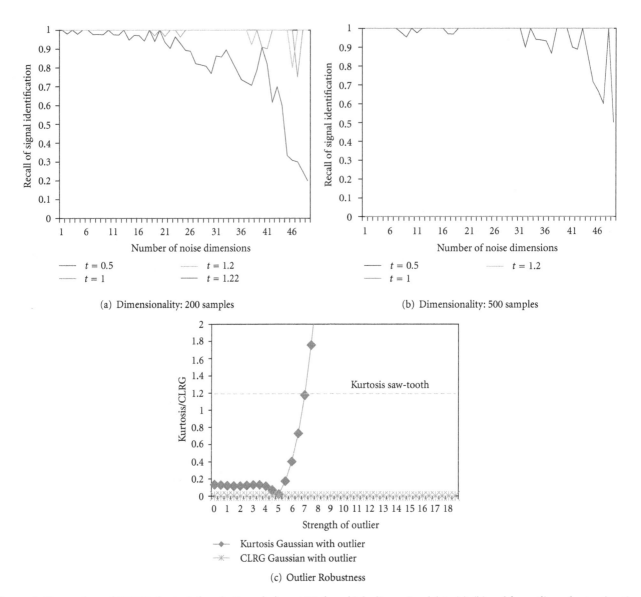

(a) Dimensionality: 200 samples   (b) Dimensionality: 500 samples

(c) Outlier Robustness

FIGURE 3: Comparison of CLRG to kurtosis for selection of relevant ICs from high-dimensional data (a)-(b) and for outlier-robust estimation of IC quality (c).

display the recall of signal identification for a dataset consisting of highly non-Gaussian saw-tooth signals and a varying number of noise dimensions for various thresholds of kurtosis. Kurtosis is measured as the absolute deviation from Gaussianity. The recall of signal identification is defined as the number of signals which have been correctly identified by the selection criterion divided by the overall number of signals. Figure 3(a) displays the results for various thresholds on a dataset with 200 samples. For this signal length, a threshold of $t = 1.2$ offers the best recall in signal identification for various numbers of noise dimensions. A slightly higher threshold of 1.22 leads to a complete break down in recall to 0, which implies that all noise signals are rated as non-Gaussian by kurtosis. For the dataset of 500 samples, however, $t = 1.0$ is a suitable threshold and for $t = 1.2$, we can observe a complete breakdown in recall. Even on these synthetic examples with a very clear distinction into highly

non-Gaussian signals and Gaussian noise, the range for suitable thresholding is very narrow. Moreover, the threshold depends on the signal length and of course strongly on the type of the particular signal. A reasonable approach to select a suitable threshold is to try out a wide range of candidate thresholds and to select the threshold maximizing the area under ROC. For most of our example datasets with 200 samples, a threshold of $t = 1.2$ maximizes the area under ROC. For the datasets with 20 to 36 noise dimensions, this threshold yields a perfect result with an area under ROC of 1.0. For 500 samples, however, a lower threshold is preferable on most datasets. Supported by information theory, CLRG automatically identifies the relevant dimensions without requiring any parameters or thresholds. For all examples, CLRG identifies the relevant dimensions as those dimensions allowing data compression with a precision and a recall of 100%.

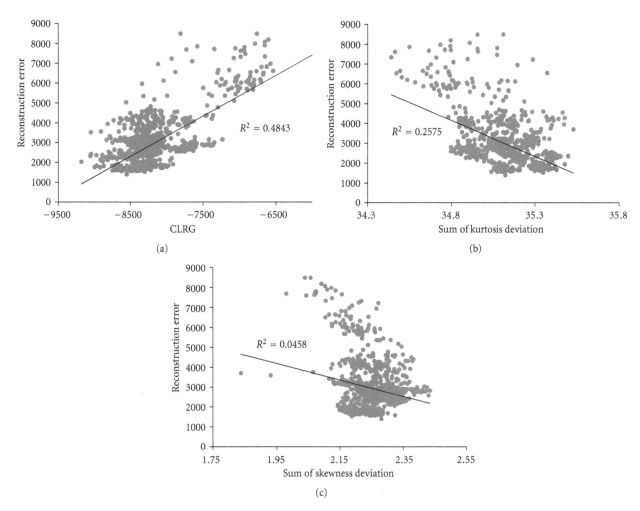

Figure 4: CLRG in comparison to kurtosis and skewness for assessing the quality of ICA-results. For 1,000 results obtained with FastIca on de-mixing speech signals, CLRG best correlates with the reconstruction error of the ICs.

4.1.2. Stable Estimation of the IC Quality. Commonly used approximations of neg-entropy are sensitive to single outliers. Outliers may cause an overestimation of the quality of the IC. CLRG is an outlier-robust measure for the interestingness of a signal. Figure 3(c) displays the influence of one single outlier on the kurtosis (displayed in terms of deviation from Gaussian) and CLRG of a Gaussian noise signal with 500 samples with respect to various outlier strengths (displayed in units of standard deviation). For reference, also the kurtosis of a highly non-Gaussian saw-tooth signal is displayed with a dotted line. Already for moderate outlier strength, the estimation of kurtosis becomes unstable. In case of a strong single outlier, kurtosis severely overestimates the interestingness of the signal. CLRG is not sensitive with respect to single outliers: even for strongest outliers, the noise signal is scored as not interesting with a CLRG of zero. For comparison, the saw-tooth curve allows an effective data compression with a CLRG of −553.

4.1.3. Comparing ICA Results. CLRG is a very general criterion for assessing the quality of ICA results which does not rely on any assumptions specific to certain algorithms. In

this experiment, we compare CLRG to kurtosis and skewness on the benchmark dataset acspeec16 form ICALAB (http://www.bsp.brain.riken.go.jp/ICALAB/ICALABSignalProc/benchmarks/). This dataset consists of 16 speech signals which we mixed with a uniform random mixing matrix. Figure 4 displays 1,000 results of FastIca [2] generated with the nonlinearity tanh and different random starting conditions. For each result, we computed the reconstruction error as the sum of squared deviations of the ICs found by FastIca to the original source signals. For each IC, we used the best matching source signal (corrected for sign ambiguity) and summed up the squared deviations. Figure 4(a) shows that CLRG correlates best with the reconstruction error. In particular, ICA results with a low reconstruction error also allow effective data compression. For comparison, we computed the sum of kurtosis deviations and the sum of skewness deviations from Gaussianity. Kurtosis and even more skewness show only a slight correlation with the reconstruction error. As an example, Figure 5(a) shows the first extracted IC from the result best scored by CLRG and the corresponding IC (Figure 5(b)) from the result best scored by kurtosis. For each of the two ICs the scatter plots with

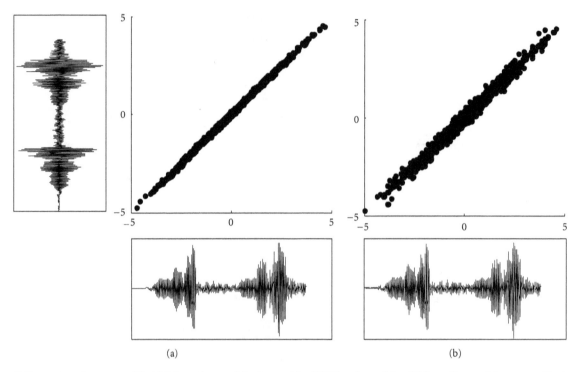

(a)   (b)

FIGURE 5: Reconstruction error of first IC from the result best scored by CLRG and matching IC from the result best scored by kurtosis.

the original signal are displayed. Obviously, the left IC better matches the true signal than the right IC resulting in a lower reconstruction error.

4.1.4. Selecting Relevant Components from fMRI Data. Functional magnetic resonance imaging (fMRI) yields time series of 3-d volume images allowing to study the brain activity, usually while the subject is performing some task. In this experiment, a subject has been visually stimulated in a block-design by alternately displaying a checkerboard stimulus and a central fixation point on a dark background as control condition [21]. fMRI data with 98 images (TR/TE = 3000/60 msec) were acquired with five stimulation and rest periods having each a duration of 30 s. After standard preprocessing, the dimensionality has been reduced with PCA. FastIca has been applied to extract the task-related component. Figure 6(a) displays an example component with strong correlation to the experimental paradigm. This component is localized in the visual cortex which is responsible for processing photic stimuli, see Figure 6(b). We compared CLRG to kurtosis and skewness with respect to their scoring of the task-related component. In particular, we performed PCA reductions with varying dimensionality and identified the component with the strongest correlation to the stimulus protocol. Figure 6(c) shows that CLRG scores the task-related component much better than skewness and kurtosis. Regardless of the dimensionality, the task-related component is always among the top-ranked components by CLRG, in most cases among the top 3 to 5. By kurtosis and skewness, the interest of task-related component often rated close to the average.

4.2. Discussion of CLRG Estimation Techniques. Phi-transformed histograms and equidistant Gaussian mixture models represent different possibilities to estimate the code length relative to Gaussianity (CLRG). As elaborated in Section 3, to estimate the code length in bits, we need a probability density function (PDF) and the two variants differ in the way the PDF is defined. The major benefit of equidistant Gaussian mixture models over Phi-transformed histograms is that the PDF is defined by a continuous function which tends to represent some signals better than phi-transformed histograms. A better representation of the non-Gaussian characteristics of a signal results in more effective data compression expressed by a lower CLRG.

Figure 7 provides a comparison of phi-transformed histograms and equidistant Gaussian mixture models (eGMMs) regarding the CLRG estimated for the 16 signals of the aspeech16 dataset. For most signals, the CLRG estimated by both variants is very similar, for example, signals number 1 to 3, 10, and 16. Eight signals can be most effectively compressed using phi-transformed histograms, most evidently signals number 11 to 13. The other eight signals can be most effectively compressed using eGMM. In average on the aspeech16 dataset, the average CLRG 6,028 bits for phi-transformed histograms, 6,148 bits for eGMM.

We found similar results on other benchmark datasets also available at the ICALAB website: the 19 signals of the eeg19 dataset tend to be better represented by eGMM with an average CLRG of 17,691 (11 signals best represented by eGMM) followed by phi-transformed histograms with an average CLRG of 17,807 (8 signals best represented by phi-transformed).

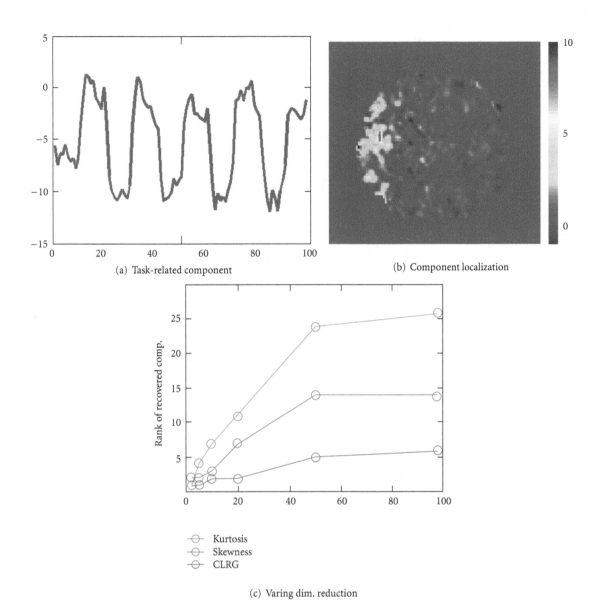

(a) Task-related component

(b) Component localization

(c) Varing dim. reduction

FIGURE 6: fMRI experiment: (a) Task-related IC extracted by FastIca from a fMRI experiment where the subject performed a visual task while in the scanner. (b) Color-coded spatial activation pattern of this IC in an axial brain slice. (c) The rank of this IC according to CLRG and the comparison methods for varying dimensionality reduction. This interesting IC is always identified among the top-ranked components by CLRG.

Also, the abio7 data tends to be better represented by eGMM with an average CLRG of 6,480 (5 out of 7 signals best represented by GMM). Phi-transformed histograms perform with an average CLRG of 7,023 (2 best represented signals).

To summarize, we found only minor differences in performance among the two techniques estimating CLRG. Whenever a continuous representation of the PDF is required, the eGMM techniques should be preferred. A continuous representation allows, for example, incremental assessment of streaming signals. In this case, the CLRG can be reestimated periodically when enough novel data points have arrived from the stream.

5. Conclusion

In this paper, we introduced CLRG (code length relative to gaussianity) as an information-theoretic measure to evaluate the quality of single independent components as well as complete ICA results. Our experiments demonstrated that CLRG is an attractive complement to existing measures for non-Gaussianity, for example, kurtosis and skewness for the following reasons: relating the relevance of an IC to its usefulness for data compression, CLRG identifies the most relevant ICs in a dataset without requiring any parameters or thresholds. Moreover, CLRG is less sensitive to outliers

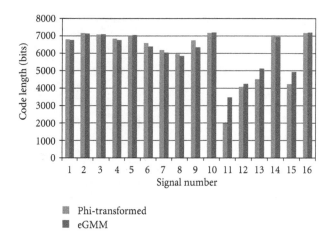

FIGURE 7: Comparison of CLRG estimation techniques regarding the compression of speech signals.

than comparison measures. On fMRI data, CLRG clearly outperforms the comparison techniques in identifying the relevant task-specific components.

The basic idea that a good model provides efficient data compression is very general. Therefore, not only different ICs and ICA results obtained by different algorithms can be unbiasedly compared. Given a dataset, we can also compare the quality completely different models, for example, obtained by ICA, PCA, and projection pursuit. Moreover, it might lead to the best data compression to apply different models to different subsets of the dimensions as well as different subsets of the data objects. In our ongoing and future work, we will extend CLRG to support various models and will explore algorithms for finding subsets of objects and dimensions which can be effectively compressed together.

Acknowledgment

Claudia Plant is supported by the Alexander von Humboldt Foundation.

References

[1] O. Sporns, "The human connectome: a complex network," *Annals of the New York Academy of Sciences*, vol. 1224, no. 1, pp. 109–125, 2011.

[2] A. Hyvärinen, "Fast and robust fixed-point algorithms for independent component analysis," *IEEE Transactions on Neural Networks*, vol. 10, no. 3, pp. 626–634, 1999.

[3] A. Hyvärinen, J. Karhunen, and E. Oja, *Independent Component Analysis*, John Wiley & Sons, New York, NY, USA, 2001.

[4] P. M. Rasmussen, M. Mørup, L. K. Hansen, and S. M. Arnfred, "Model order estimation for independent component analysis of epoched EEG signals," in *Proceedings of the 1st International Conference on Bio-inspired Systems and Signal Processing (BIOSIGNALS '08)*, pp. 3–10, January 2008.

[5] C. J. James and C. W. Hesse, "Independent component analysis for biomedical signals," *Physiological Measurement*, vol. 26, no. 1, pp. R15–R39, 2005.

[6] A. Hyvärinen and E. Oja, "Independent component analysis: algorithms and applications," *Neural Networks*, vol. 13, no. 4-5, pp. 411–430, 2000.

[7] J. Himberg and A. Hyvärinen, "Icasso: software for investigating the reliability of ica estimates by clustering and visualization," in *Proceedings of the IEEE Workshop on Neural Networks for Signal Processing (NNSP '03)*, pp. 259–268, 2003.

[8] F. Meinecke, A. Ziehe, M. Kawanabe, and K. R. Müller, "A resampling approach to estimate the stability of one-dimensional or multidimensional independent components," *IEEE Transactions on Biomedical Engineering*, vol. 49, no. 12, pp. 1514–1525, 2002.

[9] G. Qian, "Computing minimum description length for robust linear regression model selection," in *Proceedings of the Pacific Symposium on Biocomputing*, pp. 314–325, 1999.

[10] S. R. Rao, H. Mobahi, A. Y. Yang, S. S. Sastry, and Y. Ma, "Natural image segmentation with adaptive texture and boundary encoding," in *Proceedings of the Asian Conference on Computer Vision (ACCV '09)*, vol. 5994 of *Lecture Notes in Computer Science*, pp. 135–146, 2009.

[11] T. Wekel and O. Hellwich, "Selection of an optimal polyhedral surface model using the minimum description length principle," in *Proceedings of the 32nd Symposium of the German Association for Pattern Recognition (DAGM '10)*, vol. 6376 of *Lecture Notes in Computer Science*, pp. 553–562, 2010.

[12] J. Sun, C. Faloutsos, S. Papadimitriou, and P. S. Yu, "Graph-Scope: parameter-free mining of large time-evolving graphs," in *Proceedings of the 13th ACM SIGKDD International Conference on Knowledge Discovery and Data Mining (KDD '07)*, pp. 687–696, August 2007.

[13] D. Pelleg and A. W. Moore, "X-means: extending k-means with efficient estimation of the number of clusters," in *Proceedings of the 17th International Conference on Machine Learning (ICML '00)*, pp. 727–734, 2000.

[14] C. Böhm, C. Faloutsos, J. Y. Pan, and C. Plant, "Robust information-theoretic clustering," in *Proceedings of the 12th ACM SIGKDD International Conference on Knowledge Discovery and Data Mining (KDD '06)*, pp. 65–75, August 2006.

[15] C. Böhm, C. Faloutsos, and C. Plant, "Outlier-robust clustering using independent components," in *Proceedings of the ACM SIGMOD International Conference on Management of Data (SIGMOD '08)*, pp. 185–198, June 2008.

[16] C. Böhm, K. Haegler, N. S. Müller, and C. Plant, "CoCo: coding cost for parameter-free outlier detection," in *Proceedings of the 15th ACM SIGKDD International Conference on Knowledge Discovery and Data Mining (KDD '09)*, pp. 149–157, July 2009.

[17] P. Gruber, F. Theis, A. Tome, and E. Lang, "Automatic denoising using local independent component analysis," in *Proceedings of the 4th International ICSC Symposium on Engineering of Intelligent Systems (EIS '04)*, 2004.

[18] A. Barron, J. Rissanen, and B. Yu, "The Minimum Description Length Principle in Coding and Modeling," *IEEE Transactions on Information Theory*, vol. 44, no. 6, pp. 2743–2760, 1998.

[19] T. C. M. Lee, "Regression spline smoothing using the minimum description length principle," *Statistics and Probability Letters*, vol. 48, no. 1, pp. 71–82, 2000.

[20] T. W. Lee, M. S. Lewicki, and T. J. Sejnowski, "ICA mixture models for unsupervised classification of non-Gaussian classes and automatic context switching in blind signal separation," *IEEE Transactions on Pattern Analysis and Machine Intelligence*, vol. 22, no. 10, pp. 1078–1089, 2000.

[21] A. Wismüller, O. Lange, D. R. Dersch et al., "Cluster analysis of biomedical image time-series," *International Journal of Computer Vision*, vol. 46, no. 2, pp. 103–128, 2002.

13

Globally Exponential Stability of Impulsive Neural Networks with Given Convergence Rate

Chengyan Liu, Xiaodi Li, and Xilin Fu

Department of Mathematics, Shandong Normal University, Ji'nan 250014, China

Correspondence should be addressed to Xiaodi Li; sodymath@163.com

Academic Editor: Manwai Mak

This paper deals with the stability problem for a class of impulsive neural networks. Some sufficient conditions which can guarantee the globally exponential stability of the addressed models with given convergence rate are derived by using Lyapunov function and impulsive analysis techniques. Finally, an example is given to show the effectiveness of the obtained results.

1. Introduction

Recently, special interest has been devoted to the dynamics analysis of neural networks due to their potential applications in different areas of science. Particularly, there has been a significant development in the theory of neural networks with impulsive effects [1–9], since such neural networks with impulsive effect can be used as an appropriate description of the phenomena of abrupt qualitative dynamical changes of essential continuous time systems. Based on the theory of impulsive differential equations [10–17], some sufficient conditions guaranteeing the exponential stability are derived [18–24]. For example, in [8], the author has obtained a criterion of exponential stability for a Hopfield neural network with periodic coefficients; in [18], by constructing the extended impulsive delayed Halanay inequality and Lyapunov functional methods, authors have got some sufficient conditions ensuring exponential stability of the unique equilibrium point of impulsive Hopfield neural networks with time delays. They all have obtained exponential stability for some kinds of neural networks through different methods. However, most of the existing results about the exponential stability of impulsive neural networks have a common feature that the exponential convergence rate cannot be derived, or derived but not the given one [8, 18, 23, 24]. The purpose of this paper is to establish some criteria which can guarantee the globally exponential stability of impulsive neural networks with the given convergence rate by using Lyapunov function and impulsive analysis techniques. This work is organized as follows. In Section 2, we introduce some basic definitions and notations. In Section 3, the main results are presented. In Section 4, an example is discussed to illustrate the results.

2. Preliminaries

Let $\mathbb{R}$ denote the set of real numbers, $\mathbb{R}_+$ denote the set of nonnegative real numbers, $\mathbb{Z}_+$ denote the set of positive integers and $\mathbb{R}^n$ denote the n-dimensional real space equipped with the Euclidean norm $\|\cdot\|$.

Consider the following impulsive neural networks:

$$\dot{x}_i(t) = -a_i(t) x_i(t)$$

$$+ \sum_{j=1}^{n} b_{ij}(t) f_j(x_j(t)) + I_i(t), \quad t \geq t_0, \ t \neq t_k,$$

$$\Delta x_i|_{t=t_k} = x_i(t_k) - x_i(t_k^-), \quad k \in \mathbb{Z}_+, \ i \in \Lambda,$$

$$(1)$$

where $\Lambda = \{1, 2, \ldots, n\}$. $n \geq 2$ corresponds to the number of units in a neural network; the impulse times t_k satisfy $0 \leq t_0 < t_1 < \cdots < t_k < \cdots$, $\lim_{k \to \infty} t_k = \infty$; x_i corresponds to the state of the neurons, f_j denotes the measures of response to its incoming potentials of the unit j at time t; $I_i(t)$ is the input of the unit i at time t. $PC[I, \mathbb{R}] \triangleq \{\varphi : I \to \mathbb{R} \mid \varphi(t^+) = \varphi(t)$ for $t \in I$, $\varphi(t^-)$ exists for $t \in I$, $\varphi(t^-) = \varphi(t)$ for all but points $t_k \in I\}$, where $I \subset \mathbb{R}$ is an interval, $\varphi(t^+)$ and $\varphi(t^-)$ denote the left limit and right limit of function $\varphi(t)$, respectively. $a_i(t) > 0$, $b_{ij}(t), I_i(t) \in PC[[t_0, +\infty), \mathbb{R}]$. For given $t_0, x(t_0) = x_0 = (x_1^0, x_2^0, \ldots, x_n^0) \in \mathbb{R}^n$, we denote by $x(t)$ the solution of system (1) with initial value $(t_0, x(t_0))$.

In this paper, we assume that some conditions are satisfied so that the equilibrium point of system (1) does exist, see [16, 17]. Assume that $x^* = (x_1^*, x_2^*, \ldots, x_n^*)^T$ is an equilibrium point of system (1). Impulsive operator is viewed as perturbation of the point x^* of such system without impulsive effects. We assume that the following impulsive condition holds.

(H_0) $\Delta x_i|_{t=t_k} = x_i(t_k) - x_i(t_k^-) = \sigma_{ik}(x_i(t_k^-) - x_i^*)$, $\sigma_{ik} \in \mathbb{R}$, $i \in \Lambda$, $k \in \mathbb{Z}_+$.

Furthermore, we will assume that the response function f_i satisfies the following condition.

(H_1) f_i is globally Lipschizian with Lipschitz constant $l_i > 0$, that is, $|f_i(s_1) - f_i(s_2)| \le l_i|s_1 - s_2|$, for all $s_1, s_2 \in \mathbb{R}$, $i \in \Lambda$.

Note that x^* is an equilibrium point of system (1), one can derive from system (1) that the transformation $z_i = x_i - x_i^*$, $i \in \Lambda$ transforms such system into the following system:

$$\dot{z}_i(t) = -a_i(t)z_i(t)$$
$$+ \sum_{j=1}^n b_{ij}(t)F_j(z_j(t)), \quad t \ge t_0, \ t \ne t_k, \quad (2)$$
$$z_i(t_k) = (1 + \sigma_{ik})z_i(t_k^-), \quad i \in \Lambda, \ k \in \mathbb{Z}_+,$$

where $F_j(z_j(t)) = f_j(x_j^* + z_j(t)) - f_j(x_j^*)$, and from the condition (H_1), it holds that $\|F_j(z_j(t))\| \le l_j\|z_j(t)\|$, $j \in \Lambda$.

Furthermore, let $y_i(t) = z_i(t)e^{\alpha(t-t_0)}$, $i \in \Lambda$, then system (2) becomes as follows:

$$\dot{y}_i(t) = (\alpha - a_i(t))y_i(t)$$
$$+ e^{\alpha(t-t_0)}\sum_{j=1}^n b_{ij}(t)F_j(y_j(t)e^{-\alpha(t-t_0)}), \quad t \ge t_0, \ t \ne t_k,$$
$$y_i(t_k) = (1 + \sigma_{ik})y_i(t_k^-), \quad i \in \Lambda, \ k \in \mathbb{Z}_+.$$
$$(3)$$

To prove the stability of x^* of system (1), it is equal to prove the stability of the zero solution of system (2), and also equal to the boundedness of system (3).

In the following, the notion A^T means the transpose of a square matrix A. We will use the notation $A > 0$ (or $A < 0$, $A \ge 0$, $A \le 0$) to denote that the matrix A is a positive definite (negtive definite, positive semidefinite, an negative semidefinite) marix.

Let $y(t) = (y_1(t), y_2(t), \ldots, y_n(t))^T$, $A(t) = \text{diag}[a_1(t), a_2(t), \ldots, a_n(t)]$, $B(t) = (b_{ij}(t))_{n \times n}$, $L = \text{diag}[l_1, l_2, \ldots, l_n]$, $I = \text{diag}[1, 1, \ldots, 1]$, $D_k = \text{diag}[1 + \sigma_{1k}, 1 + \sigma_{2k}, \ldots, 1 + \sigma_{nk}]$, $F(y) = (F_1(y_1), F_2(y_2), \ldots, F_n(y_n))^T$ then system (3) with initial condition becomes as follows:

$$\dot{y}(t) = (\alpha I - A(t))y(t)$$
$$+ e^{-\alpha(t-t_0)}B(t)F(y(t)e^{-\alpha(t-t_0)}), \quad t \ge t_0, \ t \ne t_k,$$
$$y(t_k) = D_ky(t_k^-), \quad i \in \Lambda, \ k \in \mathbb{Z}_+.$$
$$(4)$$

We introduce a definition as follows.

Definition 1. Assume $x^* = (x_1^*, x_2^*, \ldots, x_n^*)^T \in \mathbb{R}^n$ is the equilibrium point of system (1), then the equilibrium point x^* of system (1) is said to be globally exponential stable with given convergence rate $\alpha > 0$. If for any initial data $x(t_0) = x_0 \in \mathbb{R}$, there exists a constant $M \ge 1$, such that

$$\|x(t, t_0, x_0) - x^*\| \le \|x_0 - x^*\| Me^{-\alpha(t-t_0)}, \quad t \ge t_0. \quad (5)$$

From the transformation $z_i = x_i - x_i^*$, $i \in \Lambda$, and $z(t_0) = z_0 = x_0 - x^*$, the globally exponential stability of the equilibrium point x^* of system (1) can be transformed into the globally exponential stability of trivial solution of system (2), so (5) can be rewritten as follows:

$$\|z(t, t_0, z_0)\| \le \|z(t_0)\| Me^{-\alpha(t-t_0)}, \quad t \ge t_0. \quad (6)$$

Furthermore, form the transformation $y(t) = z(t, t_0, z_0)e^{\alpha(t-t_0)}$, $i \in \Lambda$, the globally exponential stability of trivial solution of system (2) can be transformed into the boundedness of the solution of system (4) and it can be rewritten as follows:

$$\|y(t)\| \le \|y(t_0)\| M, \quad t \ge t_0. \quad (7)$$

3. Main Results

Theorem 2. Given constant $\alpha > 0$. The equilibrium point of the system (1) is globally exponentially stable with the given convergence rate α, if the conditions (H_0) and (H_1) are fulfilled; moreover, suppose that

(i) $\alpha I - A(t) + B(t)L \le 0$, for all $t > t_0$,

(ii) $\prod_{k=1}^\infty \max_{i \in \Lambda}(1 + \sigma_{ik}) < \infty$, and $\sigma_{ik} \ge 0$, $i \in \Lambda$, $k \in \mathbb{Z}_+$.

Proof. We only need to prove $y(t) = z(t)e^{\alpha(t-t_0)}$ is bounded when $t \ge t_0$, where $z(t) = z(t, t_0, z_0)$ is a solution of (3) through (t_0, z_0).

Consider the Lyapunov function as follows:

$$V(t) = y(t)^T y(t) = \sum_{i=1}^n y_i^2(t). \quad (8)$$

Particularly, $V(t_0) = \sum_{i=1}^n y_i^2(t_0)$.

Then from conditions (H_0)-(H_1) and (i), we get the upper right-hand derivative of $V(t)$ along the solutions of system (3), for $t \in [t_k, t_{k+1})$, $k \in \mathbb{Z}_+$

$$D^+V(t) = 2\sum_{i=1}^n y_i(t)\dot{y}_i(t)$$
$$= 2\sum_{i=1}^n z_i(t)e^{2\alpha(t-t_0)}[\dot{z}_i(t) + \alpha z_i(t)]$$
$$= 2\sum_{i=1}^n z_i(t)e^{2\alpha(t-t_0)}$$
$$\times \left[-a_i(t)z_i(t) + \sum_{j=1}^n b_{ij}(t)F_j(z_j(t)) + \alpha z_i(t)\right]$$

$$= 2\sum_{i=1}^{n} e^{2\alpha(t-t_0)}$$

$$\times \left[\left(\alpha - a_i(t)\right) z_i^2(t) + z_i(t) \sum_{j=1}^{n} b_{ij}(t) F_j\left(z_j(t)\right) \right]$$

$$\leq 2\sum_{i=1}^{n} e^{2\alpha(t-t_0)}$$

$$\times \left[\left(\alpha - a_i(t)\right) z_i(t)^2 + z_i(t) \sum_{j=1}^{n} b_{ij}(t) l_j \left\| z_j(t) \right\| \right]$$

$$= 2\sum_{i=1}^{n} e^{2\alpha(t-t_0)} z_i^2(t) \left(\alpha - a_i(t)\right)$$

$$+ 2\sum_{i=1}^{n} e^{2\alpha(t-t_0)} z_i(t) \sum_{j=1}^{n} b_{ij}(t) l_j \left\| z_j(t) \right\|$$

$$= 2y(t)^T \left[\alpha I - A(t) + B(t) L\right] y(t)$$

$$\leq 0,$$

$$(9)$$

which implies the functional $V(t)$ is nonincreasing for $t \in [t_k, t_{k+1})$, $k \in \mathbb{Z}_+$. By condition (ii), it holds that

$$V(t_k) = \sum_{i=1}^{n} y_i^2(t_k) = \sum_{i=1}^{n} z_i^2(t_k) e^{2\alpha(t_k-t_0)}$$

$$= \sum_{i=1}^{n} e^{2\alpha(t-t_0)} \left[z_i\left(t_k^-\right) + J_i\left(z_i\left(t_k^-\right)\right)\right]^2$$

$$= \sum_{i=1}^{n} e^{2\alpha(t-t_0)} \left(1 + \sigma_{ik}\right)^2 z_i^2\left(t_k^-\right)$$

$$\leq \max_{i\in\Lambda} \left(1 + \sigma_{ik}\right)^2 V\left(t_k^-\right).$$

$$(10)$$

For any $t \in [t_0, t_1)$, since $V(t)$ is nonincreasing, it holds that $V(t) \leq V(t_0)$; moreover,

$$V(t_1) \leq \max_{i\in\Lambda} \left(1 + \sigma_{i1}\right)^2 V\left(t_1^-\right) \leq \max_{i\in\Lambda} \left(1 + \sigma_{i1}\right)^2 V\left(t_0\right).$$

$$(11)$$

Similarly, for any $t \in [t_1, t_2)$, it holds that $V(t) \leq V(t_1) \leq \max_{i\in\Lambda}(1 + \sigma_{i1})^2 V(t_0)$, and

$$V(t_2) \leq \max_{i\in\Lambda}\left(1 + \sigma_{i2}\right)^2 V\left(t_2^-\right)$$

$$\leq \max_{i\in\Lambda}\left(1 + \sigma_{i2}\right)^2 \max_{i\in\Lambda}\left(1 + \sigma_{i1}\right)^2 V\left(t_0\right).$$

$$(12)$$

Thus, it can be deduced that for $t \in [t_k, t_{k+1})$, $k \in \mathbb{Z}_+$,

$$V(t) \leq \prod_{j=1}^{k} \max_{i\in\Lambda}\left(1 + \sigma_{ij}\right)^2 V(t_0).$$

$$(13)$$

Hence, we obtain that for any $t \geq t_0$,

$$V(t) \leq \prod_{j=1}^{\infty} \max_{i\in\Lambda}\left(1 + \sigma_{ij}\right)^2 V(t_0),$$

$$(14)$$

which implies that

$$\left\| y(t) \right\| \leq M \left\| y(t_0) \right\|, \quad t \geq t_0,$$

$$(15)$$

where $M = \prod_{k=1}^{\infty} \max_{i\in\Lambda}(1 + \sigma_{ik}) < \infty$.

The proof of Theorem 2 is complete. $\square$

Remark 3. Most of the existing results about the exponential stability of impulsive neural networks cannot effectively control the convergence rate. It is interesting to see that Theorem 2 can guarantee the globally exponential stability of impulsive neural networks with the given convergence rate.

Remark 4. In particular, if $A(t) \equiv A$, $B(t) \equiv B$ in Theorem 2, where A, B are constant matrices, then condition $\alpha I - A + BL < 0$ can be easily checked via Matlab.

Theorem 5. *Given constant* $\alpha > 0$. *The equilibrium point of the system (1) is globally exponentially stable with the given convergence rate* α, *if the conditions* (H_0)-(H_1) *are fulfilled; moreover, suppose that*

(i) *there exists a constant* $\lambda > 0$, *such that* $(\alpha + \lambda)I - A(t) + B(t)L < 0$, *for all* $t > t_0$,

(ii) $\tau \triangleq \min_{k\in\mathbb{Z}_+}\{t_{k+1} - t_k\}$, $\max_{i\in\Lambda}(1 + \sigma_{ik}) \leq M_k e^{\lambda\tau}$, *where* $1 \leq M_k < \infty$ *and* $\prod_{k=1}^{\infty} M_k < \infty$, $i \in \Lambda$, $k \in \mathbb{Z}_+$.

Proof. We only need to prove that $y(t) = z(t)e^{\alpha(t-t_0)}$ is bounded when $t \geq t_0$, where $z(t) = z(t, t_0, z_0)$ is a solution of (3) through (t_0, z_0).

Consider the Lyapunov function as follows:

$$V(t) = y(t)^T y(t) = \sum_{i=1}^{n} y_i^2(t).$$

$$(16)$$

In particular, $V(t_0) = \sum_{i=1}^{n} y_i^2(t_0)$.

Then from conditions (H_0)-(H_1) and (i), we get the upper right-hand derivative of $V(t)$ along the solutions of system (3), for $t \in [t_k, t_{k+1})$, $k \in \mathbb{Z}_+$

$$D^+ V(t) = 2\sum_{i=1}^{n} y_i(t) \dot{y}_i(t)$$

$$\leq 2y(t)^T \left(\alpha I - A(t) + B(t) L\right) y(t) < -2\lambda V(t).$$

$$(17)$$

Thus,

$$V(t) < V(t_k) e^{-2\lambda(t-t_k)} < V(t_k) e^{-2\lambda\tau}, \quad t \in [t_k, t_{k+1}),$$

$$k \in \mathbb{Z}_+.$$

$$(18)$$

By condition (ii), it holds that

$$V(t_k) = \sum_{i=1}^{n} y_i^2(t_k) = \sum_{i=1}^{n} e^{2\alpha(t-t_0)}(1+\sigma_{ik})^2 z_i^2(t_k^-)$$

$$\leq M_k^2 e^{2\lambda\tau} \sum_{i=1}^{n} e^{2\alpha(t-t_0)} z_i^2(t_k^-) \qquad (19)$$

$$\leq M_k^2 e^{2\lambda\tau} V(t_k^-).$$

For any $t \in [t_0, t_1)$, it holds that $V(t) \leq V(t_0)e^{-2\lambda\tau}$, moreover

$$V(t_1) \leq M_1^2 e^{2\lambda\tau} V(t_1^-) \leq M_1^2 V(t_0). \qquad (20)$$

Similarly, for any $t \in [t_1, t_2)$, it holds that $V(t) \leq V(t_1)e^{-2\lambda\tau} \leq M_1^2 V(t_0)e^{-2\lambda\tau}$, and

$$V(t_2) \leq M_2 e^{2\lambda\tau} V(t_2^-) \leq M_2^2 M_1^2 V(t_0). \qquad (21)$$

Without loss of generality, when $t \in [t_k, t_{k+1})$, $k \in \mathbb{Z}_+$, it can be deduced that

$$V(t) \leq \prod_{j=1}^{k} M_j^2 e^{-2\lambda\tau} V(t_0). \qquad (22)$$

Hence, we obtain that for any $t \geq t_0$,

$$V(t) \leq \prod_{j=1}^{\infty} M_j^2 V(t_0), \qquad (23)$$

which implies that

$$\|y(t)\| \leq M \|y(t_0)\|, \quad t \geq t_0, \qquad (24)$$

where $M = (\prod_{j=1}^{\infty} M_j) < \infty$.
The proof of Theorem 5 is complete. □

Remark 6. Although Theorem 5 enhances the restriction on condition (i), the impulsive restriction in (ii) is weaker; that is, σ_{ik} is not necessary to converge to 0 as k is large enough, provided that the impulsive intervals are not too small.

Theorem 7. *Given constant $\alpha > 0$. The equilibrium point of the system (1) is globally exponentially stable with the given exponential convergence rate α, if the conditions (H_0)-(H_1) are fulfilled; moreover, suppose that*

(i) *there exists a constant $\lambda > 0$, such that $(\alpha - \lambda)I - A(t) + B(t)L < 0$, for all $t > t_0$,*

(ii) *$\tau \triangleq \max_{k \in \mathbb{Z}_+}\{t_{k+1} - t_k\}$ and $\beta_k e^{\lambda\tau} \leq 1$, where $\beta_k = \max_{i \in \Lambda}(1 + \sigma_{ik})$, $-1 \leq \sigma_{ik} \leq 0$, $i \in \Lambda$, $k \in \mathbb{Z}_+$.*

Proof. We only need to prove that $y(t) = z(t)e^{\alpha(t-t_0)}$ is bounded when $t \geq t_0$, where $z(t) = z(t, t_0, z_0)$ is a solution of (3) through (t_0, z_0).
Consider the Lyapunov functional as follows:

$$V(t) = y(t)^T y(t) = \sum_{i=1}^{n} y_i^2(t). \qquad (25)$$

Particularly, $V(t_0) = \sum_{i=1}^{n} y_i^2(t_0)$.

Then from conditions (H_0)-(H_1) and (i), we get the upper right-hand derivative of $V(t)$ along the solutions of system (1), for $t \in [t_k, t_{k+1})$, $k \in \mathbb{Z}_+$

$$D^+ V(t) = 2\sum_{i=1}^{n} y_i(t) \dot{y}_i(t)$$

$$= 2y(t)^T(\alpha I - A(t) + B(t)L)y(t) < 2\lambda V(t). \qquad (26)$$

Thus,

$$V(t) < V(t_k) e^{2\lambda(t-t_k)} < V(t_k) e^{2\lambda\tau}, \quad t \in [t_k, t_{k+1}), \ k \in \mathbb{Z}_+. \qquad (27)$$

By condition (ii), it holds that

$$V(t_k) = \sum_{i=1}^{n} y_i^2(t_k) \leq \max_{i \in \Lambda}(1 + \sigma_{ik})^2 V(t_k^-) \qquad (28)$$

$$= \beta_k^2 V(t_k^-), \quad k \in \mathbb{Z}_+.$$

By simple induction, we can prove that for any $t \in [t_k, t_{k+1})$, $k \in \mathbb{Z}_+$,

$$V(t) \leq \prod_{j=1}^{k} \beta_j^2 e^{2(k+1)\lambda\tau} V(t_0) \leq e^{2\lambda\tau} V(t_0), \qquad (29)$$

which implies that

$$\|y(t)\| \leq M \|y(t_0)\|, \quad t \geq t_0, \qquad (30)$$

where $M = e^{\lambda\tau}$.
The proof of Theorem 7 is complete. □

4. Applications

The following illustrative example will demonstrate the effectiveness of our results.

Example 8. Consider the following impulsive neural networks:

$$\dot{x}_1(t) = -a_1(t) x_1(t) + b_{11}(t) f_1(x_1(t))$$
$$+ b_{12}(t) f_2(x_2(t)) + I_1(t),$$

$$\dot{x}_2(t) = -a_2(t) x_2(t) + b_{21}(t) f_1(x_1(t))$$
$$+ b_{22}(t) f_2(x_2(t)) + I_2(t), \qquad (31)$$

$$x_1(t_k) = (1 + \sigma_{1k}) x_1(t_k^-) - \sigma_{1k}, \quad k \in \mathbb{Z}_+,$$

$$x_2(t_k) = (1 + \sigma_{2k}) x_2(t_k^-) - \sigma_{2k}, \quad k \in \mathbb{Z}_+,$$

where $f_1(u) = f_2(u) = (|u+1| - |u-1|)/2$.
It is easy to see that f_j, $j = 1, 2$ satisfying hypothesis (H_1) with $l_1 = l_2 = 1$. We have $a_1(t) = 3$, $a_2(t) = 2 - (3/2)\cos(2t)$, $b_{11}(t) = |\sin t|/2$, $b_{12}(t) = 1/2$, $b_{21}(t) = 2$, $b_{22}(t) = -1 - (\cos(2t)/2)$, $I_1 = (5/2) - (|\sin t|/2)$, $I_2 = 1 - \cos(2t)$, $\sigma_{1k} = \sqrt{1 + (1/5k^2)} - 1$, $\sigma_{2k} = \sqrt{1 + (1/6k^2)} - 1$.

Let $\alpha = 3$. It can be deduced that $\alpha I - A(t) + B(t)L \leq 0$ and $\prod_{k=1}^{\infty} \max_{i=1,2} |1 + \sigma_{ik}| < \infty$. Hence, all the conditions of Theorem 2 are satisfied; then the equilibrium point $x^* = (1, 1)$ of the above system (31) is globally exponentially stable with the given convergence rate $\alpha = 3$.

Acknowledgments

This work was jointly supported by the Project of Shandong Province Higher Educational Science and Technology Program (J12LI04), Research Fund for Excellent Young and Middle-aged Scientists of Shandong Province (BS2012DX039), and National Natural Science Foundation of China (11226136, 11171192).

References

[1] Z. Yang and D. Xu, "Stability analysis of delay neural networks with impulsive effects," *IEEE Transactions on Circuits and Systems II*, vol. 52, no. 1, pp. 517–521, 2005.

[2] J. Cao, "Global stability analysis in delayed cellular neural networks," *Physical Review E*, vol. 59, no. 5, pp. 5940–5944, 1999.

[3] J. Shen, Y. Liu, and J. Li, "Asymptotic behavior of solutions of nonlinear neutral differential equations with impulses," *Journal of Mathematical Analysis and Applications*, vol. 332, no. 1, pp. 179–189, 2007.

[4] B. Kosko, *Neural Networks and Fuzzy Systems*, Prentice Hall, New Delhi, India, 1992.

[5] J. Cao, "On stability of delayed cellular neural networks," *Physics Letters A*, vol. 261, no. 5-6, pp. 303–308, 1999.

[6] K. Gopalsamy, "Stability of artificial neural networks with impulses," *Applied Mathematics and Computation*, vol. 154, no. 3, pp. 783–813, 2004.

[7] R. Samidurai, S. Marshal Anthoni, and K. Balachandran, "Global exponential stability of neutral-type impulsive neural networks with discrete and distributed delays," *Nonlinear Analysis: Hybrid Systems*, vol. 4, no. 1, pp. 103–112, 2010.

[8] B. Lisena, "Exponential stability of Hopfield neural networks with impulses," *Nonlinear Analysis: Real World Applications*, vol. 12, no. 4, pp. 1923–1930, 2011.

[9] S. Wu, C. Li, X. Liao, and S. Duan, "Exponential stability of impulsive discrete systems with time delay and applications in stochastic neural networks: a Razumikhin approach," *Neurocomputing*, vol. 82, pp. 29–36, 2012.

[10] A. Berman and R. J. Plemmons, *Nonnegative Matrices in The Mathematical Sciences*, Academic Press, New York, NY, USA, 1979.

[11] D. D. Baïnov and P. S. Simeonov, *Systems with Impulsive Effect Stability Theory and Applications*, Halsted Press, New York, NY, USA, 1989.

[12] V. Lakshmikantham, D. D. Baïnov, and P. S. Simeonov, *Theory of Impulsive Differential Equations*, World Scientific, Singapore, 1989.

[13] X. L. Fu, B. Q. Yan, and Y. S. Liu, *Introduction of Impulsive Differential Systems*, Science Press, Beijing, China, 2005.

[14] I. M. Stamova, *Stability Analysis of Impulsive Functional Differential Equations*, Walter de Gruyter, New York, NY, USA, 2009.

[15] X. Liu and Q. Wang, "The method of Lyapunov functionals and exponential stability of impulsive systems with time delay," *Nonlinear Analysis: Theory, Methods and Applications*, vol. 66, no. 7, pp. 1465–1484, 2007.

[16] X. D. Li, "New results on global exponential stabilization of impulsive functional differential equations with infinite delays or finite delays," *Nonlinear Analysis: Real World Applications*, vol. 11, no. 5, pp. 4194–4201, 2010.

[17] X. Z. Liu, "Stability of impulsive control systems with time delay," *Mathematical and Computer Modelling*, vol. 39, no. 4-5, pp. 511–519, 2004.

[18] X. Fu and X. Li, "Global exponential stability and global attractivity of impulsive Hopfield neural networks with time delays," *Journal of Computational and Applied Mathematics*, vol. 231, no. 1, pp. 187–199, 2009.

[19] X. Li, X. Fu, P. Balasubramaniam, and R. Rakkiyappan, "Existence, uniqueness and stability analysis of recurrent neural networks with time delay in the leakage term under impulsive perturbations," *Nonlinear Analysis: Real World Applications*, vol. 11, no. 5, pp. 4092–4108, 2010.

[20] X. D. Li and Z. Chen, "Stability properties for Hopfield neural networks with delays and impulsive perturbations," *Nonlinear Analysis: Real World Applications*, vol. 10, no. 5, pp. 3253–3265, 2009.

[21] X. D. Li and M. Bohner, "Exponential synchronization of chaotic neural networks with mixed delays and impulsive effects via output coupling with delay feedback," *Mathematical and Computer Modelling*, vol. 52, no. 5-6, pp. 643–653, 2010.

[22] H. Akça, R. Alassar, V. Covachev, Z. Covacheva, and E. Al-Zahrani, "Continuous-time additive Hopfield-type neural networks with impulses," *Journal of Mathematical Analysis and Applications*, vol. 290, no. 2, pp. 436–451, 2004.

[23] Z. T. Huang, Q. G. Yang, and X. S. Luo, "Exponential stability of impulsive neural networks with time-varying delays," *Chaos, Solitons and Fractals*, vol. 35, no. 4, pp. 770–780, 2008.

[24] I. M. Stamova and R. Ilarionov, "On global exponential stability for impulsive cellular neural networks with time-varying delays," *Computers and Mathematics with Applications*, vol. 59, no. 11, pp. 3508–3515, 2010.

14

Evaluation of a Nonrigid Motion Compensation Technique Based on Spatiotemporal Features for Small Lesion Detection in Breast MRI

F. Steinbruecker,[1] A. Meyer-Baese,[2] T. Schlossbauer,[3] and D. Cremers[1]

[1] Department of Computer Science, Technical University of Munich, 85748 Garching, Germany
[2] Department of Scientific Computing, Florida State University, Tallahassee, FL 32306, USA
[3] Institute for Clinical Radiology, University of Munich, 81679 Munich, Germany

Correspondence should be addressed to A. Meyer-Baese, ameyerbaese@fsu.edu

Academic Editor: Olivier Bastien

Motion-induced artifacts represent a major problem in detection and diagnosis of breast cancer in dynamic contrast-enhanced magnetic resonance imaging. The goal of this paper is to evaluate the performance of a new nonrigid motion correction algorithm based on the optical flow method. For each of the small lesions, we extracted morphological and dynamical features describing both global and local shape, and kinetics behavior. In this paper, we compare the performance of each extracted feature set under consideration of several 2D or 3D motion compensation parameters for the differential diagnosis of enhancing lesions in breast MRI. Based on several simulation results, we determined the optimal motion compensation parameters. Our results have shown that motion compensation can improve the classification results. The results suggest that the computerized analysis system based on the non-rigid motion compensation technique and spatiotemporal features has the potential to increase the diagnostic accuracy of MRI mammography for small lesions and can be used as a basis for computer-aided diagnosis of breast cancer with MR mammography.

1. Introduction

Breast cancer is one of the leading death cases among women in the US. MR technology has advanced tremendously and became a highly sensitive method for the detection of invasive breast cancer [1]. While only dynamic signal intensity characteristics are integrated in today's CAD systems leaving morphological features to the interpretation of the radiologist, an automated diagnosis based on a combination of both should be strived for. Clinical studies have shown that combinations of different dynamic and morphologic characteristics [2] achieve diagnostic sensitivities up to 97% and specificities up to 76.5%.

However, most of these techniques have not been applied to small enhancing foci having a size of less than 1 cm. These diagnostically challenging cases found unclear ultrasound or mammography indications can be adequately visualized in magnetic resonance imaging (MRI) [3] with MRI providing an accurate estimation of invasive breast cancer tumor size [4].

Automatic motion correction represents an important prerequisite to a correct automated small lesion evaluation [5]. Motion artifacts are caused either by the relaxation of the pectoral muscle or involuntary patient motion and invalidate the assumption of same spatial location within the breast of the corresponding voxels in the acquired volumes for assessing lesion enhancement. Especially for small lesions, the assumption of correct spatial alignment often leads to misinterpretation of the diagnostic significance of enhancing lesions [6]. Therefore, spatial registration has to be performed before enhancement curve analysis. Due to the elasticity and heterogeneity of breast tissue, only nonrigid image registration methods are suitable. Although there has been a significant amount of research on nonrigid motion

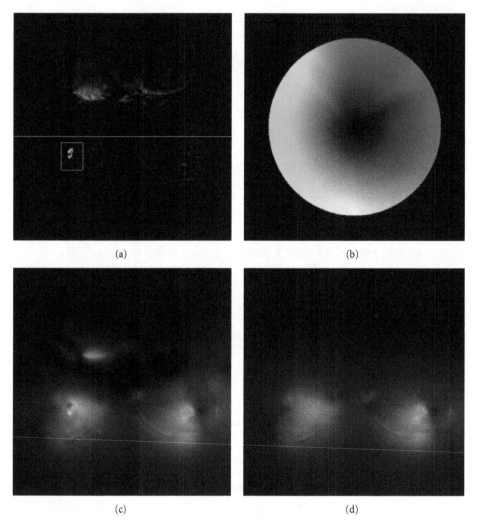

(a)   (b)

(c)   (d)

FIGURE 1: Motion detection on a transverse image. (a) Masking the data term: the green lines separate the boundary between masked and unmasked areas. (b) Color code describing motion from the interior of the image. (c) Motion in two directions determined without mask and (d) based on the mask from (a). The values for the standard deviation of the Gaussian presmoothing kernel and for the smoothness term are $\sigma = 3$ and $\alpha = 500$.

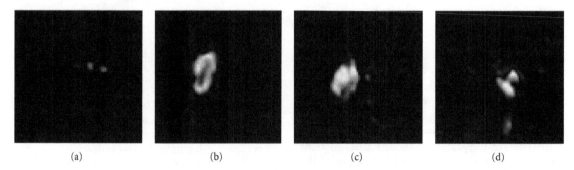

(a)   (b)   (c)   (d)

FIGURE 2: Tumor in adjacent transverse slices of a $512 \times 512 \times 32$ image.

compensation techniques in brain imaging, few methods have been so far proposed for breast MRI. Most proposed techniques employ physically motivated deformation models [6, 7], transformations based on the deformation of B-splines, [8, 9], elastic transformations [10], and more recently adaptive grid generation algorithms [11]. We present in this paper a novel elastic image registration method based on the variational optical flow computation and will study its impact on the shape of the enhancement curves for small lesions.

Evaluation of a Nonrigid Motion Compensation Technique Based on Spatiotemporal Features for Small Lesion Detection in Breast MRI

139

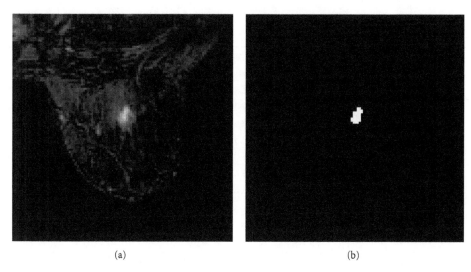

(a)

(b)

FIGURE 3: Example of an MR images segmentation showing the transverse image of a tumor in the right breast (a) and the binary segmentation of the tumor (b).

TABLE 1: Motion compensation parameters for two or three directions. σ represents the standard deviation for presmoothing and α the regularization parameter.

01	No motion compensation
02	3 directions, $\sigma = 1$, $\alpha = 100$
03	3 directions, $\sigma = 1$, $\alpha = 500$
04	3 directions, $\sigma = 3$, $\alpha = 100$
05	3 directions, $\sigma = 13$, $\alpha = 500$
06	2 directions, $\sigma = 1$, $\alpha = 100$
07	2 directions, $\sigma = 1$, $\alpha = 500$
08	2 directions, $\sigma = 3$, $\alpha = 100$
09	2 directions, $\sigma = 13$, $\alpha = 500$

The automated evaluation is a multistep system which includes a non-rigid motion compensation technique based on the optical flow, global and local feature extraction methods as shape descriptors, dynamical features, and spatiotemporal features combining both morphology and dynamics aspects to determine the optimal motion compensation parameters.

The paper is organized as follows. Section 2 describes the materials and methods, Section 3 the motion compensation technique, Section 4 the feature extraction techniques, and Section 5 the results. In Section 3, we present the non-rigid motion compensation technique, the feature extraction based on geometrical features, morphological features, dynamical features, and scaling index method for simultaneous time and space descriptions, and as classification technique the Fisher's discriminant analysis.

2. Material and Methods

2.1. Patients. A total of 40 patients, all female and age range 42–73, with indeterminate small mammographic breast lesions were examined. All patients were consecutively selected after clinical examinations, mammography in standard projections (craniocaudal and oblique mediolateral projections) and ultrasound. Only lesions BIRADS 3 and 4 were selected where at least one of the following criteria was present: nonpalpable lesion, previous surgery with intense scarring, or location difficult for biopsy (close to chest wall). All patients had histopathologically confirmed diagnosis from needle aspiration/excision biopsy and surgical removal. Breast cancer was diagnosed in 17 out of the total 31 cases. The average size of both benign and malignant tumors was less than 1.1 cm.

2.2. MR Imaging. MRI was performed with a 1.5 T system (Magnetom Vision, Siemens, Erlangen, Germany) with two different protocols equipped with a dedicated surface coil to enable simultaneous imaging of both breasts. The patients were placed in a prone position. First, transversal images were acquired with a STIR (short TI inversion recovery) sequence (TR = 5600 ms, TE = 60 ms, FA = 90°, IT = 150 ms, matrix size 256 × 256 pixels, slice thickness 4 mm). Then a dynamic T-weighted gradient echo sequence (3D fast low angle shot sequence) was performed (TR = 11 ms and TR = 9 ms, TE = 5 ms, FA = 25°) in transversal slice orientation with a matrix size of 256 × 256 pixels and an effective slice thickness of 4 mm or 2 mm.

The dynamic study consisted of 6 measurements with an interval of 83 s. The first frame was acquired before injection of paramagnetic contrast agent (gadopentetate dimeglumine, 0.1 mmol/kg body weight, Magnevist, Schering, Berlin, Germany) immediately followed by the 5 other measurements. The initial localization of suspicious breast lesions was performed by computing difference images, that is subtracting the image data of the first from the fourth acquisition. As a preprocessing step to clustering, each raw gray level time-series $S(\tau)$, $\tau \in \{1,\ldots,6\}$ was transformed into a signal time-series of relative signal enhancement $x(\tau)$

TABLE 2: Areas under the ROC curves for contour features using FLDA. The rows represent the motion compensation as given in Table 1. Numbers in boldface show the best results.

Feature type	Area under the ROC curve (%)								
	01	02	03	04	05	06	07	08	09
Radius min.	70.2	**85.1**	79.0	72.9	63.9	80.3	66.8	74.4	71.2
Radius max.	**83.4**	76.3	81.7	84.0	84.2	80.7	80.0	79.6	83.4
Radius mean	**83.2**	80.0	83.0	83.4	79.8	81.1	76.7	82.6	84.2
Radius st. dev.	82.4	70.4	76.1	80.3	80.7	76.9	79.2	75.0	76.9
Radius entropy	83.0	76.7	79.6	84.0	74.8	79.6	75.0	80.7	80.9
Azimuth entropy	80.7	81.9	77.7	79.6	77.5	81.9	79.0	78.4	79.6
Compactness	69.5	**77.1**	73.7	75.6	67.9	68.9	68.7	71.4	65.8

TABLE 3: Areas under the ROC curves for morphological features (geometric moments I_1 to I_6) using FLDA. The rows represent the motion compensation as given in Table 1. Numbers in boldface show the best results.

Feature type	Area under the ROC curve (%)								
	01	02	03	04	05	06	07	08	09
I_1	**64.5**	54.4	64.7	60.3	63.2	**67.6**	65.8	64.1	66.2
I_2	56.3	58.0	56.7	54.2	69.5	60.7	63.7	66.8	59.7
I_3	56.3	**78.8**	65.5	58.0	59.0	67.2	68.1	61.6	62.2
I_4	56.3	55.9	61.8	63.4	56.3	58.2	63.9	59.2	54.0
I_5	56.3	52.9	58.8	66.2	64.5	64.5	64.5	61.8	59.2
I_6	56.3	56.3	63.7	59.9	60.1	67.2	66.0	64.3	66.4

for each voxel, the precontrast scan at $\tau = 1$ serving as reference. Thus, we ensure that the proposed method is less sensitive to changing between different MR scanners and/or protocols.

3. Motion Compensation Technique

The employed motion compensation algorithm is based on the Horn and Schunck method [12] and represents a variational method for computing the displacement field, the so-called optical flow, in an image sequence. It is based on two typical assumptions for variational optical flow methods, the brightness constancy, and smoothness assumption.

In this context, the MR image sequence f_0 is a differentiable function of brightness values on a four-dimensional spatiotemporal image domain Ω:

$$f_0 : \underbrace{\Omega}_{\subset \mathbb{R}^3} \times \mathbb{R}_+ \longrightarrow \mathbb{R}_+. \tag{1}$$

From this image sequence, we want to compute a dense vector field $\mathbf{u} = (u_1, u_2, u_3)^\top : \Omega \to \mathbb{R}^{\{2,3\}}$ that describes the motion between the precontrast image at time point t and a postcontrast image at time point $t + k$, either for all three dimensions ($\mathbb{R}^3$) or only in one transversal slice ($\mathbb{R}^2$).

The initial image sequence f_0 is preprocessed and convolved with a Gaussian K_σ of a standard deviation σ to remove noise in the image:

$$f = K_\sigma * f_0. \tag{2}$$

The brightness constancy assumption dictates that under the motion $\mathbf{u}$, the image brightness values of the precontrast

image at time t and the postcontrast image at time $t + k$ remain constant in every pixel:

$$f(\mathbf{x} + \mathbf{u}(\mathbf{x}), t + k) = f(\mathbf{x}, t), \quad \forall \mathbf{x} \in \Omega. \tag{3}$$

Naturally, this condition by itself is not sufficient to describe the motion field $\mathbf{u}$ properly, since for a brightness value in an image voxel in the precontrast image, there are generally many voxels in the postcontrast image with the same brightness value, or, in the presence of noise, possibly even none at all. Therefore, we include the smoothness assumption, dictating that neighboring voxels should move in the same direction, which is expressed as the gradient magnitude of the flow field components is supposed 0 to be as follows:

$$|\nabla u_{\{1,2,3\}}(\mathbf{x})| = 0, \quad \forall \mathbf{x} \in \Omega. \tag{4}$$

This constraint by itself would force the motion field to be a rigid translation, which is not the case in MR images. However, if we use both the brightness constancy assumption and the smoothness assumption as weak constraints in an energy formulation, the motion field $\mathbf{u}$ that minimizes this energy matches the postcontrast image to the precontrast image and is spatially smooth.

The variational method is based on the minimization of the continuous energy functional which penalizes all deviations from model assumptions:

$$E(\mathbf{u}) = \int_\Omega \underbrace{(f(\mathbf{x} + \mathbf{u}(\mathbf{x}), t + k) - f(\mathbf{x}, t))^2}_{\text{Data term}}$$

$$+ \alpha \underbrace{\left(|\nabla u_1(\mathbf{x})|^2 + |\nabla u_2(\mathbf{x})|^2 + |\nabla u_3(\mathbf{x})|^2 \right)}_{\text{Smoothness term}} d\mathbf{x}. \tag{5}$$

Evaluation of a Nonrigid Motion Compensation Technique Based on Spatiotemporal Features for Small Lesion Detection in Breast MRI

141

TABLE 4: Areas under the ROC curves for dynamic features (slope) using FLDA. The rows represent the motion compensation as given by Table 1.

Feature type	Area under the ROC curve (%)								
	01	02	03	04	05	06	07	08	09
Slope	70.4	75.6	74.2	75.0	75.0	73.9	75.8	72.7	75.4

The weight term $\alpha > 0$ represents the regularization parameter where larger values correspond to smoother flow fields. This technique is a global method where the filling-in-effect yields dense flow fields, and no subsequent interpolation is necessary as with the technique proposed in [13]. This method works within a single variational framework.

Given the computed motion from the precontrast image to a postcontrast image, the postcontrast image is being registered backwards before its difference image with the precontrast image is being computed for tumor classification:

$$f_{\text{post-registered}}(\mathbf{x}) = f_{\text{post}}(\mathbf{x} + \mathbf{u}(\mathbf{x})). \tag{6}$$

Since this registration explicitly yields the brightness constancy assumption, if the motion has been estimated correctly, the registered postcontrast image is equal to the precontrast image.

Breast MR images are mostly characterized by brightness, since bright regions are created by fatty tissue or contrast agent enhancing tumor tissue, while dark regions describe glandular tissue and background. Tumors are mainly located in the glandular tissue and proliferate either into the fatty tissue (invasive) or along the boundary inside the glandular tissue (noninvasive).

Two major concerns have to be addressed when applying the optical flow approach to breast MRI: (1) The constancy assumption does not hold for objects appearing from one image to the next such as lesions the contrast agent enhancement of which is much stronger than in the surrounding tissue and (2) The lack of constant grid size in all directions since voxel size is smaller than the slice thickness. The first concern is alleviated by masking suspicious areas by a radiologist and by detecting the sharp gradients in the motion field in the unmasked image. Figure 1 shows the masking of the entire upper image and visualizes the motion in the inner slice by a color code. This color code describes the motion direction based on the hue and the motion magnitude based on the brightness and thus identifies suspicious regions by detecting the sharp gradients. The mask $m : \Omega \rightarrow \{0, 1\}$ can be easily incorporated in the energy formulation and it forces the data term to disappear in suspicious regions:

$$E(\mathbf{u}) = \int_{\Omega} m(\mathbf{x}) \big(f(\mathbf{x} + \mathbf{u}(\mathbf{x}), t + k) - f(\mathbf{x}, t) \big)^2$$
$$+ \alpha \big(|\nabla u_1(\mathbf{x})|^2 + |\nabla u_2(\mathbf{x})|^2 + |\nabla u_3(\mathbf{x})|^2 \big) d\mathbf{x}. \tag{7}$$

In addition, there can be gaps between the slices where no nuclei are being excited in order to avoid overlapping of the slices. Figure 2 shows an example of a tumor considerably shifting its position on adjacent transversal slices.

To overcome the second concern, it is important to decide whether the motion in transverse direction is having a significant impact. The present research has shown that there is no significant difference in visual quality if motion is computed in two or three directions. In the following notation, we will consider the motion in three directions, the one in two directions is analogous.

Based on the work of Horn and Schunck, a vast variety of research in optical flow estimation has been conducted, most of it on more robust, edge preserving regularity terms, for example [14]. In our work however, we favor the original quadratic formulation, since we explicitly need the filling-in effect of a non-robust regularizer to fill in the information in masked regions. To overcome the problem of having a non-convex energy in (5), we use the coarse-to-fine warping scheme detailed in [14], which linearizes the data term as in [12] and computes incremental solutions on different image scales.

For this, we approximate the image f at the distorted point $(\mathbf{x} + \mathbf{u}(\mathbf{x}), t + k)$ by a first-order Taylor approximation:

$$f(\mathbf{x} + \mathbf{u}(\mathbf{x}), t + k) - f(\mathbf{x}, t)$$
$$\approx f(\mathbf{x}, t + k) + \nabla f(\mathbf{x}, t + k)^\top \mathbf{u}(\mathbf{x}) - f(\mathbf{x}, t). \tag{8}$$

Alternatively, one can develop the Taylor series at time t, getting

$$f(\mathbf{x} + \mathbf{u}(\mathbf{x}), t + k) - f(\mathbf{x}, t)$$
$$\approx f(\mathbf{x}, t) + \nabla f(\mathbf{x}, t)^\top \mathbf{u}(\mathbf{x}) + \frac{\partial}{\partial t} f(\mathbf{x}, t) k - f(\mathbf{x}, t). \tag{9}$$

Since the term $f(\mathbf{x}, t)$ cancels and the temporal derivative is again approximated by the difference between the two images at point $\mathbf{x}$, the only difference between (8) and (9) is the time at which the spatial derivative ∇f is being computed. In optical flow computation, one usually uses the arithmetic mean $(1/2)(\nabla f(\mathbf{x}, t + k) + \nabla f(\mathbf{x}, t))$. For the purpose of registration, the scalar factor k can be neglected since it is arbitrary whether one computes a motion for a $k \neq 1$ and then scales the motion later on with k when registering the image, or simply sets k to 1. Incorporating this into the energy formulation and leaving out the indices for better readability, the linearized energy functional then reads as

$$E_{\text{lin}}(\mathbf{u}) = \int_{\Omega} m \left(\frac{\partial}{\partial t} f + \nabla f^\top \mathbf{u} \right)^2$$
$$+ \alpha \big(|\nabla u_1|^2 + |\nabla u_2|^2 + |\nabla u_3|^2 \big) d\mathbf{x}. \tag{10}$$

This functional is convex in **u**, and a minimizer can be found by solving its Euler-Lagrange equations:

$$0 = m\left(\frac{\partial f}{\partial x}\frac{\partial f}{\partial x}u_1 + \frac{\partial f}{\partial x}\frac{\partial f}{\partial y}u_2 + \frac{\partial f}{\partial x}\frac{\partial f}{\partial z}u_3 + \frac{\partial f}{\partial x}\frac{\partial f}{\partial t}\right) - \alpha\Delta u_1$$

$$\forall \mathbf{x} \in \Omega,$$

$$0 = m\left(\frac{\partial f}{\partial x}\frac{\partial f}{\partial y}u_1 + \frac{\partial f}{\partial y}\frac{\partial f}{\partial y}u_2 + \frac{\partial f}{\partial y}\frac{\partial f}{\partial z}u_3 + \frac{\partial f}{\partial y}\frac{\partial f}{\partial t}\right) - \alpha\Delta u_2$$

$$\forall \mathbf{x} \in \Omega,$$

$$0 = m\left(\frac{\partial f}{\partial x}\frac{\partial f}{\partial z}u_1 + \frac{\partial f}{\partial y}\frac{\partial f}{\partial z}u_2 + \frac{\partial f}{\partial z}\frac{\partial f}{\partial z}u_3 + \frac{\partial f}{\partial z}\frac{\partial f}{\partial t}\right) - \alpha\Delta u_3$$

$$\forall \mathbf{x} \in \Omega. \tag{11}$$

Since the linearization in (8) or (9) is only valid for small motions in the subpixel range, a typical strategy to overcome the problem of large motions is to downsample the MR images to a coarse resolution, compute an approximate motion on the coarse resolution, interpolate this motion to the next finer resolution, register the second image with the approximate motion, compute the incremental motion from the first image to the registered second image, add the incremental motion to the approximate motion, and repeat this iteration up to the original resolution.

4. Segmentation

Before we proceed with feature extraction, each MR image has to be segmented into two regions, the region of interest (ROI), that is, the voxels belonging to the tumor, and the background. We are using an interactive region growing algorithm, creating a binary mask the tumor voxels of which are true, and all other voxels are false. The image used for the region growing algorithm was the difference image of the second postcontrast image and the native precontrast image. The center of the lesion was interactively marked on one slice of the subtraction images and then a region growing algorithm included all adjacent contrast-enhancing voxels also those from neighboring slices. Thus a 3D form of the lesion was determined. An interactive ROI was necessary whenever the lesion was connected with diffuse contrast enhancement, as it is the case in mastopathic tissue.

Figure 3 shows a transverse image of a tumor in the right breast and its binary segmentation, created with region growing.

5. Feature Extraction

The complexity of the spatio-temporal tumor representation requires specific morphology and/or kinetic descriptors. We analyzed geometric and dynamical features as shape descriptors, provided a temporal enhancement modeling for kinetic feature extraction and the scaling index method for the simultaneous morphological and dynamics representation.

5.1. Contour Features. To represent the shape of a tumor, we compute the following features: the maximal, the minimum, the mean, and the standard deviation of a radius as well as the azimuth, entropy, and compactness.

First, we determine the center of mass of the tumor as

$$\bar{v} := \frac{1}{n}\sum_{i=1}^{n} v_i, \tag{12}$$

where n is the number of voxels belonging to the tumor, and v_i is location of the ith voxel.

We define for each contour voxel c_i, the radius r_i and the azimuth ω_i (i.e, the angle between the vector from the center of mass to the voxel c_i and the sagittal plane) and give in the following the definitions of the geometrical features to be used in context with the motion compensation technique.

From the set of the values $r_1, \ldots, r_m$ representing the radii, we determine the minimum value $r_{\min}$ and the maximum value $r_{\max}$ as well as

the radius:

$$r_i := \|c_i - \bar{v}\|_2, \tag{13}$$

the azimuth:

$$\omega_i := \arcsin\left(\frac{c_{ix} - \bar{v}_x}{(c_{ix} - \bar{v}_x)^2 + (c_{iy} - \bar{v}_y)^2}\right), \tag{14}$$

the mean value:

$$\bar{r} := \frac{1}{m}\sum_{i=1}^{m} r_i \tag{15}$$

the standard deviation:

$$\sigma_r := \sqrt{\frac{1}{m}\sum_{i=1}^{m}(r_i - \bar{r})^2}, \tag{16}$$

and the entropy:

$$h_r := -\sum_{i=1}^{100} p_i \cdot \log_2(p_i). \tag{17}$$

The subscripts x and y denote the position of the voxel in sagittal and coronal direction respectively. ω_i was also extended to the range from $-\pi$ to π by taking into account the sign of $(c_{iy} - \bar{v}_y)$.

The entropy h_r was computed from the normalized distribution of the values into 100 "buckets," where p_i is defined as follows:

For $0 \le i \le 99$:

$$p_i := \frac{\left|\{r_j \mid i \le (r_j - r_{\min})/(r_{\max} - r_{\min}) \cdot 100 < i+1\}\right|}{m}. \tag{18}$$

From the radius, $r_{\min}$, $r_{\max}$, $\bar{r}$, σ_r, and h_r were used as morphological features of the tumor. From the azimuth, only the entropy h_ω (computed for ω as in (17) and (18)) was used

Evaluation of a Nonrigid Motion Compensation Technique Based on Spatiotemporal Features for Small Lesion Detection in Breast MRI

143

as a feature, since the values $\omega_{\min}$ and $\omega_{\max}$ are always around π and $-\pi$, and the values $\bar{\omega}$, and σ_ω are not invariant under rotation of the tumor image.

An additional measurement describing the compactness of the tumor, which was also used as a feature, is the number of contour voxels, divided by the number of all voxels belonging to the tumor.

5.2. Geometric Moments. The spatial and morphological variations of a tumor can be easily captured by shape descriptors. Here, we will employ geometric moments [15] as shape descriptors for our lesions. For each lesion, we determine 6 three-dimensional moments that are invariant under rotation, translation, and scaling and are able to completely characterize the shape of the tumor.

Geometric moments are defined in the discrete three-dimensional case as

$$m_{\mathrm{pqr}} = \sum_x \sum_y x^p y^q z^r f(x, y, z), \qquad (19)$$

with $f(x, y, z)$ being the image intensity function (gray values). Finally, we compute three-dimensional moment invariants [16] that are not computational intensive and provide results stable to noise and distortion.

5.3. Dynamical Features. For each lesion, the time/intensity curve is computed based on the average signal intensity of the tumor before contrast agent administration (SI) and after contrast agent administration (SI_C), the relative enhancement as

$$\Delta\mathrm{SI} := \frac{\mathrm{SI}_C - \mathrm{SI}}{\mathrm{SI}} \cdot 100\%. \qquad (20)$$

To capture the slope of the curve of relative signal intensity enhancement (RSIE) versus time in the late postcontrast time, we compute the linear approximation of the RSIE curve for the last three time scans. The slope of this curve represents an important parameter for lesion classification.

5.4. Simultaneous Morphology and Dynamics Representations. The scaling index method [17] describes mathematically an estimation of the local scaling properties of a point represented in an n-dimensional embedding space. For every single point in the distribution, the number N of points is determined, which are included in an n-dimensional sphere of a radius r centered at $\mathbf{x_i}$

$$N(\mathbf{x_i}, r) = \sum_j \Theta\left(r - \left|\mathbf{x_j} - \mathbf{x_i}\right|\right), \qquad (21)$$

where Θ represents the Heaviside function. The function $N(\mathbf{x_i}, r)$, is usually determined within a specified range $r \in [r_1, r_2]$, the so-called scaling range.

If the scaling region is large, then $N(\mathbf{x_i}, r)$ becomes $N(\mathbf{x_i}, r) \propto \mathbf{r}^\alpha$ where α is the scaling index. A first-order approximation yields

$$\alpha_i = \frac{(\log N(\mathbf{x_i}, r_2) - \log N(\mathbf{x_i}, r_1))}{(\log r_2 - \log r_1)} \qquad (22)$$

with r_1 and r_2 being the lower and upper limit of the scaling range.

This technique can easily distinguish between point-like ($\alpha = 0$), string-like ($\alpha = 1$), and sheet-like ($\alpha = 2$) structures, in images and be thus employed for texture extraction. In the context of breast MRI, such a point consists of the sagittal, coronal, and transverse positions of a tumor voxel and its third-time scan gray value, and the scaling index serves as an approximation of the dimension of local point distributions.

The scaling index serves as a descriptor of the simultaneous enhancement kinetics and morphology. In particular, it can capture the blooming and the hook sign [18] and identify cancers with benign-like kinetics, discriminate normal tissue showing cancer-like enhancement curves, and thus improve the performance of computer-assisted detection of small enhancing lesions.

5.5. Morphologic Blooming. Another feature relying on morphology as well as on dynamics is the so-called *blooming*: the tumor contour becoming blurred and proliferating over the time of contrast agent enhancement is an indication for malignancy [19]. Beside blooming, [PTL+ 06] also attributes "centripetal" enhancement (strong, contrast agent enhancement near the tumor contour, weak enhancement in the tumor center with advancing time), and inhomogeneous contrast agent enhancement in general to a high probability of malignancy of the tumor.

To capture the blooming of a tumor, the difference of the relative signal intensity enhancement (RSIE) of every contour voxel and the average RSIE of its nontumor neighbor voxels was computed, and their mean, standard deviation and entropy from the 3rd to the 5th postcontrast image were used as features. Unlike for computation of the radial transform, for these features not only voxels in the contour of each transverse slice were considered contour voxels, but also voxels of the tumor with a non-tumor neighbor voxel on an adjacent transverse slice. The minimum and maximum values were neglected as features, since the gray values in the images are sensitive to noise.

The general irregularity of contrast agent enhancement in the tumor interior was computed as the standard deviation and entropy of the RSIE $s_{i,j}$ described above for the time scans 1, 3, and 5 ($i \in \{1, 3, 5\}$), and for all tumor voxels j. For each of the three time scans, the standard deviation and entropy were used as a feature.

In order to compensate general contrast and brightness differences between the images, for all features described in this section, the images were normalized to have the same mean as the precontrast image, and the standard deviation was divided by the standard deviation of the precontrast image.

6. Results

In the following, we will explore the applicability of the previously described motion compensation algorithm under different motion compensation parameters and features sets. The results will elucidate the applicability of motion

TABLE 5: Areas under the ROC curves for scaling index (SI) method using FLDA. The rows represent the motion compensation as given by Table 1. Numbers in boldface show the best results.

Feature type	Area under the ROC curve (%)								
	01	02	03	04	05	06	07	08	09
SI max.	74.6	66.6	64.3	69.3	62.8	**80.3**	69.1	60.9	62.8
SI mean	**80.3**	79.8	79.6	80.0	78.6	80.5	77.1	79.6	77.5
SI st. dev.	52.7	**81.5**	73.3	70.8	74.4	61.1	67.4	79.2	72.5
SI entropy	70.8	71.4	75.0	72.7	71.6	68.9	65.1	75.0	**76.5**

TABLE 6: Areas under the ROC curves for spatio-temporal features using FLDA. The rows represent the motion compensation as given in Table 1.

Feature type	Area under the ROC curve (%)								
	01	02	03	04	05	06	07	08	09
RSIE st. dev. (3)	56.7	52.5	55.0	52.3	48.1	52.5	55.5	58.4	55.3
RSIE st. dev. (4)	64.9	65.8	68.5	62.8	63.7	66.6	66.8	69.5	64.5
RSIE st. dev. (5)	64.7	70.6	70.0	64.9	68.3	69.7	65.8	66.8	69.5
RSIE entropy (3)	**80.9**	84.2	**85.3**	83.0	79.4	84.5	81.3	81.5	83.4
RSIE entropy (4)	77.9	87.4	81.9	80.7	76.7	83.8	78.8	77.3	78.4
RSIE entropy (5)	**74.6**	79.8	81.7	81.7	73.3	**81.5**	76.3	76.9	73.5
Contour RSIE mean (3)	54.4	51.7	52.7	52.3	54.0	55.7	52.7	52.7	55.5
Contour RSIE mean (4)	63.7	56.9	62.8	59.2	61.1	59.5	59.5	59.0	59.9
Contour RSIE mean (5)	62.2	64.9	60.3	68.5	68.7	62.6	63.9	62.6	66.6
Contour RSIE st. dev. (3)	55.3	57.4	58.0	52.1	55.7	58.0	55.0	57.4	57.8
Contour RSIE st. dev. (4)	58.4	59.9	57.1	56.7	61.3	60.7	58.6	56.9	62.4
Contour RSIE st. dev. (5)	63.7	63.2	67.6	60.5	65.1	58.6	58.2	66.2	64.3
Contour RSIE entropy (3)	77.5	81.3	77.1	74.2	76.9	77.1	74.8	75.4	74.4
Contour RSIE entropy (4)	83.2	84.5	82.8	79.8	77.9	84.9	77.5	81.3	79.6
Contour RSIE entropy (5)	80.5	81.3	78.2	80.7	72.9	79.6	78.2	77.5	78.4

compensation as an artefact correction method and also the descriptive power of several tumor features with and without motion correction.

Table 1 describes the motion compensation parameters used in the subsequent evaluations.

The effect of the motion compensation based on motion compensation parameters such as the amount of presmoothing and the regularization parameter was analyzed based on different combinations of feature groups.

We analyzed the performance of each proposed feature set and combinations of those for tumor classification based on receiver-operating characteristic (ROC) and compare the area-under-the-curve (AUC) values.

As a classification method to evaluate the effect of motion compensation on breast MR images, we chose the Fisher's linear discriminant analysis. Discriminant analysis represents an important area of multivariate statistics and finds a wide application in medical imaging problems. The most known approaches are linear discriminant analysis (LDA), quadratic discriminant analysis (QDA), and Fisher's canonical discriminant analysis.

Let us assume that $\mathbf{x}$ describes a K-dimensional feature vector, that there are J classes and there are N_j samples available in group j. The mean in group j is given by μ_j, and the covariance matrix is given by Σ_j.

The underlying idea of Fisher's linear discriminant analysis (FLDA) is to determine the directions in the multivariate space that allow the best discrimination between the sample classes. FLDA is based on a common covariance estimate and finds the most dominant direction and afterwards searches for "orthogonal" directions with the same property. The technique can extract at most $J - 1$ components, and for visualization purposes scores of the first component are plotted against that of the second one, thus yielding the optimal separation among the classes.

This technique identifies the first discriminating component based on finding the vector $\mathbf{a}$ that maximizes the discrimination index given as

$$\frac{\mathbf{a}^\mathrm{T}\mathbf{B}\mathbf{a}}{\mathbf{a}^\mathrm{T}\mathbf{W}\mathbf{a}}, \tag{23}$$

with $\mathbf{B}$ denoting the interclass sum-of-squares matrix and $\mathbf{W}$ the intraclass sum-of-squares matrix.

6.1. Effectiveness of Contour Features. The contour features described in Section 5.1 show for almost all motion compensation parameters high ROC values as shown in Table 2. Without motion compensation, the entropy as well as radius mean and maximum yield the best results. The radius minimum followed by the compactness show a significant improvement for motion compensation in 3D directions.

Evaluation of a Nonrigid Motion Compensation Technique Based on Spatiotemporal Features for Small Lesion Detection in Breast MRI

145

TABLE 7: Areas under the ROC curves for all combined features and for the optimal number of PCs using FLDA. The rows represent the motion compensation as given by Table 1.

| | Area under the ROC curve (%) | | | | | | | | |
	01	02	03	04	05	06	07	08	09
FLDA classification	85.1	80.0	77.1	78.6	84.2	76.3	83.8	84.7	84.0
Number of PC	14	20	19	17	20	5	12	11	21

6.2. Effectiveness of Geometric Moments. The geometric moments describe a representation of average shape parameters. Table 3 shows that motion compensations in two directions yields better results than in three directions for almost all geometric moments. However, the geometric moments seen not to be an adequate mean to extract features for small lesions.

6.3. Effectiveness of Kinetic Features. The slope is derived from the first-order approximation of relative signal intensity enhancement from the last three scans. Table 4 shows that both 2D as well as 3D motion compensation yield almost equally good results.

6.4. Effectiveness of Spatiotemporal Features. For the two radii r_1 and r_2, we used radii in the size of tumor structures, $r_1 = 3$ mm and $r_2 = 6$ mm. The maximum, mean, and standard deviation and entropy of the set of scaling-indices, computed from tumor points as in (15)–(17), were used as features of the tumor. The minimum was neglected, since for almost every tumor it was 0, due to isolated points.

Table 5 shows the ROC values for the scaling index method for different motion compensation parameters shown in Table 1. The scaling index mean value yields the highest results without motion compensation and for both 2D and 3D motion compensation.

The performance results for the spatio-temporal features related to both contour and tumor relative signal intensity enhancement are shown in Table 6 for the third, fourth, and fifth scans. For both the tumor and contour, the entropy showed the best results in the ROC analysis: the third scan for the tumor entropy and the fourth for the contour entropy for both uncompensated and compensated motion.

6.5. Effectiveness of All Combined Features. In a final step, we considered all determined features as a vector, reduced its dimension with PCA and used FLDA as a classification method. The AUCvalues for the optimal number of PCs and depending on the motion compensation parameters are shown in Table 7. We observe again that motion compensation in 2D yields promising results for a CAD for small lesions.

7. Conclusion

Breast MRI reading is often impeded by motion artifacts of different grades. Motion correction algorithms become a necessary correction tool in order to improve the diagnostic value of these mammographic images. We applied a new motion compensation algorithm based on the Horn and Schunck method for motion correction and determined the optimal parameters for lesion classification. Several novel lesion descriptors such as morphologic, kinetic, and spatiotemporal are applied and evaluated in context with benign and malignant lesion discrimination. The optimal motion correction results were achieved for motion compensation in two directions for mostly small standard deviations of the Gaussian kernel and smoothing parameter. Consistent with the only study known for evaluating the effect of motion correction algorithms [20], the proposed motion compensation technique achieved good results for weak motion artifacts.

The performed ROC-analysis shows that an integrated motion compensation step in a CAD system represents a valuable tool for supporting radiological diagnosis in dynamic breast MR imaging.

Acknowledgments

The research was supported by NIH Grant 5K25CA106799-04.

References

[1] S. G. Orel, M. D. Schnall, C. M. Powell et al., "Staging of suspected breast cancer: effect of MR imaging and MR-guided biopsy," *Radiology*, vol. 196, no. 1, pp. 115–122, 1995.

[2] B. Szabó, P. Aspelin, M. Wiberg, and B. Bone, "Dynamic mr imaging of the breast—analysis of kinetic and morphologic diagnsotic criteria," *Acta Radiologica*, vol. 44, no. 4, pp. 379–386, 2003.

[3] A. P. Schouten van der Velden, C. Boetes, P. Bult, and T. Wobbes, "Variability in the description of morphologic and contrast enhancement characteristics of breast lesions on magnetic resonance imaging," *The American Journal of Surgery*, vol. 192, no. 2, pp. 172–178, 2006.

[4] G. M. Grimsby, R. Gray, A. Dueck et al., "Is there concordance of invasive breast cancer pathologic tumor size with magnetic resonance imaging?" *The American Journal of Surgery*, vol. 198, no. 4, pp. 500–504, 2009.

[5] S. Behrens, H. Laue, T. Boehler, B. Kuemmerlen, H. Hahn, and H. O. Peitgen, "Computer assistance for MR based diagnosis of breast cancer: present and future challenges," *Computerized Medical Imaging and Graphics*, vol. 31, no. 4-5, pp. 236–247, 2007.

[6] A. Hill, A. Mehnert, S. Crozier, and K. McMahon, "Evaluating the accuracy and impact of registration in dynamic contrast-enhanced breast MRI," *Concepts in Magnetic Resonance B*, vol. 35, no. 2, pp. 106–120, 2009.

[7] W. R. Crum, C. Tanner, and D. J. Hawkes, "Anisotropic multi-scale fluid registration: evaluation in magnetic resonance

breast imaging," *Physics in Medicine and Biology*, vol. 50, no. 21, pp. 5153–5174, 2005.

[8] T. Rohlfing, C. R. Maurer, D. A. Bluemke, and M. A. Jacobs, "Volume-preserving nonrigid registration of MR breast images using free-form deformation with an incompressibility constraint," *IEEE Transactions on Medical Imaging*, vol. 22, no. 6, pp. 730–741, 2003.

[9] D. Rueckert, L. Sonoda, C. Hayes, D. Hill, M. Leach, and D. Hawkes, "Nonrigid registration using free-form deformations: application to breast mr images," *IEEE Transactions on Medical Imaging*, vol. 18, no. 8, pp. 712–721, 1999.

[10] R. Lucht, S. Delorme, J. Heiss et al., "Classification of signal-time curves obtained by dynamic magnetic resonance mammography: statistical comparison of quantitative methods," *Investigative Radiology*, vol. 40, no. 7, pp. 442–447, 2005.

[11] M. Y. Chu, H. M. Chen, C. Y. Hsieh et al., "Adaptive grid generation based non-rigid image registration using mutual information for breast MRI," *Journal of Signal Processing Systems*, vol. 54, no. 1–3, pp. 45–63, 2009.

[12] B. K. P. Horn and B. G. Schunck, "Determining optical flow," *Artificial Intelligence*, vol. 17, no. 1–3, pp. 185–203, 1981.

[13] K. H. Herrmann, S. Wurdinger, D. R. Fischer et al., "Application and assessment of a robust elastic motion correction algorithm to dynamic MRI," *European Radiology*, vol. 17, no. 1, pp. 259–264, 2007.

[14] N. Papenberg, A. Bruhn, T. Brox, S. Didas, and J. Weickert, "Highly accurate optic flow computation with theoretically justified warping," *International Journal of Computer Vision*, vol. 67, no. 2, pp. 141–158, 2006.

[15] S. Theodoridis and K. Koutroumbas, *Pattern Recognition*, Academic Press, 1998.

[16] D. Xu and H. Li, "Geometric moment invariants," *Pattern Recognition*, vol. 41, no. 1, pp. 240–249, 2008.

[17] F. Jamitzky, R. W. Stark, W. Bunk et al., "Scaling-index method as an image processing tool in scanning-probe microscopy," *Ultramicroscopy*, vol. 86, no. 1-2, pp. 241–246, 2001.

[18] W. A. Kaiser, *Signs in MR Mammography*, Springer, 2008.

[19] A. Penn, S. Thompson, C. Lehman et al., "Morphologic blooming in breast mri as a characterization of margin for discriminating benign from malignant lesions," *Academic Radiology*, vol. 13, no. 11, pp. 1344–1354, 2006.

[20] U. Schwarz-Boeger, M. Mueller, G. Schimpfle et al., "Moco—comparison of two different algorithms for motion correction in breast mri," *Onkologie*, vol. 31, no. 2, pp. 141–158, 2008.

15

Combining Neural Methods and Knowledge-Based Methods in Accident Management

Miki Sirola and Jaakko Talonen

Department of Information and Computer Science, Aalto University, P.O. Box 15400, 00076 Aalto, Finland

Correspondence should be addressed to Miki Sirola, miki.sirola@aalto.fi

Academic Editor: Wilson Wang

Accident management became a popular research issue in the early 1990s. Computerized decision support was studied from many points of view. Early fault detection and information visualization are important key issues in accident management also today. In this paper we make a brief review on this research history mostly from the last two decades including the severe accident management. The author's studies are reflected to the state of the art. The self-organizing map method is combined with other more or less traditional methods. Neural methods used together with knowledge-based methods constitute a methodological base for the presented decision support prototypes. Two application examples with modern decision support visualizations are introduced more in detail. A case example of detecting a pressure drift on the boiling water reactor by multivariate methods including innovative visualizations is studied in detail. Promising results in early fault detection are achieved. The operators are provided by added information value to be able to detect anomalies in an early stage already. We provide the plant staff with a methodological tool set, which can be combined in various ways depending on the special needs in each case.

1. Introduction

Accident management grew into an own and popular research branch in the early 1990s. This trend was a kind of delayed reflection of the two serious industrial accidents in the 1980s in Bhopal (1984) and in Chernobyl (1986). It was noticed that most of the earlier studies about abnormal events did not cover very well the severe accident cases. Already the Three Mile Island accident (1979) made the nuclear power plant control room a major focus for the studies of human factors, human reliability, and man-machine interface technology [1]. The Fukushima accident in 2011 has risen the accident management issue up again, although the nature and origin of this accident were completely different.

The problem area in the 1990s was identified to begin with information needs and reliability, to be completed with accident mitigation. The presentation methods and information structuring were located to central issues, as the human being was considered often to be the weakest link in the safety systems. The fault diagnosis of abnormal events and the support of operator decision making were naturally completing this entity [2].

Computerized accident management was studied in the 1990s, for instance, in OECD Halden Project, and prototyping systems including also strategic planning features in operator support or technical support centre were carried out in several projects the author is participating in [3]. Methodology was developed and decision models were built for selected application areas.

Early fault detection and information visualization are important key issues in accident management also today that we have been concentrating on in our recent studies [4]. We have combined different methods, including knowledge-based techniques and neural methods, to help the decision making of operators and experts in the control room of nuclear power plants. Self-organizing map (SOM) method [5] has been one of the important methods used.

2. Background

Research in computerized decision support systems has been carried out for the last fifty years. The field of computerized support systems (CSSs) can be divided into two main branches: decision support systems (DSSs) and expert systems (ESs). The introduction of knowledge-based systems (KBSs) in the 1980s led to the development of intelligent decision support systems (IDSSs). A large variety of different types of computerized support systems with a large variety of properties and characteristics can be recognized in later studies of this field [6].

The CAMS project [7] was an attempt to build a large-scale computerized support system for nuclear industry that would cover also severe accident management [8]. The CAMS (computerized accident management support) system was planned to provide support to various user groups in all states of the nuclear power plant, including accident states. The CAMS was composed from the following components: signal validation, tracking simulator, predictive simulator, strategy generator, critical function monitoring, and an MMI (man-machine interface) system.

As a part of CAMS project and a followup, a knowledge-based decision support system was developed [9]. The concept was based partly on decision theory including value theory, utility theory, and decision analysis [10, 11]. In addition to the control room tool prototype, a decision tool including a case-based criteria database in maintenance was developed [12]. In maintenance the problem area is somewhat different. Two important areas can be recognized: event-driven decisions and plant life management.

During the last decade we have added the neural methods to the decision support concept. We participated a few years ago in a large industrial research program studying nonlinear temporal and spatial forecasting: modeling and uncertainty analysis, called NoTeS project. In cooperation with a Finnish nuclear power plant, we studied early fault detection with various methods and developed many decision support visualizations mostly based on neural methods [4]. The self-organizing map method was combined with knowledge-based methods in a decision support system prototype. The following tasks were studied more in detail: process and progress visualization, failure detection and separations, leakage detection with adaptive modeling, feature selection and process fault detection, and detecting the prestage of a process fault.

The fault dynamics and dependencies of power plant elements and variables were inspected in our recent studies to open the way for modeling and creating useful statistics to detect process faults. We succeeded in using data mining to learn from industrial processes and finding out dependencies between variables by principal component analysis (PCA) [13] and self-organizing map (SOM). Also a segmentation method was developed to detect automatically different process states of stored datasets.

3. Self-Organizing Map Method in Decision Support

Self-organizing map (SOM) [5] is an effective method in neural computing for analysis and visualization of multidimensional data. An SOM consists of neurons organized in an array. The SOM is trained iteratively. The best-matching unit (BMU) is calculated with a selected distance measure. The SOM map is updated with the SOM update rule at each time step.

Originally the SOM algorithm was not designed for temporal data mining. The SOM is able to analyze ideally only static sets of data. Many attempts to use SOM method in the analysis of dynamic data have been made. The problems of using it in time-related problems in process modeling and monitoring are discussed in [14]. One possibility to describe dynamical behaviour is the visualization of trajectories, which link together the adjacent winner neurons (BMU) in the SOM grid.

The self-organizing map (SOM) is used here in data analysis for resolving and visualizing nonlinear relationships in a complex process. An application of the SOM describing the state and progress of the real-time process is studied. The self-organizing map is used as a visual regression model for estimating the state configuration and progress of and observation in process data. One important tool is the process state trajectory in the process component plane. The failure detection is done with prototype systems.

Early detection of faults is a key issue in nuclear industry. Tools have been developed to help the operators in their daily work and to help experts to understand better various phenomena in the process. Older nuclear power plants are going through modernization projects. This development has initialized new needs. Wide monitoring screens set up new requirements for presentation techniques, for instance. New contents are needed.

We have developed new visualizations and visualization techniques and developed prototypes of control room tools for testing various combinations of methodologies [4]. Two examples are presented in this paper more in detail. Information visualization concentrates on the use of computer-supported tools to explore large amount of process data. Visualization technique is the technical realization of information visualization. The new aspects in these visualizations and visualization techniques are the versatile use of self-organizing map (SOM) method and also combining it with various other methods as well in the field of data analysis and other fields such as knowledge-based methods.

A decision support system that combines knowledge-based methods and neural methods is seen in Figure 1. It is a prototype of a control room tool for operators or an analysis tool for experts [4]. It is developed for failure management in nuclear power plants. It gives informative decision support visualizations based mostly on self-organizing map (SOM) method and gives advice produced by rule-based reasoning. A Finnish nuclear power plant in Olkiluoto has tested the control room tool.

The prototype is a Matlab software program built on the top of Matlab extension SOM Toolbox [15]. It includes visualizations of SOM maps of normal data and failure data, state U-matrix, quantisation error for both state U-matrix and component planes, progress visualization, and time curves. Note the U-matrix trajectory showing the dynamical behavior in the process in Figure 1. U-matrix is visualization technique that reveals the clustering structure of the data.

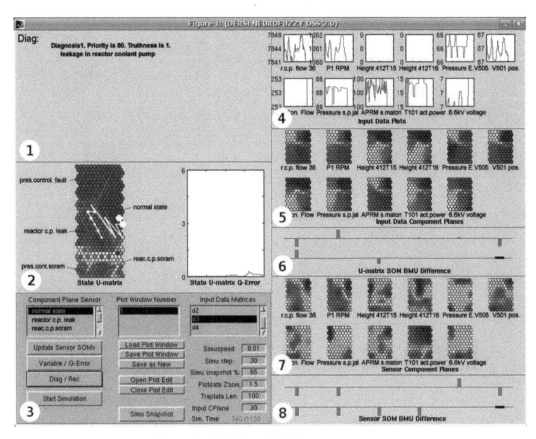

FIGURE 1: A SOM-based decision support system.

Quantisation includes the numerical evaluating. Quantisation error is a cumulative measure notifying differences in the data.

The failure management scenario analyzed in Figure 1 is simulated with the Olkiluoto training simulator. A leakage has appeared at the primary circuit near the main circulation pump. The control room tool has just identified the leak, and the rule base is reasoning the first diagnosis of the event; see Field 1 in Figure 1. The U-matrix trajectory is revealing the problem as well as the U-matrix quantisation error; see Field 2 in Figure 1. The trajectory (white line) is moving from the normal operation area into the specific leak problem area in the U-matrix, and the quantisation error is increasing. Clear differences can be seen in the normal operation SOM maps and the failure SOM maps; see Fields 5 and 7 in Figure 1. Variable correlations should be observed. If, for example, two variables have similar colouring shape, then they strongly correlate. Many strong variable correlations in normal operation get weaker in the failure, for instance, the reverse correlation of flow and pressure. Also time curves (see Field 4 in Figure 1) and the quantisation errors of component planes (see Fields 6 and 8 in Figure 1) point out abnormal behaviour. In this particular case, these differences are not as clear as those in the SOM maps and U-matrix. Field 3 in Figure 1 is for the user to control this decision tool.

Feature subset selection is essential in data mining applications. Here the feature subset selection is integrated into real-time process fault detection [4]. Methods based both on dependency measures and cluster separability measures are used. A tool for process visualization is developed; see Figure 2. Experiments on nuclear power plant data are carried out to assess the effectiveness and performance of the methods. We show with a leak scenario produced by the Olkiluoto Nuclear Power Plant training simulator that the visualizations help in the early detection of failures.

Already in an early phase of the scenario, the colouring of the SOM mapping begins to change, see upper left part of Figure 2. Some colours in the SOM map are already out of the normal operation colourbar. In addition the statistical Kolmogorov-Smirnov test (KS-test) detect anomalies in an early phase (lower left part of Figure 2), when changes, for instance, in the time curves are still very small (lower right part of Figure 2). In KS test the most varying variables are marked with red coloured bars. Also the locations of the interesting variables selected at each moment are marked in the PI diagram; see the upper right part of Figure 2.

These two examples show the value and effectiveness of the SOM method together with some other methods in visualization and early fault detection. These visualizations make the operators or analysts aware of the problems already when the changes in the process variables are still rather small and difficult to notice. Suitable visual changes figure the mental model of the operator more effectively than small changes in numbers or curves and give remarkable aid in the difficult decision-making process.

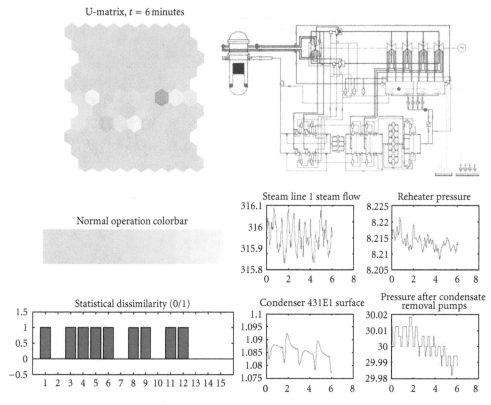

FIGURE 2: Control room visualization detecting abnormalities in an early phase of a leak scenario.

4. Detecting Pressure Drift on the Boiling Water Reactor by Multivariate Methods

Multivariate methods make it possible to model process offline, and research results can be used to understand the process dynamics. The transmitters that have drifted out of tolerance have to be identified. It provides cost savings for utilities, including direct reductions in working hours and indirect savings, caused by improved instrument reliability and plant safety.

A large amount of high-dimensional data is monitored by the univariate control charts. Redundant or in some cases high correlating signal measurements are compared with each other to detect deviation and a need for calibration. This makes it possible to know when instrument adjustment is necessary. In practice a sensor drift is detected when the sensor readings deviate from the calibrated value.

Continuous online validation will provide the most expedient status identification. The principal component regression (PCR) and the partial least square (PLS) are introduced as techniques to indicate calibration status. PCR is a regression analysis that uses principal component analysis (PCA) when estimating regression coefficients. It is a procedure to overcome problems which arise when the explanatory variables are close to being collinear. PLS is a statistical method that bears some relation to PCR. PLS family of methods is known as bilinear factor models.

In this paper the calibration status is measured as index value, which is a correlation between predicted and measurement values. When the difference of index and calibration value is considered significant by a certain criterion (e.g., D(index) > 5%), the channel is suspected to be out of calibration. After each transmitter calibration, the model is updated.

The nuclear industry currently practices a conservative approach by testing the process, such as temperature sensors and pressure transmitters. These components are fully calibrated on the refueling outages.

The dataset was captured in May 2009 from the Finnish Olkiluoto Nuclear Power Plant. More than 700 signals were recorded: 10 hours, every 10 seconds. About 100 signals have quality problems, and missing values. These variables were not used in the analysis. Because we did not have separate training data, the data was divided into training and testing parts. In our experiments it is assumed that the training part is recorded after the calibration. It was used for the input signal selection to find redundant or high correlating signals; see Figure 3. Techniques for removing noise were not used.

In Figure 3 on the y-axis are the variable names, and on the x-axis the corresponding Matlab variable indexes (variable codes). As the variable has always strongest correlation with itself, the corresponding variable name of these variable indexes can be found by following the diagonal, which have the largest values. The colourings of the variable values are in the right side of the Figure 3.

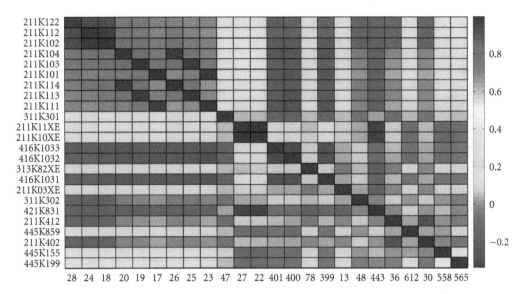

FIGURE 3: The target variable 211K122 (reactor pressure) is modelled by correlating variables. Variable code names are shown on y-axis and variable codes on x-axis. z-axis is correlation (colour coding in the figure), for example, the reactor pressure has the largest negative correlation with the variable 421K831 (Matlab variable index 443) and the largest positive correlation with the variable 211K112.

Normalized data was divided into separate sets for estimation and validation. Simple validation was performed, and 2/3 of the data in the learning set and 1/3 in the validation set were selected.

First 2400 samples were selected for the learning set. Two sampling types of were tested: (a) first 2400 points are in the learning set and the rest are for validation; (b) points were selected randomly. Methods like multilinear regression (MLR), principal component regression (PCR), and partial least squares (PLSs) do not take into account the time dimension; see Figure 4. Random sampling is used to get more reliable results.

In Figure 4 the parameters are the explanation stage of the teaching set (R2) and the explanation stage of the test set (R2v). Explanation stage is a related concept to correlation (in both, 1 is the highest possible value). The blue curve presents the teaching set and the green curve the test set.

Mostly, the problem with the MLR is multicollinearity when there is a lot of data available. The collinearity problem is essentially caused by redundancy in the data. However, none of the measurements is completely useless, because each of them delivers some information. The solution is dimension reduction. Feature extraction transforms the data on the high-dimensional space to a space of fewer dimensions. The data transformation may be linear, as in the principal component analysis (PCA), but also many nonlinear dimensionality reduction techniques exist.

The principal component analysis (PCA) is a useful tool for finding relevant variables for the system and the model. It is a linear transformation to a new lower-dimensional coordinate system while retaining as much as possible of the variation. In the PCR the components are used as dependent model variables. In the PLS again a small number of latent variables are used between the input and output. Now the goal is to maximize covariance between dependability and interpretability.

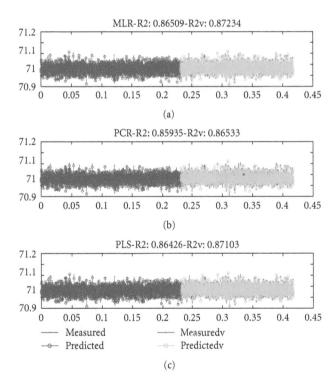

FIGURE 4: Modelling example: in this case all these multivariate methods indicate that process variable is in a good calibration. Correlation between model and measured values is even better before than after the calibration. x-axis: time in days. y-axis: interpretative variable 211K122 (reactor pressure). Calibration limits (5%) in this case are MLR: 0.8218, PCR: 0.8164, PLS: 0.821.

5. Discussion

With the self-organizing map, promising results in early fault detection have been achieved. The developed visualizations can reveal to the operator or plant expert in an early phase that something exceptional is going on in the process. The used methodologies have advantages in given information value compared to the traditional methods used in the control rooms. The combination of many rather different methods together gives the best results in this respect. The difficulty of new concepts may require extra training for the operators to be properly understood. The severe accident management has special needs that need to be taken into account.

The SOM method shows the dynamical development of the process with the U-matrix trajectories. U-matrix also reveals the cluster structure of the data. The component plane SOM maps show clearly, for example, the variable correlations. Quantisation error is one good indicator in detecting failures. The SOM method has strength also in analyzing nonlinear behaviour, compared to, for instance, the PCA method.

The case example shows in a concrete way how these methods work in practice. The variable selection, multilinear regression, and principal component regression including their visualization structures in each phase show in an offline process model how to increase instrument reliability and plant safety in some limits of measurement accuracy.

The prototyping is used as a research methodology, because it is not possible to produce such solid experimental setups and proofs that are common in pure methodological studies. Using prototyping as an analysis tool is used also, for example, in robotics, where exist similar difficulties in the experimental setup.

The suitability of these methods in accident management needs still careful assessment, as the licensing path in nuclear industry is rather long and tricky. It is not easy to convince that more traditional methods are not enough in all circumstances. In the research laboratories always new concepts have been tried out, but only very few of them end up to the control rooms of the real nuclear power plants. Still the modernization of control rooms brings many changes anyway, and also the used methodology behind all displays should be rethought.

Our methodology has been developed during a rather long period and has perspective from many generations. The knowledge-based methods used together with neural methods are introduced based on long experience in this field. The most suitable combination of methods varies case by case. The methodology can therefore be seen as a kind of tool set available for various needs.

References

[1] B. K. H. Sun and D. G. Cain, "Computer applications for control room operator support in nuclear power plants," *Reliability Engineering and System Safety*, vol. 33, no. 3, pp. 331–340, 1991.

[2] G. Salvendy, *Handbook of Human Factors*, John Wiley & Sons, New York, NY, USA, 1986.

[3] M. Sirola, "Generating strategies for managing accidents," *Nuclear Engineering International*, vol. 39, no. 478, pp. 50–551, 1994.

[4] M. Sirola, J. Talonen, J. Parviainen, and G. Lampi, "Decision support with data-analysis methods in a nuclear power plant," TKK Reports in Information and Computer Science (TKK-ICS-R29), TKK, Espoo, Finland, 2010.

[5] T. Kohonen, *Self-Organizing Map*, Springer, Berlin, Germany, 1995.

[6] S. B. Eom, "Mapping the intellectual structure of research in decision support systems through author cocitation analysis (1971–1993)," *Decision Support Systems*, vol. 16, no. 4, pp. 315–338, 1996.

[7] P. Fantoni, G. Meyer, P. Nurmilaukas, M. Sirola, and A. Sørenssen, *CAMS Prototype*, vol. 2, NKS, Halden, Norway, 1995.

[8] W. E. Kastenberg, "Uncertainties and severe accident management," *Transactions of the American Nuclear Society*, vol. 63, pp. 266–2267, 1991.

[9] M. Sirola, *Computerized Decision Support Systems in Failure and Maintenance Management of Safety Critical Processes*, VTT, Espoo, Finland, 1999.

[10] D. Bunn, *Applied Decision Analysis*, McGraw-Hill, New York, NY, USA, 1984.

[11] S. French, *Decision Theory: An Introduction to Mathematics Rationality*, Ellis Horwood, Chichester, UK, 1986.

[12] K. Laakso, M. Sirola, and J. Holmberg, "Decision modelling for maintenance and safety," *International Journal of Comadem*, vol. 23, pp. 13–117, 1999.

[13] J. A. Lee and M. Verleysen, *Dimensionality Reduction. Information Science and Statistics*, Springer, 1st edition, 2007.

[14] G. Barreto, A. Araujo, and H. Ritter, "Time in self-organizing maps: an overview of models," *International Journal of Computer Research*, vol. 10, no. 2, pp. 139–179, 2001.

[15] J. Vesanto, J. Himberg, E. Alhoniemi, and J. Parhankangas, "Self-organizing map in matlab: the SOM toolbox," in *Proceedings of the Matlab DSP Conference*, 1999.

16

Unsupervised Neural Techniques Applied to MR Brain Image Segmentation

A. Ortiz,[1] **J. M. Gorriz,**[2] **J. Ramirez,**[2] **and D. Salas-Gonzalez**[2]

[1] *Department of Communication Engineering, University of Malaga, 29071 Malaga, Spain*
[2] *Department of Signal Theory, Networking and Communications, University of Granada, 18071 Granada, Spain*

Correspondence should be addressed to A. Ortiz, aortiz@ic.uma.es

Academic Editor: Anke Meyer-Baese

The primary goal of brain image segmentation is to partition a given brain image into different regions representing anatomical structures. Magnetic resonance image (MRI) segmentation is especially interesting, since accurate segmentation in white matter, grey matter and cerebrospinal fluid provides a way to identify many brain disorders such as dementia, schizophrenia or Alzheimer's disease (AD). Then, image segmentation results in a very interesting tool for neuroanatomical analyses. In this paper we show three alternatives to MR brain image segmentation algorithms, with the Self-Organizing Map (SOM) as the core of the algorithms. The procedures devised do not use any a priori knowledge about voxel class assignment, and results in fully-unsupervised methods for MRI segmentation, making it possible to automatically discover different tissue classes. Our algorithm has been tested using the images from the Internet Brain Image Repository (IBSR) outperforming existing methods, providing values for the average overlap metric of 0.7 for the white and grey matter and 0.45 for the cerebrospinal fluid. Furthermore, it also provides good results for high-resolution MR images provided by the Nuclear Medicine Service of the "Virgen de las Nieves" Hospital (Granada, Spain).

1. Introduction

Nowadays, magnetic resonance imaging (MRI) systems provide an excellent spatial resolution as well as a high tissue contrast. Nevertheless, since actual MRI systems can obtain 16-bit depth images corresponding to 65535 gray levels, the human eye is not able to distinguish more than several tens of gray levels. On the other hand, MRI systems provide images as slices which compose the 3D volume. Thus, computer-aided tools are necessary to exploit all the information contained in an MRI. These are becoming a very valuable tool for diagnosing some brain disorders such as Alzheimer's disease [1–5]. Moreover, modern computers, which contain a large amount of memory and several processing cores, have enough process capabilities for analyzing the MRI in reasonable time.

Image segmentation consists in partitioning an image into different regions. In MRI, segmentation consists of partitioning the image into different neuroanatomical structures which corresponds to different tissues. Hence, analyzing the neuroanatomical structures and the distribution of the tissues on the image, brain disorders or anomalies can be figured out. Hence, the importance of having effective tools for grouping and recognizing different anatomical tissues, structures and fluids is growing with the improvement of the medical imaging systems. These tools are usually trained to recognize the three basic tissue classes found on a healthy brain MR image: white matter (WM), gray matter (GM), and cerebrospinal fluid (CSF). All of the nonrecognized tissues or fluids are classified as suspect, to be pathological.

The segmentation process can be performed in two ways. The first consists of manual delimitation of the structures present within an image by an expert. The second consists of using an automatic segmentation technique. As commented before, computer image processing techniques allow exploiting all the information contained in an MRI.

There are several automatic segmentation techniques. Some of them use the information contained in the image histogram [6–11]. This way, since different contrast areas should correspond with different tissues, the image histogram can be used for partitioning the image. Nevertheless, variations on the contrast of the same tissue are found in an image due to RF noise or shading effects due to magnetic field variations, resulting in tissue misclassification. Other methods use statistical classifiers based on the expectation-maximization (EM) algorithms [12–14], maximum likelihood (ML) estimation [15], or Markov random fields [16, 17]. Other segmentation techniques are based on artificial neural network classifiers [8, 18–21] such as *self-organizing maps* (SOMs) [18, 19, 21–23].

In this paper we present three segmentation alternatives based on SOMs, which provide good results over the internet brain image repository (IBSR) [16] images.

2. SOM Algorithm

SOM is an unsupervised classifier proposed by Kohonen and it has been used for a large number of applications regarding classification or modelling [24]. The self-organizing process is based on the distance (usually the Euclidean distance) computation among each training sample and all the units on the map as a part of a competitive learning process. On the other hand, several issues such as topological map, number of units on the map, initialization of weights, and the training process on the map are decisive for the classification quality. Regarding the topology, a 2D hexagonal grid was selected since it fitted better in the feature space as shown in the experiments.

The SOM algorithm can be summarized as follows. Let $X \subset \mathbb{R}^d$ be the data manifold. In each iteration, the winning unit is computed according to

$$U_\omega(t) = \arg \min_i \{\|x(t) - \omega_i(t)\|\}, \qquad (1)$$

where $x(t), x \in X$, is the input vector at time t and $\omega_i(t)$ is the prototype vector associated with the unit i. The unit closer to the input vector $U_\omega(t)$ is referred to as *winning unit* and the associated prototype is updated. To complete the adaptive learning process on the SOM, the prototypes of the units in the neighborhood of the *winning unit* are also updated according to:

$$\omega_i(t+1) = \omega_i(t) + \alpha(t)h_{Ui}(t)(x(t) - \omega_i(t)), \qquad (2)$$

where $\alpha(t)$ is the exponential decay learning factor and $h_{Ui}(t)$ is the neighborhood function associated with the unit i. Both, the learning factor and the neighborhood function decay with time; thus the prototypes adaptation becomes slower as the neighborhood of the unit i contains less number of units:

$$h_{Ui}(t) = e^{(-\|r_U - r_i\|^2/2\sigma(t)^2)}. \qquad (3)$$

Equation (3) shows the neighbourhood function, where r_i represents the position on the output space and $\|r_U - r_i\|$ is the distance between the winning unit and the unit i on the output space. The neighbourhood is defined by a Gaussian function which shrinks in each iteration as shown in (4). In this competitive process, the winning unit is named the best matching unit (BMU). On the other hand, $\sigma(t)$ controls the reduction of the Gaussian neighborhood in each iteration. τ_1 is a time constant which depends on the number of iterations and the map radius and computed as $\tau_1 =$ number_of_iterations/map_radius:

$$\sigma(t) = \sigma_0 e^{(-t/\tau_1)}. \qquad (4)$$

The quality of the trained map can be computed by the means of two measures. These two measures are the quantization error (t_e), which determines the average distance between each data vector and its best matching unit (BMU) and the topological error (q_e), which measures the proportion of all data vectors for which first and second BMUs are not adjacent units. Both, the quantization error and the topological error are defined by the following:

$$t_e = \frac{1}{N} \sum_{i=1}^{N} u(\vec{x}_i), \qquad (5)$$

$$q_e = \sum_{i=1}^{N} \|\vec{x}_i - \vec{b}_{\vec{x}_i}\|. \qquad (6)$$

In (5), N is the total number of data vectors, and $u(\vec{x}_i)$ is 1 if the first and the second BMU for $\vec{x}_i$ are nonadjacent and 0 otherwise. In (6) the quantization error is defined where $\vec{x}_i$ is the ith data vector on the input space and $b_{\vec{\omega}_i}$ is the weight (prototype) associated with the best matching unit for the data vector $\vec{x}_i$. Therefore, lower values of t_e and q_e imply a better topology preservation, which is equivalent to a better clustering result. That is to say, the lower the values on the quantization error (q_e) and the topological error (t_e), the better the goodness of the SOM [25, 26]. In this paper, *SOM toolbox* [27] has been used to implement SOM.

3. MR Image Segmentation with SOM

In this section we present two image segmentation algorithms based on unsupervised SOM. The first uses the histogram to segment the whole volume (i.e., classify all the voxels on the volumetric image). The second extracts a set of features from each image slice and uses an SOM to classify the feature vectors into clusters using the devised entropy gradient clustering method. Thus, Figure 1 shows the block diagram of the presented segmentation algorithms.

3.1. Image Preprocessing. Once the MR image has been acquired, a preprocessing is performed in order to remove noise and to homogenize the image background. The brain extraction for undesired structures removal (i.e., skull and scalp) can be done at this stage. There are several algorithms for this purpose such as brain surface extractor (BSE), brain extraction tool (BET) [8], Minneapolis consensus strip (McStrip), or hybrid watershed algorithm (HWA) [2]. Since IBSR 1.0 images have these undesired structures already removed, brain extraction is not required. Nevertheless, images provided by IBSR 2.0 are distributed without the scalp/skull already removed. In these images, the brain has been extracted in the preprocessing stage using BET.

3.2. Segmentation Using the Volume Image Histogram (HFS-SOM). The first step after preprocessing the image consists

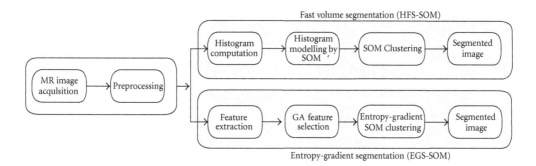

FIGURE 1: Block diagram of the segmentation methods.

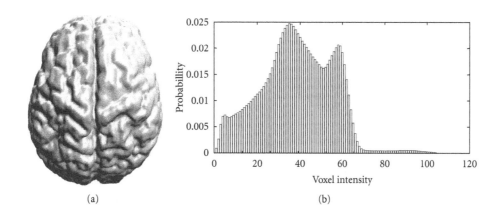

(a)

(b)

FIGURE 2: Rendered brain surface extracted from IBSR_12 volume (a) and computed histogram (b).

in computing the volume image histogram which describes the probability of occurrence of voxel intensities in the volume image and provides information regarding different tissues. A common approach to avoid processing the large number of voxels present on MR images consists in modelling the intensity values as a finite number of prototypes, which deals to improve the computational effectiveness. After computing the histogram, the bin 0 is removed since it contains all the background voxels. Thus, only information corresponding to the brain is stored.

Figure 2 shows the rendered brain surface from the IBSR volume 12, and its histogram.

Histogram data including the intensity occurrence probabilities (p_i) and the relative position (bin number), b_i, are used to compose the feature vectors $\vec{F} = (p_i, b_i), p_i \in \mathbb{R}, b_i \in \mathbb{Z}$, to be classified by the SOM.

On a trained SOM, the output layer is composed by a reduced number of prototypes (the number of units on the output layer) modelling the input data manifold. In addition, the most similar prototypes are closely located in the output map at the time the most dissimilar are located apart. Nevertheless, since all the units have an associated prototype, it is necessary to cluster the SOMs in order to define the borders between clusters. In other words, each prototype is grouped so that it belongs to a cluster. Thus, the k-means algorithm is used to cluster the SOMs, grouping the prototypes into a number of different classes, and the DBI [28], which gives

lower values for better clustering results, is computed for different k values to provide a measurement of the clustering validity.

The clusters on the SOM group the units so that they belong to a specific class. As each of these units will be the BMU of a specific set of voxels, the clusters define different voxel classes. This way, each voxel is labeled as belonging to a class (i.e., segment).

3.3. MR Image Segmentation with SOM and the Entropy-Gradient Algorithm (EGS-SOM).
The method described in this section is also based on SOM for voxel classification, but histogram information from the image volume is replaced by computing a set of features, selecting the most discriminant ones. After that, SOM clustering is performed by the EGS-SOM method described here in after, which allows us to obtain higher-resolution images providing good segmentation results as shown in the experiments.

3.3.1. Feature Extraction and Selection.
In this stage some significant features from the MR image are extracted to be subjected to classification. As commented before, we perform the image processing slice by slice on each plane. Thus, the feature extraction is carried out by using an overlapping and sliding window of 7×7 pixels on each slice of a specific plane.

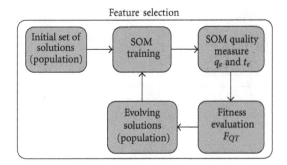

FIGURE 3: Feature selection process with genetic algorithm.

In the feature extraction process, window size plays an important role since smaller windows are not able to capture the second-order features, that is, texture information. The use of higher window sizes results in loosing resolution. Therefore the 7×7 size gives a good trade-off between complexity and performance.

In this paper we use first- and second-order statistical features [29]. The first-order features we extract from the image are intensity, mean, and variance. The intensity is referred to the gray level of the center pixel on the window. The mean and variance are calculated taking into account the gray level present on the window. On the other hand, we additionally use second-order features such as textural features. Haralick et al. [30] proposed the use of 14 features for image classification, computed using the gray level coocurrence matrix (GLCM) method. The set of second-order features we have used are energy, entropy, contrast, angular second moment (ASM), sum average, autocorrelation, correlation, inverse difference moment, maximum probability, cluster prominence, cluster shade, dissimilarity, and second-order variance as well as moment invariants [31].

In order to select the most discriminant features, a genetic algorithm is used to minimize the topological and the quantization error on the SOM through the fitness function shown in (7)

$$F_{QT} = (0.5q_e + 0.5t_e). \tag{7}$$

The feature selection process is summarized in Figure 3.

The stop criterion is reached when the performance of the proposed solutions does not improve the performance significantly (1%) or the maximum number of generations is reached (500).

Once the dimension of the feature space has been reduced, we use the vectors of this space for training a SOM. The topology of the map and the number of units on the map are decisive for the SOM quality. In that sense, we use a hexagonal grid since it allows better fitting the prototypes to the feature space vectors. Each BMU on the SOM has an associated pixel on the image. This association is made through a matrix computed during the feature extraction phase which stores the coordinates of the central pixel on each window. This allows associating a feature vector to an image pixel.

Nevertheless, these clusters roughly define the different areas (segments) on the image, and a further fine-tuning phase is required. This fine-tuning phase is accomplished by the entropy-gradient method.

Entropy-Gradient Method. The procedure devised consists of using the feature vectors associated with each BMU to compute a similarity measurement among the vectors belonging with each BMU and the vectors associated to each other BMU. Next, the BMUs are sorted in ascending order of the contrast. Finally, the feature vectors of each BMU are included on a cluster. For each map unit, we compute the accumulated entropy:

$$H_{m_i} = \sum_{n=1}^{N_p} H_n, \tag{8}$$

where i is the map unit index and N_p the number of pixels belonging to the map unit in the classification process. This means that the unit i has a number of N_p-associated pixels. Since the output layer on the SOM is a two-dimensional space, we calculate the entropy-gradient vector from each map unit (8) and move to the opposite direction for clustering.

4. Results and Discussion

In this section we show the segmentation results obtained using real MR brain images from two different sources. One of these sources is the IBSR database [32] in two versions, IBSR and IBSR 2.0.

Figures 4(a) and 4(b) show the segmentation results for the IBSR volume 100_23 using the HFS-SOM algorithm and the EGS-SOM algorithm, respectively. In these images, WM, GM, and CSF are shown for slices 120, 130, 140, 150, 160, and 170 on the axial plane. Expert segmentation from IBSR database is shown in Figure 4(c).

Figure 5(a) shows the segmentation results for the IBSR 2.0 volume 12 using the fast volume segmentation algorithm. In this figure, each row corresponds to a tissue and each image column corresponds to a different slice. In the same way, Figure 5(b) shows the same slices of Figure 5(b) but the segmentation is performed using the EGS-SOM algorithm. Figure 5(c) shows the segmentation performed by expert radiologists provided by the IBSR database (ground truth).

Visual comparison between automatic segmentation and the ground truth points up that the EGS-SOM method outperforms the fast volume segmentation method.

This fact is also stated in Figure 6 where Tanimoto's index is shown for different segmentation algorithms, where SSOM corresponds to our entropy-gradient algorithm, BMAP is biased map [33], AMAP is adaptative map [33], MAP is maximum a posteriori probability [34], MLC is maximum likelihood [35], FUZZY is fuzzy k-means [36] and TSKMEANS is tree-structured k-means [36]. The performance of the presented segmentation techniques has been evaluated by computing the average overlap rate through Tanimoto's index, as it has been widely used by other authors

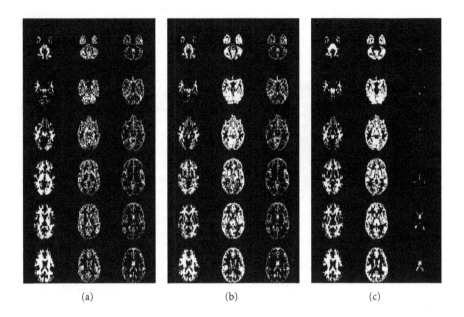

FIGURE 4: Segmentation of the IBSR volume 100_23 using the HFS-SOM algorithm (a) and the EGS-SOM algorithm (b). Ground Truth is shown in (c). Slices 120, 130, 140, 150, 160, and 170 on the axial plane are shown on each column. First column corresponds to WM, second column to GM, and third column to CSF.

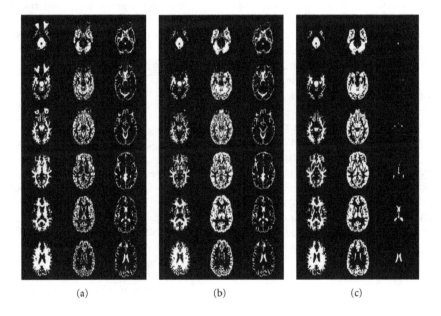

FIGURE 5: Segmentation of the IBSR 2.0 volume 12 using the HFS-SOM algorithm (a) and the EGS-SOM algorithm (b). Ground Truth is shown in (c). Slices 110, 120, 130, 140, 150, and 160 on the axial plane are shown on each column. First column corresponds to WM, second column to GM, and third column to CSF.

to compare the segmentation performance of their proposals [13, 16, 17, 21, 26, 37–41]. Tanimoto's index can be defined as

$$T(S_1, S_2) = \frac{|S_1 \cap S_2|}{|S_1 \cup S_2|}, \tag{9}$$

where S_1 is the segmentation set and S_2 is the ground truth.

5. Conclusions

In this paper we presented fully unsupervised segmentation methods for MR images based on hybrid artificial intelligence techniques for improving the feature extraction process and self-organizing maps for pixel classification. The use of a genetic algorithm provides a way for training the Self-Organizing map used as a classifier in the most efficient way. This is because the dimension of the training samples

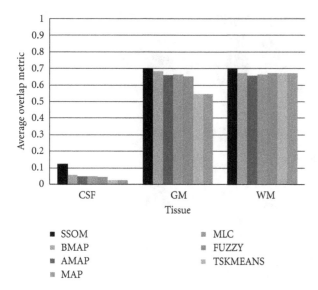

FIGURE 6: Average overlap metric comparison for different segmentation methods.

(feature vectors) has been reduced in order to be enough discriminant but not redundant. As a result, the number of units (neurons) on the map is also optimized as well as the classification process. Thus, we take advantage of the competitive learning model of the SOM which groups the pixels into clusters. This competitive process discovers discriminant among the pixels, resulting in an unsupervised way to segment the image. Moreover, the clusters' borders are redefined by using the entropy-gradient method presented on this paper. The whole process allows figuring out the segments present on the image without using any a priori information.

The results shown in Section 4 have been compared with the segmentations provided by the IBSR database that outperform the results obtained by other algorithms such as k-means or fuzzy k-means. The number of segments or different tissues found in an MR image is figured out automatically making possible to find out tissues which could be identified with a pathology.

Acknowledgment

This work was partly supported by the *Consejería de Innovación, Ciencia y Empresa* (Junta de Andalucía, Spain) under the Excellence Projects TIC-02566 and TIC-4530.

References

[1] I. A. Illán, J. M. Górriz, J. Ramírez et al., "18F-FDG PET imaging analysis for computer aided Alzheimer's diagnosis," *Information Sciences*, vol. 181, no. 4, pp. 903–916, 2011.

[2] I. A. Illán, J. M. Górriz, M. M. López et al., "Computer aided diagnosis of Alzheimer's disease using component based SVM," *Applied Soft Computing Journal*, vol. 11, no. 2, pp. 2376–2382, 2011.

[3] J. M. Górriz, F. Segovia, J. Ramírez, A. Lassl, and D. Salas-Gonzalez, "GMM based SPECT image classification for the diagnosis of Alzheimer's disease," *Applied Soft Computing Journal*, vol. 11, no. 2, pp. 2313–2325, 2011.

[4] M. Kamber, R. Shinghal, D. L. Collins, G. S. Francis, and A. C. Evans, "Model-based 3-D segmentation of multiple sclerosis lesions in magnetic resonance brain images," *IEEE Transactions on Medical Imaging*, vol. 14, no. 3, pp. 442–453, 1995.

[5] J. Ramírez, J. M. Górriz, D. Salas-Gonzalez et al., "Computer-aided diagnosis of Alzheimer's type dementia combining support vector machines and discriminant set of features," *Information Sciences*. In press.

[6] D. N. Kennedy, P. A. Filipek, and V. S. Caviness, "Anatomic segmentation and volumetric calculations in nuclear magnetic resonance imaging," *IEEE Transactions on Medical Imaging*, vol. 8, no. 1, pp. 1–7, 1989.

[7] A. Khan, S. F. Tahir, A. Majid, and T. S. Choi, "Machine learning based adaptive watermark decoding in view of anticipated attack," *Pattern Recognition*, vol. 41, no. 8, pp. 2594–2610, 2008.

[8] Z. Yang and J. Laaksonen, "Interactive retrieval in facial image database using self-organizing maps," in *Proceedings of the MVA*, 2005.

[9] M. García-Sebastián, E. Fernández, M. Graña, and F. J. Torrealdea, "A parametric gradient descent MRI intensity inhomogeneity correction algorithm," *Pattern Recognition Letters*, vol. 28, no. 13, pp. 1657–1666, 2007.

[10] E. Fernández, M. Graña, and J. R. Cabello, "Gradient based evolution strategy for parametric illumination correction," *Electronics Letters*, vol. 40, no. 9, pp. 531–532, 2004.

[11] M. García-Sebastián, A. Isabel González, and M. Graña, "An adaptive field rule for non-parametric MRI intensity inhomogeneity estimation algorithm," *Neurocomputing*, vol. 72, no. 16-18, pp. 3556–3569, 2009.

[12] T. Kapur, L. Grimson, W. M. Wells, and R. Kikinis, "Segmentation of brain tissue from magnetic resonance images," *Medical Image Analysis*, vol. 1, no. 2, pp. 109–127, 1996.

[13] Y. F. Tsai, I. J. Chiang, Y. C. Lee, C. C. Liao, and K. L. Wang, "Automatic MRI meningioma segmentation using estimation maximization," in *Proceedings of the 27th Annual International Conference of the Engineering in Medicine and Biology Society (IEEE-EMBS '05)*, pp. 3074–3077, September 2005.

[14] J. Xie and H. T. Tsui, "Image segmentation based on maximum-likelihood estimation and optimum entropy-distribution (MLE-OED)," *Pattern Recognition Letters*, vol. 25, no. 10, pp. 1133–1141, 2004.

[15] Y. Zhang, M. Brady, and S. Smith, "Segmentation of brain MR images through a hidden Markov random field model and the expectation-maximization algorithm," *IEEE Transactions on Medical Imaging*, vol. 20, no. 1, pp. 45–57, 2001.

[16] N. A. Mohamed, M. N. Ahmed, and A. Farag, "Modified fuzzy c-mean in medical image segmentation," in *Proceedings of the IEEE International Conference on Acoustics, Speech, and Signal Processing (ICASSP '99)*, pp. 3429–3432, March 1999.

[17] W. M. Wells III, W. E. L. Crimson, R. Kikinis, and F. A. Jolesz, "Adaptive segmentation of mri data," *IEEE Transactions on Medical Imaging*, vol. 15, no. 4, pp. 429–442, 1996.

[18] D. Tian and L. Fan, "A brain MR images segmentation method based on SOM neural network," in *Proceedings of the 1st International Conference on Bioinformatics and Biomedical Engineering (ICBBE '07)*, pp. 686–689, July 2007.

[19] I. Güler, A. Demirhan, and R. Karakiş, "Interpretation of MR images using self-organizing maps and knowledge-based expert systems," *Digital Signal Processing*, vol. 19, no. 4, pp. 668–677, 2009.

[20] P. K. Sahoo, S. Soltani, and A. K. C. Wong, "A survey of thresholding techniques," *Computer Vision, Graphics and Image Processing*, vol. 41, no. 2, pp. 233–260, 1988.

[21] W. Sun, "Segmentation method of MRI using fuzzy Gaussian basis neural network," *Neural Information Processing*, vol. 8, no. 2, pp. 19–24, 2005.

[22] J. Alirezaie, M. E. Jernigan, and C. Nahmias, "Automatic segmentation of cerebral MR images using artificial neural networks," *IEEE Transactions on Nuclear Science*, vol. 45, no. 4, pp. 2174–2182, 1998.

[23] A. Ortiz, J. M. Górriz, J. Ramírez, and D. Salas-Gonzalez, "MR brain image segmentation by hierarchical growing SOM and probability clustering," *Electronics Letters*, vol. 47, no. 10, pp. 585–586, 2011.

[24] T. Kohonen, *Self-Organizing Maps*, Springer, 2001.

[25] E. Arsuaga and F. Díaz, "Topology preservation in SOM," *International Journal of Mathematical and Computer Sciences*, vol. 1, no. 1, pp. 19–22, 2005.

[26] K. Taşdemir and E. Merényi, "Exploiting data topology in visualization and clustering of self-organizing maps," *IEEE Transactions on Neural Networks*, vol. 20, no. 4, pp. 549–562, 2009.

[27] E. Alhoniemi, J. Himberg, J. Parhankagas, and J. Vesanta, "SOM Toolbox for Matlab v2.0," 2005, http://www.cis.hut. fi/projects/somtoolbox.

[28] M. O. Stitson, J. A. E. Weston, A. Gammerman, V. Vork, and V. Vapnik, "Theory of support vector machines," Tech. Rep. CSD-TR-96-17, Department of Computer Science, Royal Holloway College, University of London, 1996.

[29] M. Nixson and A. Aguado, *Feature Extraction and Image Processing*, Academic Press, 2008.

[30] R. M. Haralick, K. Shanmugam, and I. Dinstein, "Textural features for image classification," *IEEE Transactions on Systems, Man and Cybernetics*, vol. 3, no. 6, pp. 610–621, 1973.

[31] M. Hu, "Visual pattern recognition by moments invariants," *IRE Transactions on Information Theory*, vol. 8, pp. 179–187, 1962.

[32] Internet Brain Database Repository, Massachusetts General Hospital, Center for Morphometric Analysis, 2010, http://www.cma.mgh.harvard.edu/ibsr/data.html.

[33] J. C. Rajapakse and F. Kruggel, "Segmentation of MR images with intensity inhomogeneities," *Image and Vision Computing*, vol. 16, no. 3, pp. 165–180, 1998.

[34] J. L. Marroquin, B. C. Vemuri, S. Botello, F. Calderon, and A. Fernandez-Bouzas, "An accurate and efficient Bayesian method for automatic segmentation of brain MRI," *IEEE Transactions on Medical Imaging*, vol. 21, no. 8, pp. 934–945, 2002.

[35] J. C. Bezdek, L. O. Hall, and L. P. Clarke, "Review of MR image segmentation techniques using pattern recognition," *Medical Physics*, vol. 20, no. 4, pp. 1033–1048, 1993.

[36] L. P. Clarke, R. P. Velthuizen, M. A. Camacho et al., "MRI segmentation: methods and applications," *Magnetic Resonance Imaging*, vol. 13, no. 3, pp. 343–368, 1995.

[37] C. T. Su and H. C. Lin, "Applying electromagnetism-like mechanism for feature selection," *Information Sciences*, vol. 181, no. 5, pp. 972–986, 2011.

[38] K. Tan, E. Khor, and T. Lee, *Multiobjective Evolutionary and Applications*, Springer, 1st edition, 2005.

[39] T. Tasdizen, S. P. Awate, R. T. Whitaker, and N. L. Foster, "MRI tissue classification with neighborhood statistics: a non-parametric, entropy-minimizing approach," in *Proceedings of the International Conference on Medical Image Computing and Computer Assisted Intervention (MICCAI '05)*, 2005.

[40] I. Usman and A. Khan, "BCH coding and intelligent watermark embedding: employing both frequency and strength selection," *Applied Soft Computing Journal*, vol. 10, no. 1, pp. 332–343, 2010.

[41] Y. Wang, T. Adali, S. Y. Kung, and Z. Szabo, "Quantification and segmentation of brain tissues from MR images: a probabilistic neural network approach," *IEEE Transactions on Image Processing*, vol. 7, no. 8, pp. 1165–1181, 1998.

17

A Unified Framework for GPS Code and Carrier-Phase Multipath Mitigation Using Support Vector Regression

Quoc-Huy Phan,[1] **Su-Lim Tan,**[2] **Ian McLoughlin,**[3] **and Duc-Lung Vu**[1]

[1] *University of Information Technology, Km 20, Ha Noi Highway, Linh Trung Ward, Thu Duc, HCMC 70000, Vietnam*
[2] *Singapore Institute of Technology, 25 North Bridge Road, Singapore 179104*
[3] *School of Information Science and Technology, University of Science and Technology of China, No. 443 Huangshan Road, Hefei, Anhui 230027, China*

Correspondence should be addressed to Quoc-Huy Phan; huypq@uit.edu.vn

Academic Editor: Paolo Gastaldo

Multipath mitigation is a long-standing problem in global positioning system (GPS) research and is essential for improving the accuracy and precision of positioning solutions. In this work, we consider multipath error estimation as a regression problem and propose a unified framework for both code and carrier-phase multipath mitigation for ground fixed GPS stations. We use the kernel support vector machine to predict multipath errors, since it is known to potentially offer better-performance traditional models, such as neural networks. The predicted multipath error is then used to correct GPS measurements. We empirically show that the proposed method can reduce the code multipath error standard deviation up to 79% on average, which significantly outperforms other approaches in the literature. A comparative analysis of reduction of double-differential carrier-phase multipath error reveals that a 57% reduction is also achieved. Furthermore, by simulation, we also show that this method is robust to coexisting signals of phenomena (e.g., seismic signals) we wish to preserve.

1. Introduction

Multipath is defined as one or more indirect replicas of the line-of-sight (LOS) signal from satellites arriving at a receiver's antenna from a satellite. It normally occurs due to reflection from objects in the vicinity of the receiver and constitutes a major error source that contaminates receivers' measurements, resulting in performance degradation of GPS positioning solutions. The errors induced by multipath are typically up to 15 meters for C/A code [1] and a few centimeters for carrier-phase measurements [2]. Multipath mitigation is hence important for a variety of applications which utilize this data, such as ionospheric monitoring [3], geodesy [4, 5], and navigation [6].

On the one hand, multipath mitigation is a very challenging task. As multipath is site-dependent, differencing measurements among multiple short-baseline receivers (DGPS) are unlikely to help. Furthermore, aggressively removing multipath error may harm wanted coexisting information and perturbations such as seismic signals induced by an earthquake, as their frequency spectra likely overlap with that of the contaminating multipath error.

Various mitigation approaches have been proposed in the literature, classified into either frequency-domain or time-domain processing. The former is based on spectral analysis of multipath error in the frequency domain using fast fourier transform (FFT) [7], or wavelet decomposition [8, 9]. However, they unintentionally rule out other coexisting signals. To overcome this issue, signal-to-noise (SNR) measurements [10, 11] can be used as alternative for analysis. Unfortunately, this suffers from unavailability and inconsistency in units from different types of receivers. Time-domain methods range from the popular carrier smoothing filter (CSF) [12, 13], band-pass finite impulse response (FIR) filter [14, 15] to stacking [16–18]. These methods also tend to filter out coexisting signals of interest and require high-rate data to boost their performance [16].

In previous works [19, 20], we propose a regression model, which integrates kernel support vector regression (SVR) with geometrical features to deal with the code multipath error prediction on ground fixed GPS stations. To the best of the authors' knowledge, this is the first work using machine learning to address GPS multipath error estimation. This paper extends our previous work to define a unified framework for both code and carrier-phase multipath mitigation. The contribution of this paper is threefold: (1) deriving geometric models for code and carrier-phase multipath errors, (2) formulating multipath error estimation as a regression problem with geometrical features, and (3) unifying the framework for code and carrier-phase multipath estimation using support vector regression.

The rest of this paper is organized as follows. Section 2 briefly reviews the mathematical models of GPS measurements and derives the geometrical models of multipath errors. By posing multipath estimation as a nonlinear regression problem, Section 3 defines the framework for multipath mitigation. Experimental results and discussions for code and carrier-phase multipath mitigation will be presented in Sections 4 and 5, respectively. The conclusion will follow in Section 6.

2. GPS Measurements and Code Multipath Extraction

In this section, we briefly review the GPS measurement data as generated by GPS receivers. Following this, geometrical models will be derived for both code and carrier-phase multipath errors.

2.1. GPS Measurements. The code measurement ρ_1 and carrier-phase measurement ϕ_1 for channel L1 are given as in (1) and (2), respectively [13, 21]. The measurements for L2 are similar,

$$\rho_1 = r + c\left(\delta_u - \delta_s\right) + I_1 + T + M_1^\rho + \varepsilon_1^\rho, \tag{1}$$

$$\phi_1\lambda_1 = r + c\left(\delta_u - \delta_s\right) - I_1 + T + N_1\lambda_1 + M_1^\phi + \varepsilon_1^\phi, \tag{2}$$

where r represents the true range from a satellite to a receiver, δ is clock bias, the subscripts u and s refer to the user (receiver) and the satellite, respectively, c is the speed of light, T, I, M^ρ, ε^ρ, M_1^ϕ, and ε_1^ϕ denote tropospheric delay, ionospheric delay, code multipath error, random receiver noise on code, carrier-phase multipath error, and random receiver noise on carrier-phase, respectively, and the symbols λ_1 denote wavelengths of L1. The term N_1 is the *ambiguous integer* of L1. The opposite signs of the ionospheric delays in (1) and (2) are due to the fact that the ionosphere affects code and carrier measurements equally but in opposite directions when the signals travel through the dispersive ionospheric layer in the atmosphere [2].

2.2. Geometrical Model of Code Multipath. Ideally, in a multipath-free environment, only one direct signal is received by the antenna from each satellite. However, no environment is completely multipath-free in practice. A receiver antenna receives one or more replicas of the direct signal reflected from objects near the LOS path, particularly those in the

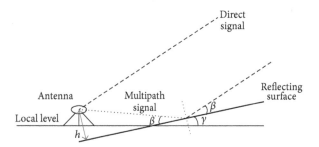

FIGURE 1: The direct signal and one multipath signal with simplified geometry.

vicinity of the receiver. As a result, the receiver will track a composite signal that is a combination of the direct path and the multipath replicas.

For clarity, let us consider the simplified case of one multipath signal. Let A_d and A_m denote the amplitudes of the direct signal and the multipath signal, respectively, δ the path delay, ψ the multipath relative phase in radians, $\alpha = A_m/A_d \leq 1$ the ratio of the multipath and direct amplitudes, and θ and μ the azimuth and elevation angles, respectively. The position of any reflecting object is described as a planar surface tilted relative to the local level with a tilt angle γ at a distance h from the antenna centre as illustrated in Figure 1.

Let β denote the reflection angle relative to the reflecting surface; the induced code multipath error is given as [16]:

$$M^\rho = \frac{\alpha\delta\cos\psi}{1 + \alpha\cos\psi}. \tag{3}$$

In order to obtain the geometrical model, we need to relate multipath error with geometrical parameters, that is, azimuth and elevation angles. Assuming that the satellite, antenna, and normal vector to the reflecting surface are coplanar, multipath reflections fall into two categories: *forward-scatter* and *backscatter* [22] as in Figure 2.

In both forward-scatter and backscatter scenarios, it is easily to obtain

$$\delta = 2h\sin\beta, \tag{4}$$

$$\psi = \frac{2\pi}{\lambda}\delta = \frac{2\pi}{\lambda}2h\sin\beta. \tag{5}$$

Furthermore, using the convention of angles measured anticlockwise over the interval $[0°\,180°]$, $\beta + \gamma = \theta$ for forward-scatter whereas $\beta + \theta = \gamma$ for backscatter. To generalize,

$$\beta = |\theta - \gamma|. \tag{6}$$

Substituting (4), (5), and (6) into (3), the code multipath equations corresponding to one reflecting signal can be rewritten as

$$M^\rho = \frac{\alpha 2h\sin\left(|\theta - \gamma|\right)\cos\left((4\pi h/\lambda)\sin\left(|\theta - \gamma|\right)\right)}{1 + \alpha\cos\left((4\pi h/\lambda)\sin\left(|\theta - \gamma|\right)\right)}. \tag{7}$$

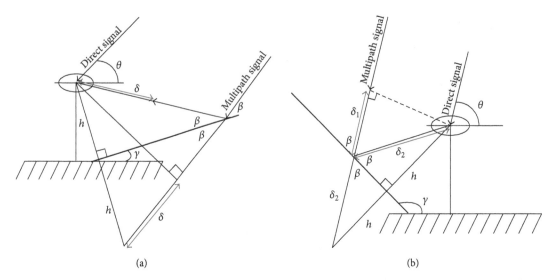

FIGURE 2: Multipath reflections: (a) forward-scatter and (b) backscatter.

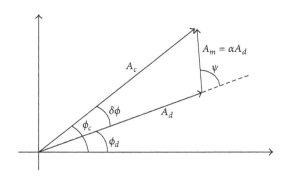

FIGURE 3: Effect of multipath to carrier-phase measurement.

In the general case of m reflecting signals, the total code multipath is the sum of the individual code multipath:

$$M^p = \frac{\sum_{i=1}^{m} \alpha_i 2 h_i \sin\left(|\theta - \gamma_i|\right) \cos\left((4\pi h_i/\lambda) \sin\left(|\theta - \gamma_i|\right)\right)}{1 + \sum_{i=1}^{m} \alpha_i \cos\left((4\pi h_i/\lambda) \sin\left(|\theta - \gamma_i|\right)\right)}. \tag{8}$$

2.3. Geometrical Model of Carrier-Phase Multipath. The effect of multipath on carrier-phase measurement can be demonstrated by the phasor diagram in Figure 3. Additionally, let A_c denote the amplitude of the composite signal which is the combination of the multipath signal and the direct signal. ϕ_d, ϕ_c, and ψ are the direct signal's phase, the composite signal's phase and the multipath relative phase with respect to the direct signal, respectively. δ_ϕ denotes the phase error due to multipath.

The phase error due to multipath is easily derived in terms of multipath parameters as follows:

$$\tan\left(\delta\phi\right) = \frac{A_m \sin\left(\psi + \phi_0\right)}{A_d + A_m \cos\left(\psi + \phi_0\right)} = \frac{\alpha \sin\left(\psi + \phi_0\right)}{1 + \alpha \cos\left(\psi + \phi_0\right)}, \tag{9}$$

where ϕ_0 is a possible phase offset at time 0. Therefore,

$$\delta\phi = \arctan\left(\frac{\alpha \sin\left(\psi + \phi_0\right)}{1 + \alpha \cos\left(\psi + \phi_0\right)}\right). \tag{10}$$

Substituting (5) into (10), we obtain the phase error caused by one multipath signal:

$$\delta\phi = \arctan\left(\frac{\alpha \sin\left((4\pi h/\lambda) \sin\left(|\theta - \gamma|\right) + \phi_0\right)}{1 + \alpha \cos\left((4\pi h/\lambda) \sin\left(|\theta - \gamma|\right) + \phi_0\right)}\right). \tag{11}$$

In general case of m multipath signals,

$$\delta\phi = \arctan\left(\frac{\sum_{i=1}^{m} \alpha \sin\left((4\pi h_i/\lambda) \sin\left(|\theta - \gamma_i|\right) + \phi_0^i\right)}{1 + \sum_{i=1}^{m} \alpha \cos\left((4\pi h_i/\lambda) \sin\left(|\theta - \gamma_i|\right) + \phi_0^i\right)}\right). \tag{12}$$

3. Multipath Mitigation Framework Using Nonlinear Support Vector Regression

In this section, we will define the unified framework for code and carrier-phase multipath mitigation followed by the formulation to solve multipath estimation as nonlinear regression using support vector regression algorithm.

3.1. Multipath Mitigation Framework. Under assumption that the multipath environment around a ground fixed receiver is held fixed, then quantities α_i, h_i, γ_i in (8) and (12) will remain constant. As a result, code multipath error M^p and carrier-phase multipath error $\delta\phi$ are complicated functions of satellite-relative elevation angle θ and azimuth angle μ in the general case which characterizes the geometry of the satellite with respect to the receiver. Give these functions, in order to compute multipath errors, it is necessary to somehow evaluate the functions in (8) and (12) given as an azimuth/elevation pair. Viewed as a regression problem, these functions will be approximated by learning from the historical multipath data and satellite orbital information. Specifically, estimating code and carrier-phase multipath errors is a 2-dimensional regression setting:

$$\text{multipath} = f\,(\text{azimuth, elevation})\,. \tag{13}$$

The rationale behind this approach is the observation that a fixed receiver experiences highly sidereal day-to-day correlation of satellite-receiver geometry and multipath error. It is well known that the GPS satellite orbits were selected to have a period of half a sidereal day (23 hours 56 minutes 4 seconds) with a daily repeating ground track [23, 24]. Because of this, satellite visibility from any point on earth is the same from day to day, with the satellites appearing in their positions approximately 4 minutes or 236 seconds earlier each day due to the time difference between the sidereal and solar day. Furthermore, for a fixed station, its surroundings and the antenna usually do not change significantly across consecutive days. Therefore, GPS multipath signals are expected to largely repeat over the same time period. Our proposed approach leverages this observation with a regression approach to approximate the function of the repeatable multipath error.

Code and carrier-phase multipath errors can be estimated independently, but the procedure for training the estimators is the same. Satellite-specific multipath estimator will be trained using ε-SVR [25], a well-known support vector regression algorithm. After being trained, the code and carrier-phase multipath estimators will be used to provide estimate of multipath errors. Afterwards, these estimates will be used to correct code and carrier-phase measurements to achieve multipath mitigation.

3.2. Nonlinear Regression for Multipath Estimation.
Among various kinds of regression models, SVRs [25, 26] are well known to have more potential advantages than traditional models, such as neural networks [27]. They are based on the strong statistical learning theory and have been shown to be less prone to overfitting as well as being independent of the dimensionality of the input space. We employ ε-SVR [25], which is most commonly used for regression problem. In the hard margin loss setting for ε-SVR, the estimate has at most ε deviation from the actual target for all training data, meaning that one does not care about errors as long as they are less than ε, but will not accept any deviation larger than this. Nevertheless, owing to noise in data, we usually use soft margin loss setting to allow for some errors by introducing slack variables in the formulation of ε-SVR.

We denote input vector as $x \in \mathfrak{R}^n$ and denote a value of multipath error as $y \in \mathfrak{R}$. Given the multipath model in (8) and (12), our goal is to learn a function $f : \mathfrak{R}^n \mapsto \mathfrak{R}$ mapping from an observation vector x to an estimate of multipath error $\hat{y}$. Formally, this can be accomplished by first choosing a set of N training samples $\{(x_1, y_1), \ldots, (x_N, y_N)\} \in \mathfrak{R}^n \times \mathfrak{R}$. Due to noise in the training data, it is unlikely that $f(x_i)$ will be equal to y_i for all x_i, so a loss function $L(f(x), y)$ must also be chosen to quantify the penalty for $f(x_i)$ differing from y_i. The estimator f can be found by minimizing the total loss over the training data.

For each satellite, the multipath estimator is trained using ε-SVR [25]. We denote the regression function $f(x) = \langle w, \varphi(x) \rangle + b$, where w is the weight vector in the kernel feature space, $b \in \mathfrak{R}$ is a bias term, $\langle \cdot, \cdot \rangle$ denotes the dot product, and φ is the kernel feature map of data point x. The ε-insensitive loss function given by (14) is chosen so that the function $f(x)$ is found to have at most ε deviation from the targets y_i for all training samples:

$$L\,(f\,(x)\,,y) = \begin{cases} 0, & \text{if } |f\,(x) - y| < \varepsilon, \\ |f\,(x) - y| - \varepsilon, & \text{otherwise,} \end{cases} \tag{14}$$

$f(x)$ can be solved through the following optimization problem [25]:

$$
\begin{aligned}
\text{minimize} \quad & \frac{1}{2}\|w\|^2 + C\sum_{i=1}^{N}\left(\xi_i + \xi_i^*\right) \\
\text{subject to} \quad & \begin{aligned} y_i - \langle w, \varphi\,(x_i) \rangle - b &\leq \varepsilon + \xi_i \\ \langle w, \varphi\,(x_i) \rangle + b - y_i &\leq \varepsilon + \xi_i^* \\ \xi_i, \xi_i^* > 0, \quad i &= 1, \ldots, N, \end{aligned}
\end{aligned} \tag{15}
$$

where $\varepsilon > 0$ is the parameter of the ε-insensitive loss function that controls the accuracy of the regressor. The constant $C > 0$ adjusts the tradeoff between the regression error and the regularization on f. $\xi = \{\xi_1, \ldots, \xi_N\} \in \mathfrak{R}^N$ and $\xi^* = \{\xi_1^*, \ldots, \xi_N^*\} \in \mathfrak{R}^N$ are slack variables allowing errors around the regression function. After solving the optimization problem, the form of the estimator is

$$
\begin{aligned}
f\,(x) &= \sum_{i=1}^{N_{\mathrm{SV}}} \omega_i \left\langle \varphi\,(x), \varphi\,(p_i) \right\rangle + b \\
&= \sum_{i=1}^{N_{\mathrm{SV}}} \omega_i \kappa\,(x, p_i) + b,
\end{aligned} \tag{16}
$$

where $\omega_1, \ldots, \omega_{N_{\mathrm{SV}}}$ are scalar coefficients, $p_1, \ldots, p_{N_{\mathrm{SV}}}$ are support vectors, and $\kappa : \mathfrak{R}^n \times \mathfrak{R}^n \mapsto \mathfrak{R}$ is a kernel function. $f(x)$ depends only on the training samples having nonzero coefficients (support vectors) through the representation of the kernel function κ. The Gaussian kernel given by (17) is reasonably chosen due to its ability to handle nonlinearity:

$$\kappa\,(x_i, x_j) = \exp\left(-\eta \|x_i - x_j\|^2\right), \tag{17}$$

where η is kernel bandwidth. Solving the regression problem by ε-SVR, learning from training data, code multipath error can be estimated for each visible satellite.

4. Experiment I: Code Multipath Mitigation

In this section, we will describe experiments conducted to train multipath estimators and subsequently use them for multipath mitigation. We demonstrate that our approach outperforms state-of-the-art results in code multipath mitigation in terms of standard deviation. The advantages of the exploited methods will be also discussed.

FIGURE 4: The observation site on the rooftop of N2 building (NTU campus).

4.1. Experimental Data Set. The data set used for evaluation was recorded at a sampling rate of 0.1 Hz from a GPS monitoring station equipped with a Trimble NetRS receiver on the rooftop of the N2 building in Nanyang Technological University (NTU) campus (Singapore) during five consecutive days: from the day of year (Day) 306 to 310 of 2010. The nominal position of the observation site is (−1507932.6167, 6195587.6757, 148897.9990) in the earth-centered, earth-fixed (ECEF) Cartesian coordinate system [13]. Rooftops are usually bad multipath environments since there are often many vents and other reflective objects within the GPS antenna field of view. In the photographs shown in Figure 4, it can be seen that the observation site is surrounded by many buildings and reflectors which make multipath potentially more severe. During the evaluation period there were 31 visible satellites ranging from PRN 2 to PRN 32 observed at this site.

To illustrate the repeatability of GPS satellite geometries, Figure 5 plots the geometries of 4 visible satellites with respect to the observation site during 4 consecutive days from Day 306 to Day 309. For the sake of simplicity and clarity, only 4 of 31 in-view satellites whose full arcs completely fall in each day period are plotted. As seen from these plots, the footprints of the day-to-day repeated geometries of the satellites are obviously exposed.

Likewise, in order to illustrate the day-to-day repeatability of code multipath error, Figures 6(a) and 6(b) plotted the code multipath sequences extracted from the recorded data set during four observation days from Day 306 to Day 309. The code multipath error can be extracted in batch mode from code measurements using code-minus-carrier (CmC) combination on a whole arc [9, 13]. The correlation is more clearly revealed after we smoothed the sequences with a CSF [9] having a 50-second window to largely remove high-frequency noise. The original multipath sequences are plotted in blue and CSF-smoothed multipath sequences are plotted in red. Day-to-day correlation of the two multipath sequences is numerically evaluated by their normalized

TABLE 1: Normalized cross-correlation of PRN 12's multipath sequences for original data shown in blue and for CSF-smoothed data shown in red.

	Day 306	Day 307	Day 308	Day 309
Day 306	N/A	0.6668	0.5215	0.5215
Day 307	0.9055	N/A	0.6513	0.5254
Day 308	0.8775	0.8988	N/A	0.6260
Day 309	0.8649	0.8630	0.8851	N/A

cross-correlation. Pair-wise normalized cross-correlation values of the multipath sequences are tabulated in Table 1 for PRN 12 with blue and red values representing the original and smoothed multipath sequences, respectively. The day-to-day correlation is around 89% between two consecutive days and slowly degrades with time. This is understandable since cumulative environmental changes become noticeable as the time span increases.

4.2. Training Code Multipath Estimators. For each satellite, the training data is prepared using 4-day data from Day 306 to Day 309 extracted from the experimental data set, which we have found to be redundant enough to capture distribution of multipath sequences. Azimuth and elevation angles of the satellites in degrees with respect to the receiver, which are inputs for training, are computed from the broadcast navigation data [13]. For the desired multipath outputs, after being detached from observation data, the CmC sequences containing multipath errors are filtered with CSF to remove high-frequency noise. The effect of this smoothing on the multipath error is negligible as long as the smoothing window is shorter than the highest rate multipath. The smoothing window is set to 50 seconds (equivalent to 5 epochs) which is only a fraction of the shortest anticipated multipath fading period of 200 seconds [9, 28]. Thus, the receiver noise was significantly reduced without removing the multipath which was to be quantified. This smoothing operation helps to

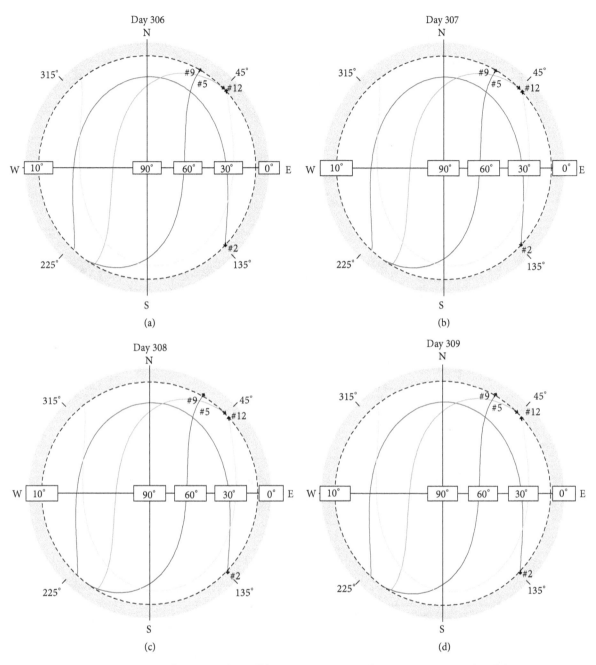

FIGURE 5: Geometry footprints of 4 satellites PRN 02, 05, 09, and 12 in 4 consecutive sidereal days.

clearly expose multipath patterns and, as a result, to enhance the estimators' generalization.

Scaling is applied to the training data before use. Azimuth angles, elevation angles, and code multipath values are scaled to the range $[-1; +1]$. The main advantage of scaling is not only to avoid numerical difficulties during the calculation but also to prevent domination of values in greater numeric ranges over those in smaller numeric ranges.

The *libSVM* package (http://www.csie.ntu.edu.tw/~cjlin/ libsvm), which implements ε-SVR, was used to find the support vectors and coefficients of each satellite-specific code multipath estimator. ε, the kernel parameter η and the penalty

parameter of the error term C, must be chosen as a priori. It is not known beforehand which parameter values are best for a given problem; consequently, some kind of model selection (parameter search) must be done. For η and C, grid search and cross-validation were applied for parameter search. Following the recommended *libSVM* approach, a coarse grid search was firstly performed on exponentially growing sequences of $\eta = 2^{-15}, 2^{-13}, \ldots, 2^3$ and $C = 2^{-5}$, $2^{-3}, \ldots, 2^{15}$ followed by cross-validation for each pair of (η, C) with a fixed $\varepsilon = 0.01$. The result with the best 6-fold cross-validation accuracy was picked. With this strategy, better region on the grid can be identified and finer grid-search

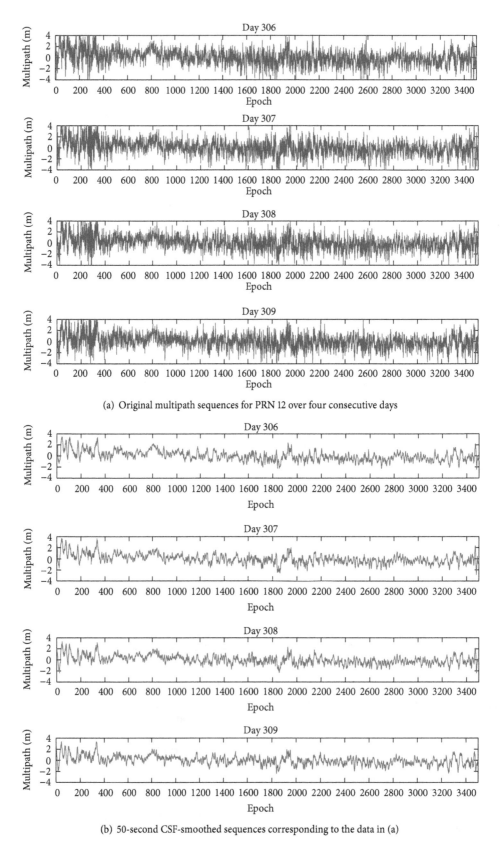

(a) Original multipath sequences for PRN 12 over four consecutive days

(b) 50-second CSF-smoothed sequences corresponding to the data in (a)

FIGURE 6: Multipath sequences of PRN 12 in four sidereal days from Day 306 to Day 309 of 2010.

across those regions. ε was searched separately in the range (0.005–0.1) with step size of 0.005 after the best pair (η, C) has been chosen.

Learning from the training data set, the support vectors and coefficients in (16) are found for multipath estimation of each satellite. Each separately trained estimator should estimate multipath error when presented with a new observation of azimuth/elevation angles thereafter.

4.3. Experimental Results. In order to evaluate the performance of code multipath estimators, the proper multipath correction is directly applied to code measurements for Day 310. Note that the inputs must be scaled as they were during the training phase, and the estimated multipath values subsequently need to be descaled.

For the sake of demonstration, Figure 7 presents pseudorange multipath errors and responses of the multipath estimator corresponding to PRN 12 in the Day. As observed, standard deviation of the multipath sequence is significantly reduced after being corrected with the responses of the SVR estimator.

Performance of all multipath estimators corresponding to the visible satellites is tabulated in Table 2 where multipath reduction is measured in terms of the reduced standard deviation of multipath errors. The percentages of reduction range from 68% to 91%. On average, calibrating the data with CSF followed by the SVR estimators gains improvement from 36.68% to 78.99%. With the assumption about unchanged surroundings of this approach, performance of the multipath estimators would depend upon how fast the reflecting surfaces along the propagation direction change. The environmental changes are expected to be different for different propagation directions of the GPS satellites. Therefore, the variation in performance of the estimators as seen in Table 2 is expected.

The goodness of the corrections can also be illustrated in the positional domain. Figure 8 shows the variation of the solved positions from the nominal position of the receiver. Weighted least mean square single-point positioning [13] with broadcast navigation data was applied to the data of Day 310. The measurements were only multipath corrected while other noises and biases (e.g., atmosphere delays, etc.) were not calibrated. The plot reveals noticeably higher centralization of the solution on the data corrected with SVR estimators over those obtained from the original data and the 50-second CSF-smoothed data. The reduction of standard deviation of coordinate time series North, East, and Up is tabulated separately in Table 3.

5. Discussions

For comparison, Table 4 tabulates numerical performance of different methods in terms of percentage of reduced multipath error. The performance of CSF is reported with a 100-second smoothing window [13]. The performance range of the frequency analysis method using fast fourier transform (FFT) [7] is reported with block sizes of 256 and 512, respectively, whilst the block size of the frequency analysis method using wavelet analysis [9] is 100 seconds. In particular, the

TABLE 2: Standard deviation (m) of noise before and after correction applied with CSF and SVR estimators.

PRN	Original	CSF corrected	SVR corrected
02	1.4927	0.9992 (33.06%)	0.3671 (75.41%)
03	1.1479	0.6741 (41.28%)	0.2478 (78.41%)
04	1.4009	0.8913 (36.38%)	0.2201 (84.29%)
05	1.2474	0.7722 (38.10%)	0.2325 (81.36%)
06	1.3194	0.6957 (47.28%)	0.2946 (77.67%)
07	1.2561	0.8768 (30.20%)	0.2711 (78.42%)
08	1.2806	0.8680 (32.22%)	0.2409 (81.19%)
09	1.3406	0.7955 (40.66%)	0.3599 (73.15%)
10	1.2084	0.7954 (34.18%)	0.2193 (81.85%)
11	1.4290	0.9993 (30.07%)	0.2995 (79.04%)
12	1.4813	0.9943 (32.87%)	0.2509 (83.06%)
13	1.5451	0.9960 (35.54%)	0.4969 (67.84%)
14	1.4514	0.8575 (40.92%)	0.2880 (80.16%)
15	1.3496	0.9539 (29.32%)	0.3034 (77.52%)
16	1.2200	0.7730 (36.64%)	0.3902 (68.01%)
17	1.4946	0.9515 (36.34%)	0.2763 (81.51%)
18	1.7889	1.1555 (35.40%)	0.3425 (80.85%)
19	1.1336	0.6832 (39.73%)	0.2506 (77.90%)
20	1.3501	0.8263 (38.80%)	0.2020 (85.04%)
21	1.1886	0.7329 (38.34%)	0.3492 (70.62%)
22	1.2568	0.8065 (35.83%)	0.3058 (75.67%)
23	1.2730	0.8483 (33.36%)	0.3378 (73.47%)
24	1.4779	0.9000 (39.11%)	0.1706 (88.46%)
25	1.4986	0.9260 (38.21%)	0.2914 (80.55%)
26	1.4292	0.9721 (31.99%)	0.2940 (79.43%)
27	1.9437	1.1705 (39.78%)	0.2504 (87.12%)
28	1.2519	0.8063 (35.59%)	0.2662 (78.74%)
29	1.6434	1.0105 (38.51%)	0.5116 (68.87%)
30	1.3446	0.8137 (39.48%)	0.1207 (91.02%)
31	1.3725	0.8317 (39.40%)	0.2569 (81.28%)
32	1.3985	0.8607 (38.46%)	0.2675 (80.87%)
Average reduction		36.68%	78.99%

TABLE 3: Standard deviation (m) of coordinate time series.

	Original	CSF corrected	SVR corrected
North	0.9136	0.7223 (20.94%)	0.5902 (35.40%)
East	1.2180	0.9997 (17.92%)	0.9033 (25.94%)
Up	2.6069	2.1715 (16.70%)	1.9496 (25.21%)

performance of the FIR filter method [14] is unreliable as only one satellite (PRN 9) was used for analysis. It is clear that SVR estimators significantly outperform the other reported methods. The state-of-the-art performance of SVR estimators on pseudorange multipath reduction emphasizes the efficiency of the proposed method. However, as the accumulative environmental changes become more and more severe over time, the performance of the estimators would temporally degrade. Therefore, the multipath estimators need to be equipped with adaptability, which has not been addressed so far.

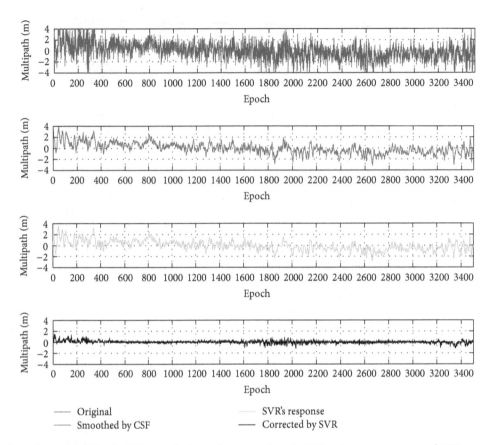

FIGURE 7: Original pseudorange multipath, CSF-smoothed pseudorange multipath, SVR-estimator response, and SVR-corrected pseudorange multipath of PRN 12 of the orbital plane B in Day 310 of 2010.

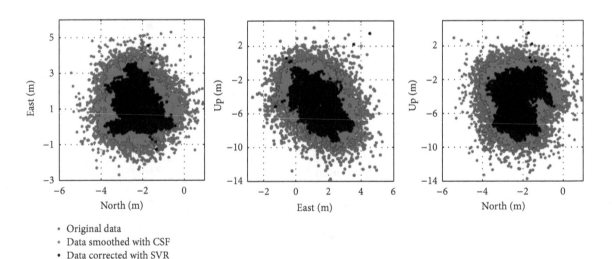

FIGURE 8: Positioning solution on original data, CSF-smoothed data, and SVR-corrected data of Day 310 of 2010.

Unlike the multipath stacking-based approaches [16, 17, 29], modeling multipath errors as functions of continuous variables (i.e., azimuth and elevation angles) does not experience the difficulty in the determination of the time-shifting period. In addition, the interpolation ability of the trained estimators makes them applicable for different data rates provided that training data is adequate to capture the underlying distribution of multipath errors. Furthermore, with the nature of sparsity, the multipath estimators just count on a subset of training data, being simpler while requiring less storage. All of these imply better scalability.

Another distinct advantage of the proposed approach is that it is able to preserve other signals of studied phenomena such as deformation caused by earthquakes. This is achieved

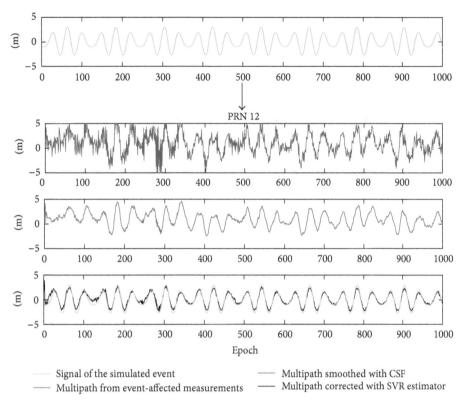

FIGURE 9: Simulation of event signal added to pseudorange measurements of PRN 12. It can be seen that the event signal is indeed left intact from correction of the PRN 12's SVR estimator.

TABLE 4: Performance comparison of code multipath mitigation methods.

CSF [13]	58%
FIR Filter [14]	75%
FFT [7]	50%–70%
Wavelet [9]	55%–65%
SVR estimator	68%–91%

by training the models with data on normal days without displacement before using them to correct data on the subsequent days where a phenomenon occurs. For the purpose of demonstration, we simulated an earthquake-like event by adding the signal given in (18) to PRN 12's pseudorange measurements for Day 310:

$$e(t) = 2\cos\left(\frac{\pi}{10}t + \pi\right) + \cos\left(\frac{\pi}{15}t\right). \quad (18)$$

Since signals of phenomena are usually low frequency [14, 23], the frequencies of the simulated event were chosen to exhibit diminishing effects of CSF, which is a low-pass filter [9, 12]. The PRN 12's pseudorange multipath sequence was smoothed by CSF with a 50-second smoothing window and then corrected by the trained PRN 12's SVR estimator. As shown in Figure 9, the corrected multipath sequence aligns very well with the event signal; that is, the event signal is not affected significantly.

Although carrier-phase multipath error is more sensitive to environmental variation, it also saw correlation on a sidereal daily basis [15, 29]. Therefore, the proposed method could be extended to apply to carrier-phase multipath mitigation.

6. Experiment 2: Carrier-Phase Multipath Mitigation

6.1. Double-Differential Carrier-Phase Multipath. Unlike code multipath error, carrier-phase multipath error cannot be isolated using combinations of code and carrier-phase measurements of one receiver alone. In order to do that, double differential (DD) combination of two short-baseline receivers (<10 km) is used. In practice, high-precision applications rely on this combination for relative positioning. The DD combination of two satellites a and b observed at two receivers A and B is given by

$$\phi_{AB}^{ab} = \Delta T^{ab} - \Delta I^{ab} + \Delta M^{\phi,ab} + \lambda\Delta N^{ab} + \Delta\varepsilon^{\phi,ab}. \quad (19)$$

In (19), clock error terms are eliminated through the differencing process. Furthermore, for a short baseline, atmospheric effects are approximately equal, leading to $\Delta T^{ab} \approx 0$ and $\Delta M^{ab} \approx 0$. The integer ambiguity term ΔN^{ab} can be computed by debiasing over the entire DD sequence as long as there are no cycle slips. The multipath effect, hence, is

(a)   (b)

FIGURE 10: IGS observation stations: (a) KIRU and (b) KIR0.

dominant in the DD measurements which can now be written as

$$\phi_{AB}^{ab} = \Delta M^{\phi,ab} + \Delta \varepsilon^{\phi,ab}. \tag{20}$$

The DD multipath error is the composition of four multipath errors of the four carrier-phase components. Denote θ_j^i and φ_j^i the elevation and azimuth angles of the satellite i with respect to the receiver j, DD multipath error actually depends on eight geometrical variables:

$$\Delta M^{\phi,ab} = f_\phi \left(\theta_A^a, \varphi_A^a, \theta_B^a, \varphi_B^a, \theta_A^b, \varphi_A^b, \theta_B^b, \varphi_B^b \right). \tag{21}$$

Fortunately, at each epoch, eight variable parameters can be calculated given the orbital information of the satellites broadcast to the receivers and nominal positions of the receivers which are known beforehand. Therefore, the DD multipath function f_ϕ can be learned from historical data.

6.2. Experimental Data Set. In this experiment, two short-baseline stations from the IGS monitoring network were chosen. Their continuous 1-second data during two consecutive days (Day 050 and 051 of 2011) were downloaded from IGS data archive (http://igscb.jpl.nasa.gov/components/prods.html). The stations named KIR0 and KIRU whose corresponding geodetic coordinates are (21.0602°, 67.8776°, 497.9000 m) and (20.9684, 67.8573, 391.1000 m) (20.9684°, 67.8573°, 391.1000 m) in (longitude, latitude, and height) triplet or equivalent to (2242.624 km, 5516.729 km, 2277.795 km) and (2245.915 km, 5519.218 km, 2268.268 km) in ECEF coordinate system. They are located in Kiruna, Sweden, with a separation distance of approximately 10 km. Figure 10 shows photographs of the locations and surroundings of the two stations. As seen in Figure 10, the stations' vicinity is covered by snow; therefore, the multipath environment is expected to change quickly even in a short time span as the weather changes. If so, the performance of the multipath estimator would degrade.

The station KIRU is selected as the reference station. With predetermined nominal positions of the stations, the geometrical parameters of the satellites with respect to the stations can be computed easily at every epoch given the

broadcast navigation data. In order to extract DD multipath as described earlier, a satellite with high elevation is usually selected as a reference to form the DD combination [1, 13]. The pair of satellites PRN 8 and PRN 18 with the longest DD sequences are thus selected for analysis. PRN 8, with higher elevation peak, is used as the reference satellite. Their geometries with respect to the two stations are illustrated in Figure 11.

6.3. Training Multipath Estimator. In order to train a DD multipath estimator for the satellite pair, the steps that have been done previously for code multipath estimation will again be performed. The geometrical data and multipath errors in Day 050 are scaled to $[-1; +1]$ before feeding to the training program. The *libSVM* package that implements ε-SVR algorithm is employed to train the multipath estimators. The values of ε, the Gaussian kernel parameter η, and the penalty parameter of the error term C are again chosen using grid search and cross-validation with the same strategy as described previously for code multipath mitigation.

Learning from the training data set, the support vectors and coefficients of the DD multipath estimator are found. Finally, the multipath estimator f_ϕ should estimate DD multipath error when presented with a new observation of azimuth/elevation angles thereafter. The estimated multipath error will be used to correct carrier-phase DD of the satellite pair in the successive days.

6.4. Experimental Results. In order to demonstrate the ability of the proposed method, the trained estimator is used to estimate the carrier-phase multipath error of the following Day 051. From top to bottom, Figure 12 shows the original multipath sequence, the response of the trained estimator, and the corrected multipath sequence with the response. The standard deviations of the original multipath sequence and the corrected multipath sequence are 2.15 cm and 0.92 cm, respectively. In other words, the multipath error has been reduced by 57.2% using the trained multipath estimator. Although only two data sets for one satellite pair have been presented here, this preliminary result provides a strong indication that the proposed technique can be applied to the carrier-phase multipath mitigation problem.

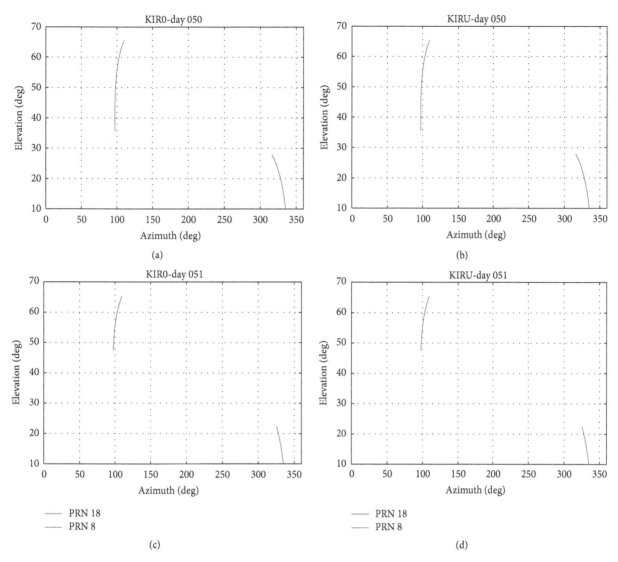

FIGURE 11: Geometries of PRN 8 and PRN 18 with respect to KIR0 and KIRU in Day 050 and Day 051.

7. Discussion

As expected, the response of the multipath estimator can capture the dominant trend of the multipath sequence which is the dominant component of the multipath error [8, 9]. However, the result of the proposed method when applied to carrier-phase multipath mitigation seems to be lower than what was achieved for code multipath mitigation. It is explainable as there is no equivalent smoothing algorithm like CSF to smooth the multipath sequence to attenuate high-frequency noise during training and correction. Although it is unwise to conclude firmly since the experimental result is only for one pair of satellites, for the sake of comparison, the proposed method outperforms the FIR filter method (39.8%–56.1%) [15], and the frequency-domain processing methods relying on analysis of SNR measurements (20%) [10, 22]. It provides a motivation for further exploration of the proposed method on the carrier-phase multipath mitigation problem.

However, this result is incomparable to that of the direct frequency-domain processing methods using wavelets such as those of Elhabiby et al. [8], which can reduce carrier-phase DD multipath up to 84%. It is because these methods can attenuate both errors from low to high frequencies to achieve better mitigation effects at the cost of filtering out other signals if their frequency content overlaps with multipath's frequency content. Although it has not been proven and more comprehensive experiments need to be conducted in future work, the proposed method should share similar advantages of code multipath estimators that it, intuitively, does not affect other phenomena signals. This could be fulfilled if data without displacement is used for training before estimating multipath error for data with displacement. Therefore, for applications where additional important signals such as seismic signals exist, the proposed method is promising.

As carrier-phase multipath is much more sensitive to environmental changes than pseudorange multipath, the data training over a short time span is more suitable for training SVR estimators under the constant environment assumption. It leads to higher data rates being required for training in

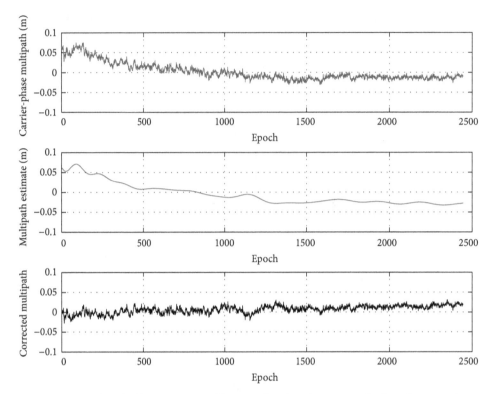

FIGURE 12: Original carrier-phase multipath (blue), response of the trained multipath estimator (red), and corrected carrier-phase multipath (black) sequences of the satellite pair PRN 18–PRN 8.

order to retain data density. However, it does not strictly require high-rate data (≥1 Hz) as stacking-based approaches do [17, 29]; only data rates that can capture the underlying distribution of the multipath error are required. Fortunately, the proposed method is also scalable with data rate due to its inherent sparsity. In other words, only a subset of training data which are support vectors are kept and involved in the computation. However, if the number of support vectors is significantly large, computational complexity may still be a concern for real-time operation. This issue needs further exploration.

8. Conclusion

This paper has presented a unified framework based on nonlinear support vector regression to address the GPS code and carrier-phase multipath mitigation problems for ground fixed GPS stations. Based on analysis of the geometry of multipath signal reflections, geometrical models of multipath errors are developed. More specifically, multipath errors corresponding to a satellite are mathematically formulated as functions of the satellite's geometry with respect to a receiver, which is parameterized by azimuth and elevation angles. As a result, the problem of multipath error estimation amounts to regression problem where the multipath functions are approximated by learning from training data using ε-SVM algorithm. Finally, the trained multipath estimators are employed to correct measurements for successive days. The proposed method demonstrates good performance and is

scalable to data rate. Furthermore, the multipath estimators do not affect the simulated signal of phenomena.

Acknowledgment

This work was done while Q.-H. Phan was a graduate research student at School of Computer Engineering, Nanyang Technological University, Singapore.

References

[1] B. Hoffmann-Wellenhof, H. Lichtenegger, and J. Collins, *GPS: Theory and Practice*, Springer, Wien, Austria, 2001.

[2] A. Leick, *GPS Satellite Surveying*, 3rd John Wiley & Sons, New York, NY, USA, 2004.

[3] G. J. Bishop, D. S. Coco, P. H. Kappler, and E. A. Holland, "Studies and performance of a new technique for mitigation of pseudorange multipath effects in GPS ground stations," in *Proceedings of the 1994 National Technical Meeting of The Institute of Navigation*, pp. 231–242, San Diego, Calif, USA, January 1994.

[4] N. Kubo and A. Yasuda, "How multipath error influences on ambiguity resolution," in *Proceedings of the 16th International Technical Meeting of the Satellite Division of The Institute of Navigation (ION GPS/GNSS '03)*, pp. 2142–2150, Portland, Ore, USA, 2003.

[5] Y. Zhang, *High performance differential global positioning system for long baseline application [Ph.D. thesis]*, Ohio University, 2005.

[6] B. Parkinson and P. Enge, "Differential GPS," in *Global Positioning System*, B. Parkinson, J. Spilker, P. Axelrad, and P. Enge, Eds., vol. 2, pp. 3–49, American Institute of Aeronautics and Astronautics, Washington, DC, USA, 1996.

[7] Y. Zhang and C. Bartone, "Multipath mitigation in the frequency domain," in *Proceedings of the IEEE/ION Position Location and Navigation Symposium (PLANS '04)*, pp. 486–495, Athens, Ga, USA, April 2004.

[8] M. Elhabiby, A. El-Ghazouly, and N. El-Sheimy, "A new wavelet-based multipath mitigation technique," in *Proceedings of the 21st International Technical Meeting of the Satellite Division of the Institute of Navigation (ION GNSS '08)*, pp. 625–631, Savannah, Ga, USA, September 2008.

[9] Y. Zhang and C. Bartone, "Real-time multipath mitigation with WaveSmoothǓ technique using wavelets," in *Proceedings of the 17th International Technical Meeting of the Satellite Division of the Institute of Navigation (ION GNSS '04)*, pp. 1181–1194, Long Beach, Calif, USA, September 2004.

[10] A. Bilich, K. M. Larson, and P. Axelrad, "Modeling GPS phase multipath with SNR: case study from the Salar de Uyuni, Boliva," *Journal of Geophysical Research B*, vol. 113, no. 4, Article ID B04401, 2008.

[11] C. Rost and L. Wanninger, "Carrier phase multipath mitigation based on GNSS signal quality measurements," *Journal of Applied Geodesy*, vol. 3, no. 2, pp. 81–87, 2009.

[12] P. Y. Hwang, G. A. McGraw, and J. R. Bader, "Enhanced Differential GPS carrier-smoothed code processing using dual-frequency measurements," *Navigation*, vol. 46, no. 2, pp. 127–137, 1999.

[13] P. Misra and P. Enge, *Global Positioning System: Signals, Measurements, and Performance*, IGanga-Jamuna Press, Lincoln, Mass, USA, 2nd edition, 2006.

[14] L. Ge, S. Han, and C. Rizos, "Multipath mitigation of continuous GPS measurements using an adaptive filter," *GPS Solutions*, vol. 4, pp. 19–30, 2000.

[15] H. Liu, X. Li, L. Ge, C. Rizos, and F. Wang, "Variable length LMS adaptive filter for carrier phase multipath mitigation," *GPS Solutions*, vol. 15, no. 1, pp. 29–38, 2011.

[16] P. Axelrad, K. Larson, and B. Jones, "Use of the correct satellite repeat period to characterize and reduce site-specific multipath errors," in *Proceedings of the 18th International Technical Meeting of the Satellite Division of The Institute of Navigation (ION GNSS '05)*, pp. 2638–2648, Long Beach, Calif, USA, September 2005.

[17] K. M. Larson, A. Bilich, and P. Axelrad, "Improving the precision of high-rate GPS," *Journal of Geophysical Research*, vol. 112, no. B5, 2007.

[18] P. Zhong, X. Ding, L. Yuan, Y. Xu, K. Kwok, and Y. Chen, "Sidereal filtering based on single differences for mitigating GPS multipath effects on short baselines," *Journal of Geodesy*, vol. 84, no. 2, pp. 145–158, 2010.

[19] Q. H. Phan and S. L. Tan, "Mitigation of GPS periodic multipath using nonlinear regression," in *Proceedings of 19th European Signal Processing Conference (EUSIPCO '11)*, pp. 1795–1799, Barcelona, Spain, 2011.

[20] Q. H. Phan, S. L. Tan, and I. McLoughlin, "GPS multipath mitigation: a nonlinear regression approach," *GPS Solutions*, 2012.

[21] B. Parkinson, "Introduction and heritage of NAVSTAR, the Global Positioning System," in *Global Positioning System*, B. Parkinson, J. Spilker, P. Axelrad, and P. Enge, Eds., vol. 1, pp. 3–28, American Institute of Aeronautics and Astronautics, Washington, DC, USA, 1996.

[22] A. Bilich and K. M. Larson, "Mapping the GPS multipath environment using the signal-to-noise ratio (SNR)," *Radio Science*, vol. 42, no. 6, 2007.

[23] Y. Bock, R. M. Nikolaidis, P. J. de Jonge, and M. Bevis, "Instantaneous geodetic positioning at medium distances with the Global Positioning System," *Journal of Geophysical Research B*, vol. 105, no. 12, pp. 28223–28253, 2000.

[24] J. F. Genrich and Y. Bock, "Rapid resolution of crustal motion at short ranges with the Global Positioning System," *Journal of Geophysical Research*, vol. 97, no. 3, pp. 3261–3269, 1992.

[25] A. J. Smola and B. Schölkopf, "A tutorial on support vector regression," *Statistics and Computing*, vol. 14, no. 3, pp. 199–222, 2004.

[26] V. Vapnik, *The Nature of Statistical Learning Theory*, Springer, New York, NY, USA, 1995.

[27] C. M. Bishop, *Neural Networks for Pattern Recognition*, Oxford University Press, Oxford, UK, 1996.

[28] J. Dickman, C. Bartone, Y. Zhang, and B. Thornburg, "Characterization and performance of a prototype wideband airport pseudolite multipath limiting antenna for the local area augmentation system," in *Proceedings of the 2003 National Technical Meeting of The Institute of Navigation*, pp. 783–793, Anaheim, Calif, USA, 2003.

[29] K. Choi, A. Bilich, K. M. Larson, and P. Axelrad, "Modified sidereal filtering: implications for high-rate GPS positioning," *Geophysical Research Letters*, vol. 31, no. 22, pp. 1–4, 2004.

18

Inverse Analysis of Crack in Fixed-Fixed Structure by Neural Network with the Aid of Modal Analysis

Dhirendranath Thatoi[1] and Prabir Kumar Jena[2]

[1] *Department of Mechanical Engineering, I.T.E.R, Bhubaneswar 751030, Odisha, India*
[2] *Department of Mechanical Engineering, Silicon Institute of Technology, Bhubaneswar 751024, Odisha, India*

Correspondence should be addressed to Prabir Kumar Jena; prabirkumarjena07@gmail.com

Academic Editor: Kyong Joo Oh

In this research, dynamic response of a cracked shaft having transverse crack is analyzed using theoretical neural network and experimental analysis. Structural damage detection using frequency response functions (FRFs) as input data to the back-propagation neural network (BPNN) has been explored. For deriving the effect of crack depths and crack locations on FRF, theoretical expressions have been developed using strain energy release rate at the crack section of the shaft for the calculation of the local stiffnesses. Based on the flexibility, a new stiffness matrix is deduced that is subsequently used to calculate the natural frequencies and mode shapes of the cracked beam using the neural network method. The results of the numerical analysis and the neural network method are being validated with the result from the experimental method. The analysis results on a shaft show that the neural network can assess damage conditions with very good accuracy.

1. Introduction

Vibration-based methods for detection of cracks offer some advantages over conventional methods. This methodology can help to determine the location and size of the cracks from the vibration data collected from the cracked beam structure. Development of cracks in a vibrating structure leads to reduction in the stiffness and increase in its damping [1] which, in turn, gives rise to a change in natural frequencies and mode shapes. So it may be possible to estimate the location and size of the cracks by measuring changes in the vibration parameters.

Tada et al. [2] have proposed the basis for calculation of compliance matrix for different types of beams. Sekhar and Prabhu [3] have derived a method to calculate the vibration characteristics using a model based on finite element. Paviglianiti et al. [4] have devised a scheme for detecting and isolating sensor faults in industrial robot manipulators. They have adopted a procedure for decoupling of the disturbance effect from the effect of the fault generated in the system. The dynamics of the proposed scheme has been improved by using radial basis functions neural network. Behera et al. [5]

have studied the vibration characteristics of a shaft with two open cracks rotating in a fluid medium by using the influence coefficient method to find frequency of the cracked shaft and frequency contours with respect to crack depths and locations. Wang et al. [6] have investigated the bending and torsional vibration of a fiber reinforced composite cantilever with a surface crack. They have suggested that the coupling of bending and torsion is the result of material properties or the surface crack. Lee [7] has presented a method to identify multiple cracks in a beam by modeling the cracks as rotational springs. He has claimed that the results are in excellent agreement with the actual ones. Artificial neural networks (ANN) can be used as an alternative effective tool for solving the inverse problems because of the pattern-matching capability. The results of ANN are quite encouraging and prove the robustness of the proposed damage assessment algorithm [8–10].

The paper is organized as following. In Section 2, a general framework to address local flexibility matrix at the vicinity of the crack is introduced. Neural controller mechanism for crack detection of the shaft with the aid of modal analysis is discussed in Section 3. Section 4 provides

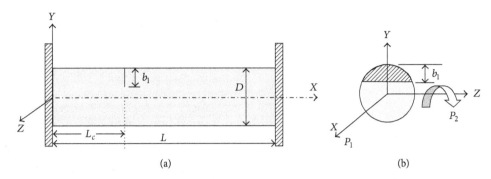

FIGURE 1: Geometry of the shaft. (a) Fixed-Fixed shaft, (b) cross-sectional view of the shaft.

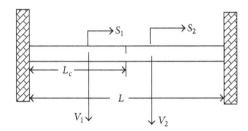

FIGURE 2: Shaft model.

a detailed description of the experimental method deployed, and the results obtained from this has been compared with that obtained from the theoretical and ANN results. A good agreement between the results has been observed.

2. Problem Formulation and Theory

2.1. Local Flexibility of a Cracked Beam under Bending and Axial Loading. The presence of a transverse surface crack of depth "b_1" on a shaft of diameter D introduces a local flexibility, which can be defined in matrix form, the dimension of which depends on the degrees of freedom. Here a 2×2 matrix is considered. A fixed-fixed shaft is subjected to axial force (P_1) and bending moment (P_2), shown in Figure 1, which is coupled to give both longitudinal and transverse motion. The cross-sectional view of the shaft is shown in Figure 1(b).

Using strain energy release rate, the local stiffness of a cracked shaft can be obtained in the matrix form as [2]

$$K = \begin{bmatrix} K_{11} & K_{12} \\ K_{21} & K_{22} \end{bmatrix} = \begin{bmatrix} C_{11} & C_{12} \\ C_{21} & C_{22} \end{bmatrix}^{-1}, \tag{1}$$

where, C_{ij} represents the compliance matrix.

2.2. Analysis of Vibration Characteristics of the Cracked Shaft

2.2.1. Free Vibration. A shaft of length "L" with a crack of depth "b_1" at a distance "L_c" from the left-fixed end is considered (shown in Figure 1). Taking $S_1(x, t)$ and $S_2(x, t)$ as the amplitudes of longitudinal vibration for the sections before and after the crack position, and $V_1(x, t)$ and $V_2(x, t)$ are the amplitudes of bending vibration for the same sections as shown in Figure 2.

The normal functions for the cracked shaft in nondimensional form for both the longitudinal and bending vibration in steady state can be defined as

$$\overline{S}_1(\overline{x}) = B_1 \cos\left(\overline{H}_s \overline{x}\right) + B_2 \sin\left(\overline{H}_s \overline{x}\right) \tag{2a}$$

$$\overline{S}_2(\overline{x}) = B_3 \cos\left(\overline{H}_s \overline{x}\right) + B_4 \sin\left(\overline{H}_s \overline{x}\right) \tag{2b}$$

$$\overline{V}_1(\overline{x}) = B_5 \cosh\left(\overline{H}_v \overline{x}\right) + B_6 \sinh\left(\overline{H}_v \overline{x}\right)$$
$$+ B_7 \cos\left(\overline{H}_v \overline{x}\right) + B_8 \sin\left(\overline{H}_v \overline{x}\right) \tag{2c}$$

$$\overline{V}_2(\overline{x}) = B_9 \cosh\left(\overline{H}_v \overline{x}\right) + B_{10} \sinh\left(\overline{H}_v \overline{x}\right)$$
$$+ B_{11} \cos\left(\overline{H}_v \overline{x}\right) + B_{12} \sin\left(\overline{H}_v \overline{x}\right), \tag{2d}$$

where $\overline{x} = x/L$, $\overline{S} = S/L$, $\overline{V} = V/L$, $\alpha = L_c/L$, $\overline{H}_s = \omega L/D_s$, $D_s = (E/\rho)^{1/2}$, $\overline{H}_V = \left(\omega L^2/D_v\right)^{1/2}$, $D_v = (EI/\mu)^{1/2}$, and $\mu = A\rho$, B_i, ($i = 1, 12$). Constants are to be determined from boundary conditions.

Boundary conditions are as follows.
At the left-fixed end

$$\overline{S}_1(0) = 0; \qquad \overline{V}_1(0) = 0; \qquad \frac{\partial \overline{V}_1}{\partial \overline{X}}(0) = 0. \tag{3}$$

At the right-fixed end

$$\overline{S}_1(1) = 0; \qquad \overline{V}_1(1) = 0; \qquad \frac{\partial \overline{V}_1}{\partial \overline{X}}(1) = 0. \tag{4}$$

At the cracked section

$$\overline{S}_1(\alpha) = \overline{S}_2(\alpha); \qquad \overline{V}_1(\alpha) = \overline{V}_2(\alpha);$$
$$\frac{\partial^2 \overline{V}_1}{\partial \overline{X}^2}(\alpha) = \frac{\partial^2 \overline{V}_2}{\partial \overline{X}^2}(\alpha); \qquad \frac{\partial^3 \overline{V}_1}{\partial \overline{X}^3}(\alpha) = \frac{\partial^3 \overline{V}_2}{\partial \overline{X}^3}(\alpha). \tag{5}$$

Also at the cracked section, by force balancing

$$AE\frac{dS_1(L_c)}{dx} = K_{11}(S_2(L_c) - S_1(L_c))$$

$$+ K_{12}\left(\frac{dV_2(L_c)}{dx} - \frac{dV_1(L_c)}{dx}\right) \quad (6)$$

$$\implies N_1 N_2 \overline{S}'_1(\alpha) = N_2\left(\overline{S}_2(\alpha) - \overline{S}_1(\alpha)\right)$$

$$+ N_1\left(\overline{V}'_2(\alpha) - \overline{V}'_1(\alpha)\right).$$

Similarly, by moment balancing

$$EI\frac{d^2V_1(L_c)}{dx^2} = K_{21}(S_2(L_c) - S_1(L_c))$$

$$+ K_{22}\left(\frac{dV_2(L_c)}{dx} - \frac{dV_1(L_c)}{dx}\right) \quad (7)$$

$$\implies N_3 N_4 \overline{V}''_1(\alpha) = N_3\left(\overline{S_2}(\alpha) - \overline{S_1}(\alpha)\right)$$

$$+ N_4\left(\overline{V}'_2(\alpha) - \overline{V}'_1(\alpha)\right),$$

where $N_1 = AE/LK_{11}$, $N_2 = AE/K_{12}$, $N_3 = EI/LK_{22}$, and $N_4 = EI/L^2 K_{21}$.

The normal functions, (2a), (2b), (2c), and (2d), along with the boundary conditions as mentioned above, yield the characteristic equation of the system as $|\Omega| = 0$.

Ω is a 12×12 matrix (the Appendix) whose determinant is a function of natural circular frequency (ω), the nondimensional location of the crack (α), and the local stiffness matrix (K) which in turn is a function of the nondimensional crack depth $\delta_1 = (b_1/T)$.

3. Analysis of Neural Controller for Crack Detection

The presence of damage, in general, in a structure undermines the viability of the structure, leads to shorter life time period, and opens the way for complete failure of the system. Hence, development of an automated method to identify cracks accurately in an engineering application is desirable. As it is known that the cracks present in a mechanical element increase the flexibility, decrease the vibration frequencies, and modify the amplitude of vibration, and those changes can be potentially used to locate the crack positions and crack depths. So it is of interest to design and develop an AI-based technique for online multiple crack diagnosis to avoid catastrophic failure of structural system. In this Section, an intelligent controller has been designed using artificial neural network to detect the presence of a crack in structural members. The proposed neural controller has been modeled with feed forward network trained with back propagation technique. Finally, the results from the controller have been compared with the experimental results to establish the robustness of the proposed neural method.

The back propagation technique can be used to train the multilayer networks. This technique is an approximate steepest algorithm in which the performance of the network is based on mean square error. In order to train the neural network, the weights for each input to the neural system should be so adjusted that the error between the actual output and desired output is minimum. The multilayer neural system would calculate the change in error due to increase or decrease in the weights. The algorithm first computes each error weight by computing the rate of the error changes with the change in synaptic weights. The error in each hidden layer, just before the output layer in a direction opposite to the way activities propagate through the network, have to be computed and fed to the network by back propagation algorithm to minimize the error in the actual output and desired output by adjusting the parameters of the network.

The main features of the neural model are as follows

(1) The inputs to the neuron are assigned with synaptic weights, which in turn affect the decision making ability of the neural network. The inputs to the neuron are called weighted inputs.

(2) These weighted inputs are then summed together in an adder and if they exceed a preset threshold value, the neuron fires. In any other case the neuron does not fire.

(3) An activation function for limiting the amplitude of the output of a neuron has been adopted in the current model. Generally, the normalized amplitude range of the output of a neuron is given as the closed unit interval $[0, 1]$ or alternatively $[-1, 1]$.

A back propagation neural network controller has been developed for detection of the relative crack location and relative crack depth (Figure 3). The neural network has got six input parameters and two output parameters.

The inputs to the neural network controller are as follows:

$\overline{\Delta}_{nf_1}$ = relative first natural frequency,

$\overline{\Delta}_{nf_2}$ = relative second natural frequency,

$\overline{\Delta}_{nf_3}$ = relative third natural frequency,

$\overline{\Delta}_{m_1}$ = relative first mode shape difference;

$\overline{\Delta}_{m_2}$ = relative second shape difference,

$\overline{\Delta}_{m_3}$ = relative third mode shape difference.

The outputs from the neural network are as follows;

relative crack location = α and relative crack depth = δ_1.

The back propagation neural network controller has got 5 layers (i.e., input layer, output layer, and three hidden layers). The neurons associated with the input and output layers are six and two, respectively. The input layer neurons represent relative deviation of the first three natural frequencies and the first three relative mode shape differences. The output layer neurons represent relative crack location and relative crack depth. The neurons are taken in order to give the neural network a diamond shape.

TABLE 1: Examples of the training patterns for training of the neural network controller.

Serial number	Input to the neural network controller						Desired output from the neural network controller	
	$\overline{\Delta}_{nf_1}$	$\overline{\Delta}_{nf_2}$	$\overline{\Delta}_{nf_3}$	$\overline{\Delta}_{m_1}$	$\overline{\Delta}_{m_2}$	$\overline{\Delta}_{m_3}$	α	δ_1
1	0.9184	0.9232	0.9602	0.2007	0.4218	0.2035	0.149	0.505
2	0.9264	0.9772	0.9854	0.1426	0.2233	0.1821	0.099	0.412
3	0.9430	0.9806	0.9862	0.1008	0.1624	0.2064	0.172	0.398
4	0.9456	0.9810	0.9876	0.0958	0.1593	0.2052	0.072	0.199
5	0.9578	0.9862	0.9878	0.0709	0.1492	0.1968	0.273	0.536
6	0.9662	0.9872	0.9894	0.0460	0.1305	0.1936	0.214	0.249
7	0.9678	0.9908	0.9936	0.0351	0.1219	0.1604	0.382	0.513
8	0.9726	0.9922	0.9938	0.0182	0.0458	0.1319	0.425	0.491
9	0.9804	0.9936	0.9964	0.0147	0.0299	0.0912	0.503	0.540
10	0.9882	0.9980	0.9982	0.0063	0.0132	0.0349	0.489	0.430

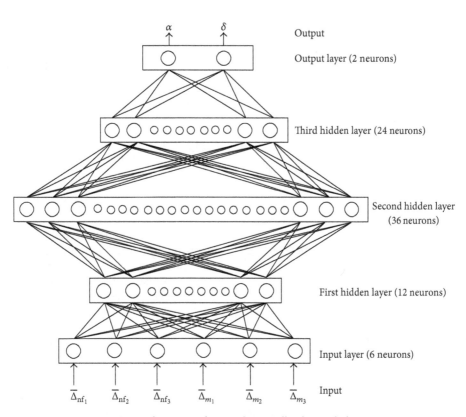

FIGURE 3: Five-layer neural network controller for crack detection.

TABLE 2: Material properties of aluminium-alloy, 2014-T$_4$.

Young's modulus, E	Density, ρ	Poisson's ratio, μ	Length, L	Diameter, D
72.4 GPa	2.8 gm/cc	0.33	800 mm	150 mm

The relative crack depth ($\delta_1 = b_1/D$) = varies from 0.05 to 0.8.
The relative crack location ($\alpha = L_c/L$) = varies from 0.0125 to 0.95.

3.1. Neural Controller Mechanism for Crack Detection.
The neural network used is a five-layer perceptron [11]. The chosen number of layers was found empirically to facilitate training. The input layer has six neurons, three for the first three relative natural frequencies and the other three for the first three relative mode shape differences. The output layer has two neurons, which represent relative crack location and relative crack depth. These numbers of hidden neurons are also found empirically. Figure 4 depicts the neural network with its input and output signals.

The neural network is trained with 500 patterns representing typical scenarios, some of which are depicted in Table 1. The neural network is trained to give outputs such

TABLE 3: Comparison of results between neural network controller, numerical analysis, and experimental setup.

Slerial number	$\overline{\Delta}_{nf_1}$	$\overline{\Delta}_{nf_2}$	$\overline{\Delta}_{nf_3}$	$\overline{\Delta}_{m_1}$	$\overline{\Delta}_{m_2}$	$\overline{\Delta}_{m_3}$	Neural network controller		Numerical		Experimental	
							δ_1	α	δ_1	α	δ_1	α
1	0.9429	0.9534	0.9554	0.1354	0.1186	0.1579	0.195	0.071	0.194	0.067	0.197	0.072
2	0.9265	0.9457	0.9523	0.1984	0.1623	0.1961	0.414	0.079	0.411	0.077	0.413	0.082
3	0.9217	0.9525	0.9558	0.0907	0.0139	0.0387	0.526	0.156	0.516	0.156	0.546	0.154
4	0.9345	0.9555	0.9552	0.0691	−0.0412	0.0949	0.374	0.183	0.378	0.183	0.375	0.184
5	0.9433	0.9563	0.9583	0.0051	−0.4339	0.1286	0.218	0.233	0.222	0.231	0.221	0.235
6	0.9313	0.9541	0.9404	0.0973	0.0336	0.2052	0.531	0.281	0.534	0.277	0.524	0.28
7	0.9409	0.9456	0.9497	0.0363	0.1283	0.1997	0.432	0.397	0.433	0.396	0.429	0.397
8	0.9432	0.9396	0.9512	0.0449	0.1577	0.1961	0.475	0.415	0.477	0.415	0.475	0.415
9	0.9444	0.9192	0.9563	−0.016	0.1611	0.1982	0.408	0.493	0.409	0.491	0.408	0.494
10	0.9419	0.9277	0.9554	0.0189	0.2279	0.1753	0.516	0.523	0.521	0.524	0.514	0.522

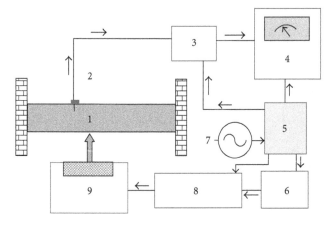

(1) Fixed-fixed beam specimen
(2) Vibration pickup (accelerometer)
(3) Vibration analyzer (pulse lite type)
(4) Vibration indicator with software
    (PULS LabShop software)
(5) Distribution box
(6) Function generator
(7) Power supply
(8) Power amplifier
(9) Vibration exciter

FIGURE 4: Schematic block diagram of experimental setup for fixed-fixed cracked beam.

as relative crack depth and relative crack location. During training and during normal operation, the input patterns fed to the neural network comprise the following components.

$\Delta_1^{\{1\}}$, $\Delta_2^{\{1\}}$, and $\Delta_3^{\{1\}}$ are the relative deviations of first, second, and third natural frequencies and $\Delta_4^{\{1\}}$, $\Delta_5^{\{1\}}$, and $\Delta_6^{\{1\}}$ are the relative deviations of first, second, and third mode shape differences.

These input values are distributed to the hidden neurons which generate outputs given by [11]

$$\Delta_j^{\{lay\}} = g\left(V_j^{\{lay\}}\right), \tag{8}$$

where

$$V_j^{\{lay\}} = \sum_i w_{ji}^{\{lay\}} \cdot \Delta_i^{\{lay-1\}} \tag{9}$$

lay = layer number (2 or 4),

j = label for jth neuron in hidden layer "lay" and i = label for ith neuron in hidden layer "lay-1",

$w_{ji}^{\{lay\}}$ = weight of the connection from neuron i in layer "lay-1" to neuron j in layer "lay".

$g(\cdot)$ = activation function, chosen in this work as the hyperbolic tangent function as

$$g(x) = \frac{e^x - e^{-x}}{e^x + e^{-x}}. \tag{10}$$

During training, the network output $\theta_{actual,n}$ ($i = 1, 2$) may differ from the desired output $\theta_{desired,n}$ ($n = 1, 2$) as specified in the training pattern presented to the network. A measure of the performance of the network is the instantaneous sum-squared difference between $\theta_{desired,n}$ and $\theta_{actual,n}$ for the set of presented the following training patterns:

$$error = \frac{1}{2} \sum_{all\ training\ patterns} \left(\theta_{desired,n} - \theta_{actual,n}\right)^2, \tag{11}$$

where $\theta_{actual,n}$ ($n = 1$) represents relative crack location (α), and $\theta_{actual,n}$ ($n = 2$) represents relative crack depth (δ_1).

The error back propagation method is employed to train the network. This method requires the computation of local error gradients in order to determine appropriate weight corrections to reduce error. For the output layer, the error gradient $\exists^{\{5\}}$ is

$$\exists^{\{5\}} = g'\left(V_1^{\{5\}}\right)\left(\theta_{desired,n} - \theta_{actual,n}\right). \tag{12}$$

The local gradient for neurons in hidden layer lay is given by

$$\exists_j^{\{lay\}} = g'\left(V_j^{\{lay\}}\right)\left(\sum_k \exists_k^{\{lay+1\}} W_{kj}^{\{lay+1\}}\right). \tag{13}$$

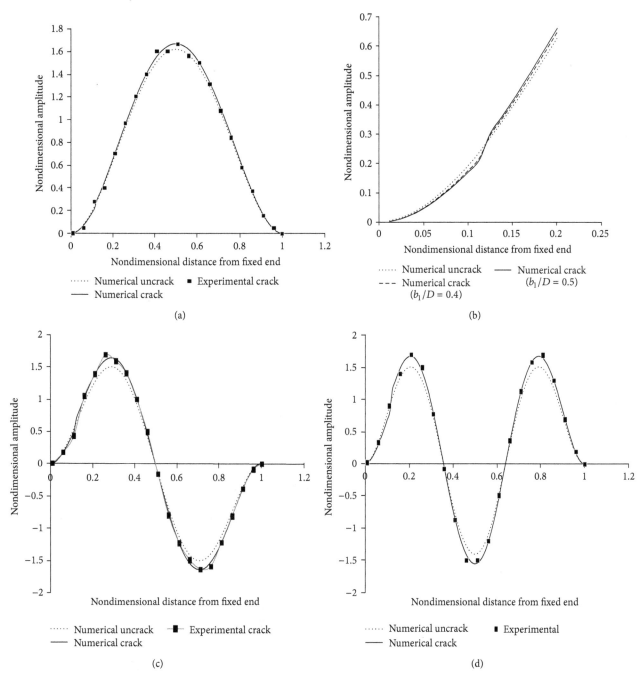

FIGURE 5: (a) Nondimensional amplitude versus nondimensional distance from left end (1st mode of vibration), $b_1/D = 0.4$, $L_c/L = 0.125$. (b) Magnified view of Figure 5(a) at the vicinity of the crack location. (c) Nondimensional amplitude versus nondimensional distance from left end (2nd mode of vibration), $b_1/D = 0.4$, $L_c/L = 0.125$. (d) Nondimensional amplitude versus nondimensional distance from left end (3rd mode of vibration), $b_1/D = 0.4$, $L_c/L = 0.125$.

The synaptic weights are updated according to the following expressions:

$$w_{ji}(t+1) = w_{ji}(t) + (\Delta w)_{ji}(t+1),$$

$$(\Delta w)_{ji}(t+1) = \beta(\Delta w)_{ji}(t) + \eta \exists_j^{\{lay\}} \Delta_i^{\{lay-1\}}, \quad (14)$$

β = momentum coefficient (chosen empirically as 0.2 in this work),

η = learning rate (chosen empirically as 0.35 in this work),

t = iteration number, each iteration consisting of the presentation of a training pattern and correction of the weights.

The final output from the neural network is

$$\theta_{\text{actual},n} = g\left(V_n^{\{5\}}\right), \quad \text{where } V_n^{\{5\}} = \sum_i w_{ni}^{\{5\}} \Delta_i^{\{4\}}. \quad (15)$$

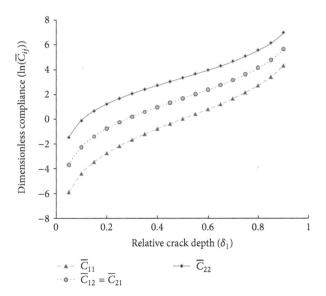

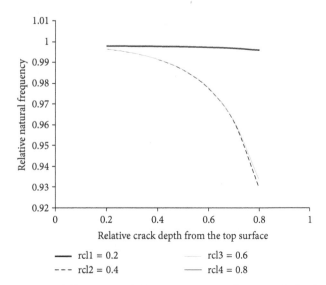

FIGURE 6: Dimensionless compliance ($\ln(\overline{C}_{ij})$) versus relative crack depth (δ_1).

FIGURE 8: Relative natural frequency versus relative crack depth from the top surface (1st mode vibration).

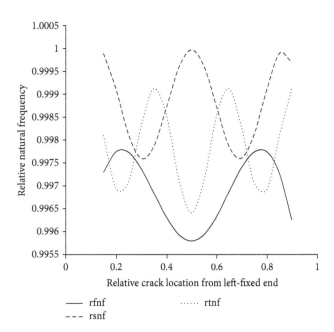

FIGURE 7: Relative natural frequency versus relative crack location from the fixed end $b_1/T = 0.3$.

4. Experimental Validation

Experiments are performed to determine the natural frequencies and mode shapes for different crack depths on aluminum shaft specimen having 800 mm in length and 150 mm in diameter on the experimental setup shown in schematic diagram Figure 4. The amplitude of transverse vibration at different locations along the length of the aluminum beam is recorded by positioning the vibration pickup and tuning the vibration generator at the corresponding resonant frequencies. These results for first three modes are plotted in Figure 5. Corresponding numerical results for the

cracked and uncracked beam are also presented in the same graph for comparison.

4.1. Shaft Specimen Specification. In the current investigation, using both numerical and experimental analysis of a cracked shaft, the following (Table 2) specifications are being considered.

5. Discussion

In this section, the results from the theoretical neural network and experimental analysis performed on the cracked fixed-fixed shaft are discussed. Figure 1 presents the cracked shaft with its cross-sectional view. A comparison between the first three mode shapes of numerical crack, numerical un-crack, and the magnified view of the shaft (at the vicinity of the crack location) are also shown in Figure 5. A neural controller has been shown in Figure 3. Examples of the training patterns for training of the neural network controller are presented in Table 1. An experimental setup has been developed (Figure 4) to perform experiments on aluminum shaft specimen for validation of results obtained from theoretical and neural network analysis. The results from theoretical analysis and experimental setup are compared and the results for cracked and uncracked shaft are presented in Figure 5.

The dimensionless compliances ($\overline{C}_{11}, \overline{C}_{12} = \overline{C}_{21}, \overline{C}_{22}$) increase with the increase in relative crack depth as shown in Figure 6. Figure 7 explains how the natural frequencies vary with the location of crack. Since fixed-fixed beam is geometrically symmetric, the variations are symmetric between left half and right half. Higher modes of vibration show both maximaly and minimaly more numbers of times because of more number of nodes. As shown in Figure 8, natural frequencies are in decreasing trend with depth of crack. The variations of frequencies are sharper for cracks located far away from either end of the beam.

The results of the numerical analysis, the neural network method, and the experimental method are shown in Table 3. This proposed NN scheme shows very high accuracy in predicting damage location and severity. The high detection performance, combined with the simple computation structure and high learning efficiency, could lead to a promising real-time damage detection system.

6. Conclusions

The conclusions drawn from the above analyses are described in this section. From the analysis of the vibration characteristics a clear-cut deviation of the mode shapes and natural frequencies has been observed for the cracked and uncracked shaft. Comparisons of results from neural network method and theoretical and experimental analysis have been carried out and they show a very good agreement. This method can be utilized for condition monitoring of cracked vibrating structures, and, in future, hybrid techniques can be developed for fault identification in damaged vibrating structures.

Appendix

$$Q =$$

$$\begin{bmatrix}
1 & 0 & 1 & 0 & 0 & 0 & 0 & 0 & 0 & 0 & 0 & 0 \\
0 & 1 & 0 & 1 & 0 & 0 & 0 & 0 & 0 & 0 & 0 & 0 \\
0 & 0 & 0 & 0 & G_3 & G_4 & -G_7 & -G_8 & 0 & 0 & 0 & 0 \\
0 & 0 & 0 & 0 & G_4 & G_3 & G_8 & -G_7 & 0 & 0 & 0 & 0 \\
G_1 & G_2 & -G_5 & -G_6 & -G_1 & -G_2 & G_5 & G_6 & 0 & 0 & 0 & 0 \\
G_2 & G_1 & G_6 & -G_5 & -G_2 & -G_1 & -G_6 & G_5 & 0 & 0 & 0 & 0 \\
G_1 & G_2 & G_5 & G_6 & -G_1 & -G_2 & -G_5 & -G_6 & 0 & 0 & 0 & 0 \\
S_1 & S_2 & S_3 & S_4 & -G_2 & -G_1 & G_6 & -G_5 & S_5 & S_6 & S_7 & S_8 \\
0 & 0 & 0 & 0 & 0 & 0 & 0 & 0 & 1 & 0 & 0 & 0 \\
0 & 0 & 0 & 0 & 0 & 0 & 0 & 0 & 0 & 0 & -T_8 & T_7 \\
0 & 0 & 0 & 0 & 0 & 0 & 0 & 0 & -T_6 & T_5 & T_6 & -T_5 \\
S_9 & S_{10} & S_{11} & S_{12} & S_{13} & S_{14} & S_{15} & S_{16} & S_{17} & S_{18} & -T_5 & -T_6
\end{bmatrix},$$

(A.1)

where

$$S_1 = G_2 + N_3 \overline{H}_V G_1, \qquad S_2 = G_1 + N_3 \overline{H}_V G_2,$$

$$S_3 = -G_6 - N_3 \overline{H}_V G_5, \qquad S_4 = G_5 - N_3 \overline{H}_V G_6,$$

$$S_5 = \frac{N_{34}}{\overline{H}_V} T_5, \qquad S_6 = \frac{N_{34}}{\overline{H}_V} T_6, \qquad S_7 = \frac{-N_{34}}{\overline{H}_V} T_5,$$

$$S_8 = \frac{-N_{34}}{\overline{H}_V} T_6, \qquad S_9 = N_{12} \overline{H}_V G_2, \qquad S_{10} = N_{12} \overline{H}_V G_1,$$

$$S_{11} = -N_{12} \overline{H}_V G_6, \qquad S_{12} = N_{12} \overline{H}_V G_5,$$

$$S_{13} = -N_{12} \overline{H}_V G_2, \qquad S_{14} = -N_{12} \overline{H}_V G_1,$$

$$S_{15} = N_{12} \overline{H}_V G_6, \qquad S_{16} = -N_{12} \overline{H}_V G_5,$$

$$S_{17} = T_5 - N_1 \overline{H}_S T_6, \qquad S_{18} = T_6 + 6 N_1 \overline{H}_S T_5,$$

$$G_1 = \text{Cosh}\left(\overline{H}_V \alpha\right), \qquad G_2 = \text{Sinh}\left(\overline{H}_V \alpha\right),$$

$$G_3 = \text{Cosh}\left(\overline{H}_V\right), \qquad G_4 = \text{Sinh}\left(\overline{H}_V\right),$$

$$G_5 = \text{Cos}\left(\overline{H}_V \alpha\right), \qquad G_6 = \text{Sin}\left(\overline{H}_V \alpha\right),$$

$$G_7 = \text{Cosh}\left(\overline{H}_V\right), \qquad G_8 = \text{Sin}\left(\overline{H}_V\right),$$

$$T_5 = \text{Sin}\left(\overline{H}_S \alpha\right), \qquad T_6 = \text{Sin}\left(\overline{H}_S \alpha\right),$$

$$T_7 = \text{Cos}\left(\overline{H}_S\right), \qquad T_8 = \text{Sin}\left(\overline{H}_S\right),$$

$$N_{12} = \frac{N_1}{N_2}, \qquad N_{34} = \frac{N_3}{N_4}.$$

(A.2)

References

[1] R. D. Adams, D. Walton, J. E. Flitcroft, and D. Short, "Composite Reliability, Philadelphia: American Society for Testing Materials," Vibration testing as a nondestructive test tool for composite materials, ASTM STP 580, pp.159–175, 1975.

[2] H. Tada, P. C. Paris, and G. R. Irwin, *The Stress Analysis of Cracks Hand Book*, Del Research, Hellertown, Pennsylvania, 1973.

[3] A. S. Sekhar and B. S. Prabhu, "Crack detection and vibration characteristics of cracked shafts," *Journal of Sound and Vibration*, vol. 157, no. 2, pp. 375–381, 1992.

[4] G. Paviglianiti, F. Pierri, F. Caccavale, and M. Mattei, "Robust fault detection and isolation for proprioceptive sensors of robot manipulators," *Mechatronics*, vol. 20, no. 1, pp. 162–170, 2010.

[5] R. K. Behera, D. R. K. Parhi, and S. K. Sahu, "Vibration analysis of a cracked rotor surrounded by viscous liquid," *JVC/Journal of Vibration and Control*, vol. 12, no. 5, pp. 465–494, 2006.

[6] K. Wang, D. J. Inman, and C. R. Farrar, "Modeling and analysis of a cracked composite cantilever beam vibrating in coupled bending and torsion," *Journal of Sound and Vibration*, vol. 284, no. 1-2, pp. 23–49, 2005.

[7] J. H. Lee, "Identification of multiple cracks in a beam using natural frequencies," *Journal of Sound and Vibration*, vol. 320, no. 3, pp. 482–490, 2009.

[8] M. Sahin and R. A. Shenoi, "Quantification and localisation of damage in beam-like structures by using artificial neural networks with experimental validation," *Engineering Structures*, vol. 25, no. 14, pp. 1785–1802, 2003.

[9] B. Sahoo and D. Maity, "Damage assessment of structures using hybrid neuro-genetic algorithm," *Applied Soft Computing Journal*, vol. 7, no. 1, pp. 89–104, 2007.

[10] S. Suresh, S. N. Omkar, R. Ganguli, and V. Mani, "Identification of crack location and depth in a cantilever beam using a modular neural network approach," *Smart Materials and Structures*, vol. 13, no. 4, pp. 907–915, 2004.

[11] S. Haykin and Neural Networks, *A Comprehensive Foundation*, Pearson Education, 2006.

19

Dynamical Behavior in a Four-Dimensional Neural Network Model with Delay

Changjin Xu[1] and Peiluan Li[2]

[1] *Guizhou Key Laboratory of Economics System Simulation, School of Mathematics and Statistics,*
  Guizhou College of Finance and Economics, Guiyang 550004, China
[2] *Department of Mathematics and Statistics, Henan University of Science and Technology, Luoyang 471003, China*

Correspondence should be addressed to Changjin Xu, xcj403@126.com

Academic Editor: Songcan Chen

A four-dimensional neural network model with delay is investigated. With the help of the theory of delay differential equation and Hopf bifurcation, the conditions of the equilibrium undergoing Hopf bifurcation are worked out by choosing the delay as parameter. Applying the normal form theory and the center manifold argument, we derive the explicit formulae for determining the properties of the bifurcating periodic solutions. Numerical simulations are performed to illustrate the analytical results.

1. Introduction

The interest in the periodic orbits of a delay neural networks has increased strongly in recent years and substantial efforts have been made in neural network models, for example, Wei and Zhang [1] studied the stability and bifurcation of a class of n-dimensional neural networks with delays, Guo and Huang [2] investigated the Hopf bifurcation behavior of a ring of neurons with delays, Yan [3] discussed the stability and bifurcation of a delayed trineuron network model, Haji-hosseini et al. [4] made a discussion on the Hopf bifurcation of a delayed recurrent neural network in the frequency domain, and Liao et al. [5] did a theoretical and empirical investigation of a two-neuron system with distributed delays in the frequency domain. For more information, one can see [6–23]. In 1986 and 1987, Babcock and Westervelt [24, 25] had analyzed the stability and dynamics of the following simple neural network model of two neurons with inertial coupling:

$$\frac{dx_1}{dt} = x_3,$$

$$\frac{dx_2}{dt} = x_4,$$

$$\frac{dx_3}{dt} = -2\xi x_3 - x_1 + A_2 \tanh(x_2),$$

$$\frac{dx_4}{dt} = -2\xi x_4 - x_2 + A_1 \tanh(x_1),$$

$$(1)$$

where x_i $(i = 1, 2)$ denotes the input voltage of the ith neuron, x_j $(j = 3, 4)$ is the output of the jth neuron, $\xi > 0$ is the damping factor and A_i $(i = 1, 2)$ is the overall gain of the neuron which determines the strength of the nonlinearity. For a more detailed interpretation of the parameters, one can see [24, 25]. In 1997, Lin and Li [26] made a detailed investigation on the bifurcation direction of periodic solution for system (1).

Considering that there exists a time delay (we assume that it is τ) in the response of the output voltages to changes in the input, then system (1) can be revised as follows:

$$\frac{dx_1}{dt} = x_3,$$

$$\frac{dx_2}{dt} = x_4,$$

$$\frac{dx_3}{dt} = -2\xi x_3 - x_1 + A_2 \tanh(x_2(t - \tau)),$$

$$\frac{dx_4}{dt} = -2\xi x_4 - x_2 + A_1 \tanh(x_1(t - \tau)).$$

$$(2)$$

As is known to us that the research on the Hopf bifurcation, especially on the stability of bifurcating periodic solutions and direction of Hopf bifurcation is very critical. When delays are incorporated into the network models, stability, and Hopf bifurcation analysis become much complex. To obtain a deep and clear understanding of dynamics of neural network model with delays, we will make a investigation on system (2), that is, we study the stability, the local Hopf bifurcation for system (2).

The remainder of the paper is organized as follows. In Section 2, local stability for the equilibrium state of system (2) is discussed. We investigate the existence of the Hopf bifurcations for system (2) choosing time delay as the bifurcation parameter. In Section 3, the direction and stability of the local Hopf bifurcation are analyzed by using the normal form theory and the center manifold theorem by Hassard et al. [27]. In Section 4, numerical simulations for justifying the theoretical results are illustrated.

2. Stability of the Equilibrium and Local Hopf Bifurcations

The object of this section is to investigate the stability of the equilibrium and the existence of local Hopf bifurcations for system (2). It is easy to see that if the following condition:

(H1) $A_1A_2 < 1$

holds, then (2) has a unique equilibrium $E(0,0,0,0)$. To investigate the local stability of the equilibrium state we linearize system (2). We expand it in a Taylor series around the orgin and neglect the terms of higher order than the first order. The linearization of (2) near $E(0,0,0,0)$ can be expressed as:

$$\frac{dx_1}{dt} = x_3,$$

$$\frac{dx_2}{dt} = x_4,$$

$$\frac{dx_3}{dt} = -x_1 - 2\xi x_3 + A_2 x_2(t - \tau),$$

$$\frac{dx_4}{dt} = -x_2 - 2\xi x_4 + A_1 x_1(t - \tau),$$

(3)

whose characteristic equation has the form

$$\det\begin{pmatrix} \lambda & 0 & -1 & 0 \\ 0 & \lambda & 0 & -1 \\ 1 & -A_2 e^{-\lambda\tau} & \lambda + 2\xi & 0 \\ -A_1 e^{-\lambda\tau} & 1 & 0 & \lambda + 2\xi \end{pmatrix} = 0,$$

(4)

namely,

$$\lambda^4 + 4\xi\lambda^3 + (4\xi^2 + 2)\lambda^2 + 4\xi\lambda + 1 - A_1 A_2 e^{-2\lambda\tau} = 0.$$

(5)

In order to investigate the distribution of roots of the transcendental equation (5), the following Lemma is necessary.

Lemma 1 (see [28]). *For the transcendental equation:*

$$P\left(\lambda, e^{-\lambda\tau_1}, \ldots, e^{-\lambda\tau_m}\right)$$

$$= \lambda^n + p_1^{(0)}\lambda^{n-1} + \cdots + p_{n-1}^{(0)}\lambda + p_n^{(0)}$$

$$+ \left[p_1^{(1)}\lambda^{n-1} + \cdots + p_{n-1}^{(1)}\lambda + p_n^{(1)}\right]e^{-\lambda\tau_1} + \cdots$$

$$+ \left[p_1^{(m)}\lambda^{n-1} + \cdots + p_{n-1}^{(m)}\lambda + p_n^{(m)}\right]e^{-\lambda\tau_m} = 0,$$

(6)

as $(\tau_1, \tau_2, \tau_3, \ldots, \tau_m)$ vary, the sum of orders of the zeros of $P(\lambda, e^{-\lambda\tau_1}, \ldots, e^{-\lambda\tau_m})$ in the open right half plane can change, and only a zero appears on or crosses the imaginary axis.

For $\tau = 0$, (5) becomes

$$\lambda^4 + 4\xi\lambda^3 + (4\xi^2 + 2)\lambda^2 + 4\xi\lambda + 1 - A_1A_2 = 0.$$

(7)

In view of the Routh-Hurwitz criteria, we know that all roots of (7) have a negative real part if the following condition:

(H2) $4\xi^2 + A_1A_2 > 0$

is satisfied.

For $\omega > 0$, $i\omega$ is a root of (5) if and only if

$$\omega^4 - 4\xi\omega^2 i - (4\xi^2 + 2)\omega^2 + 4\xi\omega i + 1$$

$$- A_1A_2(\cos 2\omega\tau - i\sin 2\omega\tau) = 0.$$

(8)

Separating the real and imaginary parts gives

$$A_1A_2 \cos 2\omega\tau = \omega^4 - (4\xi^2 + 2)\omega^2 + 1,$$

$$A_1A_2 \sin 2\omega\tau = 4\xi\omega^2 - 4\xi\omega.$$

(9)

It follows from (9) that

$$\left[\omega^4 - (4\xi^2 + 2)\omega^2 + 1\right]^2 + \left[4\xi\omega^2 - 4\xi\omega\right]^2 = A_1^2A_2^2,$$

(10)

which is equivalent to

$$\omega^8 + m_1\omega^6 + m_2\omega^4 + m_3\omega^3 + m_4\omega^2 + m_5 = 0,$$

(11)

where

$$m_1 = -4(2\xi^2 + 1), \quad m_2 = 16\xi^4 + 32\xi^2 + 6,$$

$$m_3 = -32\xi^2, \quad m_4 = 8\xi^2 - 4, \quad m_5 = 1 - A_1^2A_2^2.$$

(12)

Without loss of generality, we assume that (11) has eight positive roots, denoted by $\omega_k(k = 1, 2, 3, \ldots, 8)$. Then by (9), we derive

$$\tau_k^{(j)} = \frac{1}{2\omega_k}\left\{\arccos\left[\frac{\omega^4 - (4\xi^2 + 2)\omega^2 + 1}{A_1A_2}\right] + 2j\pi\right\},$$

(13)

where $k = 1, 2, 3, \ldots, 8$; $j = 0, 1, \ldots$, then $\pm i\omega_k$ are a pair of purely imaginary roots of (5) when $\tau = \tau_k^{(j)}$. Define

$$\tau_0 = \tau_{k_0}^{(0)} = \min_{k \in \{1,2,3,\ldots,8\}}\left\{\tau_k^{(0)}\right\}.$$

(14)

The above analysis leads to the Lemma as follows.

Lemma 2. *If* (H1) *and* (H2) *hold, then all roots of* (5) *have a negative real part when* $\tau \in [0, \tau_0)$ *and* (5) *admits a pair of purely imaginary roots* $\pm\omega_k$ *when* $\tau = \tau_k^{(j)}(k = 1, 2, 3, \ldots, 8; \ j = 0, 1, 2, \ldots)$.

Let $\lambda(\tau) = \alpha(\tau) + i\omega(\tau)$ be a root of (5) near $\tau = \tau_k^{(j)}$, and $\alpha(\tau_k^{(j)}) = 0$, and $\omega(\tau_k^{(j)}) = \omega_k$. Due to functional differential equation theory, for every $\tau_k^{(j)}, k = 1, 2, \ldots, 8; \ j = 0, 1, 2, \ldots$, there exists $\varepsilon > 0$ such that $\lambda(\tau)$ is continuously differentiable in τ for $|\tau - \tau_k^{(j)}| < \varepsilon$. Substituting $\lambda(\tau)$ into the left hand side of (5) and taking derivative with respect to τ, we have

$$\left[\frac{d\lambda}{d\tau}\right]^{-1} = \frac{2\lambda^3 + 6\xi\lambda^2 + 2(2\xi^2 + 1)\lambda + 2\xi}{\lambda A_1 A_2 e^{-2\lambda\tau}} - \frac{\tau}{\lambda}. \quad (15)$$

Then

$$\left[\frac{d(\mathrm{Re}\,\lambda(\tau))}{d\tau}\right]^{-1}_{\tau = \tau_k^{(j)}}$$

$$= \mathrm{Re}\left\{\frac{2\lambda^3 + 6\xi\lambda^2 + 2(2\xi^2 + 1)\lambda + 2\xi}{\lambda A_1 A_2 e^{-2\lambda\tau}}\right\}_{\tau = \tau_k^{(j)}}$$

$$= \mathrm{Re}\left\{\frac{2\xi - 6\xi\omega_k^2 + \left(4\xi^2\omega_k + 2\omega_k - 2\omega_k^3\right)i}{A_1 A_2 \omega_k \sin 2\omega_k\tau_k^{(j)} + iA_1 A_2 \omega_k \cos 2\omega_k\tau_k^{(j)}}\right\}$$

$$= \frac{1}{A_1^2 A_2^2 \omega_k^2}\left\{\left(2\xi - 6\xi\omega_k^2\right)A_1 A_2 \omega_k \sin 2\omega_k\tau_k^{(j)}\right.$$

$$\left. - \left(4\xi^2\omega_k + 2\omega_k - 2\omega_k^3\right)A_1 A_2 \omega_k \cos 2\omega_k\tau_k^{(j)}\right\}$$

$$= \frac{1}{A_1^2 A_2^2 \omega_k^2}\left\{\left(2\xi - 6\xi\omega_k^2\right)\omega_k\left(4\xi\omega_k^2 - 4\xi\omega_k\right)\right.$$

$$- \left(4\xi^2\omega_k + 2\omega_k - 2\omega_k^3\right)\omega_k$$

$$\left. \times\left[\omega_k^4 - (4\xi^2 + 2)\omega_k^2 + 1\right]\right\}$$

$$= \frac{2\Lambda}{A_1^2 A_2^2}, \quad (16)$$

where

$$\Lambda = 4\omega_k^6 - 3(2\xi^2 + 1)\omega_k^4 - 12\xi\omega_k^3$$

$$+ (8\xi^4 + 8\xi^2 + 12\xi + 3)\omega_k^2 \quad (17)$$

$$+ 4\xi^2\omega_k - (6\xi^2 + 1).$$

We assume that the following condition holds:

(H3) $\Lambda \neq 0$.

According to above analysis and the results of Kuang [29] and Hale [30], we have the following theorem

Theorem 3. *If* (H1) *and* (H2) *hold, then the equilibrium $E(0, 0, 0, 0)$ of system* (2) *is asymptotically stable for* $\tau \in [0, \tau_0)$. *Under the conditions* (H1) *and* (H2), *if the condition* (H3)

holds, then system (2) undergoes a Hopf bifurcation at the equilibrium $E(0, 0, 0, 0)$ when $\tau = \tau_k^{(j)}$, $k = 1, 2, 3, \ldots, 8; \ j = 0, 1, 2, \ldots$.

3. Direction and Stability of the Hopf Bifurcation

In this section, we discuss the direction, stability and the period of the bifurcating periodic solutions. The used methods are based on the normal form theory and the center manifold theorem introduced by Hassard et al. [27]. From the previous section, we know that if $\tau = \tau_k^{(j)}$, $k = 1, 2, 3 \ldots, 8; \ j = 0, 1, 2, \ldots$, any root of (5) of the form $\lambda(\tau) = \alpha(\tau) + i\omega(\tau)$ satisfies $\alpha(\tau_k^{(j)}) = 0$, $\omega(\tau_k^{(j)}) = \omega_k$ and $d\alpha(\tau)/d\tau|_{\tau = \tau_k^{(j)}} \neq 0$.

For convenience, let $\bar{x}_i(t) = x_i(\tau t)$ $(i = 1, 2, 3, 4)$ and $\tau = \tau_k^{(j)} + \mu$, where $\tau_k^{(j)}$ is defined by (13) and $\mu \in R$, drop the bar for the simplification of notations, then system (3) can be written as an FDE in $C = C([-1, 0], R^4)$ as

$$\dot{u}(t) = L_\mu(u_t) + F(\mu, u_t), \quad (18)$$

where $u(t) = (x_1(t), x_2(t), x_3(t), x_4(t))^T \in C$ and $u_t(\theta) = u(t + \theta) = (x_1(t + \theta), x_2(t + \theta), x_3(t + \theta), x_4(t + \theta))^T \in C$, and $L_\mu : C \to R$, $F : R \times C \to R$ are given by

$$L_\mu\phi = \left(\tau_k^{(j)} + \mu\right)\begin{pmatrix} 0 & 0 & 1 & 0 \\ 0 & 0 & 0 & 1 \\ -1 & 0 & -2\xi & 0 \\ 0 & 0 & -1 & -2\xi \end{pmatrix}\begin{pmatrix} \phi_1(0) \\ \phi_2(0) \\ \phi_3(0) \\ \phi_4(0) \end{pmatrix}$$

$$+ \left(\tau_k^{(j)} + \mu\right)\begin{pmatrix} 0 & 0 & 0 & 0 \\ 0 & 0 & 0 & 0 \\ 0 & A_2 & 0 & 0 \\ A_1 & 0 & 0 & 0 \end{pmatrix}\begin{pmatrix} \phi_1(-1) \\ \phi_2(-1) \\ \phi_3(-1) \\ \phi_4(-1) \end{pmatrix}, \quad (19)$$

$$f(\mu, \phi) = \left(\tau_k^{(j)} + \mu\right)\begin{pmatrix} 0 \\ 0 \\ A_2\phi_2^3(-1) + \text{h.o.t.} \\ A_1\phi_1^3(-1) + \text{h.o.t.} \end{pmatrix},$$

respectively, where $\phi(\theta) = (\phi_1(\theta), \phi_2(\theta), \phi_3(\theta), \phi_4(\theta))^T \in C$.

From the discussion in Section 2, we know that if $\mu = 0$, then system (18) undergoes a Hopf bifurcation at the equilibrium $E(0, 0, 0, 0)$ and the associated characteristic equation of system (18) has a pair of simple imaginary roots $\pm\omega_k\tau_k^{(j)}$.

By the representation theorem, there is a matrix function with bounded variation components $\eta(\theta, \mu)$, $\theta \in [-1, 0]$ such that

$$L_\mu\phi = \int_{-1}^{0} d\eta(\theta, \mu)\phi(\theta) \quad \text{for } \phi \in C. \quad (20)$$

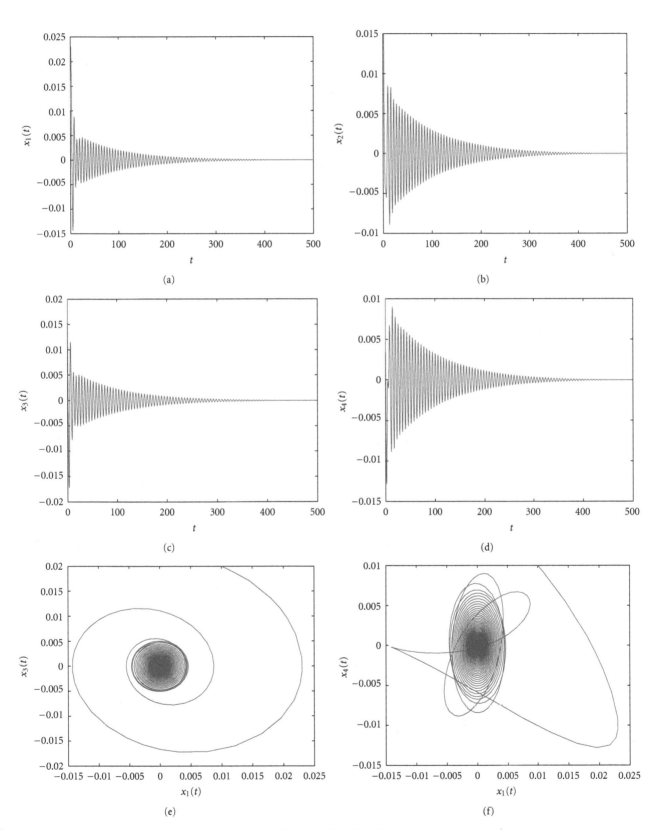

FIGURE 1: Continued.

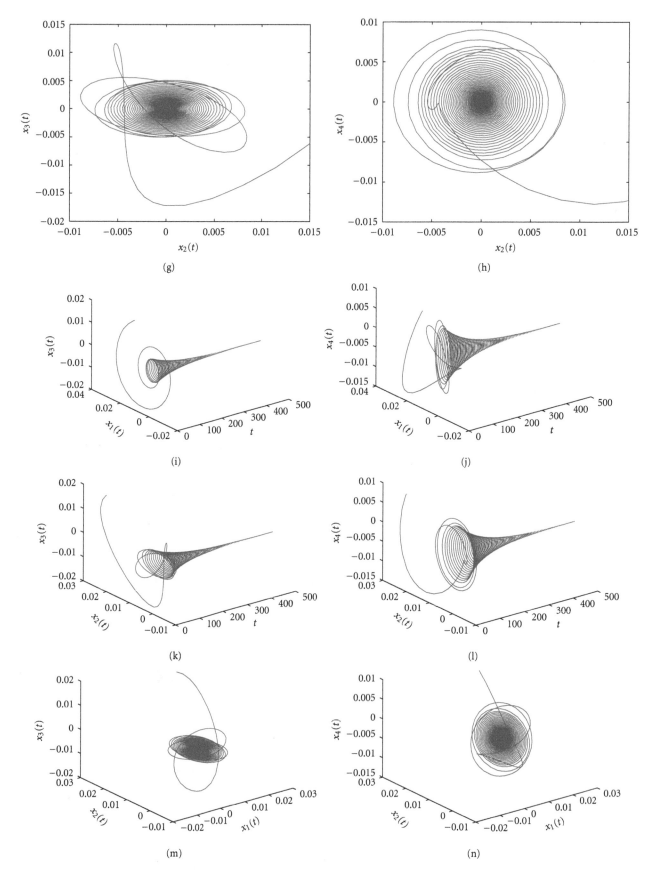

FIGURE 1: Continued.

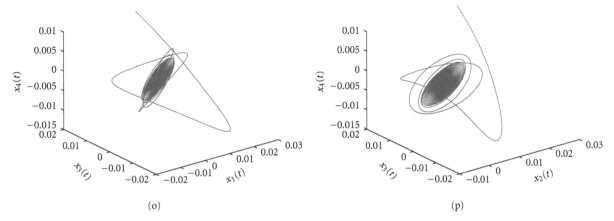

(o)   (p)

FIGURE 1: (a)–(p) The dynamical behavior of system (37) with $\tau = 0.7 < \tau_0 \approx 0.9$ and the initial value $(0.01, 0.02, 0.02, 0.01)$. The equilibrium $E_0(0,0,0,0)$ is asymptotically stable.

In fact, we can choose

$$\eta(\theta, \mu) = \left(\tau_k^{(j)} + \mu\right) \begin{pmatrix} 0 & 0 & 1 & 0 \\ 0 & 0 & 0 & 1 \\ -1 & 0 & -2\xi & 0 \\ 0 & -1 & 0 & -2\xi \end{pmatrix} \delta(\theta)$$

$$- \left(\tau_k^{(j)} + \mu\right) \begin{pmatrix} 0 & 0 & 0 & 0 \\ 0 & 0 & 0 & 0 \\ 0 & A_2 & 0 & 0 \\ A_1 & 0 & 0 & 0 \end{pmatrix} \delta(\theta + 1),$$

(21)

where δ is the Dirac delta function.

For $\phi \in C([-1, 0], R^4)$, define

$$A(\mu)\phi = \begin{cases} \dfrac{d\phi(\theta)}{d\theta}, & -1 \le \theta < 0, \\ \displaystyle\int_{-1}^{0} d\eta(s, \mu)\phi(s), & \theta = 0, \end{cases}$$

(22)

$$R\phi = \begin{cases} 0, & -1 \le \theta < 0, \\ f(\mu, \phi), & \theta = 0. \end{cases}$$

Then (18) is equivalent to the abstract differential equation

$$\dot{u}_t = A(\mu)u_t + R(\mu)u_t,$$

(23)

where $u_t(\theta) = u(t + \theta)$, $\theta \in [-1, 0]$. For $\psi \in C([0, 1], (R^4)^*)$, define

$$A^*\psi(s) = \begin{cases} -\dfrac{d\psi(s)}{ds}, & s \in (0, 1], \\ \displaystyle\int_{-1}^{0} d\eta^T(t, 0)\psi(-t), & s = 0. \end{cases}$$

(24)

For $\phi \in C([-1, 0], R^4)$ and $\psi \in C([0, 1], (R^4)^*)$, define bilinear form

$$\langle \psi, \phi \rangle = \overline{\psi}(0)\phi(0) - \int_{-1}^{0} \int_{\xi=0}^{\theta} \psi^T(\xi - \theta) d\eta(\theta)\phi(\xi) d\xi,$$

(25)

where $\eta(\theta) = \eta(\theta, 0)$, the $A = A(0)$ and A^* are adjoint operators. By the discussions in Section 2, we know that $\pm i\omega_k \tau_k^{(j)}$ are eigenvalues of $A(0)$, and they are also eigenvalues of A^* corresponding to $i\omega_k \tau_k^{(j)}$ and $-i\omega_k \tau_k^{(j)}$ respectively. By direct computation, we can obtain

$$q(\theta) = (1, \alpha, \beta, \gamma)^T e^{i\omega_k \tau_k^{(j)} \theta},$$

$$q^*(s) = D(1, \alpha^*, \beta^*, \gamma^*) e^{i\omega_k \tau_k^{(j)} s},$$

(26)

where

$$\alpha = \frac{1 - \omega_k^2 + 2\xi\omega_k i}{A_2 e^{-i\omega_k \tau_k^{(j)}}}, \qquad \beta = i\omega_k,$$

$$\gamma = \frac{i\omega_k\left(1 - \omega_k^2 + 2\xi\omega_k i\right)}{A_2 e^{-i\omega_k \tau_k^{(j)}}}, \qquad \alpha^* = \frac{1 - \omega_k^2 - 2\xi\omega_k i}{A_1 e^{-i\omega_k \tau_k^{(j)}}},$$

$$\beta^* = \frac{1}{2\xi - i\omega_k}, \qquad \gamma^* = \frac{1 - \omega_k^2 - 2\xi\omega_k i}{A_1 e^{-i\omega_k \tau_k^{(j)}}(2\xi - i\omega_k)},$$

$$D = \frac{1}{1 + \overline{\alpha}\alpha^* + \overline{\beta}\beta^* + \overline{\gamma}\gamma^* + \tau_k^{(j)}(A_1\gamma^* + A_2\beta^*\overline{\alpha})e^{i\omega_k \tau_k^{(j)}}}.$$

(27)

Furthermore, $\langle q^*(s), q(\theta) \rangle = 1$ and $\langle q^*(s), \overline{q}(\theta) \rangle = 0$.

Next, we use the same notations as those in Hassard et al. [27] and we first compute the coordinates to describe the center manifold C_0 at $\mu = 0$. Let u_t be the solution of (18) when $\mu = 0$.

Define

$$z(t) = \langle q^*, u_t \rangle, \qquad W(t, \theta) = u_t(\theta) - 2\,\mathrm{Re}\{z(t)q(\theta)\},$$

(28)

on the center manifold C_0, and we have

$$W(t, \theta) = W(z(t), \overline{z}(t), \theta),$$

(29)

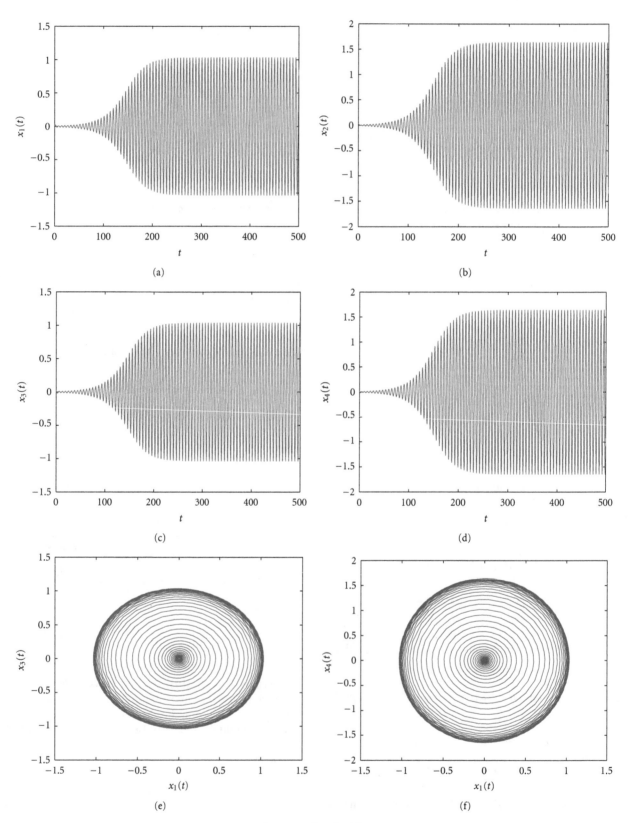

FIGURE 2: Continued.

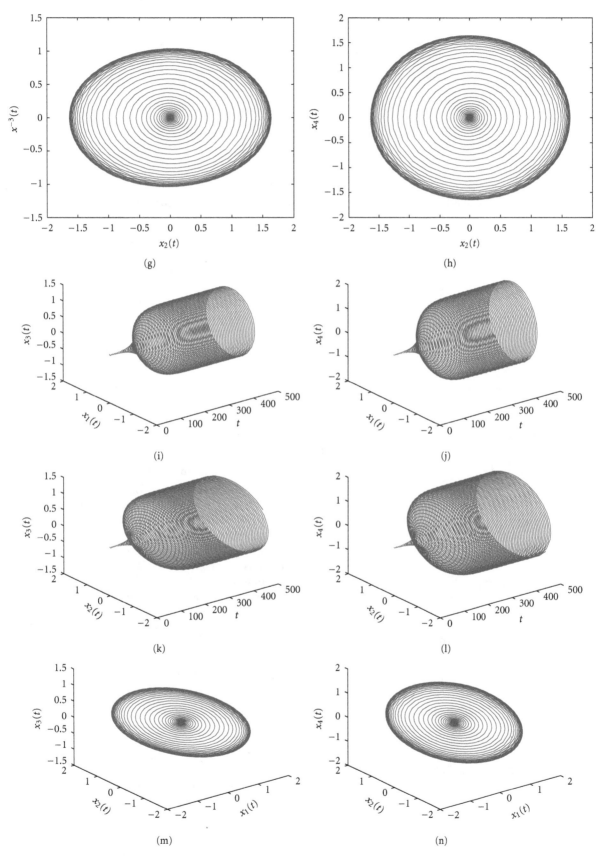

FIGURE 2: Continued.

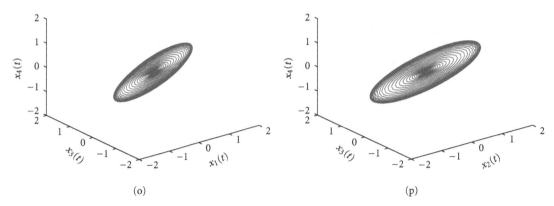

FIGURE 2: (a)–(p) The dynamical behavior of system (37) with $\tau = 1.5 > \tau_0 \approx 0.9$ and the initial value $(0.01, 0.02, 0.02, 0.01)$. Hopf bifurcation occurs from the equilibrium $E_0(0, 0, 0, 0)$.

where

$$W(z(t), \overline{z}(t), \theta) = W(z, \overline{z})$$
$$= W_{20}\frac{z^2}{2} + W_{11}z\overline{z} + W_{02}\frac{\overline{z}^2}{2} + \cdots, \tag{30}$$

and z and $\overline{z}$ are local coordinates for center manifold C_0 in the direction of q^* and $\overline{q}^*$. Noting that W is also real if u_t is real, we consider only real solutions. For solutions $u_t \in C_0$ of (18),

$$\dot{z}(t) = i\omega_k\tau_k^{(j)}z + \overline{q}^*(\theta)f\left(0, W(z, \overline{z}, \theta) + 2\,\mathrm{Re}\{zq(\theta)\}\right) \tag{31}$$
$$\overset{\mathrm{def}}{=} i\omega_k\tau_k^{(j)}z + \overline{q}^*(0)f_0.$$

That is,

$$\dot{z}(t) = i\omega_k\tau_k^{(j)}z + g(z, \overline{z}), \tag{32}$$

where

$$g(z, \overline{z}) = g_{20}\frac{z^2}{2} + g_{11}z\overline{z} + g_{02}\frac{\overline{z}^2}{2} + g_{21}\frac{z^2\overline{z}}{2} + \cdots. \tag{33}$$

Hence we have

$$g(z, \overline{z}) = \overline{q}^*(0)f_0(z, \overline{z}) = \overline{q}^*(0)f(0, u_t)$$
$$= \tau_k^{(j)}\overline{D}\left(1, \overline{\alpha^*}, \overline{\beta^*}, \overline{\gamma^*}\right)\begin{pmatrix} 0 \\ 0 \\ A_2x_{2t}^3(-1) + \text{h.o.t.} \\ A_1x_{1t}^3(-1) + \text{h.o.t.} \end{pmatrix}$$
$$= \overline{D}\tau_k^{(j)}\left[3\beta^*e^{-i\omega_k\tau_k^{(j)}} + 3\gamma^*\alpha^2\overline{\alpha}e^{-2i\omega_k\tau_k^{(j)}}\right]z^2\overline{z} + \text{h.o.t.} \tag{34}$$

and we obtain

$$g_{20} = g_{11} = g_{02} = 0,$$
$$g_{21} = 2\overline{D}\tau_k^{(j)}\left[3\beta^*e^{-i\omega_k\tau_k^{(j)}} + 3\gamma^*\alpha^2\overline{\alpha}e^{-2i\omega_k\tau_k^{(j)}}\right]. \tag{35}$$

Therefore, we can compute the following values:

$$c_1(0) = \frac{i}{2\omega_k\tau_k^{(j)}}\left(g_{20}g_{11} - 2\left|g_{11}\right|^2 - \frac{\left|g_{02}\right|^2}{3}\right) + \frac{g_{21}}{2},$$
$$\mu_2 = -\frac{\mathrm{Re}\{c_1(0)\}}{\mathrm{Re}\left\{\lambda'\left(\tau_k^{(j)}\right)\right\}}, \tag{36}$$
$$\beta_2 = 2\,\mathrm{Re}(c_1(0)),$$
$$T_2 = -\frac{\mathrm{Im}\{c_1(0)\} + \mu_2\,\mathrm{Im}\left\{\lambda'\left(\tau_k^{(j)}\right)\right\}}{\omega_k\tau_k^{(j)}},$$

which determine the quantities of bifurcation periodic solutions on the center manifold at the critical value $\tau_k^{(j)}$ ($k = 1, 2, 3, \ldots, 8$; $j = 0, 1, 2, 3, \ldots$), μ_2 determines the direction of the Hopf bifurcation: If $\mu_2 > 0$ ($\mu_2 < 0$), then the Hopf bifurcation is supercritical (subcritical); β_2 determines the stability of the bifurcating periodic solutions: the periodic solutions are stable (unstable) if $\beta_2 < 0$ ($\beta_2 > 0$); and T_2 determines the period of the bifurcating periodic solutions: the period is increases (decreases) if $T_2 > 0$ ($T_2 < 0$).

4. Numerical Examples

To illustrate the analytical results found, let $\xi = 0.1$, $A_1 = 0.4$, $A_2 = 0.2$, then system (2) becomes

$$\frac{dx_1}{dt} = x_3,$$
$$\frac{dx_2}{dt} = x_4,$$
$$\frac{dx_3}{dt} = -0.2x_3 - x_1 + 0.2\tanh(x_2(t - \tau)), \tag{37}$$
$$\frac{dx_4}{dt} = -0.2x_4 - x_2 + 0.4\tanh(x_1(t - \tau)),$$

which has a unique equilibrium $E_0(0, 0, 0, 0)$ and satisfies the conditions indicated in Theorem 3. The equilibrium $E_0(0, 0, 0, 0)$ is asymptotically stable for $\tau = 0$. For $j = 0$, using the software Matlab, we derive $\omega_0 \approx 3.4233$, $\tau_0 \approx 0.9$, $\lambda'(\tau_0) \approx 0.2556 - 2.3588i$, $g_{21} \approx -0.2409 - 3.7451i$. Thus by the algorithm (36) derived in Section 3, we get $c_1(0) \approx -0.1205 - 1.8726i$, $\mu_2 \approx -0.4714$, $\beta_2 \approx -0.2410$, $T_2 \approx 0.9687$. Thus the equilibrium $E_0(0,0,0,0)$ is stable when $\tau < \tau_0 \approx 0.9$. Figures 1(a)–1(j) show that the equilibrium $E_0(0,0,0,0)$ is asymptotically stable when $\tau = 0.7 < \tau_0 \approx 0.9$. When τ passes through the critical value $\tau_0 \approx 0.9$, the equilibrium $E_0(0,0,0,0)$ loses its stability and a Hopf bifurcation occurs, that is, a family of periodic solutions bifurcate from the equilibrium $E_0(0,0,0,0)$. Since $\mu_2 > 0$ and $\beta_2 < 0$, the direction of the Hopf bifurcation is $\tau > \tau_0 \approx 0.9$, and these bifurcating periodic solutions from $E_0(0,0,0,0)$ at $\tau_0 \approx 0.9$ are stable. Figures 1(j)–2(d) suggest that Hopf bifurcation occurs from the equilibrium $E_0(0,0,0,0)$ when $\tau = 1.5 > \tau_0 \approx 0.9$.

Acknowledgments

This work is supported by National Natural Science Foundation of China (no. 60902044), the Doctoral Foundation of Guizhou College of Finance and Economics (2010), and the Science and Technology Program of Hunan Province (no. 2010FJ6021).

References

[1] J. Wei and C. Zhang, "Bifurcation analysis of a class of neural networks with delays," *Nonlinear Analysis: Real World Applications*, vol. 9, no. 5, pp. 2234–2252, 2008.

[2] S. Guo and L. Huang, "Hopf bifurcating periodic orbits in a ring of neurons with delays," *Physica D*, vol. 183, no. 1-2, pp. 19–44, 2003.

[3] X. P. Yan, "Hopf bifurcation and stability for a delayed tri-neuron network model," *Journal of Computational and Applied Mathematics*, vol. 196, no. 2, pp. 579–595, 2006.

[4] A. Hajihosseini, G. R. Rokni Lamooki, B. Beheshti, and F. Maleki, "The Hopf bifurcation analysis on a time-delayed recurrent neural network in the frequency domain," *Neurocomputing*, vol. 73, no. 4–6, pp. 991–1005, 2010.

[5] X. Liao, S. Li, and G. Chen, "Bifurcation analysis on a two-neuron system with distributed delays in the frequency domain," *Neural Networks*, vol. 17, no. 4, pp. 545–561, 2004.

[6] B. Zheng, Y. Zhang, and C. Zhang, "Global existence of periodic solutions on a simplified BAM neural network model with delays," *Chaos, Solitons and Fractals*, vol. 37, no. 5, pp. 1397–1408, 2008.

[7] S. Guo, X. Tang, and L. Huang, "Stability and bifurcation in a discrete system of two neurons with delays," *Nonlinear Analysis: Real World Applications*, vol. 9, no. 4, pp. 1323–1335, 2008.

[8] S. Guo, "Equivariant Hopf bifurcation for functional differential equations of mixed type," *Applied Mathematics Letters*, vol. 24, no. 5, pp. 724–730, 2011.

[9] J. Wei and C. Zhang, "Bifurcation analysis of a class of neural networks with delays," *Nonlinear Analysis: Real World Applications*, vol. 9, no. 5, pp. 2234–2252, 2008.

[10] J. Wei and M. Y. Li, "Global existence of periodic solutions in a tri-neuron network model with delays," *Physica D*, vol. 198, no. 1-2, pp. 106–119, 2004.

[11] S. Li, X. Liao, C. Li, and K. W. Wong, "Hopf bifurcation of a two-neuron network with different discrete time delays," *International Journal of Bifurcation and Chaos*, vol. 15, no. 5, pp. 1589–1601, 2005.

[12] W. Yu and J. Cao, "Stability and hopf bifurcation on a two-neuron system with time delay in the frequency domain," *International Journal of Bifurcation and Chaos*, vol. 17, no. 4, pp. 1355–1366, 2007.

[13] Y. Song, M. Han, and J. Wei, "Stability and Hopf bifurcation analysis on a simplified BAM neural network with delays," *Physica D*, vol. 200, no. 3-4, pp. 185–205, 2005.

[14] C. Zhang, B. Zheng, and L. Wang, "Multiple Hopf bifurcations of symmetric BAM neural network model with delay," *Applied Mathematics Letters*, vol. 22, no. 4, pp. 616–622, 2009.

[15] H. Zhao and L. Wang, "Hopf bifurcation in Cohen-Grossberg neural network with distributed delays," *Nonlinear Analysis: Real World Applications*, vol. 8, no. 1, pp. 73–89, 2007.

[16] C. Xu, X. Tang, and M. Liao, "Frequency domain analysis for bifurcation in a simplified tri-neuron BAM network model with two delays," *Neural Networks*, vol. 23, no. 7, pp. 872–880, 2010.

[17] C. Xu, X. Tang, and M. Liao, "Stability and bifurcation analysis of a six-neuron BAM neural network model with discrete delays," *Neurocomputing*, vol. 74, no. 5, pp. 689–707, 2011.

[18] W. Yu and J. Cao, "Stability and Hopf bifurcation analysis on a four-neuron BAM neural network with time delays," *Physics Letters A*, vol. 351, no. 1-2, pp. 64–78, 2006.

[19] P. D. Gupta, N. C. Majee, and A. B. Roy, "Stability, bifurcation and global existence of a Hopf-bifurcating periodic solution for a class of three-neuron delayed network models," *Nonlinear Analysis: Theory, Methods and Applications*, vol. 67, no. 10, pp. 2934–2954, 2007.

[20] R. Curtu, "Singular Hopf bifurcations and mixed-mode oscillations in a two-cell inhibitory neural network," *Physica D*, vol. 239, no. 9, pp. 504–514, 2010.

[21] H. Zhao, L. Wang, and C. Ma, "Hopf bifurcation and stability analysis on discrete-time Hopfield neural network with delay," *Nonlinear Analysis: Real World Applications*, vol. 9, no. 1, pp. 103–113, 2008.

[22] S. A. Campbell, S. Ruan, and J. Wei, "Qualitative analysis of a neural network model with multiple time delays," *International Journal of Bifurcation and Chaos*, vol. 9, no. 8, pp. 1585–1595, 1999.

[23] L. Olien and J. Bélair, "Bifurcations, stability, and monotonicity properties of a delayed neural network model," *Physica D*, vol. 102, no. 3-4, pp. 349–363, 1997.

[24] K. L. Babcock and R. M. Westervelt, "Dynamics of simple electronic neural networks," *Physica D*, vol. 28, no. 3, pp. 305–316, 1987.

[25] K. L. Babcock and R. M. Westervelt, "Stability and dynamics of simple electronic neural networks with added inertia," *Physica D*, vol. 23, no. 1–3, pp. 464–469, 1986.

[26] Y. P. Lin and J. B. Li, "The Hopf bifurcation direction of a four dimensional electronic neural network system," *System Science and Mathematical Sciences*, vol. 10, no. 4, pp. 337–343, 1997.

[27] B. Hassard, D. Kazarino, and Y. Wan, *Theory and Applications of Hopf Bifurcation*, Cambridge University Press, Cambridge, UK, 1981.

[28] S. Ruan and J. Wei, "On the zeros of transcendental functions with applications to stability of delay differential equations with two delays," *Dynamics of Continuous, Discrete and Impulsive Systems Series A: Mathematical Analysis*, vol. 10, no. 6, pp. 863–874, 2003.

[29] Y. Kuang, *Delay Differential Equations With Applications in Population Dynamics*, Academic Press, New York, NY, USA, 1993.

[30] J. Hale, *Theory of Functional Differential Equation*, Springer, New York, NY, USA, 1977.

20

Visualizing Clusters in Artificial Neural Networks Using Morse Theory

Paul T. Pearson

Department of Mathematics, Hope College, P.O. Box 9000, Holland, MI 49422-9000, USA

Correspondence should be addressed to Paul T. Pearson; pearsonp@hope.edu

Academic Editor: Songcan Chen

This paper develops a process whereby a high-dimensional clustering problem is solved using a neural network and a low-dimensional cluster diagram of the results is produced using the Mapper method from topological data analysis. The low-dimensional cluster diagram makes the neural network's solution to the high-dimensional clustering problem easy to visualize, interpret, and understand. As a case study, a clustering problem from a diabetes study is solved using a neural network. The clusters in this neural network are visualized using the Mapper method during several stages of the iterative process used to construct the neural network. The neural network and Mapper clustering diagram results for the diabetes study are validated by comparison to principal component analysis.

1. Introduction

Topological data analysis (TDA) is an emerging field of mathematics that focuses on constructing topological models for data and calculating algebraic invariants of such models [1–3]. The fundamental idea is to use methods from topology to determine shapes or patterns in high-dimensional data sets [4]. One method from TDA called Mapper constructs a low-dimensional topological model for a data set $X \subset \mathbb{R}^m$ from the clusters in the level sets of a function $h : X \rightarrow \mathbb{R}^n$ on the data set [5]. This topological model for X is a cluster diagram that shows the clusters in the level sets of h (i.e., clusters in the layers of a stratification of X) and how clusters in adjacent, overlapping level sets are connected (i.e., how the neighboring layers are glued together). The topological model built in this way is analogous to how Morse theory is used to construct a cell decomposition of a manifold using sublevel sets of a Morse function on the manifold [5–7]. The resolution of the cluster diagram produced by Mapper can be adjusted by changing the level sets by varying the number, size, and shape of the regions used to cover the image of the function h. Further, the Mapper method allows for different clustering algorithms to be used. The most important step for obtaining a useful topological model from Mapper is finding a function

$h : X \rightarrow \mathbb{R}^n$ that solves a particular clustering problem of interest for a data set X. This study examines the case when the function h is a neural network.

A feedforward, multilayer perceptron artificial neural network (hereafter called a neural network) is a function $f : \mathbb{R}^m \rightarrow \mathbb{R}^n$ constructed by an iterative process in order to approximate a training function $g : P \rightarrow T$ between two finite sets of points P and T called the inputs and target outputs, where $P \subseteq X \subset \mathbb{R}^m$ and $T \subset \mathbb{R}^n$. In a context where a target output value represents the classification of an input point, the neural network f is a solution to a classification or clustering problem because f has been trained to learn the rule of association of inputs with target outputs given by g. In this manner, many clustering problems for high dimensional data sets $X \subset \mathbb{R}^m$ have been solved by finding collections of points in the domain of f that have similar output values, which is to say that the level sets of a neural network are solutions to a clustering problem [8–12]. Although neural networks are adept at solving clustering problems, it is hard to visualize these clusters when the neural network's domain has dimension $m > 3$. To address this limitation, Mapper will be used to construct a low-dimensional, visualizable topological model that shows the clusters in the level sets of f as well as how clusters in neighboring level sets are connected. More generally, using Mapper to make a cluster diagram of the level sets of a neural network will provide a low-dimensional picture of the solution to a clustering problem that makes interpreting the neural network results much easier.

The research presented in this paper uses the Miller-Reaven diabetes study data [13, 14] as a case study for the method of using a neural network to solve a clustering problem and Mapper to visualize and interpret the results. A neural network is constructed that classifies patients of a diabetes study as overt diabetic, chemical diabetic, or not diabetic based on the results of five medical tests. The neural network is trained using the five medical tests as inputs and the diagnosis of diabetes type as the target output. At several intermediate stages of the weight update process during the construction of this neural network, the Mapper method is used to create a topological model of the level sets of the neural network at that stage of its formation. The results are compared to principal component analysis (PCA) as a means to validate the method. The general method presented in this paper for solving and visualizing clustering problems combines the efficacy of neural networks, which are nonlinear functions that have a proven track record for solving a wide variety of clustering problems whenever a training function is available [15], with the clarity and simplicity of the cluster diagrams produced by the Mapper method to make the neural network's solution to the clustering problem readily comprehensible.

The Mapper method has been used previously in the context of unsupervised learning by using functions such as density and eccentricity estimates to study diabetes data, breast cancer data, and RNA hairpin folding [4, 5, 16, 17]. Since neural networks employ supervised learning, using neural networks together with Mapper may provide more accurate and precise results than what could be attained by unsupervised learning on the same data. Other techniques for visualization of high-dimensional data sets such as projection pursuit, Isomap, locally linear embedding, and multidimensional scaling are discussed in relation to Mapper in [5]. Methods for visualizing the clusters in a neural network have been constructed by a variety of other dimension reduction techniques. Such techniques include linear and nonlinear projection methods [18], principal component analysis [19], Sammon's mapping [20], multidimensional scaling and nonlinear mapping networks [21], and fuzzy clustering [22]. These dimension reduction techniques produce useful two- and three-dimensional models of the data set and have varying degrees of success in solving specific real-world problems. Some of these constructions can be quite sensitive to the distance metric chosen, outliers in the data, or other factors.

This paper is organized as follows. In Section 2, background information on neural networks is given, followed by a description of the Mapper method from topological data analysis. Section 3 describes the Miller-Reaven diabetes study, principal component analysis, and the configuration of the neural network and Mapper algorithm used to analyze the diabetes data. Section 4 demonstrates the results of applying PCA and a neural network to the diabetes data and compares the PCA results to the cluster diagram for the neural network

produced using the Mapper method. Section 5 summarizes the main results of the case study, the general method of using neural networks to solve clustering problems, and the Mapper method to visualize the resulting clustering diagrams.

2. Background

This section provides a brief overview of neural networks and the Mapper method from topological data analysis.

2.1. Brief Description of Neural Networks. A neural network is function $f : \mathbb{R}^m \to \mathbb{R}^n$ constructed via an iterative process in order to approximate a training function $g : P \to T$ between two finite sets of points $P \subseteq X \subset \mathbb{R}^m$ and $T \subset \mathbb{R}^n$ called the inputs P (which is a subset of a data set X) and target outputs T. Neural networks are universal approximators in the sense that for every training function g, there exists a globally defined neural network f that approximates g to any desired degree of accuracy [23, 24]. Even though it is possible to find a neural network f that approximates g to any predetermined degree of accuracy, in practice such a neural network f could have a very large network architecture and be impractical. Thus, it is often desirable to find a moderately sized network architecture for f that approximates g to an acceptable degree of accuracy. This study will examine a neural network with one hidden layer of h_1 nodes. Such a neural network $f : \mathbb{R}^m \to \mathbb{R}^n$ has the form

$$f(x) = f_2 \left(W_2 \left(f_1 \left(W_1 x + b_1 \right) \right) + b_2 \right), \tag{1}$$

where $x \in \mathbb{R}^m$, W_1 is a $h_1 \times m$ weight matrix, W_2 is a $n \times h_1$ weight matrix, b_1 is a $h_1 \times 1$ bias vector, b_2 is a $n \times 1$ bias vector, and $f_i : \mathbb{R} \to \mathbb{R}$ denotes an activation function. For classification problems with multiple classes of data, it is common to choose $f_1(x) = \tanh(x) = (e^x - e^{-x})/(e^x + e^{-x})$ and $f_2(x) = x$ as activation functions. An activation function is evaluated on a vector by applying the function to each entry of the vector.

The iterative process for constructing a neural network $f : \mathbb{R}^m \to \mathbb{R}^n$ from a training function $g : P \to T$ begins by initializing the weights W_i and biases b_i with random values. Points $p \in P$ are sequentially presented to the neural network, and the weights W_i and the biases b_i are adjusted to minimize the error between $f(p)$ and $g(p)$. When a generalizable neural network is desired, only a subset of the points in P are used for adjusting its weights and biases, while the remaining points in P are used for cross-validation and/or testing to ensure that the neural network does not overlearn its training data. The weights and biases are adjusted by this iterative process until a tolerable level of error is reached for all points in P, or all points in the cross-validation set, or until a predetermined number of iterations is reached. The weights and biases can be adjusted by a variety of methods, including backpropagation via gradient descent, the conjugate gradient method, or the Levenberg-Marquardt method. When the conjugate gradient method or the Levenberg-Marquardt method is used, they generally construct a neural network f in very few iterations, but each iteration is more mathematically intensive and therefore more time intensive. In contrast, the backpropagation via gradient descent method generally requires many more iterations, but each iteration is very fast. Details of how the weight update process is used to construct a neural network from a training function can be found in the neural networks literature [10–12].

After a neural network has been constructed and has reached a tolerable level of error, its level sets can be used to solve a clustering or classification problem. In particular, for any connected region $Z \subset \mathbb{R}^n$, the level set $f^{-1}(Z)$ can be thought of as a set of points in the domain of f that all map to points in the same region Z. This means that these points in the domain have a classification values close to each other because they all lie in Z. Thus, a level set $f^{-1}(Z)$ can be viewed as a cluster (or clusters) of points that solve a classification problem.

2.2. Mapper. Given a function $h : X \rightarrow \mathbb{R}^n$ on a finite data set $X \subset \mathbb{R}^m$, the Mapper method from topological data analysis uses the level sets of h to construct a topological model that shows the clusters in the level sets X and how the clusters in adjacent, overlapping level sets intersect. The topological model is a simplicial complex, which is a topological space formed by gluing together vertices, edges, filled triangular faces, solid tetrahedra, and higher dimensional analogues of these convex polytopes according to a few rules about how the gluing is allowed to be done [25]. The Mapper method abstracts ideas from Morse theory, in which a smooth real-valued function $h : M \rightarrow \mathbb{R}$ on a manifold M is used to construct a cell decomposition of the manifold.

The Mapper method for a finite data set $X \subset \mathbb{R}^m$ and a real-valued function on that data set produces a one-dimensional topological model (i.e., a graph) for X as follows.

(1) Choose a real-valued function $h : X \rightarrow \mathbb{R}$ on the data set, a clustering algorithm (e.g., single-linkage clustering), and a positive integer ℓ for the number of level sets.

(2) Find the image (or range) of the function h. Let $m = \min\{h(x) \mid x \in X\}$ and $M = \max\{h(x) \mid x \in X\}$. The image of h is then a finite subset of the interval $[m, M]$.

(3) Cover the image of h by ℓ overlapping intervals $[a_1, b_1], [a_2, b_2], \ldots, [a_\ell, b_\ell]$, where $a_1 = m$, $b_\ell = M$, and $a_{i+1} < b_i$ for all $1 \le i < \ell$.

(4) Form the level sets $X_i = h^{-1}([a_i, b_i])$ for $1 \le i \le \ell$.

(5) Apply the clustering algorithm to each level set. Let $X_{i,j}$ be the jth cluster in the ith level set X_i.

(6) Construct a graph with one vertex $v_{i,j}$ for each cluster $X_{i,j}$.

(7) Construct an edge connecting vertices in $v_{i,j}$ and $v_{i+1,k}$, for all $1 \le i < \ell$ and all j and all k, whenever $X_{i,j} \cap X_{i+1,k} \ne \emptyset$. That is, an edge is constructed whenever a pair of clusters $X_{i,j}$ and $X_{i+1,k}$ from adjacent level sets X_i and X_{i+1} have nonempty intersection.

The resolution of the model changes from coarse to fine as the number of level sets ℓ increases. The amount of overlap between intervals $[a_i, b_i]$ and $[a_{i+1}, b_{i+1}]$ determines whether the level sets X_i and X_{i+1} will have nonempty intersection, which in turn determines the number of edges in the graph. When the intervals $[a_i, b_i]$ all have the same length R and the intersection of every pair of adjacent intervals also has the same length r, the percent overlap is said to be $(r/R)\%$.

More generally, for a function $h : X \rightarrow \mathbb{R}^n$, the Mapper method constructs a topological space called a simplicial complex, of which a graph is a one-dimensional example. In its full generality, the Mapper method applied to a function $h : X \rightarrow \mathbb{R}^n$ results in a simplicial complex with one vertex (or 0-simplex) for every cluster, one edge (or 1-simplex) connecting a pair of vertices whenever 2 clusters from neighboring level sets have nonempty intersection, one triangular face (or 2-simplex) filling the region enclosed by three edges whenever 3 clusters from neighboring level sets have nonempty intersection, one solid tetrahedron (or 3-simplex) filling the region enclosed by four triangles whenever 4 clusters from neighboring level sets have nonempty intersection, and so on. The level sets, and thus the simplicial complex, are determined by the size and shape of the regions used to cover the image of h. There are several common ways to cover bounded regions in $\mathbb{R}^n$, such as using rectangles, hexagons, or circular disks in $\mathbb{R}^2$ or boxes or spherical balls in $\mathbb{R}^3$, and different coverings of the image of h will result in different level sets and thus a different simplicial complex. More details on using the Mapper method to produce a simplicial complex from a function $h : X \rightarrow \mathbb{R}^n$ with $n > 1$ can be found in the paper by Singh et al. [5].

An example of the Mapper method is given in Figure 1. In this example, the data set $X \subset \mathbb{R}^2$ is a finite set of points randomly selected on an annulus and the function $h : X \rightarrow \mathbb{R}$ is the height projection $h(x, y) = y$. Single-linkage clustering was used on each of the $\ell = 3$ level sets $X_1 = h^{-1}([-2, 0])$, $X_2 = h^{-1}([-1, 1])$, and $X_3 = h^{-1}([0, 2])$ which arise from intervals $[-2, 0]$, $[-1, 1]$, and $[0, 2]$ with 50% overlap between neighboring intervals. The level set X_2 is a disjoint union of two sets $X_{2,1}$ and $X_{2,2}$ which have points with negative and positive x-coordinates, respectively. Using single-linkage clustering, each of the sets X_1, $X_{2,1}$, $X_{2,2}$, and X_3 produces one cluster and thus one vertex in the Mapper model, while each of the nonempty intersections $X_1 \cap X_{2,1}$, $X_1 \cap X_{2,2}$, $X_{2,1} \cap X_3$, and $X_{2,2} \cap X_3$ produces one edge in the Mapper model.

3. Methods

This section provides a description of the Miller-Reaven diabetes study data, how the data will be analyzed using PCA, the configuration of the neural network, and how the Mapper method will be used to visualize the results.

3.1. Case Study: The Miller-Reaven Diabetes Data. In [13, 14, 26], Reaven and Miller describe the results obtained by applying the projection pursuit method to data obtained from a diabetes study conducted at the Stanford Clinical Research Center. The diabetes study data consisted of the (1) relative weight, (2) fasting plasma glucose, (3) area under the

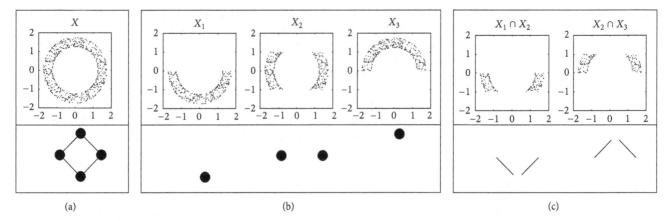

FIGURE 1: Illustration of the Mapper method applied points on an annulus with $h(x, y) = y$, single-linkage clustering, and $\ell = 3$ level sets. Top row: (a) the annular data set, (b) its level sets, and (c) intersections of adjacent, overlapping level sets. Bottom row: (a) the topological model produced by Mapper, (b) its vertices showing clusters in level sets, and (c) its edges showing adjacent level sets that intersect nontrivially.

plasma glucose curve for the three-hour glucose tolerance test (OGTT), (4) area under the plasma insulin curve for the OGTT, (5) and steady state plasma glucose response (SSPG) for 145 volunteers for a study of the etiology of diabetes [27]. The goal of the study was to determine the connection between this set of 5 variables and whether patients were classified as overt diabetic, chemical diabetic, or not diabetic. In the study, 33 patients were diagnosed as overt diabetic, 36 as chemical diabetic, and 76 as not diabetic on the basis of their oral glucose tolerance [13].

3.2. Principal Component Analysis. To establish a basis for comparison, the Miller-Reaven diabetes study data will be analyzed using principal component analysis (PCA) to project the data from $\mathbb{R}^5$ to $\mathbb{R}^3$. PCA is a variance maximizing projection of the data onto a set of orthonormal basis vectors [28–30]. As PCA is a linear projection, some of the lower variance content of the data will be lost when the dimensionality of the data is reduced. Also, since PCA identifies vectors along which the variance (or spread) of the data is greatest, it is sensitive to outliers.

3.3. Neural Networks and Mapper. The general method for analyzing the Miller-Reaven diabetes study data with a neural network and Mapper is as follows.

(1) Preprocess the data set and divide it into stratified training and testing sets. If necessary, preprocess the data to reduce noise.

(2) Use the training data to construct a neural network $h : \mathbb{R}^m \rightarrow \mathbb{R}$, meanwhile evaluating the error of the neural network on the testing set to prevent overlearning and overfitting.

(3) Apply the Mapper method (see Section 2.2) to the neural network function h to produce a diagram of the clusters formed by the neural network.

First, the Miller-Reaven diabetes study data were preprocessed by normalizing each of the five data inputs by finding z-scores. Since this normalization is an invertible affine transformation, it has no effect on the neural network's ability to solve the classification problem. The target output values for the neural network were set to -1 for overt diabetic, 0 for chemical diabetic, and 1 for not diabetic. A generalizable neural network was constructed by using 67% of the data for training and holding out 33% for testing, and these sets were stratified so that each class (overt, chemical, and not diabetic) appeared in the same proportion as in the entire data set. No extra measures were deemed necessary to denoise the Miller-Reaven data set before constructing a neural network.

Second, a feedforward, multilayer perceptron neural network was constructed with 5 input nodes, 4 hidden nodes, and 1 output node, and the method of backpropagation via gradient descent was used for weight updates. Many different numbers of hidden nodes were considered, and four hidden nodes were chosen by using mean square error on the training and testing sets as a criterion for determining whether a neural network underfits or overfits the data. The activation functions chosen were $f_1(x) = \tanh(x) = (e^x - e^{-x})/(e^x + e^{-x})$ and $f_2(x) = x$. The weights and biases in the neural network were initialized by random values between -0.5 and 0.5. This study emphasizes visualizing how the clusters in a neural network evolve during the weight update process. Thus, a learning rate of 0.1 was chosen to be small so that as the weights and biases were updated, changes in the topological model produced by Mapper could be observed. Neural network performance was evaluated after every cycle through the training data (i.e., epoch). The training data were the same (i.e., not reselected) from epoch to epoch, and they were presented to the neural network in random order to expedite learning [31]. The implementation of the neural network was written by the author in Matlab/Octave and used the standard backpropagation algorithm by stochastic gradient descent [10, Chapter 11].

Finally, the Mapper method (see Section 2.2) was applied to the neural network to produce a cluster diagram of the level sets in the neural network after several different stages of the weight update process during the formation of the neural

TABLE 1: Principal values and their percentages of the total variance in the Miller-Reaven data.

Variance in the five PCA directions				
Variance σ_i^2:	2886.6	868.2	330.6	84.4	0.0
Percent of total variance:	90.54	8.19	1.19	0.07	0.00

network. Using Mapper to visualize the clusters in the neural network as the neural network develops shows how the clusters in the neural network change as the training data is learned. Mapper was implemented in Matlab/Octave [32] and utilized GraphViz [33] to produce the graphs. The clustering algorithm used for Mapper was single-linkage clustering. The clusters in the level sets were viewed at different resolutions by varying the number of level sets and the amount of overlap between them. Decreasing the number of level sets can be used to reduce sensitivity to noise. The diagram of clusters in the neural network will be validated by visual comparison to the PCA results.

4. Results and Discussion

This section describes the results of analyzing the diabetes data using PCA and a neural network. Also, the PCA results are compared to the Mapper cluster diagrams for the neural network.

4.1. Results for Principal Component Analysis. The results of principal component analysis on the Miller-Reaven diabetes study data for dimension reduction from $\mathbb{R}^5$ to $\mathbb{R}^3$ are shown in Table 1 and Figure 2. The PCA results in $\mathbb{R}^3$ show that the data consists of a large central cluster of nondiabetic patients (red +), and that clusters of patients diagnosed as overt diabetic (blue ∘) or chemical diabetic (green ×) emanate away from the large central cluster in two different directions. The PCA results show that the classification problem is not entirely linearly separable in $\mathbb{R}^2$ by two lines, but it suggests that it may be possible to construct two planes in $\mathbb{R}^3$ (and thus also in $\mathbb{R}^5$) that separate the data into three categories with a small number of misclassified patients. The PCA results suggest that a neural network which uses a moderate number of separating hyperplanes (i.e., a neural network with one hidden layer and a moderate number of hidden nodes) might be able to solve this classification problem completely. The projections of the PCA results to $\mathbb{R}^2$ shown in Figure 2 show that from left to right there is a progression of diagnoses from not diabetic (red +) to chemical diabetic (green ×) to overt diabetic (blue ∘). The principal values in Table 1 show that almost all of the total variance in the data is captured by the first two principal components, which suggests that the original data set in $\mathbb{R}^5$ could be projected to $\mathbb{R}^2$, as in Figure 2, thereby effectively compressing the data in the three directions in which it has very little variance.

4.2. Results for a Neural Network with Mapper. The performance of the neural network during the weight update process is given in Figure 3. The number of patients misclassified

is determined by rounding the output of the neural network to the nearest integer and then counting the number of times the rounded outputs differ from the target outputs. These performance results show that the classification problem can be solved by a neural network for the entire data set. Figure 3 shows that the mean square error (MSE) on the testing set is almost always less than on the training set and that MSE on the testing set rarely increased while the MSE on the training set decreased, which indicates that the neural network did not overlearn the training set. The spikes in Figure 3 likely occur because different classes of input points are very close to each other, and thus small changes in decision boundaries (i.e., separating hyperplanes) for the neural network could lead to sudden changes in the amount of error. The positive performance results in Figure 3 after epochs 12, 32, 57, and 107 indicate four interesting neural networks which misclassified 7, 2, 2, and 0 patients. The neural network after epoch 12 would be a good choice for a compromise between performance and training time since it had a small number of misclassifications and it trained in only a few epochs. The neural network at epoch 12 had an observed success rate of 138/145 = 95.17%, and thus with 95% confidence the true success rate is between 90.37% and 97.64%. It should be noted that the data set is relatively small, so the true success rate of the resulting neural network has a somewhat large confidence interval.

The results for using $\ell = 3$ and $\ell = 10$ intervals (i.e., level sets) in Mapper are shown in Figures 4 and 5, respectively. These results show how the cluster diagrams in the neural network evolve as the number of weight updates increases. The color of each node (i.e., vertex) indicates the average neural network output value of all of the points in that node. Output values of the neural network are encoded using a color gradient in which dark blue indicates values near -1 (overt diabetic), light blue/green indicates values near 0 (chemical diabetic), and dark red indicates values near 1 (not diabetic). The size of each node is proportional to the number of patients in that node, and the number in each node is the number of patients in that cluster. Note that the results in Figures 4 and 5 are free-form cluster diagrams in the sense that the absolute position of each node is not important, but the adjacency of nodes connected by edges is important. Further, chains of nodes connected by edges reveal a partial ordering given by the neural network to patients in different nodes, who are assigned different output values by the neural network.

4.3. Discussion. The Mapper results in Figures 4 and 5 show that the graph is connected until the error becomes very low, at which point it may split into several connected components. With only three level sets and 25% overlap of intervals in Figure 4, there are only a few clusters in the neural network and they each have a large number of patients. In contrast, using ten intervals and 50% overlap in Figure 5 produces a higher resolution picture that displays chains of vertices linked by edges for much of the evolution of the neural network. The chains of vertices in Figures 4 and 5 progress from red (not diabetic) to green (chemical diabetic) to blue (overt diabetic), just as the PCA results in $\mathbb{R}^2$ do in Figure 2. The large clusters in Figure 5 are useful because they identify homogeneous groups of patients who

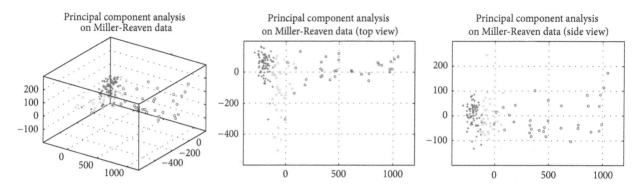

FIGURE 2: Principal component analysis of the Miller-Reaven diabetes data. The diagnosis is color coded with a red + for not diabetic, a green × for chemical diabetic, and a blue ○ for overt diabetic.

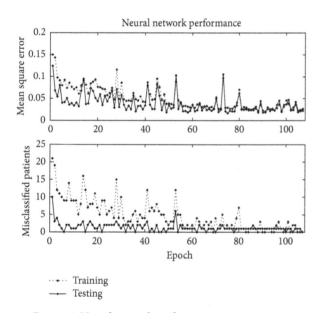

FIGURE 3: Neural network performance measurements.

have similar test results and similar diabetes classification by the neural network. When several clusters are joined together in a linear chain, the ordering of the vertices in the chain tells about the distribution of patients in a linear ordering. Larger clusters in a chain, as in Figure 5, indicate large groups of patients whose diabetes type is readily classified, whereas smaller clusters in a chain indicate patients who are closer to transitioning from one diabetes type to another. Singleton clusters in Figure 5 that are attached to a larger cluster on a chain indicate individual patients that are on the periphery of a larger cluster. The prominent Y shape in the neural network at epoch 57 in Figure 5 has two distinct blue chains at the top of the Y that result from the sparse blue points in the top view and side view of the PCA analysis in Figure 2. The red barbell shaped singleton cluster in Figure 5 occurred because the value assigned to that one outlier patient by the neural network happened to lie at the intersection of two level sets. In the neural network at epoch 107, the clustering problem has been solved with zero misclassified patients, which means that the level sets $h^{-1}([-1.5, -0.5])$, $h^{-1}([-0.5, 0.5])$, and

$h^{-1}([0.5, 1.5])$ are disjoint and have 33, 36, and 76 patients, respectively. The reason why the neural network at epoch 107 in Figure 4 is connected, rather than disjoint, is that the range of the neural network is $[-1.24, 1.15]$, and thus with 25% interval overlap, the figure shows the level sets $h^{-1}([-1.24, -0.28])$, $h^{-1}([-0.52, 0.43])$, and $h^{-1}([0.20, 1.15])$, which have nonempty intersections and contain 38, 35, and 82 patients, respectively.

Using projection pursuit instead of PCA in [13, 14], Miller and Reaven showed that in $\mathbb{R}^3$ this diabetes data looks like a central cluster of nondiabetic patients with two different "flares" of clusters of overt and chemical diabetic patients emanating from this central cluster, which is very similar to the PCA results in Figure 2. This is not surprising since PCA can be viewed as an example of projection pursuit [29]. Further, analysis of the Miller-Reaven data using Mapper with a kernel density estimator in [5], instead of a neural network, also produced a topological model for the data with a central cluster and two "flares" analogous to the projection pursuit results. Examination of the PCA results suggests that while a kernel density estimator might work well for overall shape, it might not be very accurate in differentiating between red (non-diabetic) and green (chemical diabetic) in Figure 2 because they are interspersed to some extent. Viewing the projection pursuit and PCA results in $\mathbb{R}^3$ shown in Figure 2 as a central cluster with flares, it would appear that the green (chemical diabetic) is connected to red (not diabetic) which is connected to blue (overt diabetic). However, viewing the PCA results in $\mathbb{R}^2$ shown in Figure 2 suggests that the clusters should be connected to each other in the order red to green to blue, as the neural network has done in many of the cluster diagrams in Figures 4 and 5.

According to Halkidi et al. [34], visualization of a data set is crucial for verifying clustering results. The PCA results in Table 1 indicate that the inputs in $\mathbb{R}^5$ can be projected to $\mathbb{R}^2$ without much variance being lost, so the data is very close to being two-dimensional. Further, the results of projecting the data to $\mathbb{R}^2$ shown in Figure 2 make this data set ideal for the purpose of validating a clustering method by visual comparison. The neural network performance results in Figure 3 show that the neural network was able to solve the Miller-Reaven diabetes classification problem. Visual comparison of

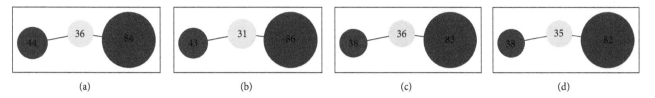

FIGURE 4: Mapper visualization of clusters in the neural network for the Miller-Reaven diabetes study data using 3 intervals with 25% overlap. From left to right: clusters in the neural network after 12, 32, 57, and 107 epochs. The neural network classification is color coded with dark blue for overt diabetic (class −1), light blue/green for chemical diabetic (class 0), and dark red for not diabetic (class 1).

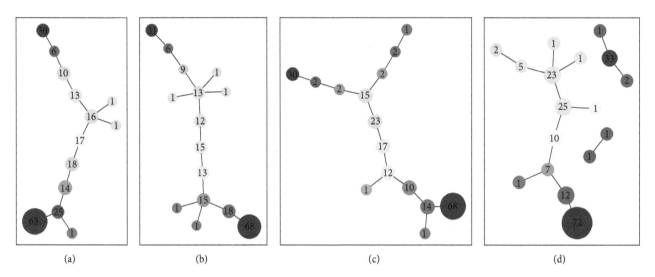

FIGURE 5: Mapper visualization of clusters in the neural network for the Miller-Reaven diabetes study data using 10 intervals with 50% overlap. From left to right: clusters in the neural network after 12, 32, 57, and 107 epochs. The neural network classification is color coded with dark blue for overt diabetic (class −1), light blue/green for chemical diabetic (class 0), and dark red for not diabetic (class 1).

the neural network and Mapper results in Figures 4 and 5 with the PCA results in Figure 2 reveal that the cluster diagram and PCA results convey the same information in compressed (i.e., clustered) and noncompressed ways, respectively. Thus, these results serve to validate the cluster diagrams generated by a neural network and Mapper.

5. Conclusions

Neural networks and the Mapper method have a symbiotic relationship for solving clustering problems and modeling the solution. The level sets of a neural network can be used to solve a clustering problem for high-dimensional data sets, and the Mapper method can produce a low-dimensional cluster diagram from these level sets that shows how they are glued together to form a skeletal picture of the data set. Using neural networks and the Mapper method together simultaneously solves the problem that visualizing the level sets of a neural network is difficult for high-dimensional data and the problem that the Mapper method only produces useful results when applied to a function that solves a clustering problem effectively. Together, they combine the efficacy of neural networks at solving clustering problems

with the clarity and simplicity of cluster diagrams produced by the Mapper method, thereby making the neural network's solution to the clustering problem much easier to interpret and understand. Further, the Mapper method allows the neural network's solution to a clustering problem to be viewed at different resolutions, which can help with developing a model that shows important features at the right scale.

The results of the case study provide evidence in support of the conclusion that using a neural network to solve a clustering problem and the Mapper method to produce a clustering diagram is a valid means of producing an accurate low-dimensional topological model for a data set. In particular, the most important pattern observed in the scatterplot of the PCA results, which was progression classifications from non-diabetic (red +) to chemical diabetic (green ×) to overt diabetic (blue ○) in Figure 2, was also observed at a finer resolution in the cluster diagram for the neural network in Figure 5. Further, the linear chains of nodes connected by edges in the clustering diagrams in Figures 4 and 5 provided a partial ordering on the neural network results that made the results easier to interpret. In order to firmly establish the validity of using a neural network with Mapper for a wide variety of applications, it is evident that in the future this method should be compared to data analysis methods other than PCA and that further case studies should be done for different types of data sets.

Acknowledgments

The author would like to thank Dr. David Housman (Goshen College) and Dr. Nancy Neudauer (Pacific University) for organizing the Research in Applied Mathematics session at the Mathematical Association of America's MathFest 2012, where preliminary results of this research were presented.

References

[1] G. Carlsson, "Topology and data," *Bulletin of the American Mathematical Society*, vol. 46, no. 2, pp. 255–308, 2009.

[2] H. Edelsbrunner and J. Harer, *Computational Topology: An Introduction*, American Mathematical Society, Providence, RI, USA, 2010.

[3] A. Zomorodian, *Topology for Computing*, Cambridge University Press, New York, NY, USA, 2005.

[4] P. Y. Lum, G. Singh, A. Lehman et al., "Extracting insights from the shape of complex data using topology," *Scientific Reports*, vol. 3, article 1236, 2013.

[5] G. Singh, F. Mémoli, and G. Carlsson, "Topological methods for the analysis of high dimensional data sets and 3D object recognition," in *Eurographics Symposium on Point-Based Graphics (Prague '07)*, pp. 91–100.

[6] H. Adams, A. Atanasov, and G. Carlsson, "Morse theory in topological dataanalysis," http://arxiv.org/abs/1112.1993.

[7] C. Marzban and U. Yurtsever, "Baby morse theory in data analysis," in *Proceedings of the Workshop on Knowledge Discovery, Modeling and Simulation (KDMS '11)*, pp. 15–21, August 2011.

[8] K.-L. Du, "Clustering: a neural network approach," *Neural Networks*, vol. 23, no. 1, pp. 89–107, 2010.

[9] J. Herrero, A. Valencia, and J. Dopazo, "A hierarchical unsupervised growing neural network for clustering gene expression patterns," *Bioinformatics*, vol. 17, no. 2, pp. 126–136, 2001.

[10] M. Hagan, H. Demuth, and M. Beale, *Neural Network Design*, PWS Publishing, Boston, Mass, USA, 1995.

[11] R. Marks and R. Reed, *Neural Smithing: Supervised Learning in Feedforward Artificial Neural Networks*, Denver, Bradford, UK, 1999.

[12] R. Rojas, *Neural Networks: A Systematic Introduction*, Springer, New York, NY, USA, 1996.

[13] G. M. Reaven and R. G. Miller, "An attempt to define the nature of chemical diabetes using a multidimensional analysis," *Diabetologia*, vol. 16, no. 1, pp. 17–24, 1979.

[14] R. Miller, "Discussion—projection pursuit," *Annals of Statistics*, vol. 13, no. 2, pp. 510–513, 1985.

[15] S. Walczak, "Methodological triangulation using neural networks for business research," *Advances in Artificial Neural Systems*, vol. 2012, Article ID 517234, 12 pages, 2012.

[16] M. Nicolau, A. J. Levine, and G. Carlsson, "Topology based data analysis identifies a subgroup of breast cancers with a unique mutational profile and excellent survival," *Proceedings of the National Academy of Sciences of the United States of America*, vol. 108, no. 17, pp. 7265–7270, 2011.

[17] G. R. Bowman, X. Huang, Y. Yao et al., "Structural insight into RNA hairpin folding intermediates," *Journal of the American Chemical Society*, vol. 130, no. 30, pp. 9676–9678, 2008.

[18] J. Mao and A. K. Jain, "Artificial neural networks for feature extraction and multivariate data projection," *IEEE Transactions on Neural Networks*, vol. 6, no. 2, pp. 296–317, 1995.

[19] M. A. Kramer, "Nonlinear principal component analysis using autoassociative neural networks," *AIChE Journal*, vol. 37, no. 2, pp. 233–243, 1991.

[20] D. De Ridder and R. P. W. Duin, "Sammon's mapping using neural networks: a comparison," *Pattern Recognition Letters*, vol. 18, no. 11-13, pp. 1307–1316, 1997.

[21] D. K. Agrafiotis and V. S. Lobanov, "Nonlinear mapping networks," *Journal of Chemical Information and Computer Sciences*, vol. 40, no. 6, pp. 1356–1362, 2000.

[22] W. Pedrycz, "Conditional fuzzy clustering in the design of radial basis function neural networks," *IEEE Transactions on Neural Networks*, vol. 9, no. 4, pp. 601–612, 1998.

[23] G. Cybenko, "Approximation by superpositions of a sigmoidal function," *Mathematics of Control, Signals, and Systems*, vol. 2, no. 4, pp. 303–314, 1989.

[24] K. Hornik, M. Stinchcombe, and H. White, "Multilayer feedforward networks are universal approximators," *Neural Networks*, vol. 2, no. 5, pp. 359–366, 1989.

[25] P. G. Goerss and J. F. Jardine, *Simplicial Homotopy Theory*, Birkhäuser, Basel, Switzerland, 2009.

[26] P. J. Huber, "Projection pursuit," *The Annals of Statistics*, vol. 13, no. 2, pp. 435–475, 1985.

[27] D. F. Andrews and A. M. Herzberg, *Data: A Collection of Problems from Many Fields for the Student and Research Worker*, Springer, New York, NY, USA, 1985.

[28] C. R. Rao, "The use and interpretation of principal component analysis in applied research," *Sankhya Series A*, vol. 26, pp. 329–358, 1964.

[29] R. J. Bolton and W. J. Krzanowski, "A characterization of principal components for projection pursuit," *The American Statistician*, vol. 53, no. 2, pp. 108–109, 1999.

[30] C. Croux, P. Filzmoser, and M. R. Oliveira, "Algorithms for Projection-Pursuit robust principal component analysis," *Chemometrics and Intelligent Laboratory Systems*, vol. 87, no. 2, pp. 218–225, 2007.

[31] Y. LeCun, L. Bottou, G. Orr, and K. Müller, "Efficient backprop," in *Neural Networks: Tricks of the Trade*, Springer, New York, NY, USA, 1998.

[32] D. Müllner and G. Singh, "Mapper 1d for matlab," 2013, http://comptop.stanford.edu/programs/.

[33] "Graphviz—graph visualization software," 2013, http://www.graphviz.org/.

[34] M. Halkidi, Y. Batistakis, and M. Vazirgiannis, "On clustering validation techniques," *Journal of Intelligent Information Systems*, vol. 17, no. 2-3, pp. 107–145, 2001.

21

Hopfield Neural Networks with Unbounded Monotone Activation Functions

Nasser-eddine Tatar

Department of Mathematics and Statistics, King Fahd University of Petroleum and Minerals, Dhahran 31261, Saudi Arabia

Correspondence should be addressed to Nasser-eddine Tatar, tatarn@kfupm.edu.sa

Academic Editor: Chao-Ton Su

For the Hopfield Neural Network problem we consider unbounded monotone nondecreasing activation functions. We prove convergence to zero in an exponential manner provided that we start with sufficiently small initial data.

1. Introduction

Of concern is the following system:

$$x_i'(t) = - a_i(t)x_i(t)$$

$$+ \sum_{j=1}^{m} b_{ij}(t)f_j\big(x_j(t)\big) + c_i(t), \quad i = 1, \dots, m, \quad (1)$$

where $a_i(t) \geq 0$, $b_{ij}(t)$, $c_i(t)$, $i, j = 1, \dots, m$ are continuous functions, and f_j are the activation functions which will be assumed continuous and bounded by some nondecreasing (and possibly unbounded functions).

This system appears in Neural Network theory [1, 2]. As is well-known, Neural Networks are an important tool in business intelligence. Their architecture differs from the one of standard computers in that it consists of a large number of processors (neurons) with high connections between them. In contrast to computers with a single processor, (Artificial) Neural Networks perform their computations in parallel.

Just as the human brain, the neurons receive weighted signals from the neurons in the input layer, sum up these inputs and test against a threshold value. Then they decide to fire or not.

The applications are numerous, we may cite few: modelling soil behavior, design of tunnels, image processing, graph flow, data deconvolution, energy demand forecasting, ecosystem evaluation, scheduling optimization, targeted

marketing, medical diagnosis, time series analysis, and stock market.

Neural Networks are able to analyze and evaluate many phenomena in real world business as well as in industry. Some of their advantages over the conventional computers are forecasting, strategy planning, and predicting many phenomena.

Different methods have been used by many authors to study the well-posedness and the asymptotic behavior of solutions [3–20]. In particular, a lot of efforts are devoted in improving the set of conditions on the different coefficients involved in the system as well as the class of activation functions. Regarding the latter issue, the early assumptions of boundedness, monotonicity, and differentiability have been all relaxed to merely a global Lipschitz condition. Since then, it seems that, this assumption has not been weakened further considerably although there is a great need for that [21]. A slightly weaker condition: $x_i g_i(x_i) > 0$, $x_i \neq 0$ and there exist $\lambda_i > 0$ such that $\lambda_i = \sup_{x_i \neq 0}(g_i(x_i)/x_i)$, where $g_i(x_i) = f_i(x_i) - f_i(x_i^*)$ and x_i^* is the equilibrium, has been used in [22–24] (see also [25–27]).

Here we assume that the activation functions f_j are bounded by continuous monotone nondecreasing functions g_j, that is,

$$\big|f_j(x)\big| \leq g_j(|x|), \quad j = 1, \dots, m. \quad (2)$$

The functions g_j are not necessarily Lipschitz continuous and they may be unbounded (like power type functions with powers bigger than one). We can also consider activation functions with discrete delays as is explained below. We prove that, for sufficiently small initial data, solutions decay to zero exponentially.

The local existence and existence of equilibria is standard (see, the Gronwall-type Lemma 1 below) and the global existence follows from the estimation in our theorem below. However, the uniqueness of the equilibrium is not trivial. Here, as we are concerned with the convergence to zero rather than stability of equilibrium, the uniqueness of equilibrium is put aside.

The next section contains the statement and proof of our result as well as a crucial lemma we will be using.

2. Exponential Convergence

In this section it is proved that solutions converge to zero in an exponential manner when the activation functions are (or bounded by) continuous nondecreasing and unbounded functions. To this end we need a lemma due to Bainov and Simeonov [3].

Let $I \subset \mathbf{R}$ and let $g_1, g_2 : I \to \mathbf{R} \setminus \{0\}$. We write $g_1 \propto g_2$ if g_2/g_1 is nondecreasing in I.

Lemma 1. *Let $a(t)$ be a positive continuous function in $J := [\alpha, \beta)$, $k_j(t,s)$, $j = 1,\ldots,n$ are nonnegative continuous functions for $\alpha \leq s \leq t < \beta$ which are nondecreasing in t for any fixed s, $g_j(u)$, $j = 1,\ldots,n$ are nondecreasing continuous functions in $\mathbf{R}_+$, with $g_j(u) > 0$ for $u > 0$ and $u(t)$ is a nonnegative continuous functions in J. If $g_1 \propto g_2 \propto \cdots \propto g_n$ in $(0, \infty)$, then the inequality*

$$u(t) \leq a(t) + \sum_{j=1}^{n} \int_{\alpha}^{t} k_j(t,s)g_j(u(s))ds, \quad t \in J \quad (3)$$

implies that

$$u(t) \leq \omega_n(t), \quad \alpha \leq t < \beta_0, \quad (4)$$

where $\omega_0(t) := \sup_{0 \leq s \leq t} a(s)$,

$$\omega_j(t) := G_j^{-1}\left[G_j\big(\omega_{j-1}(t)\big) + \int_{\alpha}^{t} k_j(t,s)ds \right], \quad j = 1,\ldots,n,$$

$$G_j(u) := \int_{u_j}^{u} \frac{dx}{g_j(x)}, \quad u > 0\big(u_j > 0, \ j = 1,\ldots,n\big),$$

$$(5)$$

and β_0 is chosen so that the functions $\omega_j(t)$, $j = 1,\ldots,n$ are defined for $\alpha \leq t < \beta_0$.

For the statement of our theorem we will need the following notation:

$$a(t) := \min_{1 \leq i \leq m} \{a_i(t)\}, \quad (6)$$

$$\omega_0(t) := x(0) + \sum_{i=1}^{m} \int_{0}^{t} \exp\left[\int_{0}^{s} a(\sigma)d\sigma\right]|c_i(s)|ds, \quad (7)$$

$$\omega_j(t) := G_j^{-1}\left[G_j\big(\omega_{j-1}(t)\big) \right.$$

$$\left. + \int_{0}^{t} \exp\left[\int_{0}^{s} a(\sigma)d\sigma\right]\left(\sum_{i=1}^{m}\big|b_{ij}(s)\big|\right)ds \right], \quad (8)$$

$$G_j(u) := \int_{u_j}^{u} \frac{dx}{g_j(x)}, \quad u > 0\big(u_j > 0, \ j = 1,\ldots,m\big). \quad (9)$$

Theorem 2. *Assume that f_j satisfy $|f_j(x)| \leq g_j(|x|)$, $j = 1,\ldots,m$ for some continuous nondecreasing (and possibly unbounded) functions g_j, $j = 1,\ldots,m$ in $\mathbf{R}_+$, with $g_j(u) > 0$ for $u > 0$. Assume further that $a_i(t) \geq 0$, $b_{ij}(t)$, $c_i(t)$, $i,j = 1,\ldots,m$ are continuous functions. If $g_1 \propto g_2 \propto \cdots \propto g_m$ in $(0, \infty)$ then, there exists $\beta_0 > 0$ such that*

$$x(t) \leq \omega_m(t) \exp\left[-\int_{0}^{t} a(s)ds\right], \quad 0 \leq t < \beta_0, \quad (10)$$

where $x(t) := \sum_{i=1}^{m} |x_i(t)|$.

Proof. From (1) and our assumption on f_j we see that

$$D^+|x_i(t)| \leq -a_i(t)|x_i(t)| + \sum_{j=1}^{m}\big|b_{ij}(t)\big|g_j\big(\big|x_j(t)\big|\big)$$

$$+ c_i(t), \quad t > 0, \ i = 1,\ldots,m, \quad (11)$$

or

$$D^+x(t) \leq -\min_{1 \leq i \leq m}\{a_i(t)\}x(t) + \sum_{i,j=1}^{m}\big|b_{ij}(t)\big|g_j\big(\big|x_j(t)\big|\big)$$

$$+ \sum_{i=1}^{m} c_i(t), \quad t > 0, \quad (12)$$

where D^+ denotes the right Dini derivative. Hence

$$D^+x(t) \leq -a(t)x(t) + \sum_{i,j=1}^{m}\big|b_{ij}(t)\big|g_j\big(\big|x_j(t)\big|\big)$$

$$+ \sum_{i=1}^{m} c_i(t), \quad t > 0. \quad (13)$$

In virtue of (13) we derive

$$D^+ \left\{ x(t) \exp\left[\int_0^t a(s)ds \right] \right\}$$

$$\leq \exp\left[\int_0^t a(s)ds \right] \sum_{i,j=1}^m \left| b_{ij}(t) \right| g_j(x(t)) \qquad (14)$$

$$+ \exp\left[\int_0^t a(s)ds \right] \sum_{i=1}^m c_i(t),$$

and thereafter (see [28])

$$\tilde{x}(t) \leq x(0) + \sum_{j=1}^m \int_0^t \left\{ \exp\left[\int_0^s a(\sigma)d\sigma \right] \right.$$

$$\times \left(\sum_{i=1}^m \left| b_{ij}(s) \right| \right) g_j(\tilde{x}(s)) \right\} ds \qquad (15)$$

$$+ \sum_{i=1}^m \int_0^t \exp\left[\int_0^s a(\sigma)d\sigma \right] |c_i(s)|ds, \quad t > 0,$$

where

$$\tilde{x}(t) := x(t) \exp\left[\int_0^t a(s)ds \right]. \qquad (16)$$

Applying Lemma 1 we obtain the existence of β_0 such that

$$\tilde{x}(t) \leq \omega_m(t), \quad 0 \leq t < \beta_0, \qquad (17)$$

where $\omega_0(t)$, $\omega_j(t)$, and $G_j(u)$, $j = 1,\ldots,m$ are as defined in (7)–(9). □

Remark 3. To have global existence we need $\beta_0 = \infty$ and this is possible when

$$\int_0^\infty \exp\left[\int_0^s a(\sigma)d\sigma \right] \left(\sum_{i=1}^m |b_{ik}(s)| \right) ds$$

$$\leq \int_{\omega_{k-1}}^\infty \frac{dz}{g_k(z)}, \quad k = 1,\ldots,m. \qquad (18)$$

Remark 4. Assuming that $\omega_n(t)$ grows up at most polynomially, we see that the rate is exponential.

Remark 5. Note here that our assumptions in the previous remarks involve a smallness condition on the initial data.

3. Applications

Using Kirchhoff's law, Hopfield demonstrated that electrical circuits could behave as a small Neural Network. His original system has the form:

$$C_i \frac{du_i}{dt} = \sum_{i=1}^m T_{ij}v_j - \frac{u_i}{R_i} + I_i, \quad i = 1,\ldots,m,$$

$$v_j = g_j(u_j), \quad j = 1,\ldots,m, \qquad (19)$$

where $C_i > 0$: Capacity, $R_i > 0$: Resistance, I_i: Bias (external action on the ith neuron), u_i: Input (voltage) of the ith neuron, v_i: Output of the ith neuron, T_{ij}: The coupling constants of the jth neuron with the ith neuron, and $g_j(u_j)$: Activation functions.

T_{ij} are called elements of the weight matrix or connection matrix. This matrix describes the strength of connection between neurons. The expression $1/R_i$ is sometimes called the feedback factor.

The functions $g_j(u_j)$ are nonlinear functions characterizing the response of the ith neuron to changes in its state. Typical activation functions are the "Step function", the "Sign function", the "Gaussian" function, the "Hyperbolic function", and the "Exponential type function". However, it has been established that many other activation functions arise in practice which are not of these forms. Therefore there is a need to enlarge these classes of functions to more general ones.

In Neural Network Theory researchers are rather interested in designing models which are globally asymptotically stable. That is, the models must have a unique equilibrium which attracts all the solutions. Of course the rate of convergence is extremely important and it is preferable to have an exponential convergence rate. In the present work (for the case of variable coefficients) we prove that if solutions start close enough to zero then they will be attracted by zero. Our theorem shows that solutions remain bounded by

$$\omega_m(t) \exp\left[-\int_0^t a(s)ds \right], \qquad (20)$$

as long as $t < \beta_0$ defined as a bound for the interval of existence of the ω_j's (see (8)). In Remark 3 we gave a sufficient condition ensuring the existence of the ω_j's for all time. That is conditions for which $\beta_0 = +\infty$. It follows then that, under these conditions, the states actually converge to zero as t goes to infinity with an exponential rate in case $\omega_m(t)$ does not grow too fast and $\int_0^t a(s)ds \to \infty$ as $t \to \infty$.

The example below represents a possible practical situation for which our argument applies. Again we establish a sufficient explicit condition leading to exponential convergence to zero provided that the initial data are small enough.

Example 6. Consider the special (but common) functions $g_j(x) = x^{n_i}$, $n_i > 1$, $i = 1,\ldots,m$. The order $g_1 \propto g_2 \propto \cdots \propto g_m$ means $n_1 \leq n_2 \leq \cdots \leq n_m$. Clearly, in this case $G_j(x) = (x^{1-n_j}/(1 - n_j)) - (x_0^{1-n_j}/(1 - n_j))$, $G_j^{-1}(z) = [x_0^{1-n_j} - (n_j - 1)z]^{-(1/(n_j-1))}$, and for $t > 0$

$$\omega_j(t) = \left\{ \omega_{j-1}^{1-n_j}(t) - (n_j - 1) \int_0^t \exp\left[\int_0^s a(\sigma)d\sigma \right] \right.$$

$$\times \left(\sum_{i=1}^m \left| b_{ij}(s) \right| \right) ds \right\}^{-(1/(n_j-1))}. \qquad (21)$$

The value β_0 will be the largest value of t for which

$$\omega_{j-1}^{n_j-1}(t) \int_0^t \exp\left[\int_0^s a(\sigma)d\sigma\right]\left(\sum_{i=1}^m \left|b_{ij}(s)\right|\right) ds < \frac{1}{n_j-1}, \tag{22}$$

for all $j = 1,\ldots,m$. As we are interested in the long time behavior of solutions it is necessary that these conditions hold for all t. Our theorem then implies that solutions are bounded by the expression

$$\omega_m(t) \exp\left[-\int_0^t a(s)ds\right], \tag{23}$$

which provides us with an exponential decay under some fairly reasonable assumptions.

3.1. Discrete Delays. The case where we have discrete delays in the activation functions, that is,

$$x_i'(t) = -a_i(t)x_i(t) + \sum_{j=1}^m b_{ij}(t)f_j\left(x_j\left(t-\tau_{ij}\right)\right) + c_i(t), \quad i = 1,\ldots,m, \tag{24}$$

where τ_{ij} are different finite delays, can be treated similarly. We use the following functional

$$\Xi(t) := \sum_{i,j=1}^m e^{-\int_0^t a(s)ds} \int_{t-\tau_{ij}}^t e^{\int_0^{s+\tau_{ij}} a(\sigma)d\sigma} \times \left|b_{ij}\left(s+\tau_{ij}\right)\right| g_j\left(\left|x_j(s)\right|\right) ds \tag{25}$$

to get rid of the delayed terms and replace them by terms without delays.

Acknowledgment

The author is grateful for the financial support and the facilities provided by King Fahd University of Petroleum and Minerals through Grant no. IN111052.

References

[1] J. J. Hopfield, "Neural networks and physical systems with emergent collective computational abilities," *Proceedings of the National Academy of Sciences*, vol. 79, pp. 2554–2558, 1982.

[2] J. J. Hopfield and D. W. Tank, "Computing with neural circuits: a model," *Science*, vol. 233, pp. 625–633, 1986.

[3] D. Bainov and P. S. Simeonov, *Integral Inequalities and Applications*, Mathematics and Its Applications, East European Series, Kluwer Academic Publishers-Springer, London, 1992.

[4] A. Bouzerdoum and T. R. Pattison, "Neural network for quadratic optimization with bound constraints," *IEEE Transactions on Neural Networks*, vol. 4, no. 2, pp. 293–304, 1993.

[5] L. O. Chua and T. Roska, "Stability of a class of nonreciprocal cellular neural networks," *IEEE Transactions on Circuits and Systems*, vol. 37, no. 12, pp. 1520–1527, 1990.

[6] B. Crespi, "Storage capacity of non-monotonic neurons," *Neural Networks*, vol. 12, no. 10, pp. 1377–1389, 1999.

[7] M. Forti, P. Nistri, and D. Papini, "Global exponential stability and global convergence in finite time of delayed neural networks with infinite gain," *IEEE Transactions on Neural Networks*, vol. 16, no. 6, pp. 1449–1463, 2005.

[8] M. Forti and A. Tesi, "New conditions for global stability of neural networks with application to linear and quadratic programming problems," *IEEE Transactions on Circuits and Systems I*, vol. 42, no. 7, pp. 354–366, 1995.

[9] L. Huang, J. Wang, and X. Zhou, "Existence and global asymptotic stability of periodic solutions for Hopfield neural networks with discontinuous activations," *Nonlinear Analysis: Real World Applications*, vol. 10, no. 3, pp. 1651–1661, 2009.

[10] J. I. Inoue, "Retrieval phase diagrams of non-monotonic Hopfield networks," *Journal of Physics A*, vol. 29, pp. 4815–4826, 1996.

[11] M. P. Kennedy and L. O. Chua, "Neural networks for non-linear programming," *IEEE Transactions on Circuits and Systems I*, vol. 35, pp. 554–562, 1998.

[12] S. Mohamad, "Exponential stability in Hopfield-type neural networks with impulses," *Chaos, Solitons & Fractals*, vol. 32, pp. 456–467, 2007.

[13] H. Qiao, J. G. Peng, and Z. Xu, "Nonlinear measures: a new approach to exponential stability analysis for Hopfield-type neural networks," *IEEE Transactions on Neural Networks*, vol. 12, pp. 360–370, 2001.

[14] Q. Song, "Novel criteria for global exponential periodicity and stability of recurrent neural networks with time-varying delays," *Chaos, Solitons & Fractals*, vol. 36, no. 3, pp. 720–728, 2008.

[15] S. I. Sudharsanan and M. K. Sundareshan, "Exponential stability and a systematic synthesis of a neural network for quadratic minimization," *Neural Networks*, vol. 4, no. 5, pp. 599–613, 1991.

[16] P. Van Den Driessche and X. Zou, "Global attractivity in delayed hopfield neural network models," *SIAM Journal on Applied Mathematics*, vol. 58, no. 6, pp. 1878–1890, 1998.

[17] S. Y. Xu, J. Lam, D. W. C. Ho, and Y. Zou, "Global robust exponential stability analysis for interval recurrent neural networks," *Physics Letters A*, vol. 325, pp. 124–133, 2004.

[18] H. F. Yanai and S. I. Amari, "Auto-associative memory with two-stage dynamics of nonmonotonic neurons," *IEEE Transactions on Neural Networks*, vol. 7, no. 4, pp. 803–815, 1996.

[19] E. H. Yang, "Perturbations of nonlinear systems of ordinary differential equations," *Journal of Mathematical Analysis and Applications*, vol. 103, pp. 1–15, 1984.

[20] H. Y. Zhao, "Global stability of neural networks with distributed delays," *Physical Review E*, vol. 68, Article ID 051909, pp. 1–7, 2003.

[21] B. Kosko, *Neural Network and Fuzzy System—A Dynamical System Approach to Machine Intelligence*, Prentice-Hall of India, New Delhi, India, 1991.

[22] C. Feng and R. Plamondon, "On the stability analysis of delayed neural networks systems," *Neural Networks*, vol. 14, no. 9, pp. 1181–1188, 2001.

[23] H. Zhao, "Global asymptotic stability of Hopfield neural networks involving distributed delays," *Neural Networks*, vol. 17, pp. 47–53, 2004.

[24] J. Zhou, S. Y. Li, and Z. G. Yang, "Global exponential stability of Hopfield neural networks with distributed delays," *Applied Mathematical Modelling*, vol. 33, pp. 1513–1520, 2009.

[25] H. Wu, "Global exponential stability of Hopfield neural networks with delays and inverse Lipschitz neuron activations," *Nonlinear Analysis: Real World Applications*, vol. 10, pp. 2297–2306, 2009.

[26] H. Wu, F. Tao, L. Qin, R. Shi, and L. He, "Robust exponential stability for interval neural networks with delays and non-Lipschitz activation functions," *Nonlinear Dynamics*, vol. 66, pp. 479–487, 2011.

[27] H. Wu and X. Xue, "Stability analysis for neural networks with inverse Lipschizian neuron activations and impulses," *Applied Mathematical Modelling*, vol. 32, pp. 2347–2359, 2008.

[28] V. Lakshmikhantam and S. Leela, "Differential and integral inequalities: theory and applications," in *Mathematics in Sciences and Engineering*, R. Bellman, Ed., vol. 55, Academic Press, London, UK, 1969.

Permissions

The contributors of this book come from diverse backgrounds, making this book a truly international effort. This book will bring forth new frontiers with its revolutionizing research information and detailed analysis of the nascent developments around the world.

We would like to thank all the contributing authors for lending their expertise to make the book truly unique. They have played a crucial role in the development of this book. Without their invaluable contributions this book wouldn't have been possible. They have made vital efforts to compile up to date information on the varied aspects of this subject to make this book a valuable addition to the collection of many professionals and students.

This book was conceptualized with the vision of imparting up-to-date information and advanced data in this field. To ensure the same, a matchless editorial board was set up. Every individual on the board went through rigorous rounds of assessment to prove their worth. After which they invested a large part of their time researching and compiling the most relevant data for our readers. Conferences and sessions were held from time to time between the editorial board and the contributing authors to present the data in the most comprehensible form. The editorial team has worked tirelessly to provide valuable and valid information to help people across the globe.

Every chapter published in this book has been scrutinized by our experts. Their significance has been extensively debated. The topics covered herein carry significant findings which will fuel the growth of the discipline. They may even be implemented as practical applications or may be referred to as a beginning point for another development. Chapters in this book were first published by Hindawi Publishing Corporation; hereby published with permission under the Creative Commons Attribution License or equivalent.

The editorial board has been involved in producing this book since its inception. They have spent rigorous hours researching and exploring the diverse topics which have resulted in the successful publishing of this book. They have passed on their knowledge of decades through this book. To expedite this challenging task, the publisher supported the team at every step. A small team of assistant editors was also appointed to further simplify the editing procedure and attain best results for the readers.

Our editorial team has been hand-picked from every corner of the world. Their multi-ethnicity adds dynamic inputs to the discussions which result in innovative outcomes. These outcomes are then further discussed with the researchers and contributors who give their valuable feedback and opinion regarding the same. The feedback is then collaborated with the researches and they are edited in a comprehensive manner to aid the understanding of the subject.

Apart from the editorial board, the designing team has also invested a significant amount of their time in understanding the subject and creating the most relevant covers. They scrutinized every image to scout for the most suitable representation of the subject and create an appropriate cover for the book.

The publishing team has been involved in this book since its early stages. They were actively engaged in every process, be it collecting the data, connecting with the contributors or procuring relevant information. The team has been an ardent support to the editorial, designing and production team. Their endless efforts to recruit the best for this project, has resulted in the accomplishment of this book. They are a veteran in the field of academics and their pool of knowledge is as vast as their experience in printing. Their expertise and guidance has proved useful at every step. Their uncompromising quality standards have made this book an exceptional effort. Their encouragement from time to time has been an inspiration for everyone.

The publisher and the editorial board hope that this book will prove to be a valuable piece of knowledge for researchers, students, practitioners and scholars across the globe.

List of Contributors

Martin Langkvist, Lars Karlsson and Amy Loutfi
Center for Applied Autonomous Sensor Systems, Orebro University, 701 82 Orebro, Sweden

Rong Duan
AT&T Labs, Florham Park, NJ 07932, USA

Hong Man
Department of Electrical and Computer Engineering, Stevens Institute of Technology, Hoboken, NJ 07030, USA

Nicholas Ampazis
Department of Financial and Management Engineering, University of the Aegean, 82100 Chios, Greece

Stavros J. Perantonis
Institute of Informatics and Telecommunications, NCSR "Demokritos", 15310 Athens, Greece

Mohammad Heidari
Mechanical Engineering Group, Aligudarz Branch, Islamic Azad University, P.O. Box 159, Aligudarz, Iran

Hadi Homaei
Faculty of Engineering, Shahrekord University, P.O. Box 115, Shahrekord, Iran

Vladimir M. Krasnopolsky
National Centers for Environmental Prediction, NOAA, College Park, MD 20740, USA
Earth System Sciences Interdisciplinary Center, University of Maryland, College Park, MD 20740, USA

Michael S. Fox-Rabinovitz
Earth System Sciences Interdisciplinary Center, University of Maryland, College Park, MD 20740, USA

Alexei A. Belochitski
Geophysical Fluid Dynamics Laboratory, NOAA, Princeton, NJ 08540, USA
Brookhaven National Laboratory, Upton, NY 11973, USA

Steven Walczak
The Business School, University of Colorado Denver, Denver, CO 80202, USA

Ruey Kei Chiu, Renee Y. Chen and Shin-An Wang
Department of Information Management, Fu Jen Catholic University, Xinzhuang District, New Taipei City 24205, Taiwan

Yen-Chun Chang
Office of Computer Processing, En Chu Kong Hospital, Sanxia District, New Taipei City 23702, Taiwan

Li-Chien Chen
Office of Information Processing, Cardinal Tien Hospital, Xindian District, New Taipei City 231, Taiwan

Vic Norris, Maurice Engel and Maurice Demarty
Theoretical Biology Unit, EA 3829, Department of Biology, University of Rouen, 76821 Mont-Saint-Aignan, France

Tzu-Chuen Lu and Chun-Ya Tseng
Department of Information Management, Chaoyang University of Technology, Wufeng District, Taichung 41349, Taiwan

A. Meyer-Baese and C. Plant
Department of Scientific Computing, Florida State University, Tallahassee, FL 32306-4120, USA

T. Schlossbauer
Institute for Clinical Radiology, University of Munich, 81377 Munich, Germany

U. Meyer-Baese
Department of Electrical and Computer Engineering, FAMU/FSU College of Engineering, Tallahassee, FL 32310-6046, USA

Deepti Moyi Sahoo and S. Chakraverty
Department of Mathematics, National Institute of Technology Rourkela, Rourkela, Odisha 769 008, India

Claudia Plant and Anke Meyer-Baese
400 Dirac Science Library, Florida State University, Tallahassee, FL 32306-4120, USA

Son Mai Thai and Christian Bohm
Department for Informatics, Research Unit for Database Systems, University of Munich, Oettingenstraße 67, 80538Munich, Germany

Junming Shao
Klinikum rechts der Isar der TUM, Ismaninger Straße 22, 81675 Munich, Germany

Fabian J. Theis
Helmholtz Zentrum Munchen, Ingolstadter Landstraße 1, 85764 Neuherberg, Germany

Chengyan Liu, Xiaodi Li and Xilin Fu
Department of Mathematics, Shandong Normal University, Jinan 250014, China

F. Steinbruecker and D. Cremers
Department of Computer Science, Technical University of Munich, 85748 Garching, Germany

Miki Sirola and Jaakko Talonen
Department of Information and Computer Science, Aalto University, P.O. Box 15400, 00076 Aalto, Finland

A. Ortiz
Department of Communication Engineering, University of Malaga, 29071 Malaga, Spain

J. M. Gorriz, J. Ramirez and D. Salas-Gonzalez
Department of Signal Theory, Networking and Communications, University of Granada, 18071 Granada, Spain

Quoc-Huy Phan and Duc-Lung Vu
University of Information Technology, Km 20, Ha Noi Highway, Linh Trung Ward, Thu Duc, HCMC 70000, Vietnam

Su-Lim Tan
Singapore Institute of Technology, 25 North Bridge Road, Singapore 179104

Ian McLoughlin
School of Information Science and Technology, University of Science and Technology of China, No. 443 Huangshan Road, Hefei, Anhui 230027, China

Dhirendranath Thatoi
Department of Mechanical Engineering, I.T.E.R, Bhubaneswar 751030, Odisha, India

Prabir Kumar Jena
Department of Mechanical Engineering, Silicon Institute of Technology, Bhubaneswar 751024, Odisha, India

Changjin Xu
Guizhou Key Laboratory of Economics System Simulation, School of Mathematics and Statistics, Guizhou College of Finance and Economics, Guiyang 550004, China

Peiluan Li
Department of Mathematics and Statistics, Henan University of Science and Technology, Luoyang 471003, China

Paul T. Pearson
Department of Mathematics, Hope College, P.O. Box 9000, Holland, MI 49422-9000, USA

Nasser-eddine Tatar
Department of Mathematics and Statistics, King Fahd University of Petroleum and Minerals, Dhahran 31261, Saudi Arabia

Printed in the USA
CPSIA information can be obtained
at www.ICGtesting.com
JSHW051438221024
72173JS00006B/1505